BEAUTIFUL

UGLY

African and Diaspora Aesthetics
Sarah Nuttall, editor

AFRICAN AND DIASPORA

AESTHETICS

Sarah Nuttall, editor

Duke University Press
Durham and London 2006

Prince Claus
Fund Library

Copyright © 2006 Prince Claus Fund
for Culture and Development
Hoge Nieuwstraat 30
2514 EL The Hague
The Netherlands
www.princeclausfund.org

Published in 2006 by
Duke University Press
Box 90660
Durham, NC 27708-0660
www.dukeupress.edu

Assistant Editor: Henrietta Innes
Copy Editors: William Dicey, Mitch Albert
Design: Irma Boom

Printed and bound in Slovenia by Print Consult GmbH

Library of Congress Cataloging-in-Publication Data

Beautiful/ugly : African and diaspora aesthetics /
edited by Sarah Nuttall.
p. cm.

Includes bibliographical references and index.
ISBN-13: 978-0-8223-3907-6 (cloth : alk. paper)
ISBN-10: 0-8223-3907-2 (cloth : alk. paper)
ISBN-13: 978-0-8223-3918-2 (pbk. : alk. paper)
ISBN-10: 0-8223-3918-8 (pbk. : alk. paper)
1. Aesthetics, African. I. Nuttall, Sarah.
BH221.A353B43 2006
111'.8508996—dc22

2006011647

Contents

Sarah Nuttall
Introduction: Rethinking Beauty

Sarah Nuttall is a Associate Professor of Literature and Cultural Studies at the Wits Institute for Social and Economic Research, University of the Witwatersrand, Johannesburg. She is co-editor of *Text, Theory, Space: Land, Literature and History in South Africa and Australia* (1996), *Negotiating the Past: The Making of Memory in South Africa* (1998), *Senses of Culture: South African Culture Studies* (2000) and of a special issue of *Public Culture* entitled *Johannesburg – The Elusive Metropolis* (2004); she is also the author of a forthcoming collection of essays on South African literature and culture.

RETHINKING BEAUTY

I

This book is about the unpredictability, mutability and volatility of beauty and its relationship to ugliness in Africa and its intersections with the world. It is not a work of art history; nor does it belong to the realms of aesthetic theory or anthropology. It is a series of essays drawn from the contemporary African, written from different vantage points, concerning a topic the force of which is felt by many but seldom articulated. It is an exploration of the ideas that, firstly, beauty is to be found at the limits of the ugly, since it is the ugly which has so often been the sign under which the African has been read; and secondly, that beauty always stands in intimate relation to ugliness, both in Africa and elsewhere, though this configuration of the beautiful and the ugly has often been suppressed in Western-based philosophies of aesthetics. It is not a book about "African beauty" but rather a set of reflections on beauty and its forms which draws on work from Africa and its elsewheres.

Beauty in Africa, as it has been dealt with by the world at large, has an ugly history. Both Africans and that which they have made have frequently been viewed in damaging, fundamentally racist, ways. At the same time, notions of beauty which derive from an unexamined whiteness, concepts of Eurocentrism or other forms of parochialism are increasingly being contested, shaken and are even disappearing in certain contexts. The making and meanings of beauty are undergoing transformations unforeseen or unattended to in normative renderings of the aesthetic, in ways this book tries to draw out. Before we turn to contemporary histories of beauty in more detail, we might reflect on what it is to study beauty in the first place, especially beauty in Africa, and why the subject receives relatively little, often guarded, attention from scholars.

The study of beauty in Africa and its diasporas needs to be understood in several registers, four of which I draw out here. It is worth reflecting, though, that each of these registers has largely to do with constructions of Africa from the outside. This is one of the dilemmas of initiating a conversation about beauty in its African contexts: that one has, almost unavoidably, to begin with its constructions by others rather than by Africans themselves. This is because so much of the best of what Africans have thought remained for so long outside of writing and within the rich epistemologies of the spoken, but also because the hermeneutic machine of the West has long relied on Africa's otherness to stage its grandest and most exclusive theatres of the self. Africans have often come to rely on, while also disavowing aspects of, this potent Western tradition. If part of what we need to do, in order to understand our subject properly, is to revisit these dominant positions, both then and now, it is also the work of this introduction to carefully unpick metropolitan debates and breathe new life into their moments of silence or repression, in so doing contributing to the emergence of a properly global epistemology of beauty and ugliness. In the second part of this introduction, I show how the essays in the book engage with, but also depart from, concepts of the beautiful as a moral, abstract or unknowable concept. In drawing beauty into a conversation with ugliness, they also view beauty as that which works across the senses, and they consider, too, the limits of beauty and its difficulty as a concept. They read beauty as relating to a set of powerful and differentiated contexts, but not as fully contingent on those contexts. First though, and in order to properly understand the context for the essays which follow, we need to turn to the ways in which "beauty in Africa" has been read.

The first register within which discourses of beauty in Africa need to be understood, then, has to do with the inscription of Africa in dominant Western aesthetic discourses as the figure of the ugly. In his essay, "On National Characteristics So Far as They Depend upon the Distinct Feeling of the Beautiful and the Sublime" (1764), Kant argues that different "nations" have different aesthetic and moral sensibilities. The "beautiful" and the "sublime" are for him qualities of aesthetic and moral "feeling", both of which, he concludes, Africans lack. The African, he writes, "has no feeling beyond the trifling"; this he links to "the ugliness of appearance" in the "Negro", clear proof in his eyes of "stupidity".[1] Racist accounts, widely accepted into the time of European colonisation and beyond, present the African continent as the metaphor *par excellence* for physical ugliness and moral decay. According to these accounts, ugliness and decay were particularly visible in the black body, which was nothing more than a mass of organs lacking form and self-awareness.[2]

Conversely, Western theories of the beautiful, as Simon Gikandi has shown, came to be mediated through the figure of blackness, becoming in the process a source of the "sublime". Thus when Pablo Picasso, master of European modernism, began to draw inspiration from African art in a movement later known as primitivism, it was the terror – and the disgust – African objects made him feel that inspired him.[3] From the start the Primitivist sign was ambivalent: its "terror" would be recovered by Surrealist artists to "terrorise" Western civilisation and to "save it from crisis". The psychoanalyst Franz Fanon, in his diagnosis of racial being in the aftermath of European colonialism in Africa, has written about the white look that renders the black person a source of terror and desire.[4] Writing in a Fanonesque vein, African American novelist Toni Morrison called beauty one of "the most destructive ideas in the history of human thought" in her first and acclaimed novel, *The Bluest Eye*.[5] Of her character, the young black girl Pecola, who wishes to have blue eyes, Morrison observes: "she would never know her beauty. She would see only what there was to see: the eyes of other people."[6] In the novel as a whole, Morrison writes against what she sees as a particularly Western fascination with sight and the idea that beauty must always be an occasion for looking. She draws out, that is, the hegemonic act of looking which objectifies the (black) subject before it and adjudicates what is beautiful and what is not.

In a recent afterword to a new edition of *The Bluest Eye*, Morrison describes how

9

the novel emerged from the disturbance she felt when a young black girl she knew told her that she wanted blue eyes: "Until that moment I had seen the pretty, the lovely, the nice, the ugly, and although I had certainly used the word 'beautiful', I had never experienced its shock – the force of which was equalled by the knowledge that no one else recognised it, not even, or especially, the one who possessed it."[7] Morrison soon realises that the beauty she was seeing was larger than the physical beauty of a face: "It must have been more than the face I was examining: the silence of the street in the early afternoon, the light, the atmosphere of confession. In any case, it was the first time I knew beautiful. Had imagined it for myself. Beauty was not simply something to behold; it was something one could do."[8] Morrison's observations reveal the force, the "shock" of beauty, and its invocation of an active rather than a passive response to objects and people. They reveal, too, that a conversation about beauty is necessarily integrally tied to a conversation about ugliness.

The second register which has to be taken into account in relation to the study of beauty in Africa is a historical one: the degree to which "beauty" has been the purchase of anthropology on the one hand, and art history on the other. In the early to mid-20th century, "ethnological" discourse was the origin of the idea of a form of beauty which would be authentically "African". In the earliest ethnographic accounts, the beauty of the "savage" did not exist in itself, but was conferred by the white slave trader, colonial, soldier or merchant.[9] In commercial ports and major sites of colonisation such as towns, the mulatto became the perfect example of such a bestowed beauty. As T.K. Biaya has written, the "beauty" of the negress and the mulatto was part of the grammar of the exotic, and race and beauty were drawn together in a hierarchy of appearance.[10]

Ethnographic approaches were closely tied to the emergence of negrophile movements in Paris between the First and Second World Wars. These movements seized the signs and objects of "primitivism" and of "fetishism" in order to make them into the very symbols of modernity in avant-garde culture. "Negrophilia" played on a duplicity, the complexity of which should not be underestimated. On the one hand it spoke in celebratory terms of the mixing of cultures; on the other it attempted to preserve the exotic as such – the operation through which a too-threatening difference is domesticated, leading to the familiarisation of the unfamiliar. Negrophilia represented the uncovering of something in the world of the coloniser and the colonised which was repressed in the psyche – a terrible familiarity that needed to be hidden. The combination of adoration and domination (as in the reception of Josephine Baker) represented the double-bind of a discourse that precluded the possibility of the very assimilation it invited.[11] James Clifford shows that Parisian negrophilia influenced avant-garde music, literature and art. In the 1920s, Paris was flooded with things *nègre*, an expansive category that included North American jazz, syncretic Brazilian rhythms, African, Oceanian and Alaskan carvings, ritual "poetry"

10

from south of the Sahara and from the Australian outback, the literature of the Harlem Renaissance, and René Maran's *Batouala* (subtitled *veritable roman nègre*) which won the Prix Goncourt in 1921.[12] A series of stereotypes long associated with backwardness and inferiority acquired positive connotations and came to stand for liberation and spontaneity, for a simultaneous recovery of ancient sources and an access to true modernity.[13] Alongside the many more or less stereotypical appropriations of 1920s negrophilia, Clifford argues, one can discern a more complex ethnographic engagement with black cultures. The cultures studied by ethnography were sources for an enlarged Western vision of human possibilities.[14]

Writing about anthropology and Negritude, a race-based movement devoted to the liberation of blacks by themselves and a rehabilitation of blackness through language and aesthetics, Christopher Miller discusses how Léopold Senghor in particular was influenced by the German anthropologist Leo Frobenius.[15] Frobenius found in African art a genre that "has preserved itself . . . in all its originality", a preservation or mummification of an essentialised style which makes it a perfect primitivism. Senghor writes in his preface to a Frobenius anthology in French that "no one better than Frobenius revealed Africa to the world and *Africans to themselves*" – creating a strange echo, as Miller points out, with Césaire's heroic figure of Patrice Lumumba in *Une saison au Congo*, who proclaims: "I speak and restore Africa to herself."[16] For Jean-Paul Sartre, it is the frustration born from the Negritude poets' inability to grasp their constantly disappearing Negritude that is the very source of their creativity, always caught in a process of metamorphosis like the mythological figures in Ovid's *Metamorphoses*: "Negritude is a sad myth full of hope, born of Evil and pregnant with future Good . . . it is an unstable rest, an explosive fixity . . . an absolute that knows it is transitory."[17] The Negritude claimed by Senghor and Césaire is a means and not an end, a racial definition that they will ultimately have to tear away from themselves to achieve the "civilisation de l'universel" that Senghor called for.[18] Negritude, Sartre writes, is a "crossing to" and not an "arrival at".[19]

For the younger generation of post-independence African writers, Senghor's reliance on Frobenius's anthropology could only have led to cultural assimilation and the erasure of difference, for it was a sign of alienation in the first place.[20] Yambo Ouologuem, in his novel *Le Devoir de violence*, creates a character called Fritz Schrobenius, "explorer, tourist and ethnographer" and a spoof of Frobenius:

> [Schrobenius had] a groping mania for resuscitating an African universe – cultural autonomy, he called it – which has lost all living reality . . . he was determined to find a metaphysical meaning in everything . . . Gesticulating at every word, he displayed his love of Africa and his tempestuous knowledge with the assurance of a high-school student who had slipped through his final examinations by the skin of his teeth. African life, he held, was pure art.[21]

Africanist art history, somewhat like anthropology, has long been awash with paradox. On the one hand, as Dominique Malaquais has observed,[22] scholars have argued that, in objects created by Africans prior to and in the early years of the colonial period, there is an aesthetics – a sheer capacity to produce beauty – that, when it is encountered by European artists, so strikes them that it radically transforms the very course of the history of European art. On the other hand, the discipline has long denied Africans the capacity to think abstractly about beauty.[23] In the 1970s, things began to change and two notions were foregrounded: (1) that of the African sculptor/potter/musician/masker as an artist conscious of his/her identity and recognised as such by his/her African public; and (2) that of complex registers, terms and philosophies of aesthetics extant in African cultures.[24] Still, despite this breakthrough, problems remain in the literature produced since then. One is that the fascination, in European art history, with connoisseurship – the ability to recognise the individual hand – has been replaced in Africanist art history by fascination for a different kind of connoisseurship: the ability to recognise the style of an "ethnic group". Much of the research on African objects, well into the late 1980s (and despite calls to the contrary by such scholars as René Bravmann) is attached to the idea of "one tribe, one style" – an exercise in which minutiae are identified that, in theory, should allow us to recognise sub-groups and, within these, further sub-groups, down to individual villages in which genres of objects are created. The individual – the artist – is, however, given very little attention.[25]

In the late 1980s, ushered in by the show "Africa Explores" (Centre for African Art, New York), an interest emerged, among Africanist art historians and anthropologists, in "tourist" and "kitsch" art. Not everyone thought this a productive avenue for exploration, but the avant-garde in the field was fascinated.[26] In time, these "takes" on African art made their way into the journal *African Arts*.[27] While *African Arts* was grappling with the complexities of mixing "untraditional" work with what its funders (galleries and dealers whose advertisements made the publication possible) really wanted to see – "real" African art – other journals like *Revue Noire* and *Nka* were more willing to consider contemporary, non-ritual art from Africa, produced by artists who thought of themselves as such and were as abreast as their European colleagues of the written, documented history of world art. The first major exhibition of such art held outside Africa in a museum not dedicated to the arts of Africa took place in 2001/2002 and was called "The Short Century".[28] The study of beauty in this second register, then, has been largely subsumed within debates about how to study the sign of Africa as an aesthetic category.

This leads to the third and related register within which we need to place the study of beauty in Africa, which is its relationship to the marketplace of global modernity and postmodernity. The long-standing tendency amongst Euro-American art curators to sample African worlds according to a principle of cultural authenticity has distorted aesthetic productions and markets. Or, put another way, African artists have frequently been denied the use of global cultural capital which Northern artists have always taken for granted as their patrimony. Anthony Appiah wrote in 1987 about a New York show entitled "Perspectives: Angles on African Art", in preparation for which ten "co-curators" were asked to select ten pieces of African art for inclusion in the exhibition from a hundred they were shown. The only African-based "co-curator", a Baule artist, was, however, given only Baule objects to choose from, since "African informants will criticise sculptures from other ethnic groups in terms of their own traditional criteria, often assuming that such works are simply inept carvings of their own aesthetic tradition." Appiah easily shows how Euro-American "co-curators" proceed from precisely the same principle, applying their own "traditional criteria" to what is beautiful in African art. David Rockefeller's observation in relation to a Fante female figure as being "the kind of thing that goes very well with contemporary Western things. It would look good in a modern apartment or house" demonstrates this particularly well. Of more interest to Appiah is James Baldwin's choice of the "polyglot" *Yoruba Man with a Bicycle* ("it matters little who it was made *for;* what we should learn from is the imagination that produced it").[29] Appiah's essay continues to alert us not only to problems relating to "tourist art" but to the vagaries of aesthetic judgment – what Arjun Appadurai has referred to as the "traffic in criteria"[30] – as well as the geographical contingencies of beauty and ugliness within global capitalism.

Fourthly and finally, the question of beauty as it relates to Africa has often been read within the register of frivolity, and dismissed as a result in relation to the sublime power of economics or politics. Put differently, in view of the forms of human degradation of which the African continent is seen to speak, to talk about beauty has been implicitly encoded as not simply superfluous but indeed morally irresponsible if not reprehensible. According to such a view, a study of beauty would distract our attention from the multiple permutations of social distress with which we are confronted.[31]

These, then, have been some of the constraints in relation to studying beauty in Africa and its diasporas. It is precisely these constraints that suggest the need for the conversation which this collection of essays takes up. While engaging with beauty's apparent recalcitrance as a concept, we might also investigate its relationship to pleasure, to erotics and to a grammar of the future. Many questions emerge, moreover, as to beauty's implication in, or rejection of, vocabularies of the moral as well as temporalities of the human. As we attempt an approach to these questions in African contexts, we need to consider an emerging body of work in the Euro-American academy since the late 1990s, but especially since 2000, which focuses explicitly on beauty. Given this recent body of work, it is an especially apposite time to consider some of these debates in relation to Africa, and also to confront the lack of a properly global epistemology at their heart. I turn to some of this new work on beauty below.

13

II

Recent work on beauty by scholars in the US in particular reveals a set of specific preoccupations and traits. These include: firstly, an ongoing concern with the ethical and moral force of beauty; secondly, an emphasis (at the end of the culture wars and the beginning of the critique of identity politics) less on the power of the gaze and more on the power of the observed, the subjective power of the "object" of beauty, to render the observer vulnerable; thirdly, a tendency, at least among some philosophers, to belie a discussion of beauty's intimate opposite, ugliness, in arguments pertaining to beauty (despite the fact that much of 20th-century modernism has been about the ugly, so much so that Mario Vargas Llosa has remarked that "contemporary aesthetics has established the beauty of ugliness, reclaiming for art everything in human experience that artistic representation had previously rejected"[32]); fourthly, an ongoing engagement with Euro-American modernism as the principal site of debates about beauty (versus either "multiple modernities" or properly rendered global epistemologies which take into their theoretical ambit the world beyond Euro-America); and fifthly, the rise, after 2000, of a focus on male bodies in relation to the "beauty industry" and the revision of forms of heterosexual culture which have long silenced the idea of male beauty. Below I briefly examine each of these in turn.

One of the more recent and controversial books on the subject of beauty to appear within a long philosophical tradition, beginning in the early 19th century, is Elaine Scarry's *On Beauty*.[33] Scarry's work on beauty is deeply embedded in Western aesthetic philosophy. She is interested, like Kant, Hegel and Heidegger, in what constitutes consciousness and how we perceive our "being-in-the-world", and in the relationship between mind and world. She is also drawn, like Levinas, to the question of beauty as it relates to the questions of others. Scarry focuses on the "distributional power" of beauty as a form of justice. She draws on philosopher Simone Weil's idea that beauty requires us to give up our imaginary position at the centre, not because we cease to stand at the centre of the world, as we never stood there, but because we cease to stand even at the centre of our own world.[34] Scarry goes on to argue that the quality of heightened attention that beauty induces is "voluntarily extended out to other persons or things ... Through its beauty, the world continually recommits us to a rigorous standard of perceptual care". Scarry emphasises less the power of the one who gazes than the notion of looking as being overtaken by the power of another. She suggests that when an experience of someone else's beauty takes us out of ourselves, the social effect is a just one. Because an encounter with beauty in this way induces an occasion for "unselving", she sees it as contributing to a sense of justice, of caring, of paying renewed attention to others.[35]

Denis Donoghue, in his book *Speaking of Beauty*, is skeptical: "Elaine Scarry evidently wants to make the discussion of beauty respectable again by claiming that beautiful objects invite us to a renewed respect for truth and justice. It seems to me a poor defence of beauty to isolate it and then make it an instrument in the advance of other values."[36] For the same reason, Donoghue seeks to dislodge beauty from its Kantian and Keatsian triad of the beautiful, the good and the true. Yet Donoghue himself links beauty to other values: beauty, he says, confers on us "nothing beyond the capacity for humanity";[37] and "beautiful things ... are rarely called beautiful, but ... they are shown to be so by the constructed centres of care in which they are presented".[38] Or, commenting on Stendhal's notion that "beauty is only the promise of happiness", Donoghue says that "it is a figure of happiness, not a promise, but a hint of possibility".[39]

Important work on beauty has also emerged recently from scholars of the philosophy and history of art. Wendy Steiner and Arthur Danto have both argued that whereas 19th-century art was deeply concerned with beauty, modernist art of the 20th century was all about the return of the sublime. In modernism, the perennial rewards of aesthetic experience – pleasure, insight, empathy – were largely withheld, and its generous aim, beauty, was abandoned, Steiner tells us.[40] Modern artworks may often have been profoundly beautiful, but theirs was a tough beauty, hedged in with deprivation, denial and revolt.[41] Kant bequeathed to the West a taste for the sublime, an aesthetic experience in which beauty is a confrontation with the unknowable, the limitless, the superhuman.[42] In Steiner's reading, the sublime turned the act of aesthetic judgment into a brush with abstraction, alienation and death. She argues that the turn from beauty in 20th-century modernist art, or at least from a long-standing idea of beauty, was also a turn away from the female subject. The latter either was absent or incidental, or subsumed within questions of form. Modernist art, she claims, chose form and fetish over beauty.

Criticising the uncompromising "masculine" distance of the sublime and the rationalist aesthetics it entailed, Steiner makes two arguments: first, that sublimity turns woman into a victim or victimiser, but never an empathetic equal; that the pure abstraction of Kant and the pure pornography of Sade were to become the two faces of the 20th-century avant-garde.[43] Second, that the question of desire itself was transferred in this body of art from woman to the African fetish, via primitivism ("if modernist art was too sophisticated to confuse the desire aroused by a subject (woman) with the Kantian perfection of its form, it did not eliminate desire altogether. It simply quoted the desire and power of those not so 'advanced', and translated the bearers of that manna into form"[44]). Steiner, angry at the rejection of beauty and the sign of woman in art as something tawdry, self-indulgent and sentimental, argues that beauty is not a property as Kant would have us see it, but an interaction between a self and an other, a pleasurable and complex reciprocity which is precisely what the sublime disallows.[45]

Arthur Danto reads the emergence of the sublime in modernist art differently.

For him, the importance of the avant-garde, from the Surrealists onwards, has been to show us that art doesn't have to be beautiful, that beauty does not have to be part of the definition of art, and that beauty could be present in any given work or not.[46] It was the moral weight assigned to beauty that helps us to understand why 20th-century modern artists found it so urgent to dislodge beauty from its mistaken place in the philosophy of art, to put right a conceptual error. It was the energy of these artists that opened us to a much more complex sense of aesthetic experience, incorporating ugliness, repulsion, abjection, horror and disgust. Hal Foster has recently written: "for many in contemporary culture, truth resides in the traumatic or abject subject, in the diseased or damaged body. This body is the evidentiary basis of important witnessings to truth, of necessary witnessings against power".[47] Foster's comment helps us to see both the importance of Danto's argument but also how little avant-garde modernist art in fact addressed the human body as the site of suffering and the object of political outrage.

Danto is interested in freeing beauty from "taste", opening it to new ways of thinking about itself and in understanding the limits of beauty. Beauty, he argues, may be internal to the meaning of some works, such as in the case of elegy ("we understand too little about the psychology of loss to understand why the creation of beauty is so fitting as a way of marking it"[48]). But the elegiac mode may be entirely inappropriate to political catastrophe – it may distance it too abruptly – especially where death is not inevitable. It is clearly wrong to present as beautiful that which calls for action or indignation. Thus Danto finds disturbing the fact that Salgado's photographs of suffering humanity are beautiful: "Have we a right to show suffering of that order in beautiful ways? Doesn't the beauty of the representation imply that its content is somehow inevitable, like death? Are the photographs not unedifyingly dissonant, their beauty jarring with the painfulness of their content? If beauty is internally connected to the content of the work, it can be a criticism of a work that it is beautiful when it is inappropriate for it to be so."[49] Picasso's paintings of prosti-tutes, he argues, make use of beauty not as consolation but as relish, a device for enhancing the appetite, for taking pleasure in the spectacle of suffering.

Both Steiner and Danto welcome the return of beauty as a compelling problem in the 21st century and a chance to rethink its terms. Steiner argues that the violent break from an aesthetics of "passive allure" now frees us, paradoxically, "to contemplate new possibilities in beauty and its female symbolism", to re-imagine the female subject "as an equal partner in aesthetic pleasure".[50] For Danto, it is the option of whether to draw on beauty or not in the repertoires of the aesthetic that becomes so important to the future. Some theorists, by contrast, disavow the current turn to beauty. Doris Summer, for example, argues that the resources of the sublime are far more suggestive of what is essential to aesthetics, which in her view is a sense of disturbance. Summer's recent study of bilingual aesthetics draws on Freud's work on jokes as expressions of psychic strangenesss and the artful mechanisms of surprise and shock. Similarly, she argues, those who inhabit two or more languages not only escape the single-mindedness of a monolingual view of the world but revel in the pleasures of not "getting it", as well as of knowing how language can fail us. The sublimity of working in simultaneous codes, with a mode of divergent thinking based on doubt and edginess, is preferable to the symmetry of a language of assimilation and constitutes an "everyday sublime" that she posits against the contemporary concern with beauty. As we have seen in this introduction, however, beauty may also evince a sense of shock and surprise.

III

These, then, have constituted dominant contemporary debates about the philosophy of beauty. Insofar as they try to rescue the conversation about beauty from the relative silence on the topic during the second half of the 20th century, they help to point us towards some of the shifting intellectual signs of our times, and to further reflect on why discussions about beauty are increasingly less often held to be regressive and suspicious. In part this has to do, as Donoghue has convincingly argued, with the demise of socialism and Marxism as a widespread social ideal and academic practice, each of which carried with it a moralising obligation to "justify beauty".[51] It may also be that the politicisation of theory is less acrimonious than it has been, and that there is more space for themes which were often regarded as taboo. Other proponents of the "return of beauty" in the American academy, however, have dismissed the work of Scarry and others as "too abstract" for a contemporary conversation about beauty. Dave Hickey's 1993 text, *The Invisible Dragon: Four Essays on Beauty*, the first to proclaim that "the issue of the nineties will be beauty", bemoaned "our largely unarticulated concept of 'beauty'" and summarily discarded aesthetics as "old patriarchal do-dah about transcendental formal values and humane realism".[52] Peter Schjeldahl, announcing in a 1996 *New York Times Magazine* essay that "Beauty is Back", issued a call for the public to recognise "Beauty's malaise – the problem of worn-out philosophies that clutter its dictionary definition" in order to become "the historically freighted, abstract piety of 'Beauty'". "Beauty" here is a reference to Plato's timeless and universal Form of Beauty, as opposed to instantiations of "beauty" of our own time or in our own sense of the term.[53] Not only did Schjeldahl confidently herald that "[a] trampled aesthetic blooms again" but volunteered to "rescue for educated talk the vernacular sense of beauty".[54] More recently, Bill Beckley and David Shapiro, editors of a 1998 anthology of readings entitled *Uncontrollable Beauty*, also dismiss a philosophical tradition of deep if, in their view, narrow reflection on beauty.[55]

At least some of this dismissiveness seems unnecessary and misleading (as well as empirically inaccurate – it is clear that a long tradition of thought about beauty still

17

inflects many contemporary meanings of the term).[56] Equally, it is certain that we need a more capacious rendering of the term beauty than Scarry and philosophers before her have allowed for.[57] While Steiner draws in her reading on powerful feminist critiques of the construction of women as "beautiful objects",[58] increasingly the theoretical power of such critiques may also be applied to male bodies in a contemporary consumer capitalism looking for new markets. Susan Bordo is one of a number of feminist scholars now writing about male bodies, and argues that the mainstreaming of a gay male aesthetic in which the erotic charge of various sexual styles is less and less mapped onto actual sexual orientation, both offers us a rich eroticisation of the male body beautiful and results in more and more men suffering body image dysfunction, eating disorders and exercise compulsion. This is in strong contrast to a, until recently, normative heterosexual culture in which male references to beauty remain rare except when referring to dead animals, a new truck or someone's prowess with a rifle ("She's a beauty").[59] Bordo both welcomes the pleasures of looking at the male body for women and detects a more Puritan ethic in our attitudes to the body in general, in which the eros of beauty "has been turned into constant, hard work".[60]

Lastly, as Mick Taussig suggests, we might keep in mind the extent to which aesthetic experience is "far more mischievous and complicated and real" than contemporary ideological critiques of the subject and of aesthetics allow. If it seems important to pluralize aesthetics as a concept, however, Martin Jay considers that if all objects can be redeemed in aesthetic terms, we run the risk of "re-enchanting" the entire world (a danger recognised by Benjamin in his warning against the aestheticisation of politics). Jay recognises the need for a reconceptualised aesthetics adequate to our contemporary historical situation.[61]

Having considered aspects of the contemporary "beauty debate" in the Northern academy, I want to turn in the next section to the work of a number of contemporary African scholars, many of whom address the issue of beauty implicitly or under the general rubric of "aesthetics", but whose work nevertheless offers us signal points of location for the essays in this volume.

IV

The writing of African scholars in the realm of beauty falls broadly into two categories, shaped respectively by Anglophone and Francophone traditions of thought. Both Simon Gikandi and Okwui Enwezor engage in their recent work with revisionist readings of primitivism and ethnology in the contemporary art museum and with representations of Africa in Northern vocabularies and sign systems. Gikandi, in his essay "Picasso, Africa and the Schemata of Difference" in this volume, makes use of the aftermath of the Museum of Modern Art's controversial 1984 "Primitivism" exhibition in New York, to reflect on the state of the debate. He begins by recalling how in the mid-1950s, the Guyanese artist Aubrey Williams, a leading exponent of

18

Afro-modernism and black abstractionism, was introduced to Pablo Picasso by Albert Camus during a visit to Paris. Given Williams's association with various factions of Cubism and his attempt to emulate its style to capture the hybrid cultures of his native Guyana, the meeting with the famed artist was supposed to be a high-light of his career, perhaps a catalyst, Gikandi speculates, for new directions in the troubled relationship between artists of African descent and the international avant-garde. As it turned out, Williams found the encounter anticlimactic and disturbing:

> I remember the first comment he made to me when we met. He said
> that I had a very fine African head and he would like me to pose for him.
> I felt terrible. In spite of the fact that I was introduced to him as an artist,
> he did not think of me as another artist. He thought of me only as
> something he could use for his own work.[62]

Gikandi goes on to locate Williams's disappointment in his assumption that since Picasso undoubtedly had an intimate artistic relationship with African art objects, he would have equal respect for "the cultures and bodies that had made modernism possible". He goes on to show how while the influences of the African "tribal" on European modernism seem self-evident, they are still redefined by contemporary scholars as "convergences", "affinities" or "connotations" rather than in terms of formal influence or style. Gikandi probes the reasons for this ongoing "anxiety of influence" in modernism's concern with others as the enabling condition of beauty, as he analyses the continual move away from the conceptual towards the perceptual in its reading of the fetish, the mask and the sign of the "African" in general.[63]

Like Gikandi, Okwui Enwezor is interested in contemporary "exhibition systems" and in the problematic for African artists and critics of being "looked at" by the European other, as in the experience of viewing African art in the Euro-American art museum. In a recent text, Enwezor reflects on his visit to London's Tate Modern, a thematically organised collection, including a "Nude/Action/Body" section. The section begins, Enwezor notes, with large galleries exhibiting the works of European artists such as Spencer and Picasso. Adjacent to these is what he describes as a small ethnographic vitrine, in which extracts from two documentary films, travel documen-taries of naked black bodies in African villages, play. Enwezor speculates why this is necessary and how it is only made worse by the "double-speak" of the explanatory footnote which reads: "the self-awareness displayed by those under scrutiny, glimpsed observing the film-maker, subverts the supposed objectivity of the film".[64]

For Enwezor, all of this speaks of a primitivist discourse to which the Tate Modern in the 21st century is a logical heir. He wonders why the curators did not rather choose to exhibit the photographs of an artist like Rotimi Fani-Kayode, which reflect on the distinction between the nude and nakedness as it concerns the African body

Sarah Nuttall > Introduction: Rethinking Beauty

(versus the naturalised conventions of otherness). Of a small sculpture in the vitrine, untitled and undated but, we are told, owned by Jacob Epstein, Enwezor writes: "it is no use speaking about the lyrical beauty and artistic integrity of this powerful sculpture so pointlessly compromised by the rest of the detritus of colonial knowledge systems crammed into the vitrine. The sculpture's presence is not only remote from us, it seems to connote not art, above all not autonomous art, just artifact, or worse still, evidence".[65] Finally, nothing in the vitrine suggests to him an "affiliative spirit of mutual influence and recognition; only a mode of instruction on what is modern and what is not (an astonishing form of ethnographic ventriloquism)".[66] He concludes that the legacy of the Western historical avant-garde seems inadequate to do the job of producing a unified theory of contemporary art, and that paradoxically, it is globalisation that has laid open the myth of a consolidated art world.

Gikandi and Enwezor are amongst many African artists, writers and others, particularly from the Anglophone African world, who express their continued frustration towards reductive interpretations of African texts – as well as towards scholars who, as the Ghanaian writer Ama Ata Aidoo has said, do not give the full weight of their intelligence and scholarship to the works of African artists and writers.[67] Readings are perpetually produced, she argues, which have interpreted the formal innovations of African texts merely as responses to, and subversions of, Western domination. Enwezor, in his discussion of the Tate, literally abandons a conversation about the beauty of the sculpture as such, writing instead of his anger at the interpretative frames that are set up for him as the viewer, and which belie an open and engaged reading of beauty.

Francophone African scholars and those writing within their theoretical ambit have taken a rather different direction with regard to the paradigms of African beauty. In an essay called "The Thing and Its Doubles", usually ignored in favour of his work on topics in political science and history, Achille Mbembe writes of particular ontologies of violence and the marvellous that emerge from the reading of "the image" in Cameroon. He discusses "the specific activity that the activity of working with signs and graphic marks has become in the postcolony", where historically the general process of communication, the making of public statements, thinking, were performed in a context where language was not written.[68] He focuses on the fact that the scriptural process in general – the writing of things and the world – was done through masks and carvings, but above all through the spoken word, speech being the very foundation of experience and the primary form of knowledge. It was from language acts that a critical tradition was constituted – and was transmitted over time and space, recited in public and pondered in private: "to publicly articulate knowledge consisted, to a large extent, in making everything speak – that is, in constantly transforming reality into a sign and on the other hand, filling with reality things empty and hollow in appearance".[69] In these conditions,

Mbembe argues, the great epistemological – and therefore social – break was not between what was seen and what was read, but between what was seen (the visible) and what was not seen (the occult), between what was heard, spoken and memorised and what was concealed (the secret).[70] In a context where there was no forced correspondence between what was seen, heard and said, one was bringing to life not simply "something other" but "another side of all things".[71]

Colonisation and Christianity did alter the relationship with the image, yet, in spite of the scale of transformation and the discontinuities, Mbembe argues, an imaginary world has remained. It is part of the general subconscious without which the figurative expression has no status. At the same time, it imposes a framework on the uses that the post-colonial urban world makes of figurative expressions. Mbembe is interested in understanding an African ontology, how a socius without writing or the Word, as Hal Foster has called it,[72] appeared to Africans themselves and became the site of a distinctive form of creativity. Yet we can see, too, how he writes not only with the influence of Nietzsche in mind but also in the wake of debates about the power of the African image given shape in the Francophone world, in particular within the intellectual worlds of Paris in mid-century, from Negritude onwards.

Mariane Ferme has written in not dissimilar ways about beauty and ugliness, in particular in relation to the Mende mask.[73] She shows how an aesthetics of the ugly protects the incommensurability of the ritual object and enhances its efficacy. Hence nothing becomes visible for the one who does not know how to recognise disguised power. A parallel stress on the ugly in Mende masking practices (for example the paired appearance of the beautiful Sowei and the unattractive Gonde in Sande public performances) imparts an ironic dimension.[74] Some see this as an ironic continuum between beauty and ugliness; others have seen the paradox of simultaneous display of beauty and ugliness as central to an anti-aesthetic in Mende ideas of power.[75] Similar to the sublime, Ferme argues, the point here is that the aesthetic emphasis on something that appears absurd and grotesque produces a sense of awe for the transcendent. The reversibility of the beautiful into an aesthetics of the ugly leads to the question of containment. This is because secret knowledge and practice are necessary for enhancing a "big person's" aura in the community. Secrecy and power share a sociological dynamic – they are both predicated on the relationship between the subject's concealed aims and their visible manifestations in the external world. Furthermore, they are both strategies for magnifying reality through the aesthetic display of the body and through the expansion of its boundaries. Ferme, like Mbembe, offers a subtle understanding of the interwovenness of beauty, ugliness and power. It is worth underscoring the extent to which these approaches differ from more "classical" readings of the beautiful/ugly in African aesthetics as primarily expressions of the "good" and the "bad" in the articulation of heuristic models of social appropriateness.[76]

21

Sarah Nuttall > Introduction: Rethinking Beauty

For both Mbembe and Ferme, that which we consider beautiful originates at the point of confluence between appearance and imagination. It has both a material nature and a nature which exists on the other side of materiality. It is this dual dimension (material and ideal) which makes it so difficult to grasp.[77] Secondly, beauty (like ugliness) belongs to the world of sensations. Western thought, on the contrary, has always shied away from interpreting beauty within the framework of an anthropology of the senses. In its eyes, it is in the world of sensations that the failure of the "ability to know" is most clearly manifested. The world of sensations, from this point of view, is a world of delirium and aberration, of "reason in disorder", prophecies, dementia and fury, no more than "maladies of the head".[78] This was contrary to the views of Hegel, who described aesthetics as "the science of sensation or feeling".[79] Scholars such as Mbembe, Biaya and Ferme start from the premise, on the contrary, that it is in the nature of what we consider to be a beautiful object or a beautiful person to arouse sensations, and the attributes of "refinement", of "order" or even of the "sublime" (elements of the classic definitions of the beautiful) are entirely secondary. Moreover, in terms of sensations, there can be no canon. For each of them, beauty is to a large extent dependent on ugliness to be properly recognised, a point I return to below.

V

Having attempted to define some of the major debates in the field of beauty, I turn now to the essays in this book. While a number of them draw on debates within the philosophy and history of art referred to earlier in this introduction, many of them do not and it is the explicit attempt of this book to widen the range of such "beauty" debates. The essays can be read through at least three broad lenses. The first is *the integral association of beauty with a form of a largely socially defined ugliness and abjection.* Achille Mbembe articulates this early on in his essay on Congolese music: "There is no beauty which does not relate to the body … behind the sounds in this case, there is the expression of an existence in which exuberance and the gift for suffering go hand in hand with fierce and powerful desires. Because this society, so accustomed to atrocity, is playing with death, its music is both born out of tragedy and nurtured by it. So is beauty." The reality of ugliness and abjection, for him, is at the centre of the social epistemology he examines. Nietzsche's statement that "it is impossible for a man fighting for his survival to be an artist"[80] is contradicted by the insatiable enthusiasm for existence expressed in Congolese music, Mbembe finds.

Other contributors come at this concatenation of the beautiful and the ugly in different ways. While Mbembe treats the "beautiful-ugly" within an aesthetics of sensation, William Kentridge focuses on the question of form. Kentridge reflects on what it is to make drawings from photographs, in this case forensic photographs. In the act of drawing such photographs, he says, "the horror of their origin is put on hold". He goes on:

"Is the image beautiful, is it ugly?" is not the question the hand is asking. Nor, even, I think, the question, "does the drawing keep the horror to which the original photo attested?" … the drawing always attests to itself, as the example of transformation. The horror of the circumstances of the original photograph regains its place only as one of the associations the image unleashes.

For Kentridge the question of beauty is the question of form: it is the form of a work that will speak in its own way and on its own terms only to the subject "at hand". Drawing beauty has everything to do with the materiality of his medium, so that for him the call of the Germiston landscape on the South African highveld, with its slime dams, reed beds and bleakness, was specific to paper, charcoal, ruler, eraser: "the burnt wood of charcoal itself moved between the object and the drawing". For Kentridge, the excitement and the reason for doing the work has to do with the engagement of being caught between the object and the sheet of paper ("I'm not sure whether I am caught between the object and the paper or lost").

Rita Barnard, by contrast, thinks about the relationship between the beautiful and the ugly in relation to geographical and cultural contingency. She shows the word "beautiful" to be a semiotic shifter, the valence of which is frequently contested, and often dependent on both its cultural context and on the place of the observer. She points out that philosophy's emphasis on beauty as a cognitive event – a "rapt and isolated confrontation between beholder and object" – ignores the fact that human beings do many things with objects they consider beautiful: "they judge them, they sell them, they wear them, they display them, they court them, they collect them, they smuggle them, they forge them and so on". She is interested more in the mutability of beauty than in Scarry's idea of it as "clearly discernible", in the possibility that one person might find another's beautiful person or thing not simply lacking "the perfect features that obligate us to stare" or "less endowed with those qualities of perfection which arrest our attention", but, quite simply, ugly. Barnard draws out what she sees as Scarry's confident cultural centrality, despite her disclaimer that we do not "stand at the centre of the world", and thus the location of aesthetic observation, in which "beautiful" is a "translation term"[81] which emphasises the geographical and personal contingency of aesthetic values.

If Mbembe emphasises the configuration of beauty and ugliness as it relates to an anthropology of sensations, Kentridge in terms of form and Barnard in terms of the contingencies of context, Dominique Malaquais and Pippa Stein do so in terms of an aesthetics of waste. Malaquais considers how questions of beauty and ugliness bear intimate links to the fraught, intricate spaces of the post-colonial city. Things ugly here become synonymous with socio-spatial, economic and by extension political disorder, beauty with ideals of order born of the colonial era, clear-cut (if invented)

23

distinctions between formal and informal, use and refuse, art and junk. For young artists in Douala, Cameroon, beauty is decentred through an implicit critique of the manner in which the Northern world deals with Africa (via a traditional art which is celebrated for its formal perfection). Beauty in the contemporary African worlds she writes about is born rather from the sheer intractability, ugliness of the city.

Malaquais focuses on the history of a sculpture, the first work of public art in Douala, which is made entirely of waste. Stein discusses doll-child figures made by children who live in informal settlements in Gauteng, South Africa. The figures are made from that which has been discovered (used bottles, dirty scraps of cardboard, broken plastic, soiled cloths found in the veld). They are rendered from the found material of extreme poverty, the remains of the everyday, "that which cannot be eaten".[82] Stein draws out their similarities to traditional fertility dolls, using a concept of slippability to think about the way deeply embedded cultural knowledges emerge into our conceptual networks. She explores, too, an aesthetic derived from the construction of shacks from waste materials found on dumps scattered around the city.

The relation between beauty and a socially defined ugliness, then, is taken up by these authors within registers of *sensation, form, cultural contingency* and *waste*. Each engages with a study of the beautiful in cultural contexts of distress or what Barnard calls "places of insecurity" in different ways. I have drawn out only four of these, and other essays in the book can be read fruitfully in relation to each of them.

The second major lens via which, I suggest, we might approach the essays which follow is a *distributional and circulatory one* in which a notion of beauty is seen to work across the senses and across space. Several essays work beyond the visual, for instance, in the realms of sound, taste, touch and smell. Moreover, they track ways in which a visual event, say, might produce a sound event or how a photograph might lead to the making of a sculpture. Some engage with an aesthetic of distribution as it relates to space – as they consider how ideas of beauty travel, transfiguring its meanings across African diasporas.

Beauty is explored in its distributional sense by Els van der Plas and Mark Gevisser. Van der Plas considers how the Senegalese sculptor Ousmane Sow saw Leni Riefenstahl's photographs of the Nuba in Kenya and was inspired to make sculptures of human bodies, drawing on his own understanding of a complex tradition of African sculpture. (Riefenstahl herself travelled to Nairobi in 1956 after reading a Hemingway novel set there, and decided to photograph the Nuba after seeing a photograph of them in Nairobi.) Thus both Riefenstahl and Sow made important aesthetic choices via the impact of a photograph. Riefenstahl, however, was fascinated by the aesthetics of the perfect human body, and saw the Nuba as radiating "an original beauty" that "was not civilised". Sow, by contrast, does not seek physical perfection, and is interested in the body's monumentality, in facial expressions and body language. For Mark Gevisser, too, it is the impact of a series of photographs that inspired him to write the beginning of an autobiographical novel. Born in 1964 into apartheid South Africa, into a world of legislated political offences and "indecent, immoral and sexual offences", Gevisser discovers as an adult a file marked "Fringe Country – No Colour Bar, 1961", images of cross-racial desire in Johannesburg in the midst of segregation. The beauty of the images evokes "unutterable loss, a hunger that ripples down the sides of my tongue and gathers in my throat", at what might have been. Gevisser goes on to consider the "history of pain in beauty" in cross-racial same-sex men's lives in South Africa. Taken together, these two essays reflect how Sow and Gevisser look for alternative body imaginaries in the face of both Nazism and apartheid's elevation of the ideal body type, which was white, masculine and heterosexual.

Few studies of beauty work with the idea of an aesthetics of taste – taste not as the sign of high-bourgeois conceptions of beauty but, to return to the root of the metaphor, in relation to food and eating. Taste in this sense is often left to food memoirs, autobiographical recipe books or tourist guides. Célestin Monga, Françoise Vergès and Cheryl-Ann Michael reflect on how food and eating take on a profoundly aesthetic significance in African contexts and consider ways in which they might have important things to tell us about beauty. Monga focuses in his essay on the importance of eating in societies of want, and especially on the arts of enjoyment (central to the art of living), dependent on both the place and moment of eating, taking as his example a close reading of increasingly ritualised wedding feasts in Cameroon. Over and above the principle of pleasure, he shows, is the struggle against failure (scarcity, misery), and a desire for self-affirmation. Françoise Vergès, writing about Réunion Island and the worlds of the African South Indian Ocean, focuses, too, on the pleasures of eating and the eros of taste, deeply implicated in childhood and desire. Vergès makes a case for a mapping of the world around territories of food and eating, economies of plenty and shortage; mapping the cartographies of colonialism and post-colonialism and their vocabularies of cooking. She reads the aesthetics of Creole cuisine as the cuisine of a society built on destruction and erasure. Here, creativity in cooking was a matter of survival, and the result was not "fusion food", but a cuisine born rather from an incredible attention to detail.

In an essay which opens a fascinating dialogue with Vergès, Cheryl-Ann Michael reflects that while food embodies cultural fusion, just as African identities themselves are inevitably eclectic, it is possible to overlook the ways in which such hybridities often mask the inequities of their own making: for example, the centrality of Malay cuisine as a marker of a distinct Cape culture while people of Malay descent are "curiously vague figures, scarcely visible despite, or perhaps because of, their food". In this "slipperiness" of food as a cultural referent lies its value, Michael argues. She works with the idea, too, that food and food memories offer simultaneously a means of connection to particular places and people, and a refusal to limit these meanings to these particularities. Reading Vergès's essay enables Michael to gesture towards a new intra-African aesthetics:

> Françoise Vergès writes of eating mangoes with chilli. Here we share a similar childhood food memory. Now my memories of a Durban childhood where summers meant dipping slivers of green or ripe mangoes in a mixture of chilli powder and salt are tantalisingly linked to faraway Réunion, a strange and distant place made partially known. A new, composite, elusive beauty is made.

Insofar as Vergès and Michael offer a vivid sense of diasporic configurations and the effects of these on the history of beauty and its forms, their essays work in conversation with those which treat the concept of diaspora more fully. Patricia Pinho reflects on the making of Brazilian blackness which searches for references to beauty in idealised images of African aesthetics. She explores the rich Afro-Brazilian aesthetics which results and which she terms "Afro-aesthetics". "Afro" is used as an adjective to describe objects that are believed to be loaded with Africanness, conferred through impression and intuition. In exploring a transnational black aesthetics, she shows how, while elements originating in Jamaica, the US and the African continent feed Brazilian Afro-aesthetics, Brazil simultaneously feeds the production of beauty for some African-Americans. Pinho also discusses some of the limitations to and problems with a cultural process of "becoming and behaving black".

Kamari Clarke is also interested in how black Atlantic zones of exchange configure the beautiful. She focuses on the transnational imaginaries which have emerged from the dispersal of West African traditional religious practices, especially Òrìsà practices in the Americas. Clarke looks at the Africanisation of the Santería movement (a continuum of religious change in the Americas), with a particular case study of Yorùbá revivalists who live at Òyótúnjí African village in South Carolina. She does so in order to show how black beauty must be understood in relation to black moral geographies whose power lies in historical discourses of post-slavery suffering, and reveals the re-inscription of autochthonous mappings of racial authenticity onto otherwise fluid articulations of personhood, strengthening their linkages to US citizenship by producing a black aesthetics of African belonging. The idea of beauty in its distributional sense as explored in these essays, then, is one which works across the senses, reappearing and reproducing itself in various directions,[83] as well as across space (and time) in a process of scattering between here and there, then and now.[84]

The third lens which essays in this book suggest is one of *an anti-aesthetic, that which deals with the limits of beauty, or one in which beauty remains unnamed.*

Rodney Place considers the limits of an explicitly or self-consciously "African" aesthetics or idea of beauty. Working with the idea of Johannesburg as a city-in-formation from the point of view of an artist, urbanist and architect, Place chooses spaces in the city from which to take up different viewpoints, accepting neither their given meanings nor functions. He emphasises the importance of displacing oneself into other viewpoints rather than professing to define a "new" aesthetic. He conceptualises South Africa's urban landscapes as inherited machines – "up-for-grabs territorial frames waiting for waves of (cultural) occupation". The idea of an African aesthetic might lie as much in the power of (re)interpreting these structures as it would in making things "African", he argues, as he considers the "potent beauty" of Johannesburg's modernist structures – now that they are detached from their original ideological aims and meanings. ("They can now exist in pure physicality, since their instructional intentions are redundant to people already social and urban in their habits.") All of this adds up, for Place, to "ordinary urbanism", vernacular landscapes rather than "social visions" – a way of learning to act, and an ethical position gleaned from social participation, "rather than from a helicopter".

Michelle Gilbert chooses to focus entirely on the ugly rather than the beautiful – the ugly, not in terms of social distress, but in terms of the representation of the shocking or the strange, the monstrous or the fantastic. She discusses painted plywood boards on the main streets of Accra and the byways of rural market towns in Ghana, advertising "morality" plays, part of all-night, open-air concert parties. Gilbert investigates the images themselves as well as responses by young Ghanaians to the content of the paintings – a "subject matter that is fearful, raw and powerful". Her focus on the signs and graphic markers of the ugly can be usefully read in relation to Mbembe's idea that in the African image, the reverse of the world (the invisible) becomes part and parcel of its obverse (the visible), and vice versa.

Lastly, for a number of contributors, the idea of beauty or an aesthetic resides more in the ways in which words are put together than in the explicit content of their essays. This is true of essays such as those by Gevisser and Vergès as well as in the two short stories by Mia Couto included here. Couto's stories, as Isabel Hofmeyr suggests, evoke rather than name what beauty might be in contexts of the ugliness of political failure, post-colonial administrative and bureaucratic disfigurement. The language of fiction is a search for form, in particular an attempt to find a form "to bring newness into the world", shifting its axes.[85]

Sarah Nuttall > Introduction: Rethinking Beauty

Conclusion

In the early part of this introduction I proposed that the question of beauty in Africa and its diasporas has been understood historically within four modes of inscription: of Africa and Africans as the figure of the *ugly;* of beauty within the registers of anthropology, especially the "*ethnographic*"; of African aesthetics within the global *market;* and of African beauty within the registers of *frivolity.*[86]

The essays in this book offer a different set of inflections which, amongst others, can be defined as: firstly, the complex and integral association of beauty with *a socially inflected ugliness*; secondly, a *distributional* sense of beauty, crisscrossing the senses; and thirdly, an anti-aesthetic, or the notion of the *limits of beauty* or its resistance to naming as such. It seems to me significant that the essays gathered here do not in general understand beauty in ethical terms. Rather, in placing beauty in a powerfully imbricated relationship to ugliness, they strongly invoke the *senses* as integral to an understanding of beauty and they mark the *difficulty* of beauty as a concept.

Of particular preoccupation in this introduction as well as in many of the essays gathered below has been the nature of beauty's relationship to ugliness. Ugliness emerges here not as the opposite of beauty but as tied to it with an intricacy that belies a binary relationship in which one pole is always the more powerfully encoded signifier. Attention to ugliness, we could say, presents us with the properly engaged conundrum, the predicament, that beauty presents. Although this book reflects on ugliness throughout, it often foregrounds the forms and practices of the beautiful. As such, it opens the way for a more fully explored aesthetics of ugliness, about which so little has yet been written and because each is intricately part of the other.

The essays below tend to read beauty as relating to a set of (powerful and differentiated) contexts, but not, I think, as fully contingent (although there are many differences internal to the essays here). This latter is in part because the apprehension of beauty is often propelled in the writing which follows by a politics of hope and anticipation, a surge of feeling beyond the merely given present moment. Implicit in this is a sense that beauty belongs to the tense of the future (not least because it stands for something we do not yet understand, that it is something the meanings of which we have not yet exhausted).[87] Taken together, these perceptions teach us to read beauty in both its contingent and capacious senses. Few essays, moreover, seek to attempt a comprehensive definition of beauty – or to fully compromise its apparent recalcitrance as a concept.[88] Further still, in their willingness to take up in one form or another the concept of beauty, they collectively propose the question of pleasure within an ethics of globalism, and help us to begin to see what a diasporic and properly global erotics of pleasure might amount to, even in their scenes of double truth and where beauty is incommensurable or unbearable.

It seems that the signals, sensations and theoretical imperatives emitted and crafted by the essays gathered here might usefully speak to discussions about beauty anywhere. That they speak of beauty as an idea about, a feeling for, something future inflected because not entirely knowable, yet that they are cautious in employing a vocabulary of the moral, is instructive. While they gesture towards a temporality of the human, they are also careful in their knowledge that most debates on the ethical, most often invested in the idea of the human, are partisan and just as they aim to speak for all, decline to hear another view. Secondly, the powerful awareness and invocation of ugliness, in particular a socially inflected ugliness – and abjection – in relation to anything we might want to say about beauty seems to me a useful way of thinking, anywhere. In other words, it should not be possible, within the paradigm of a properly inflected global epistemology, to speak of beauty without first understanding the question of ugliness. This is as much to delineate the *consequences* of any given argument as to define what beauty really might be.

Acknowledgements

I would like to thank Cheryl-Ann Michael, with whom this project was conceived. In the course of imagining a focus on the idea of beauty I valued, as always, the power and originality of her thoughts and the clarity and richness of perception which characterise her view of our world. The project took form as an international symposium held in Cape Town, South Africa, in April 2001. It was funded, as this book has been, by the Prince Claus Fund in The Netherlands. I thank the Fund for its willingness to pursue with me the less trodden routes through the post-colonial archives of the South and to offer both shape and support to new or under-voiced terrains of the imagination in art, culture and the worlds they produce.

My thanks go as well to Achille Mbembe for his rich imaginings of the continent we share, for his presence and his help, often in less than tangible ways, in negotiating the ways of beauty; and to Dominique Malaquais for discussions around dining-room tables in Johannesburg and New York, for her intellectual companionship and especially for her help in understanding issues of contemporary African art history.

Ideas of beauty and ugliness which find expression in this book began in Cape Town but came to fruition in Johannesburg, at the University of the Witwatersrand. I am especially grateful to those with whom I work at the Wits Institute of Social and Economic Research (WISER), for their intellectual companionship, the interdisciplinary spirit in which we work and for the research time that was made possible to enable me to complete this book. The Introduction to the book was written at Yale University, and I am indebted to Paul Gilroy and Vron Ware for their invitation to spend a semester there. In large part it was due to their intellectual exchanges with me and to the resources offered by the library at Yale that I was able to gather my thoughts on the elusive topic of beauty and its complex but intimate other, ugliness. Special thanks to Vron Ware and Carol Breckenridge for their extended comments.

The book was designed in Amsterdam by Irma Boom, and I thank her for her extraordinary eye and prodigious talent for making books beautiful. It was produced in close collaboration with Els van der Plas, Geerte Wachter and Malu Halasa, to whom I am warmly indebted. It has been a pleasure to publish the book through Duke University Press and Kwela Books.

My gratitude also to three sets of the people who helped inspire the shape of the book in one way or another: Rita Barnard, Angela Bull, Mariane Ferme, Simon Gikandi, Jean Nuttall, Jolyon Nuttall, and Alistair Henderson. Also to those who have influenced my thinking about Africa, its aesthetics and space: Elleke Boehmer, Isabel Hofmeyr, Peter Geschiere, Rob Nixon, Maliq Simone and Penny Siopis. Finally, my thanks are due to those who participated in the symposium with which we started: especially Maryse Condé, Rustom Barucha, Ousmane Sow and Ray Lema; and to all the contributors whose work has so enriched this book.

Sarah Nuttall > Introduction: Rethinking Beauty

Simon Gikandi
Picasso, Africa and the Schemata of Difference

Simon Gikandi is Professor of English at Princeton University. He is the recipient of numerous awards from organisations such as the American Council of Learned Societies, the Mellon Foundation and the Guggenheim Fellowship. His many books include *Reading the African Novel* (1987), *Reading Chinua Achebe* (1987), *Writing in Limbo: Modernism and Caribbean Literature* (1992), *Maps of English-ness: Writing Identity in the Culture of Colonialism* (1996) and *Ngugi wa Thiong'o* (2000). He is also the general editor of *The Encyclopaedia of African Literature* (2003).

PICASSO, AFRICA AND THE SCHEMATA OF DIFFERENCE

Sometime in the mid-1950s the Guyanese artist Aubrey Williams, a leading member of Afro-modernism and black abstractionism, was introduced to Pablo Picasso by Albert Camus during a visit to Paris. Given Williams's association with various factions of Cubism and his attempt to emulate its style to capture the hybrid cultures of his native Guyana, the meeting with the great artist was supposed to be a highlight of his career, perhaps a catalyst for new directions in the troubled relation between artists of African descent and the international avant-garde. But as it turned out, the meeting between Williams and Picasso, far from being an epiphanic encounter, was to be remembered as anticlimactic:

> There was nothing special about meeting Picasso. It was a meeting like many others, except that meeting Picasso was a big disappointment. It was a disappointment for stupid little things. I didn't like how he looked; I didn't like how he behaved. I never thought I would not like people like that. But the total of the whole thing is that *I did not like Picasso.* He was just an ordinary past-middle-aged man. I remember the first comment he made when we met. He said that I had a very fine African head and he would like me to pose for him. I felt terrible. In spite of the fact that I was introduced to him as an artist, he did not think of me as another artist. He thought of me only as something he could use for his own work.[1]

Williams's disappointment may have arisen from a sense of heightened expectation about the master, or even the hurt that came from not being recognised as a fellow artist, but what stands out in this description of the encounter is that what Picasso found most enchanting about the Guyanese painter was a "fine African head", which he valued as a model for art. Williams was disappointed that he was appealing to Picasso merely as an object or subject of art, not as an artist, not as a body, not even as a human subject. And yet, it is possible that this disappointment arose because Williams had assumed, as many historians of art have assumed over a century of modernism, that because Picasso was the most important figure in primitivism – the movement in art when the Other, often black or brown, became a catalyst for modern art – that he must have had some respect for the cultures and bodies that had made modernism possible. How else could one make other cultures and subjects the sources of art, the agents of the major breakthroughs we have come to associate with modernism, unless one also valued the people who produced it? We now know, of course, that the relationship between Picasso and his African sources was much more complicated than Williams might have assumed. Indeed, the fascination with the "fine African head" did not simply reflect the insensitivity of an artist past middle age. On the contrary, Picasso's relationship to Africa, or his investment in a certain idea of Africa, which is evident from his early career to his high Cubist period, was a meticulous attempt to separate the African's art from his or her body; to abstract, as it were, those elements of the art form that would serve his purpose at crucial moments in his struggle with established conventions of Western art. This is the gist of the argument I want to present in this essay.

Much has been written on Picasso and primitivism but little on his specific engagement with Africa. Indeed, a major part of the argument I will be presenting here demands a separation of primitivism, as a now-canonised idea in the history of modernism, from African cultures and bodies. Picasso loved the idea of the primitive and tribal, but his relationship with the cultures and peoples of Africa and Oceania was more ambiguous. We are told, by André Malraux among others, that Picasso was irritated by "the influences that the Negroes had on me" even as he eloquently discussed the magical influence of those African objects discovered at the Old Trocadéro on that fateful day in 1906.[2] In most of his reflections on the "Negro" influence he seemed careful to make distinctions between the effect and affect of African objects and cultures. When he talked about the "Negro", he was talking about the object rather than the person.[3] The fact that Picasso had an intimate relationship with African objects is not in doubt; but there is little evidence of an interest in Africans as human beings and producers of culture beyond his general interest and involvement in anticolonial and other radical movements. Indeed, as Williams discovered in that encounter in Paris in the 1950s, Picasso seemed to be meticulous in his separation of objects of art from bodies, and it is my contention that it was in this division of bodies from artistic models that the African could be cleansed of its danger and thus be allowed into what Araeen has aptly called "the citadel of modernism".[4]

It is now claimed that in order for modernism to claim its monumentality, that is its enshrinement in the very institutions of Western culture and museum culture that it had set out to defy and deconstruct, it had to shed the contaminants of the Other as part of what D.A. Miller calls, in a different context, its "routine maintenance". In fact, the debates that have come to define modernism, the custodial commentaries on its monumentality, tend to see it as the triumph of endogamy over exogamy, of internal forces over external ones.[5] It is remarkable that except in those instances when the topic at hand is primitivism, the canonical narrative of modernism has little to say about African sources.[6] Now, this absence can be explained in one of two ways: one could argue, for instance, that the institutions of commentary have been so eager to secure the purity of modernism that they have become mechanisms of surveillance against the danger that engendered it in the first place. Africa is first acknowledged as a significant episode in the history of modernism, and then it is quickly dispatched to the space of primitivism, a place where it poses no danger to the purity of modern art. However, there is a second, even more interesting explanation, namely that the practitioners of modernism had themselves started the process of containment, that they needed the primitive in order to carry out their representational revolution, but that once this task had been accomplished, the Other needed to be evacuated from the scene of the modern so that it could enter the institutions of high art. How else can we explain the paradox that runs throughout the history of modernism, the fact that almost without exception the Other is considered to be part of the narrative of modern art yet not central enough to be considered constitutive? To put it more specifically, why is it possible to argue simultaneously that the discovery of African and Oceanic art enabled the moment of modernism yet claim that these works did not have a fundamental influence in the shaping of modernism? From Daniel-Henry Kahnweiler's dismissal of the "Negro influence" in the rise of Cubism to Pierre Daix's famous claim that "there is no 'negro' in the *Les Demoiselles d'Avignon*", one of the greatest puzzles of modern art is whether Africa has to be considered a categorical imperative in the theory and practice of modern artists or just a passing fad in the ideology of modernism.[7] My discussion will proceed in a circuitous way, but it will focus, from different directions, both on Picasso's entanglement with Africa and the critics' and art historians' entanglement with this entanglement. My goal is to show how understanding it – the entanglement that is – is crucial to our rethinking of the aesthetic of modernism and the schemata – and stigmata – of difference that both maintain and haunt it.

I

Let us start with a basic question: is there an Africa in Picasso's oeuvre? And if so, what form does is take? Is it the Africa of bodies or art forms, of material culture or abstracted ideals? At first sight this might appear to be a banal question, especially when we recall the countless debates surrounding the influence of Africa as the mark of Picasso's modernist breakthrough and, inevitably, the centrality of primitivism in his aesthetic practices. But this old question needs to be posed because with few exceptions, the major studies of the African influence in Picasso, whether for or against it, are explorations of the influence of certain African art objects on Picasso's work, or generalised explorations of how African art objects, discovered at the Old Trocadéro, triggered the "terror" that made modernism possible. The terms of reference in these studies tend to acknowledge the African influence and to dispose of it in the same breath, either by confining "Africanisms" to the realm of psychological fear or artistic structure. What these approaches seem to do, even in their detailed and meticulous study of "Africanisms" in Picasso, is also to minimise what I am calling the constitutive role of Africa in the making of modernism. In 1948 Kahnweiler would, in a single bold gesture, testify to the modernists' heavy interest in Negro Art and still proceed to "dispute the validity of the thesis of a direct influence of African art on Picasso and Braque".[8] In 1984, William Rubin would provide perhaps one of the most detailed explorations of the influence of primitive art on Picasso's major works and still conclude that tribal sculpture did not have a constitutive role in the shaping of his art.[9] From the moment Picasso began to be canonised as the most important painter of the modern period in the 1940s, the institutions of interpretation have been anxious to minimise or dismiss any direct and determinative correlation between his works and the tribal objects that surrounded him as he undertook the project of making art modern. Where the influences of the tribal seem self-evident, they are redefined as "convergences" (by Kahnweiler), "affinities" (by Rubin) or "connotations" (by Bois).[10]

My interest here is to probe the reasons for this anxiety of influence. What threat does the acknowledgement of correlativity between the modern and its Others pose? What is the basis of the hauntology that has come to define the moment of modernism and Western high culture in general?[11] Elsewhere I have argued that one of the unifying characteristics of the aesthetic ideology that has emerged in Europe since the 18th century is its concern with Others as the enabling conditions of beauty, taste and judgement and, simultaneously, with the counterpoints or opposites of these conditions. If art has come to function as the defining point of cultural achievement and civilisation, it is only because it functions within economies of desires and ideals – of purity and a chaste culture – clearly distinct from the danger and defilement represented by the Other and in need of defence from the barbarism that necessitates taste.[12] Modernism presents an immediate challenge to this thesis because its overall economy, especially its adulation of primitivism, would seem to posit the Other not as a threat that must be contained but as the source of new energies. In 1919, T.S. Eliot declared that one could no longer understand culture without knowing "something about the medicine-man and his works": "As it is certain that some study of primitive man furthers our understanding of civilised man, so it is certain that primitive man and poetry help our understanding of civilised art and poetry."[13] What is easy to miss in declarations such as this one is that the primitive was a conduit to understanding "civilised" man, art and poetry, not an endpoint in itself; there was no incentive to understand the Other unless it would lead to an understanding of Western civilisation either in its "childhood" or moments of crisis. Thus, Eliot wanted his readers to comprehend something about the medicine-man so that they could recognise the sensibility of the poet, "the most able of men to learn from the savage".[14] Savagery and the artistic sensibility would intimately be connected in the aesthetic of modernism; however, it did not follow that the moderns were willing to give up civilisation to become one with the savage. Indeed, the relation between the modern and the savage was defined by a dialectic of love and loathing, identity and difference. So it is with Picasso and Africa.

Even in his "Negro" period, Picasso seemed to prefer the African art object to the "uncultured" African body. Nevertheless, this preference for the art object over the body was something that Picasso arrived at in the process of working through his aesthetic ideology at certain crucial phases of his career, beginning with his troubled relation to academic art during his youth, his subsequent flirtation with "soft" modernism and culminating in the Cubism that marked the revolution in modern art. His oscillation between the African body and artwork appears to be the symptom of a deep and continuous engagement with the continent, the mythologies surrounding it, the fantasies it generated and ultimately the threat it posed to the idea of civilisation that the modernists both wanted to deconstruct and yet secure as the insignia of white European cultural achievement.

Under these circumstances it is best to begin a rethinking of Picasso and the haunting of Africa by comparing his figuration of the continent in the years before his "Negro Period" (1906-1908) and the erruption of modernism. It is useful to recall here that in the early years of his career, Picasso was preoccupied with what Marilyn McCully has called "classicising subjects and forms"; he was primarily attracted to the art forms of what he construed to be classical cultures, mostly Iberian and Egyptian.[15] It is important to note at the outset that he did not consider "Negro Africa" to be part of this classical heritage or classicising impulse. The absence of Africa from Picasso's classicism suggests an early awareness, on the artist's part, that the value of "Negro Africa" as a model or source of art lay elsewhere; it could not be relegated to antiquity, nor could it be considered modern; rather it occupied a middle space temporally located both in the childhood of mankind and yet very much part of the living world. This understanding of Africa was determined – and explained – by Picasso's Andalusian background much more than his French sojourn. Indeed, as Natasha Staller has shown, Picasso's engagement with the myth of Africa predates his 1904 move to Paris or his 1907 discovery of African art objects at the Old Trocadéro.[16]

My concern here, then, is the meaning of Africa in Picasso's pre-primitivism period, especially the often forgotten fact that he was the product of an Andalusia whose identity had historically been defined against an African cartography, disconnected from the "dark" continent by the Strait of Gibraltar but connected to it by history. This ambiguous connection led to "a series of complex and ambivalent racial, religious, and sexual stereotypes, and [to] the Malagueno myth of Africa, including the belief that the defeat of Africa made one modern".[17] Staller informs us that the defeat of the Moors entered Andalusian consciousness as an epochal moment: "the Middle Ages ended on 18 August 1487"; it was understood "in terms of apocalyptic rupture – a rupture explicitly understood in terms of modernity".[18] The myth that Picasso inherited from this history was one in which Africa was posited as the unmodern antithesis of the new Málaga: to become modern was to break away from Africa. Modernity, rather than classicism, defined what Picasso inherited – and resisted – as tradition. Where does resistance fit into this narrative? Since Picasso

Fig. 1. Pablo Picasso, *Two Nudes*, 1906, oil on canvas, 151.3 x 93 cm
2003 Estate of Pablo Picasso/Artists Rights Society (ARS), New York. Reprinted with permission

Fig. 2. Pablo Picasso, *Portrait of Gertrude Stein*, 1906, oil on canvas, 99.6 x 81.3 cm
2003 Estate of Pablo Picasso/Artists Rights Society (ARS), New York. Reprinted with permission

had to reject tradition in order to become an artist, or at least to break away from the artistic traditions associated with his father, he needed, paradoxically, to discover and valorise a counterpoint to the modernity of Andalusia by inventing his own version of the unmodern. He could seek this unmodern, first, in the classical tradition. But it also seems, as scholars of his early works have noted, that a mastery of classical models of painting, especially those concerning the human form, would not enable a rupture in Western systems of representation; after all, one of the uncanny moves of modernity was to embrace the classical itself as the source of its civilisational authority.[19] In this sense, it was significant that the Malagueno myth of the modern was predicated not on a break from antiquity, but from the Middle Ages, clearly associated with the Arab, Moorish and hence African influences.

Aware, then, that the classical alone could not be valorised as the alternative to the modern, Picasso's work in the early years turned to the painting of the body in order to appropriate its classical form but also to mark his difference from the inherited tradition. What stands out in his transitional works from 1906 such as the *Two Nudes* (fig. 1), is what Margaret Werth has aptly described as a historical and formal liminality.[20] Werth argues that the *Two Nudes* is liminal "in that it situates itself between formal investigation and the archaic of the primitive; between materialisation and dematerialisation of the body, between figuration and disfiguration; and between masculine and feminine".[21] But I think this liminality is also the reflection of a deep anxiety about tradition. On one hand, Picasso wanted to figure the body in the classical style, while on the other hand, he wanted his representation to be in excess of the conventions he had inherited; and this excess is marked by his drawing of the human form out of proportion and, more significantly, by his conversion of the face to a mask. As the *Portrait of Gertrude Stein* (fig. 2), also painted in 1906, was to illustrate, Picasso would turn to masking when he felt he had failed to capture the human face even after numerous sittings.[22]

But if Picasso's goal was to break away from inherited conventions – and the distortion of classical forms in the early works seems to enforce this view – then there was an even more radical way in which he could achieve the task of disfiguration, that is, by turning to Africa. We know, for example, that the artist inscribed his youthful rebellion by claiming a Moorish identity. We also know that his adolescent drawings are populated by Moorish figures and subjects, representing the danger of what I have called the "unmodern". These drawings represented juvenile fantasies about the Moorish Other. In the late 1890s, however, Picasso embarked on some academic paintings of the African body (fig. 3).[23] These paintings are important for two reasons. First, they represent the first and only time that Picasso was interested in the corporeal form of the African. After that, as I will show later, Picasso's interest in things African, even during his so-called "Negro Period", was limited solely to art objects which came to stand in for Africa itself. Second, in his academic paintings,

39

Picasso perceived Africans in a two-fold relation: the African nude represented the body in its "natural" state, one which was, nevertheless, out of proportion with the "ideal" in long-established European notions about ways of representing the human form in art. (These paintings reflected stereotypical notions of the black's excessive sexuality; indeed, what made the black body compelling, in the form of the models Picasso was painting, was its unusual distortion.) In order to defy convention – in the *Two Nudes,* for example – Picasso could draw the white body by drawing it out of proportion. Now, it seemed, the black body represented the corporeal form out of order, even in nature, and hence already in defiance of the laws of proportion and symmetry. In these early paintings, the African's body, in its disproportional form and primitive sexuality, would allow Picasso to kill two birds with one stone, both classicism (which favored idealised bodies) and modern culture (which was coy about male sexuality). Consequently, in this early phase of his career, Picasso adopted African forms as a way of thinking through the limitations of the forms of representation favored by the art academy, namely a sense of order, proportionality, and idealisation. The African body formed the embodiment of disorder.[24]

There is, of course, great irony in this narrative of Picasso's early relationship with the African: he was obsessed with African imageries and bodies before he ever laid his eyes on any real Africans; while when he first visited Paris in the year of the Universal Exhibition of 1900 and encountered colonial Africans on display, blacks seemed, in Staller's apt phrase, to slip off his "mental map".[25] What banished Africans and Moors from Picasso's consciousness? Where did they go? And why and how did they reappear in 1906? Behind these questions lies the larger problem of the repressed in representation, for, to twist the words of Frederic Jameson, it is precisely at the moment that the object of analysis (reality, history or even Africa) is repressed, or its influence is denied, that "by a wondrous dialectical transfer the historical 'object' [Africa for my purposes] itself becomes inscribed in the very form".[26] But a probing of Picasso's political unconscious must be prefaced by two additional factors. The first one is basic, namely that irrespective of the form they would take in Picasso's work, from the phantasm in the juvenile sketches to the abstractness of high Cubism, African objects were what he was later to call "intercessors", instruments for mediating the kinds of forces, often unspoken and unlicenced, which he needed in order to break through the edifice of modernity.[27] Apparently, Africa was most useful to Picasso when it was confined to the unconscious – there but not there – mediating other needs and desires, while not serving as a primary faction in itself. From this perspective, it would seem that when he was encountering real Africans in Paris at the beginning of the 20th century, they had nothing useful to perform in his artistic project in their embodied form.[28] The second factor to consider when probing Picasso's political unconscious recalls what happened during his sojourn in Gósol in the summer of 1906. Here I am interested

Fig. 3. Pablo Picasso, *Academy Study of a Black Man*, 1895–1897, charcoal and conte crayon on paper, 59.5 x 48.8 cm
2003 Estate of Pablo Picasso/Artists Rights Society (ARS), New York. Reprinted with permission

Fig. 5. Jean Auguste Dominique Ingres, *The Turkish Bath*, 1862, oil on canvas and wood, 108 cm diameter Musée du Louvre, Paris/Dagli Orti. Reprinted with permission

Fig. 4. Pablo Picasso, *The Harem*, 1906, oil on canvas, 154.3 x 110cm 2003 Estate of Pablo Picasso/Artists Rights Society (ARS), New York The Cleveland Museum of Art, Bequest of Leonard C. Hanna, Jr Reprinted with permission

Fig. 6. Pablo Picasso, *Reclining Nude*, 1906, oil on canvas, 47.3 x 61.3 cm
2003 Estate of Pablo Picasso/Artists Rights Society (ARS), New York
Reprinted with permission

Fig. 7. Francisco de Lucientes Goya, *La Maja desnuda* (The Naked Maja), 1805,
oil on canvas, 97 x 100 cm
The Art Archive/Museo del Prado, Madrid/Dagli Orti. Reprinted with permission

43

not so much in what has been referred to as Picasso's "regression to ethnic and primitive roots", or even in his turn to female figures as the intercessors of the primitive, but in his valorisation of this distortion and dissymmetry as part of his method and signature.[29] If the paintings at Gósol have one thing in common, it is their intertextual and contrapuntal relation to previous works which they acknow-ledge as part of their schema and yet displace in terms of form and meaning. Picasso's primary goal in the "Blue Period" (of which the stay at Gósol is exemplary) was the artistic deformation of the European canon of painting. This goal could best be achieved through the distortion of the white female form, a subject or figure whose ideality represented the classicism he was fighting against. This point is easily made through a comparison of Picasso's *The Harem* and Ingres's *Turkish Bath* (figs 4 and 5) and of his *Reclining Nude* and Goya's *The Naked Maja* (figs 6 and 7). What we see in these repaintings of significant works in the European canon is a reinstallation of established conventions of painting, a distillation of formalised artistic subjects and a transmutation of genres.[30] But what does this repainting of European works have to do with Africa? If we were to read *The Harem* in itself, as an isolated object of reflection, or even in relation to Ingres's *Turkish Bath*, perhaps nothing, for there is little in the painting that points to Africa or the "Orient" as the primary referent. Treated as autonomous objects, what we have in front of us is one painting *(Turkish Bath)* functioning as the intertext of another *(The Harem)*. And yet from its title and implicit motif Picasso's *Harem* does seem to echo the odalisque, and this has led commentators to read it in explicitly Orientalist terms.[31] Picasso encouraged this kind of reading by describing the quality of the picture as that of *"L'humanité féminin, la femme d'Afrique"*.[32] Still, one wonders whether this kind of strong Orientalist reading is supported by the painting itself. One could argue that Picasso has modernised the odalisque and thus distorted its terms of reference, and this may well have been his intention; nevertheless, compared to the modernist Orientalism of, let's say, Matisse, the "Eastern" referent is weak and displaced.[33] It could be said that in comparison to Matisse, Africanisms or Orientalisms would be notable in Picasso's painting simply because they were absent where they should have been present, or rather, absent where we are encouraged to look for them. However, Africa was not entirely absent from Picasso's "mental map" in the Gósol period – it had just become confined to his artistic unconscious, where it would re-emerge forcefully in *Les Demoiselles d'Avignon* (fig. 8) in ways that are still being contested.

African art objects are, of course, part of the thick description of *Les Demoiselles d'Avignon* and also its enigma. According to Malraux, Picasso was unwavering in his view that *Les Demoiselles d'Avignon* came to him unconsciously during the visit to the Old Trocadéro and that it came to him not because of the enchantment of the forms of the African art he encountered – he doesn't seem to have paid much atten-tion to these – but because what he recognised in this art was a force, or spirit, that was

Fig. 8. Pablo Picasso, *Les Desmoiselles d'Avignon*, 1907, oil on canvas, 244 x 234 cm
2003 Estate of Pablo Picasso/Artists Rights Society (ARS), New York. Reprinted with permission

hard to describe or objectify. In other words, he was attracted by what he considered to be the unconscious and inexpressible. The discovery of African art was unique for Picasso because "for the first time the discovery of an art was not the discovery of a style. African art was discovered, not *an* African style".[34] In this context, the contrast Picasso was to make between himself and Braque was revealing. For Picasso, African objects were agents of exorcism (magical wards to be used against the economy of symbolic form); for Braque, African art was valued because of its form:

> That's also what separated me from Braque. He loved the Negro pieces, but as I told you: because they were good sculptures. He was never at all afraid of them. Exorcism didn't interest him. Because he wasn't affected by what I called "the whole of it," or life, or – I don't know – the earth? – everything that surrounds us, everything that is not us – he didn't find all of that hostile. And imagine – not even foreign to him! He was always at home … Even now … He doesn't understand these things at all: he's not superstitious!
>
> Then, there was another matter. Braque reflects when he works on his paintings. Personally, when I want to prepare for a painting, I need things, people. He's lucky: he never knew what curiosity was. People stupidly mistake it for indiscretion. It's a disease. Also a passion, because it has its advantages. He doesn't know a thing about life; he never felt like doing everything with everything.[35]

Now, one of the reasons why reading Africanisms in Picasso has continuously generated conflicts of interpretation is because many attempts to read his "Negro Period" – and even Cubist phase – as both inside and outside European cultural history are imprisoned by what Jameson has aptly called the ideology of modernism, which "imposes its conceptual limitations on our aesthetic thinking and our taste and judgment, and in its own way projects an utterly distorted model of (literary or art) history".[36] The struggle for a pure Picasso, one uncontaminated by Africa, is ultimately a struggle to secure the aesthetic ideology of high modernism, especially the privileging of form as the mark of its breakthrough. It is not accidental, then, that many discussions of the influence of the African in the making of Picasso's major works tend to revolve around the absence of a formal influence, or a style. And yet in their concern with substantive formal influence, these discussions start with a logic that is bound to fail because form is not what Africa had given Picasso. Indeed, one could argue that what made the African fetish attractive was that it would lead one away from forms of representation modelled on observable experience or reality. After all, as David Simpson has argued, what makes fetishism dangerous "in all perception and representation" is that "reality itself is open to construction".[37] My contention is that it is precisely the doubleness of the fetish – as a figure that is located at the heart of culture and ritual and yet seems to appear to us only in its perceptual nature, against reality – that explains Picasso's enigmatic relationship to the African figures he discovered at the beginning of the 20th century. This doubleness is worth closer consideration because it haunts some of the most influential attempts at both connecting Picasso to, and disconnecting him from, the primitive.

II

In "Picasso", an essay written for the catalogue for MOMA's controversial exhibition "Primitivism in 20th-century Art", William Rubin provides students of modern art with one of the most meticulous and detailed examinations of Picasso's engagement with tribal arts and more specifically African objects. Employing a combination of historical documentation and a systematic comparison of some of Picasso's major works and African art objects, Rubin establishes the centrality of the artist's turn to primitivism and his empathy for the artworks of the Other as one of the turning points in the emergence of modernism. He shows, convincingly, that Picasso's turn to the primitive had promised a way around artistic conventions that "had degenerated into a rhetorical and sentimental art": "By embracing primitivism in 1906, Picasso short-circuited the continuity of these inherited conventions, and his year-long exploration of increasingly remote and alien aesthetic correlatives permitted him to rediscover pictorial authenticity for himself."[38] In Rubin's account the discovery of the tribal was an important bridge between the "soft modernism" that had characterised Picasso's art before 1906 and the "hard modernism" of his Cubist period.

But underneath his acknowledgement of the affinity between the tribal and the modern, Rubin's project is also underwritten by a troubling surreptitious intention: the need to minimise the role of the Other in the emergence of modernism as a style and, in particular, the significance of Africa as an artistic model, even when acknowledging their overall affect. In other words, the majestic reconstructive effort in Rubin's essay was driven by the desire to acknowledge the role of Africa as the source of certain powerful unconscious forces while, at the same time, minimising the significance of the continent as the source of emulous art forms, rather than simple spiritual objects. Thus in his reading of Africanisms in *Les Demoiselles d'Avignon*, Rubin sees the African masks on the *demoiselles* as instruments for accentuating the themes of sexuality and death rather than as models. His primary thesis is that the invocation of African figures and women (both subjects of love and loathing in Picasso's psychic economy and behaviour) enabled the "cohabitation of Eros and Thanatos".[39] More specifically, Rubin argues, the African faces would "finally conjure something that transcends our sense of civilised experience, something ominous and monstrous such as Conrad's Kurtz discovered in the heart of darkness".[40] Rubin acknowledged that Picasso's turn to the tribal was prompted by

47

the absence of a "Western precedent" for mask-like heads and other forms of representing the human body in distortion, but he was insistent that the precedence of
primitivism lay not in the models it provided but its psychological connotations; the
word "African", for example, evoked "something more fetishistic, magical, and
above all, potentially malefic".[41]

From this interpretation we can discern two immediate issues, which lie at the
heart of the schemata of difference in modernism. The first one is how the psycho-
logising of the relationship between the artist and his primitive art forms depended
on, or ended in, the sublimation of the perceptual in the conceptual. Building on
Picasso's own claim that the tribal objects in his studio were "more witnesses than
models", Rubin makes a crucial distinction between the kind of intertextuality that
characterised Picasso's relationship to the works of other European artists such as
Cézanne and to tribal sculpture. In this scenario, tribal sculpture could function as
a point of departure for Picasso, but its significance as an artistic source – a model –
was militated by the fact that Picasso "metamorphosised" his objects of reference.
"Picasso was impressed by aspects of its conceptual structure, principles that he
could abstract from their sources and use to his own end."[42] It would appear that
Rubin's goal here is to confer the power of psychological affect on Africa while, at
the same time, denying it a formal influence in the making of modernism. But
perhaps more important is the distinction he draws between Picasso's intertextual
relation to tribal as opposed to European art. Why is it that Picasso's intertextual
relation to Gauguin or Cézanne was considered constitutive (hence conceptual)
while his relationship to African objects was perceptual, a mere starting point to
something more profound than its degree zero?

We can clarify the issue at hand here by recalling that Picasso was one of the most
intertextual of modern artists. Indeed, the moments in his career that have come to
be considered epiphanic, such as the sojourn to Gósol, are marked by powerful
repaintings of the works of other artists. It is in his distortion of the works of his
precursors that Picasso established his difference and thus his modernism. When we
consider Picasso's relation to, let's say, Ingres or Goya during his Gósol sojourn,
Gauguin during the "Blue Period" or Cézanne during the Cubist phase, we are left in
no doubt about the centrality of intertextuality in his project. It can easily be said
that his paintings are, to borrow Jonathan Culler's words "intelligible only in terms
of a prior body of discourse – other projects and thoughts, which it implicitly or
explicitly takes up, prolongs, cites, refutes, transforms".[43]

Nevertheless, in his study of the intertextual relation between the European
modern and the African or Oceanic primitive, Rubin's categorical claim is that
Picasso transformed the tribal masks in *Les Demoiselles d'Avignon* so radically that
nothing on the canvas resembled "any African or Oceanic mask Picasso could have
seen in Paris in 1907 in the studios of his friends or at the Trocadéro museum".[44]

What makes this claim puzzling, however, is that it is not clear that a reading of Picasso's transformation of the masked figures from African or Oceanic traditions was radically different from the transformation that the works of other European artists underwent in his hands. Indeed, the transformation of figures and forms so that they could retain only a minimal relation to their artistic precursors was one of the hallmarks of the method that we now call abstraction. And as the structuralists used to argue in the 1960s and 1970s, one of the signatures of a strong, as opposed to a weak, intertextuality was the extent of the deviation from the original model. Strong intertextuality is evident when the "borrowed" textual unit is "abstracted from its context and inserted as if in a new textual syntagm as a paradigmatic element".[45]

A second problem in Rubin's psychological reading of Picasso's Africanism is the emphasis he places on the subliminal and subconscious or unconscious. It is of course true that in foregrounding the perceptual dimension of the African connection, Rubin follows a long tradition (one encouraged by Picasso himself) in which the encounter with the primitive is defined by fear and repulsion and is hence connected to the forces that modern civilisation repressed. This is, of course, the familiar narrative of primitivism in modernism. But to argue that the primitive art object appealed to the modernists because of its association with repressed psychological forces, and that those forces were the triggers for the revolutionary works of modernism, should not necessarily lead to a *de facto* negation of the more formal, conscious, conceptual influences tribal art had on Picasso and his contemporaries. The problem with Rubin's valorisation of the psychological impact of the primitive on Picasso's artistic consciousness is that it is built on the rather dubious presupposition that subconscious or unconscious influences negate formal ones, hence his expenditure of much energy trying to show that the objects that were supposed to have influenced Picasso's revision of *Les Demoiselles d'Avignon* – Dan masks, for example – were not accessible to the artist at a particular phase in his career.

Rubin's theoretical stratagem – the claim that African art objects had entered Picasso's subconscious but never rose to the level of formal models – reflects, perhaps more boldly than that of others, a significant feature of the conundrum of modernism in its relation to the Others that it considered part of its schema. Simply put, if we deny the Other as a model for new forms of art, how do we explain the resemblances between Picasso and African masks that he was not supposed to have seen? It is in response to this question that Rubin developed his influential – and quite controversial – theory of affinities:

> The resemblances between the heads in the *Demoiselles* and the masks that have been compared to them in art-historical studies are thus all fortuitous – reflections of affinities between arts that communicate through conceptual signs, rather than through pictorial conventions

49

Fig. 9. Pablo Picasso, *Guitar*, 1912, sheet metal and wire, 75.5 x 35 cm
2003 Estate of Pablo Picasso/Artists Rights Society (ARS), New York. Reprinted with permission

Fig. 10. *Grebo Mask*, Ivory Coast, painted wood and fiber, 64 cm high
Anonymous

directly derived from seeing. Yet the fact that so many more such affinities may be found between Picasso's art and that of the tribal peoples than is the case with the work of other pioneer modernists reflects, on Picasso's part, a profound identity of spirit with the tribal peoples as well as a generalised assimilation of the principles and character of their art.[46]

Here Rubin's argument depends on a fundamental distinction between influence and affinity. In influence (Ingres, Gauguin or Cézanne on Picasso, for example) the relationship between the work of art and its model takes place on the conceptual level in terms of observed formal conventions. In affinity, the influence is perceptual, almost unconscious, functioning on "an invented projection of an internal, psychological state".[47] Rubin would simply not allow for "tribal" influences on the formal, artistic level so central to the identity of modernism. It was only through the unconscious that the Other would be allowed into a now canonised modernism. An unconscious influence would not be allowed to enter the surface where form is discernible. Thus, to describe or posit an influence as unconscious is both to acknowledge its constitutive presence in the making of the object under discussion, and to deny it visibility. Apprehended in its absence and read solely in terms of its perceptual, sensual influence, the African Other would be contained and then evacuated from the edifice of high modernism.

But what are we to do with those instances where Picasso visibly modelled his works on African objects and where the relationship between the two was quite formal, as in the case of the *Guitar* and a Grebo mask (figs 9 and 10)? Rubin documents many instances of what appear to be conceptual African influences in Picasso's work, especially in 1907 and 1908, including a Fang sculpture and *Woman's Head* (figs 11 and 12), but not even his own evidence was enough to convince him that these works constituted real models, sources of formal borrowings, rather than launching pads towards a Cubism detached from its influences. Clearly, Rubin was not willing to concede to African art forms the distinctive status of art; they remained – had to remain – artifacts (ritual objects) with the capacity for psychological influence, but not sources of a formalised aesthetic. And in a curious way, this confinement of African works of art to artifacts or ritual objects seems to ignore the fact that in his own relationship with African objects, Picasso tended to prefer those works which seemed to fit his *aesthetic* interests and sensibilities rather than simple affect. Indeed, if Picasso seemed to value African art objects over bodies, and quite often to privilege the former over the latter, as I argued at the beginning of this essay, it was because he was, in a very strict aesthetic sense, self-conscious and selective about the objects he found worthy of incorporation in his art. In short, Picasso had a clear idea about which objects, among his vast African collection, could

52

be considered worthy of formal emulation and which could be consigned to the spectatorship of ritual.

It is now common to argue that Picasso was attracted to African art because of its capacity to generate terror or that he sought those subjects who would serve as what Bois calls "models for anatomical forms".[48] And yet the Africanist elements in Picasso's paintings only appear deforming to the extent that they call previous conventions of painting into question, not merely because they duplicate the syphilitics that he had encountered in French hospitals. In this sense it is striking that while he had in front of him some of the most deformed and terrifying figures in the African pantheon, real fetishes as it were, Picasso chose as models those masks that seemed to be closer to a familiar European grammar of form and symmetry, even when they challenged some established notions of representation.

Consequently, Picasso's versions of tribal art are cleansed of the terror he seemed to have experienced in his first encounter with it, streamlined in such a way that they are no longer images of the deformity we are eager to ascribe to African ritual objects. Once we recognised that Picasso modelled some of his works on African objects but also departed from them significantly, once we reject the model or no-model option, we can shift the significance of his relationship with Others elsewhere.

III

Now, one of the major criticisms levelled against the notion of affinity, the reigning paradigm in the study of modernism and primitivism, has centred on the implication that the tribal and the modern were bound together by what James Clifford called "a deeper or more natural relationship than mere resemblance or juxtaposition".[49] Clifford's major difficulty with affinity as "an allegory of kinship" is that in its universalising claims it excludes the stories and experiences of the Others that modernism seeks to reappropriate in its own image; that scholars of modernism are primarily interested in tribal art for its "informing principles" or its "elemental expressive modes".[50] True enough. But it is important to underline the point that if the proponents of affinity seem to have no difficulties mounting an exhibition built on allegories of kinship, it is precisely because the aesthetic ideology of modernism was itself driven by the same impulse, the desire to encounter the Other in its ugliness and terror and then purify it so that it could enter the modern art world as part of its symmetrical economy. The major difference between modern artists and their posthumous patrons is simply that the former were also interested in "conceptual displacement" while the latter were invested solely in "morphological coincidence".[51] What makes Picasso such a central figure in the history of modernism's relationship to its Others was his ability to make the primitive central to the aesthetic ideology of modern art while also transforming tribal art objects in such a way that they were no longer recognisable as models. This is how *Les Demoiselles d'Avignon* has come to be

53

54

Fig. 11. Fang mask, Gabon, painted wood

Fig. 12. Pablo Picasso, *Woman's Head*, 1908, oil on canvas, 73.3 x 60.3 cm
2003 Estate of Pablo Picasso/Artists Rights Society (ARS), New York. Reprinted with permission

read, in Hal Foster's majestic phrase, as both the primal scene of primitivism – "one in which its structure of narcissism and aggressivity is revealed" – and also the site of disavowal of the very difference it considers a condition of possibility.[52]

So, where exactly is Africa in Picasso's schemata? This question returns us to the problem that opened my discussion, namely the strict separation of African peoples and art objects in the artist's notion of the primitive. However, a set of more complicated questions needs to be posed: how could Picasso turn to Africa for its magic and art and yet avoid being entangled in its endangered cultures or the problems of its colonised peoples? How do we reconcile the terror and danger he felt when he first encountered African objects at the ethnographic museum with the symmetrical relationship he established between the tribal art work and abstract modernism so that the two seem almost to have been made for one another? The complaint that curators of modernism and primitivism seem to avoid tribal artworks that seem impure and asymmetrical in relation to the structures of Picasso's art is a familiar one, but I argue that the failure of such curatorial endeavours as the 1984 MOMA exhibition does not simply arise from a yearning to rescue modern works from the aesthetic influence of the primitive, or even from the institutional necessity to wink at, yet displace, tribal works from their context. A larger problem concerns the imprisonment of curators and historians in the logic of coherence and symmetry favoured by the practitioners of modern art. In the end, this logic ignores two major problems which need to be at the centre of any discussion of the relationship between modern painters and their African sources, especially when we are discussing those crucial years between 1895 and 1922 when modernism emerged: the question of African definition and authority of sources.

The question of definition was raised most poignantly by Robert Farris Thompson in 1988: "What are the indigenous *African* definitions of the impact of African art forms on the artists of the cities of Europe (like Fang masks in Paris) at the beginning of this century?"[53] Berating the arrogance of Western art historians who never once consider that "the African priests and traditional leaders might have something of intellectual substance to contribute to this most important argument", Thompson concludes that "the final definition of the impact of Africa and Oceania upon modern art remains incomplete until we take large photographs of the Africanising works of Picasso, Braque, *et al.* to traditional Africa ... and listen to indigenous comments and critical reaction".[54] We still do not have "indigenous" commentaries on works of modernism. In the few instances where indigenous artists have been given access to the institutions of commentary, they have been denied the authority of criticism.[55] Even the works of African art historians produced in the most prestigious institutions in the West are not heard across the temporal and cartographic divide that separates the study of expressive and other cultural forms between the modern and everything before or after it.

Beautiful/Ugly

But what lessons could we learn from African art historians that would be useful to modernism, to the relation between Picasso and Africa? For one, we could learn that Picasso has had a significant, though perhaps surreptitious, influence on the field of African art studies. Otherwise how can one explain the almost unquestioning assumption that the mask is the primary medium of traditional African visual expression? On the other side of the debate, however, a shift in contexts of reading – from seeing Africa from Picasso's perspective to seeing the modern artist's from the Other's angle of vision – can yield even more useful results. Consider the fact that in a large measure, the literature on Picasso and his African sources assumes that the mask in Africa was part of a unified and intelligible tradition and that its value lay in its ritualised form and function. Yet the most detailed studies of African masks, their cultural contexts and the views of their producers recognise the intersection between the ritual fields in which they are produced (and out of which they perhaps cannot be understood) and the centrality of the meaning of the mask in motion.[56] Indeed, contemporary African writers and artists who have deployed the mask in their works recognise the significance of movement in determining the form of the mask and its interpretation.[57]

A final enigma must be confronted if we are to rethink the role of the Other in the making of modern art outside the ideology of modernism: how do we transcend the established doxa that it was through the acquisition of the "mythical method" or "mystical mentality" inherent in primitivism that, to paraphrase T.S. Eliot, art was made possible for the modern world?[58] What is the source of this idea, the unquestioned notion that the art of the primitive emerged from a mystical, preconscious mentality and found its ideal form in myth? Why, indeed, did the idea of the African fetish dominate Picasso's understanding of the African primitive in that initial encounter at the Trocadéro in 1906? We are, of course, familiar with the ethnographers of the primitive mentality and the mythical method, most notably Lévi-Bruhl and Sir William Fraser, and countless studies have been devoted to the influence of their ethnography on the ideology of modernism; but we have not often paid enough attention to the ethnographers' sources. As a matter of fact, we seem to take it for granted that the ethnographers of modernism conducted field work among the primitives and that their powerful ideas on the cultures and myths of the Other came from native sources. The real story, however, is different. The primary sources behind the idea of the African primitive were not the academic ethnographers but a group of what I will call the surrogate native informants: European adventurers such as Leo Frobenius, Emily Torday and Mary Kingsley; missionary ethnographers such as Robert Nassau, John Roscoe and G.T. Basden; and colonial administrative officers such as R.S. Rattray in Ashanti and Amaury Talbot in South Eastern Nigeria. These were the first Europeans to write about African cultures and to make art central to understanding the primitive mentality. They also produced their most important work in the foundational years of modernism.

Briefly, there are three reasons why these surrogate informants are central to any rethinking of modernism and its ideas of the primitive. First, while academic ethnographers were generally critical of the colonial enterprise, most often its methods rather than objectives, the surrogate informants conceived their work in the field as crucial to colonial governmentality and as a practical contribution to the theoretical work of the intellectuals of modernism. They assumed that the work of ethnographers at major European universities needed the authority of observations made first hand in the theatre of colonialism. Indeed, surrogate informants cultivated close relations with the leading ethnographers of primitive cultures. Thus

John Roscoe, who wrote the first ethnography of the Baganda, was a protégé of Fraser at Cambridge, and Rattray, who wrote on the Ashanti, was a collaborator of C.G. Seligman at Oxford. As agents in the field of colonialism, the informants premised their authority on their contact with those Africans who, in Roscoe's words, were "uninfluenced by foreign ideas".[59] Second, the surrogate informants were the first, in those crucial years between 1905 and 1922, to promulgate the notion that the mentality of the primitive was mystical and mythical, outside modern forms of rationality, and under the hold of fetishism. One could not understand the native mind or indeed any aspect of native religion and social organisation without understanding the role of the fetish, the explanatory code that connected everything. Third, as is evident from the sheer amount of cross-reference, the surrogate informants existed in a cohesive field of discourse, and thus reinforced the idea of a core set of beliefs that were uniform across Africa.

As part of a generational project, adventurers, colonial officers, and missionaries referred to each others' work and used the parallels they saw in their respective fields of operation to reinforce the power of their ideas, to provide the thick description that made their evidence unassailable. This is why even when artists such as Picasso questioned colonial practices, they seemed to reproduce the colonialist model of African societies; they questioned the practice but not the theory of colonialism. This structure – the questioning of the practice and the acceptance of the theory – tends to be reproduced when we don't interrogate the idea of Africa in modern art; when, for example, we forget the brutality that accompanied the arrival of the African art object in the West, the number of African bodies that had to be destroyed so that the objects would arrive safely at the art museum.[60]

Finally, three challenges remain to be addressed in greater detail. The first one is how to restore the intimate relationship between the brutality of late colonialism and the emergence of the ideology of modernism; the second how to consider more closely the role the surrogate informants played in making Africa accessible to modernism. The third one is how to displace Picasso – as the representative custodian of high modernism in art – from the ritualised place that he occupies in the modern museum.[61] It is my contention that we cannot undertake the work of displacement and deritualisation without changing the language of commentary, the allegory of affinity, the contexts for reading and – eventually – our understanding of perspective and spectatorship. What were to happen, for example, if one were to exhibit *Les Demoiselles d'Avignon* next to a challenging contemporary African artwork, instead of traditional Pende Mbuya masks? Or if we examined *Woman's Head* not in relation to an indigenous Fang mask but next to *Mind ya Nnom*, a bronze sculpture by Leandro Mbomio Nsue, the contemporary Equatorial Guinean artist – a modern representation of the Fang perspective on form?

Acknowledgements
This article was first published in the journal *MODERNISM/ modernity*, 10(3), 2003, pp. 455-480. Permission to republish here kindly granted by Johns Hopkins University Press.

59

Achille Mbembe
Variations on the Beautiful in
Congolese Worlds of Sound

Achille Mbembe is a Research Professor in History and Politics and a Senior Researcher at the Wits Institute for Social and Economic Research at the University of the Witwatersrand in Johannesburg. He is the author of, amongst others, *On the Postcolony* (2001) and *The Political Life of Sovereignty* (forthcoming).

VARIATIONS ON THE BEAUTIFUL IN CONGOLESE WORLDS OF SOUND

Theodor Adorno, known for his aversion to jazz, would no doubt have disliked Congolese music.[1] It is likely that he would not have considered it to be "music" at all. In his opinion, it would probably have been nothing more than a deafening noise which is painful to listen to: the discordant emission of primitive energy. Should he have considered it music at all, it would have fallen in the category of "low art" that he was fond of using.

Low art encompassed for him the *vulgar* in both form and in content: crude simplicity, stupefying effects, propensity for encouraging social passivity and intoxication. In the context of Congolese music, "low art" would have involved the coarseness of its stimuli, the banality of its lyrics, and the rudimentary manner in which it is produced. Adorno would have viewed it as vulgar, also, because of its intended audience: people (both the Congolese elite and the masses) whom Adorno would no doubt together have deemed "cut off from what they might be" and marked by the "precariousness of their own existence";[2] in short, captive consciousnesses which had come to identify with the orchestrated humiliation to which they had been subjected throughout history. Vulgar, finally, because essentially frivolous, lacking autonomy and having been inexorably colonised by commercial concerns.

Adorno would have been wrong, however. To reduce Congolese musical experience to a sheer auto-hypnosis of the masses without any aesthetic content, which neither embodies nor reveals any element of universality, is to mistake the very nature of music. Music, first of all, exists insofar as it is an act of composition, interpretation or performance. It exists, that is, when there is an act of listening, and when the body and the senses are set in motion, whether through dance, meditation, trance or any other subjective effect. As Bernard Sève remarks, "the musical work is an organised whole of sound events, and the entire set of the effects produced by these events in the listener".[3] The formalisation of the sound event through graphic notation is merely a form of domestication. It seeks to give a linguistic equivalent to an extra-linguistic event.

To a large extent, this means that the aesthetic signification of the musical work cannot simply be measured by its ability to expose social alienation as Adorno would have us believe. Rather, its aesthetic signification is revealed through that which links that work to a world of sensations. Musical beauty therefore has meaning in – and through – its effects, or the feelings and passions that the musical work produces in the subject who is listening, is present at the performance or is dancing to it. Indeed, whether involving the polyphonic interaction of the lines, variations in speed, counterpoint or instrumental accompaniment, timbre, rhythm or tone, Congolese *rumba* and its offshoots have, throughout the second half of the 20th century, exercised an intimate power over the African imaginary.

During this period a strange and powerful energy has been manifested in this genre. Given the suffering and tragedy experienced by the Congolese people over a *longue durée*, the temptation is to imply that their music has functioned in such a way as to make its listeners forget the drama of life. Indeed, with its suave melodies, its vocal gymnastics and moving tones which are immediately recognisable and not easily forgotten, this music may have imposed itself on those who listen and dance to it as the sign of a dislocated world and a dismembered body.

More significantly, however, it has demonstrated itself to be the most successful expression of *serenity in the face of tragedy*. At once poetry, dance and prayer, it has become a dual experience of both inner freedom and possession, sadness, anguish and loss, radiant happiness and emotional expressiveness. As a result, far from resembling a narcotic religion which becomes more powerful as dissatisfaction with reality increases, this music is, on the contrary, a declaration of the most radical and the most immediate faith in a life which is necessarily contradictory and paradoxical.

If this is true, the question then is to establish what actually happens in this music, in its snatches of melody and its rhythmic beat. What makes it arouse, in the African subject hearing it, listening to it or dancing to it, a force so unique and so intimate, that the subject experiences a feeling of complete jubilation? What exactly is this unique and intimate force? How does it make the body vibrate, permeated with a wave of energy? What is the relationship between this intimate force and the idea of the beautiful? How can we understand its intimate power, its penetrating strength and energising force, and hence its aesthetic signification? What experience of joy and of life does it document, and in this *writing* how does it bring about a fusion of sound, happiness and sensation?

In responding to these questions, my starting point is that there is no beauty or ugliness other than in relation to a *form of life* of which the beautiful (or the ugly) is the manifestation, the celebration or even the contradiction. From a purely musical perspective, the beautiful is that which, judged so by the ear, touches and moves, provokes pleasure or sensory joy. As I will demonstrate, in Congolese music this sensation is evoked in the body by what might be called "sound forces", and is subsequently experienced at different levels of intensity and through different organs.[4]

Below, I attempt an aesthetic description of the works of several Congolese composers whose music gave rhythm to African life during the last ten years of the 20th century such that it etched a deep impression on our imaginary.[5] By "aesthetic description" I mean an attempt to describe the totality of sensations, pleasures and energies provoked by a particular work, or set in motion in the subject listening or dancing to it. However, for these sound forces to have the effect of touching and moving, *something has to take place both in the music itself and in the emotional nervous system (feelings, sentiments, passions) of the subject possessed by it.* This is what this essay seeks to identify.

63

Thus, what I describe below is, more than anything else, an experience of listening. As Kofi Agawu argues, "The point that African music can be legitimately listened to still needs to be made in view of long-standing views linking music and dance."[6] In contrast with other artistic forms such as painting or literature, where aesthetic theory is usually based on the visual, music allows the conflation or the juxtaposition of the textual and the sonoric, the aural (*hearing*) and the visual (*seeing*), with performance and motion (*dancing*). In music, the life of the notes is brought into an alliance with that of words through voices in order to produce songs.

To comprehend the aesthetic signification of the works studied here, it should therefore be remembered that they mobilise several senses and organs (hearing, voice, sight, touch and, further, movement and waves of energy). There is nothing more complex than verbalising that which involves the non-verbal, or describing sound, something which in essence is neither linguistic in nature nor involves the purely spontaneous practice of language. Aesthetic interpretation here supposes that sensory material is reorganised by what might be called the sound event, in the very process through which the latter frees the imagination.

Rules of the beautiful in the Congolese context

In order to understand the aesthetic dimensions of popular urban Congolese music, we need to examine the context in which that music was born and developed. While from a strictly musical perspective, the history of modern Congolese music remains to be written, the sociopolitical and economic context of its evolution is relatively well documented.[7] It has been established that this music was born out of the sounds, rhythms and ethnic dances of the Democratic Republic of the Congo, Congo-Brazzaville and a large area of Angola. Mixtures and borrowings from African and foreign styles, as well as from Christian hymnody, were then added to this base. This music emerged alongside colonial urbanisation and the accompanying social and economic transformations. At the heart of these transformations is the relationship between the categories of *being* and *time*. Belgian colonial rule was to a large extent an endeavour aimed at restructuring local time and space.

This reorganisation of autochthonous space and time proceeded in two ways. The first was conversion to Christianity.[8] Several studies have shown that this conversion involved a series of memory exchanges. It took place in stages, culminating in the convert assuming an external identity and lifestyle, which he or she subsequently assimilated and displayed in his or her daily life. As a form of disciplinary power, Christianity introduced a new calendar and a new temporality: a religious economy in which the days, the months and the years embraced a clearly defined liturgical calendar (from the Nativity to the Ascension via Calvary and the Resurrection).

Together with this new temporality went a new celestial geography, which gradually became the source of the production of all kinds of utopias and fundamental shifts in moral vocabularies.[9] Probably the most important contribution to Congolese music made by Christianity is aesthetic indoctrination (what constitutes beauty, rules concerning correct harmonic progressions, voice leading, types of vibrato and timbral characteristics) and choral singing. Thanks to Christianity, the Congolese learned how to sing Gregorian chants and, in the process, to arrange notes or phrases sparingly. They learned how to maximise breathing capacity, and were introduced to the postures required for good singing: standing straight upright, chest slightly protruding. More importantly, they were initiated into the narrational, representational and dramatic character of music. The Congolese singing body is therefore partly the work of the Christian missionaries. In the seminaries, there was also musical technical training (harmony, intonation, expression, *vibrato*) via which the whole body was transformed into a musical instrument. Nevertheless, religious music was less a form of art than that which, providing benefits to the soul, made it possible to link beauty and moral worth.

Colonial modernity was also about disciplining and cultivating the body. Complex and uneven transformations of the economy (relations of ownership, property, labour) were accompanied by the development of new social relations, especially in the cities. These entailed, among others, new uses of the body and pleasures, new ways of living and dying, novel forms of desire.[10] The process of social reproduction itself increasingly depended not only on the availability of the means to meet human survival, but also on a vast array of imaginary forms, on the circulation of dreams, fantasies and fictions.[11] The city as a space of heterogeneity profoundly transformed long-standing ideas about the meanings of belonging, the symbolics of sexuality and traditional markers of culture and identity. All of this eventually led to an increased self-consciousness about the "fashioning" of human identity as a manipulable, artful process. Disciplining the body was accomplished through labour on the one hand, and intensive techniques of caring for the self on the other.

One such technique was elegance and self-stylisation.[12] As a site on which broader institutional and political forces were inscribed, the body, humiliated and made ugly in the workplace or at the hands of a brutal colonial regime, could acquire a new value and be rehabilitated through various arts of making it beautiful or through masquerades, simulation, imitation and dissimulation. This is why appearances were accorded such importance. Within extra-customary centres, the body was to be introduced to the rudiments of colonial bourgeois civility. During the years of colonialism, a new culture of taste and leisure emerged: a global culture with its own spaces.[13] The bars (*nganda*) were one such example. This global culture also produced its own activities, especially those linked to the trade in sex (*mwasi ya leta*), to sport (football clubs) and to the consumption of alcoholic drinks.[14] In all these spaces cultural artifacts both local and originating from faraway places were used.

It can therefore be argued that from its inception, Congolese popular music was less concerned with the presentation of flawless beauty and the purity of form than by its power to act as a sign system the function of which was to free imagination.

Achille Mbembe > Variations on the Beautiful in Congolese Worlds of Sound

Fig. 1. One of Koffi Olomide's first CD covers featuring a female body, c. 1991

Fig. 2. CD cover of Wenge *Musica Maison Mère*, c. 1992. Note the importance of the guitar and the majestic pose of the lead singer

At its origins, this music was inevitably a composite of styles and a juxtapositional hybrid artwork, a result of the intermixing of various traditions. In the 1940s the *rumba* arrived from Cuba. It was brought to Africa by means of gramophone records and musical instruments such as the guitar, the accordion and the harmonica, often by immigrant workers from West Africa (*coastmen*) who were also enamoured of the *highlife* (a fusion of American jazz and European and Caribbean dance styles with the folk music of West Africa).

At the same time, new dance steps originating from Loango (the *maringa*, the *polka*, the *tango*, the waltz and the *quadrille*) were added to the repertoires originating from the villages. Following the earlier examples of the *bolero*, the *cha-cha-cha* with two rhythms, the *merenge*, the *pachanga*, the *beguine* and the *mambo*, these music and dance steps were rapidly adopted in the main urban centres as well as among traders and migrant workers in the diamond and copper mines or on the railways, within a history of mobility, displacement and regional circulation of labour (East and southern Africa).

The first bands (Congo Rumba, Victoria Brazza, Jazz Bohême) were created during the first half of the 20th century in Leopoldville, Brazzaville, Pointe Noire and San Salvador. Some combined West African and European musical practices. In the process, the techniques of playing the violin, the guitar and a variety of brass and woodwind instruments were learned by local Congolese musicians. At a later phase, these instruments were adapted to traditional melodies. The majority played Caribbean or Latin American music, which required a different instrumentation (stringed instruments such as the lead guitar, the rhythm guitar, the double bass; wind instruments such as the clarinet; and percussive instruments such as conga drums, maracas or the claves rhythm sticks).

Caribbean and Latin American music was to influence the structure as well as the process of innovation and creation of Congolese urban musical expression for decades to come. This is especially true of the *rumba*, which was to enrich the wealth of Congolese music through a number of stylistic variants, starting with the *rumba boucher*, the *rumba-odemba* and the *rumba-sukuma* at the beginning of the Second World War through to the *rumba kiri-kiri* and the *rumba-sukusu* of the 1980s. As argued by Kazadi wa Mukuna, the evolution of the rumba was, in turn, nurtured by the availability of rich and compatible rhythmic formulas, dance steps, body movements (*agbwaya, nzambele, ebongo*) and a plethora of stringed instruments (*njenje, kokolo, likembe*) and drums (*patenge*) from the various ethnic groups of the Congo.[15]

Compositions produced by the two main modern Congolese bands, Joseph Kabasele's African Jazz and OK Jazz (later under Luambo Makiadi, best known as Franco) are positioned exactly at the confluence of these external and internal influences.[16] Whether in terms of harmonies, melody, rhythm or instrumentation and formal structure, Kabasele (Grand Kalle) and Luambo Makiadi (Grand Maître) have been the main sources of Congolese musical repertoire and innovation until the present. (fig. 3) These compositions initiated the development of modern Congolese music as a form of entertainment closely mixed in with social occasion, drama and ritual.

Founded in 1953, African Jazz imposed discipline on the orchestra, restructured ways of singing, integrated the tam-tam, the electric guitar and wind instruments into the band, classified repertoires and strengthened the social status of the musician. It created a popular fusion of imported and local music with a deliberately Latin flavour. Franco's main contribution lies in his use of indigenous rhythms and folklore styles. He introduced long stretches of purely instrumental music in his pieces – a technique Fela Anikulapo Kuti was to refine later in his own drawn-out, wordless stretches of saxophone, piano and bass guitar. Franco also transformed the art of guitar-playing by adopting an aggressive style which was in marked contrast to Kalle's flowing style or the lyrical and idyllic expansion of his melodic figures.

One of Franco's original trademarks was the distinctive short-long, upbeat-downbeat attacks and reiteration on a single note from the guitar; or his apparently dissonant twinges in the first half of a piece and the chromatically tinged episodes of rhythmic irregularity in the second. Lyricism here became imbued with an undercurrent of brittleness and half-heartedness we still find in most contemporary Congolese productions. Franco rehabilitated the high-register alto and falsetto male voices that were common in traditional music and used the vibrato to create an ornate electric guitar sound. He then pushed the method of playing runs of "sixths" that have become another trademark of Congolese guitar style and he combined it with a grinding, metallic sound which reproduced the resonance of a traditional harp zither. Finally, in an attempt to increase the range of musical effects, he embarked in long songs and stunning improvisations and he unleashed the *sebene*, a master stroke consisting in taking up a musical phrase and repeating it until it becomes hypnotic.[17]

By the mid-1970s, music had become a means by which Congolese society reflected on itself, on its own identity, and on the modes of representation it adopted. In many respects, music epitomised ideals of joy, festivity and happiness, elegance and serenity. It enabled the Congolese to sing what could not be spoken about in any other kind of speech. Musical instruments, the guitar in particular, did the talking and explained how what was said was to be danced.[18] As an art form, music played a crucial role in the definition of taste and sensibilities and in the invention of formal codes of "good manners" and civility. Furthermore, music became a vehicle for both a commentary on morals and social satire. As such, it contributed to setting the rules for the stylisation of everyday life through the manipulation of signs and images, pleasures and dreams. Eventually it became the repository of a social discourse on virtues, as well as on vices and passions (pride, hate, envy, idleness, ugliness, deformities, greed, sexual predation).

69

Achille Mbembe > Variations on the Beautiful in Congolese Worlds of Sound

Under Franco and Kabasele's influence and their protean energy, popular urban Congolese music was able to evolve an identity of its own. Later generations of artists took their inspiration from Kabasele and Franco's creative canons. Such was the case for Sam Mangwana, and, later, the groups Zaiko Langa Langa and Papa Wemba. Even though they found their inspiration in the core identity of Congolese music created by Franco and Kabasele, these later generations were not mere appendages of earlier ones. In many ways, they disrupted and destabilised the rhythmic figures, tempos and musical concepts inherited from their predecessors. In so doing, they prefigured one feature of the Congolese musical scene: the recurrent splintering of groups, the power of imitation and the critical function of inter-textual borrowings and reinterpretations. Later generations of artists also distinguished themselves from the earlier ones by their stylistic expressions and by the number of musical instruments used in the band.

For instance, one of the most celebrated ensembles of the second generation, Zaiko Langa Langa, developed a musical style in which wind instruments were deliberately omitted and prominence was given to rhythmic patterns borrowed from the traditional music of the ethnic group of their composers. Zaiko Langa Langa also adopted "a compositional structure in which the *sebene* was proportionally longer than the singing section". Emphasis was therefore put on dancing rather than on the lyrics. Moreover, "the role of the lead guitar was no longer limited to the harmonic accompaniment and melodic improvisations, but expanded to interact rhythmically with the percussion instruments, especially in the *sebene* section of the composition".[19]

The 1980s were marked by the return of Congolese society to a new cycle of violence characterised by the militarisation of everyday life. Wars and rebellions, rapes and massacres, drugs and unrest, pillage, political and economic violence were added to a long history of suffering.[20] It was during this period that the languid and swaying melodies characteristic of "classic" Congolese *rumba* (1950s-1970s) were replaced by new musical styles characterised by tremendous pace, a tendency towards emotional intoxication and a more or less stereotypical choreography.[21] Through the influence of bands such as Wenge Musica and its various offshoots, Olomide and Quartier Latin, a new generation changed the character of Congolese popular music by placing an emphasis on percussion, accelerating the pace of the dance, downplaying the role of wind and brass instruments, introducing the technique of "screams" (*atalaku*) and so transforming the rules of musical beauty.

Let us now turn to the idea of the *social epistemology*, that is, the socially recognised rules which underlie the production of the beautiful in Congolese urban music. Any study of the aesthetics of Congolese musical culture must give a central role to orality and voice. Despite the pressure of a written culture, oral communication has remained predominant in urban and rural contexts. Such communication takes place in the context of plural languages and a reciprocal interpenetration between different artistic genres and improvisational practices. Thus, there is no watertight division between music, dance and theatre. Multiple languages are used in all three art forms.

Juxtaposition

The aesthetic relationship is constantly constructed within a tension between a model fixed in writing, the indiscipline arising from the linguistic creolisation needed for oral communication, and the hegemony of the image. Extremely complex relationships have therefore been established by different forms of artistic expression. For example, as Jewsiewicki explains, language depicts the image, but also allows sounds and noise to be heard. Whether a television series, a video image or popular urban painting, the image is intrinsically composite. It demonstrates an extraordinary capacity to represent, to tell a story, to "make this story, the content of which everyone is aware, real and immediate."[22] In the Congo, words themselves always refer to a plurality of references. The things they designate are multiple and their significations structurally ambivalent.

To mark the imaginary, musical composition must therefore constantly visualise representations and render audible and resonant what is happening in life and in experience. In this way, the musical work itself is transformed into an "archive" or a "relic" of this same experience. Congolese music retains a close relationship between tone and words, as evidenced through the length and pitch of Lingala (the main vernacular language in Kinshasa) syllables from which the sound is related. As in Zaiko Langa Langa's *Eureka*, sounds constantly espouse the tones, accents, sighs and inflexions of the worded voice. To a large extent, Congolese urban music does not seek to become independent of the word. Moreover, there is almost always a great deal of word play in any given song. The meanings of words are twisted. New words are invented while others are adapted from different local and foreign languages. Meaning, therefore, is often not what it seems at first sight.

The musical work also constantly resorts to neologisms, and to words from other languages to signify an experience that is constantly changing and to account for the instability of reality, its ultimate dependence on the sound that domesticates it. It can only do this by combining image and text, words and sounds, body movements and vocal gestures, the sonoric, the visual and the theatrical, thereby producing heterogeneity of representation. Whether in music, theatre or painting, "signification" takes place through the juxtaposition of words, colours and sounds, in a process in which each element must both retain and lose a part of its intrinsic power. The whole, as Jewsiewicki sums up, "is more of a kaleidoscope than a fixed image". In other terms, the beautiful, in these conditions, is a matter of a *sketch*, a *summary* and the *transient*.

71

Achille Mbembe > Variations on the Beautiful in Congolese Worlds of Sound

FRANCO
20ᵉᵐᵉ ANNIVERSAIRE
6 juin 1956
6 juin 1976

Fig. 3. CD cover, volume 2 of Franco's "library", 1956-1976

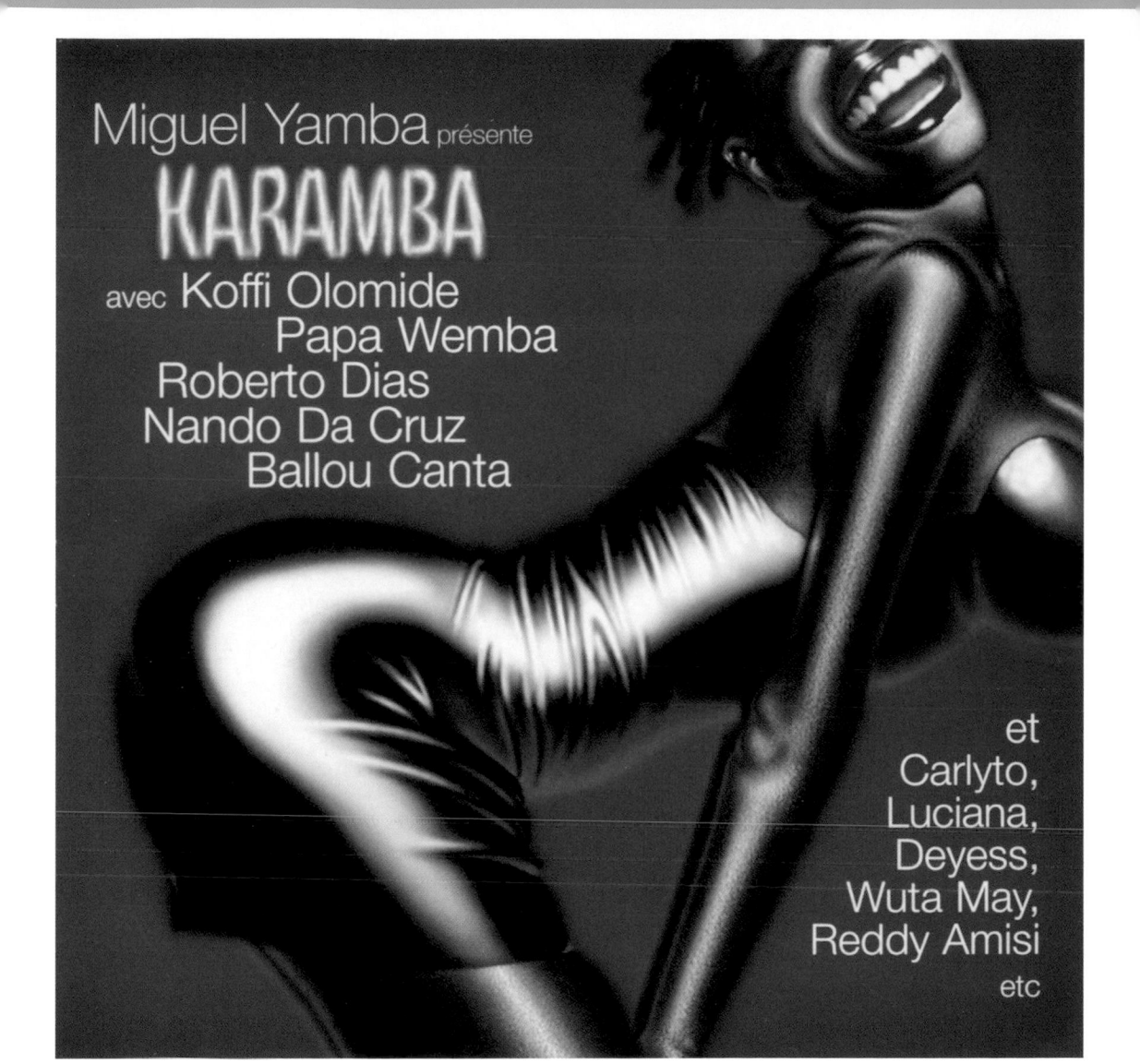

Miguel Yamba présente

KARAMBA

avec Koffi Olomide
Papa Wemba
Roberto Dias
Nando Da Cruz
Ballou Canta

et
Carlyto,
Luciana,
Deyess,
Wuta May,
Reddy Amisi
etc

Fig. 4. CD cover for a compilation of Congolese artists, c. 1995

Ugliness and abjection

The reality of ugliness and abjection is at the centre of this social epistemology. Both during the colonial and post-colonial periods, ugliness and abjection in the Congo clearly assumed a political dimension. Both originate in the violence, exploitation and economic pillage experienced over an extended period by the Congolese people. Ugliness and abjection can also be seen in the way in which sovereignty has been experienced and power has been exercised over this same period. Both the practice of sovereignty and the exercise of power have obliged human life to embrace the forms of an animal existence. In the Congolese imaginary, there is a suspicion that whether under colonial rule or after, the body of power has long sheltered a beast.[23]

The Congo has been living in this spiral of terror since the start of the colonial era. Depending on the cycle, the spiral has assumed ghostly allures while the spectacle has varied in intensity. In its most intense phases, the spectacle has resulted in situations where in terms of the human body, no one seemed to know the difference between "flesh" and "meat" any longer.[24] The distinction between what is true and what is false, what is to be believed and what is "beyond belief", became blurred.

Power could break bones and strip the subject of his or her flesh, disfiguring him or her, and forcing him or her into a demonic dance.[25] Power's *raison d'être* was now to produce carcasses and to penetrate the bodies of its subjects with nervous energy.[26] To do this, it placed them in extremely dangerous and vulnerable situations, and then aroused in them different orders of sensation – from physical pain to convulsions and spasms to envy and greed.

Conversely, it enticed them to savour *corruption* while at the same time making them "suffer like an animal". It erected the violence of genitality into a way of dealing with men, women, property and things – a practice of government. Because of the increasing power of sexual pleasure and lust in the calculus of enjoyment and the ordering of social affairs, human will and reason came to be defeated precisely in these anatomical and epileptic zones of the body that sexual organs are (figs 1 & 4). This common destiny of human beings and meat became the very trope of the Congolese regime of terror, the ugly and the abject.

From this process of slow crucifixion resulted bodies that were sometimes nailed down, sometimes spread out, sometimes standing, sometimes lying down, sometimes stretched out, and sometimes violently mounted by the "beast," shaken by terrible jerks.[27] A zone of relative indistinction was created concerning the part of animal in man and the part of man in the beast. It is in these spectral conditions that music, especially since the 1990s, broke with the limited circle of sounds it used to rely on.[28]

The range of timbres was increased and many artists undertook to play more aggressively with dissonances. This implied a willingness to blur the distinction between sound and noise, and to join art to *the world of screams* (*atalaku*) through

74

various devices.[29] Sometimes, this "scream" has taken the form of a howl – the howl of "meat", from the height of a cross, under the eye of a government transformed into a "spirit-dog".[30] Throughout the last quarter of the 20th century, Congolese music as a *noise sound* and as a *musical scream* has been endeavouring to account for the terror, cruelty and dark abyss (the ugly and the abject) that created it.[31]

Fantasy and improvisation

Another rule of musical composition in the context of the ugly and the abject described above is the capacity for improvisation and the role of fantasy. To a large extent – and particularly onstage – musical beauty is judged first by flashes of improvisation. Improvisation should not be confused with simple spontaneity. In fact, what appears to be improvisation onstage is often the result of a slow and patient process of elaboration. For example, the syntax of Congolese dance steps during the 1990s was constructed through regular repetitions, often in a local bar. Members of the public were therefore involved in the process as they were learning the new dance. As in other forms of music (for example, jazz), evidence of this slow process is modified and erased once onstage, so that the whole work often has an air of simplicity.[32]

However, there can be no improvisation without a combination of imagination and composition. Improvisation does not imply that Congolese music stands out because of the absence of a particular form or convention. In fact, there are many forms and conventions. What may appear, in the eyes of an outsider, to be an anarchic confusion of impulses and a sheer chaos of sound, in fact constitutes a medium point between prior compositional formalism and improvisation.

All of these properties give Congolese popular music a distinctive quality. These works have developed an aesthetic made up of fantasies and productive counterpoints as well as discords and distortions. This is a music in which violence and artifice cohabit with naivety, and even stupidity. Imagination is in constant conflict with formalism. The casual and at times frivolous nature of the dances contrasts with the mournful nature of the songs and melodies. Pleasure and joy are expressed through screams and writhing. And tragedy and loss are told with the nuances of comedy and festivity (fig. 5).

This interweaving of forms, genres and contents makes it possible to invent original compositions where words, the world of images, appearances and sounds merge together, producing flurries of occasional brilliance and primitive melodies which evoke tears and suffering as much as they do ecstasy (compare, for instance, with Tshala Muana's *Malu*, 2002). This is a music where the emotions are always in conflict, where the theatrical and the oneiric are superimposed on one another across a savage ocean of sounds, screams and noise. Figures and gestures drawn from popular theatre, with its farcical and comical aspects, its exaggerated disguises and its untidy and brightly coloured costumes, are brought to bear on any musical

75

performance. It can be said that this music records the fragments of a long drama, through melodies of an inexpressible melancholy, phrased both by the singers' voices and by the guitar, while the dancers are constantly required to wear their masks.

Noise and sound

Contemporary Congolese music seeks to establish a precarious balance between noise, sound and scream.[33] The music is produced in an environment itself strongly shaped by the omnipresence of noise. "Kinshasa is a town full of noises and full of smells," comments an observer. "Everywhere music is in the air, a baby crying, the sound of hooters, or portable radios singing. There is always the smell of food emanating from cooking pots or from a *nganda* (a place equipped for drinking and eating), the smell of a car's exhaust pipe or a sewage pipe, or the smell of urine against a wall or a tree bearing a sign 'No urinating here.'"[34]

Congolese musical works dip abundantly into this culture of noise. As it happens, any sound in the Congo can be used if not as a musical sound, at least to create music. Often, musical sounds are based on imitations of natural or onomatopoeic sounds. Congolese artists use noise to modify sound understood as pure form. This does not make their music less instrumentally rich, as evidenced by the virtuosity of its guitars and other forms of instrumental improvisations. What noise adds to rhythm are those spasmodic eruptions that often break the stream of slow melodies. The interest is not in any form of purity but in corruption through noise. However, this "noise" is not anarchic, not least because it expresses joy. Noise, here, is part of the practice of joy. Joy *is* noisy within this musical genre. And "noise", an "impure" sound, is used in the service of joy and beauty.

Any event involving sound is called music if it involves a certain *surplus force*. At particular moments, carried by the imagination to the brink of intoxication (especially true of the *atalaku*), the musical phrase takes the form of a volcanic effusion. Mixed with words, soaring bursts from the guitar, the screams of the *atalaku*, the rhythm of the percussion and the shape of the melody, it is transformed into an image of the very doors of hell – ear-punching frenzy, groping disorder and energy; or instead it becomes an effusion of tears provoked by the haunting memory of mourning, by jubilation and the unchained outpouring of emotion, reflecting as much the hollow tolling of reality as the pending fulfilment of still-awaited promise – an interweaving of myriad figures where the beautiful and the ugly are intertwined in the image of life itself.

Having begun to explore the beautiful in Congolese popular music, I would now like to turn in more detail to the formal and artistic dimensions of this music.

76

Rhythm

Congolese rhythm draws on the rhythms of poetry, religious song and prayer, and autochthonous dance. Rhythmic movement is not only produced by musical instruments but by gesture and voice. The rhythm subsequently imprints itself on the movements of the dancer's body and infuses the body with pulsating waves of energy. In Congolese music, the dominant rhythmic model is polyrhythmic. It is made up of bursts and sequences that are at times regular, and at others intermittent. The variations between increasing and decreasing energy, and the movement upwards to a peak and then back down again are characteristic of most musical pieces. The energetic tension is enhanced by the repetition of the same musical phrase by the solo or bass guitar, or by putting upward pressure on the rhythm by means of the "interpellations" of the screams of the *atalaku*. Very often, the sounds, syllables and slogans are simultaneously manipulated with increasing momentum.

One of the distinctive features of these works is that the rhythm is expressed as a tension. This tension may be produced by the variations in energy, as in the late works of Koffi Olomide (listen to *Mopao* MM *Mokonzi*, CDS 8983, Next Music/Sono, 2002) or Wenge Musica BCBG (listen to *Les Anges Adorables,* vol. 1, CDS 8801, Sonodisc, 1994). In these works, rhythm consists of the ordered distribution of this energy over time, in a synthesis that is more or less achieved by musical parameters (especially in guitar lines and the percussion) and figures of the vocal parts (whether the lead singer, the chorus or the *atalaku*). At certain moments during the composition, the various energy components (voice, instruments, the bodies of the dancers) may be orchestrated in convergent or divergent ways. Some evoke tension and others release or relaxation. Tension can also be induced by the sheer length of the piece.

These multiple combinations give rise to an infinite number of possible rhythmic nuances. These nuances may be translated into long and slow progressions, or intermittent breaks, which are occasionally syncopated and occasionally violent. Wenge Musica and Koffi Olomide's compositions are again excellent examples of this. Each sound is a relay between two sounds, themselves punctuated by the voice of the guitar or the endless psalmodies of the vocalist. The hiccoughs, the sudden restarts, the violent dips in energy, the residue of the voice, the beat, slow or rapid, semi-static or stationary tempos are used at different points in the number and orchestrated to produce an effect of stupefying intoxication or serene jubilation (see, for example, Tshala Muana's *Malu*, Zaiko Langa Langa's *Eureka* or Koffi Olomide's *Affaire d'Etat*).

Dance

In this section on the regulation of the beautiful in Congolese music I examine the dance form.[35] Let us take, to begin with, the female dance steps associated with the rhythms known as *soukous*.[36] There are several of them, each with a different name. The aesthetic of the names of the dance steps is in itself revealing, such as the case of the *tourniquet*. This name suggests a set of movements around a line or a circle with clearly defined limits and contours. In this dance step, it is the dancer's body that acts

77

Fig. 5. Dancers reveal the intricacy of moves required for the *ndombolo*. They are dressed in immaculate white outfits for maximum visual effect. Video still from Wenge Musica Werrason, JPS Productions

Fig. 6. The shooting of a video clip in Paris. Note the uniform worn by the dancers, and their Nike shoes.
Video still from Wenge Musica Werrason, JPS Productions

as the circular space. The movement is centred in the body itself, or, more precisely, in certain parts of the body.

The dancer lightly flexes the knees, fixes the buttocks, arches the back and then begins to turn her hips in a way that reveals those sensual and provocative curves of the body. The hips here act as a chassis for the whole body, but at the same time they are flexible, as are the buttocks. The other parts of the body follow, moving from this central pivot. To dance the *tourniquet* then basically means to rotate the pelvis. Such a movement requires both gymnastics and dexterity. The dancer's hands are also used to good effect. The position of the hands produces what is called an "attitude" or a pose. The dancer may, for example, use her wrists by flexing them firmly, but elegantly. She may also place her hands on her hips, and then repeatedly move her pelvis to the right and to the left.

The dance move called the *coucoune* differs from the *tourniquet* in the way that the legs are parted. Moreover, the term "coucoune" not only refers to the variant *coucou* (the laying of eggs), but also to *cocu* (being deceived or cuckolded) and to *coquine* (mischievous and roguish). Because it is based on a particular way of parting the legs, the *coucoune* is a sensually suggestive dance step accentuated by adding to the rotation of the pelvis to the left and right another backwards and forwards movement which is manifestly sexual because it refers specifically to sexual inter-course. The *démarreur*, in contrast, is more of a playful step. The dancer takes up her position as if about to start a motorbike, and then accelerates rapidly. But, having started the engine, the dancer suddenly almost falls forwards. At the last minute, she saves herself and avoids falling. This dance step, like the others, assigns a central role to the gyrating pelvis. But it also includes a more agile movement of the feet, thus combining fixed and mobile positions.

There are other dance steps associated with the *soukous*, such as *allumez le feu* (light the fire) or *enfoncez le clou* (hammer in the nail). In the case of "light the fire", the dancer pretends to take a match which she then tries to light by scraping it. The match does not light, however, and she tries again, fanning the flame (*moto* in Lingala) with undulating movements of the hips until the fire finally ignites. But it is hot. She then tries to extinguish it in a jerky movement, in which she moves her buttocks and her legs like a fan. *Enfoncer le clou* is very similar. The dancer pretends to hold a gun. She squats on her haunches, and moves from side to side, as if she is hammering in nails with her hips. Other dance steps include *la feinte* (the trick) in which the dancer pretends to slip, again giving the impression of falling. But at the last moment the dancer recovers and again pulsates her buttocks, just like an accordion.

The dance steps associated with the *ndombolo* also derive from the demarcation of the hips in relation to the rest of the body (figs 5 – 8). One difference compared to the *soukous* is that the body is gradually reduced to a squatting position, then raised again, and then at a specific point the dancer turns first to the right and then to the left, then forwards and backwards, at a pace dictated by the rhythm of the music (fig. 1). Another difference is that the dancer takes up a firing position as if aiming a firearm. Then, she has to lift her heels and march, gradually squat down, turn, rise again, and then break the rhythm abruptly, whether to the left or to the right, forwards or backwards. There are many steps for the *ndombolo*: *hold-up; no way, whiplash, clear off, kung-fu style, bonda style, sequence emotion, air-traffic controller,* etc.

Despite the intricacy of each of the dance steps above, the differences between these Congolese dances are actually miniscule. Whatever the dance step, the actual act of dancing consists more than anything else in a release of energy. For men, the dance aesthetics conform to certain simple rules: they should be strongly masculine, the head should be balanced, and the body should rotate in a swirling frenzy. For women, the dancer must thrill the audience with a series of interlaced movements, complex patterns that alternate the aerial movements of the arms with other, more rigid, movements of the legs. The rhythm is sometimes slow, sometimes fast. As indicated by M. Tchebwa, the circular rotation of the hips is elaborated according to a fixed ritual, from top to bottom, and from bottom to top, from left to right and from right to left. In the way in which it quivers and shakes, the dancer's bottom, well flexed, expresses elegance and skill, eroticism, sensuality and a kind of staged and calculated wildness, expressing an almost quasi-ontological relationship between sexuality and the primal state.

This is one reason that dancing to Congolese music is above all a carnal experience (figs 1 – 4). What, above all, is expressed in Congolese dance is the celebration of the flesh. Against the platonising ideology that would cast the body as the prison of the soul, dancing here is an integral part of a long history of body worship or devotion to the body. In this history, the body is absolute *flux* and music is invested with the power to enter it. Music produces psychic, somatic and emotional effects on it. The Congolese dancing body is literally subjected to the rule of waste, as evidenced by expressions such as *buka mikuwa* (to break one's bones); *bwakanka nzoto* (hurl your body); or *na zali ko bina lokolo nioka* (I dance like a snake). It is not something that one wants to "harm". It is that place in which the distinction between the transcendental and the empirical, the material and the psychic is blurred. In addition to existing as flux, the body is also a force-field of contrasts. Music engages in a struggle with these forces. Never simply a movement of organs, Congolese dance embodies something that resembles a search for original life, for perpetual genesis, and for an ideal of happiness and serenity.

Paradoxically, a state of serenity is attained through noise, screams and trance. This is the case in the *ndombolo,* where the sounds can be simplified to the extreme: hardly any high-pitched trumpets ringing out up towards the moment of triumph, as in Hugh Masekela's music; no brass instruments with thundering resonance; no saxophone, as in the style of Manu Dibango or Fela Anikulapo Kuti; rarely any

81

Fig. 7. A video clip is from a shot on a street in Brussels by Wenge Musica.
Video still from Wenge Musica Werrason, JPS Productions

swaying rhythm, as in the late Franco's rumba. Instead, orchestral clangings evoke the confusion of life. Vocal inflections and syntheses between the rhythm and a tempo are often interrupted. Furious dancing, especially by women, is interspersed, here and there, with melancholic vocal phrases, the sombre notes of a guitar, and, now and then, flowing and elegant sequences.

Everything suggests a relationship with the body made up of derision and excess, tamed fear, rage, blows and insults, extreme parody, all at the centre of an aggressive mass of sound, interrupted from time to time by a more or less pure sequence of guitar playing. Despite the torrid atmosphere in which the *ndombolo* is danced, however, its objective is to transform the body into a figure of life. In the context of the ugliness and abjection described above, the aim of the noise is to compel the body to escape from itself. To do this, the force of the music makes use of the hips and the buttocks as a pendulum. The flexed posterior pretends first to act as a parachute, then a vacuum-cleaner, and then a suction pad. It is transformed into a semi-autonomous force, maintaining a direct relationship with the world of sensation.[37]

The other path to *serenity* is through listening to the music itself, its melodies, rhythms, tensions, and lyrics. The very notion of serenity assumes that each subject is an ego endowed with its own body. The subject can dispossess or rid himself or herself of this body, even if only temporarily. Thus, in Congolese dance, the opposition between the body and the mind becomes blurred. The dance is the site where a "dual life" is unveiled, a life where there is no truth or beauty that does not have multiple meanings. In a sociological context where misery, anguish, trauma, terror and horror are not only daily realities, but constitute the state of the subject, dancing becomes a way of journeying "outside of the self".

Because death in this context is one of the general rules of life, and because, to a large extent, "everything ends by returning to the great dormant state of matter",[38] this temporary stay outside of the self – this is *joy*. This may be one reason that dancing to Congolese music involves, paradoxically, a *radicalisation of nihilism*. All meaning here emerges from an already existing radical non-meaning: *the state of the ugly and the abject.* All beauty here emerges from this state of the ugly which is almost boundless, from this otherworld of gregariousness and ecstasy, truth and lies, vulgarity and the search for dignity. Joy is what emerges in these interconnections between being and appearance, while the music serves as a vector of enjoyment, just as does general corruption: a space for wandering, until *the being towards death which has become life itself.*

Music as a sound scream

Let us move on to "interpellations" ("screams" or *animation*). These are produced by the *atalaku* or animators. *Animation* is used to accompany the guitar. Introduced in the 1970s, it was relatively insignificant until the middle of the 1980s. During the

1980s, the band Zaiko Langa Langa started a dance accompanied by screams: *"Atalaku, Zekete!"*; *"Regardez ses fesses. Voyez comment elles bougent!"* (Watch her buttocks, see how they move!) This technique was then adopted by a number of other Congolese bands.

In the middle of the 1980s, the technique of screams was transformed under the influence of charismatic figures such as Dolce Parabolic, Bill Clinton, Tutu Kalondji, Celeo Scram (Animation Maison-Mère), Al-Patchino (Animateur Nouvelle Ecriture), Robert Ekokota (Wenge Musica) and Theo Mbala (Ambassadeur). The *atalaku* have extremely revealing names drawn from the world of medicine – for example, Gentamycine (Animation Wenge BCBG); from military operations in the age of globalisation – Djuna Mumbafu Colonel Bradi (Animation Delta Force); the world of new communications technology associated with secret operations (3615 Code Niawu); and Egyptian mythology (Shora Pharaon). Each *atalaku* strives to forge his own style, but they all make use of folklore. They endeavour to coordinate screams and musical instruments to produce an effect of calling out to the dancers. This is combined with the harmonisation of the dance steps described above. The *atalaku* screams an instruction determining which specific dance step should be performed.

"Screams" endow the musical performance with a torrid and turbulent atmosphere. "The words, the phrases, in crude flights of oratory, burst forth intuitively from the mouth of the *atalaku* like lava from a volcano," observes Tchebwa. The *atalaku* cheers on the dancers and "incites them to further passion, creativity and technical brilliance ... Regular breaks and syncopations are alternated, punctuating the *seben* with a brilliant and suggestive play of guitars and synthesisers. They embellish the dance, loading it with fantasies and trills of sound, raising it ever closer to the pinnacle. The rhythm of the percussion has no sooner faded than it is replaced by the hysterical *animation* of the *atalaku*. This time, the *atalaku* is accompanied by a brisk and lively chorus, and constructs the phraseology of the screams around a theme parallel to the main text of the work, riding on the back of the dancer's skill in a mysterious journey between the gesture and the being, its being."[39]

> Darling, do you see how this girl rolls her hips? I can hardly contain myself, but look, look, look ...
>
> My brother, we have to collect the crumbs they have left us. Let's go come, if you refuse, what shall we eat?
>
> Can you feel it, this emotion? Let us destroy the elixir, right now.
>
> My young brother, I cry every day, because where are we going to live? In Europe they want no more of us, and here at home, there is nothing but trouble.
>
> Comrade in exile, why do you stab me in the back? Should we distrust our childhood friends?

85

Fig. 8. Dancers wear expensive high-fashion attire and their gestures signal victory and self-release. Video still from Wenge Musica Werrason, JPS Productions

Long live the weed!
Let's let go, my brother, let go completely!
Shamukwale: my brother is returning the money you have stolen.
There is no point in killing me, there is no point in hurting me.
My mother is the mistress of my father's best friend. My mother's best
friend is now sleeping with my father. How far can immorality go?
Empty the truck! Cemetery full!

That the technique of screams was introduced in popular Congolese musical performances in the 1980s is not coincidental. The 1980s in the Congo were characterised
by multiple crises. It is in this context that music was transformed into an
instrument of social revolt. Revolt, however, always went hand in hand with an
uneasy compromise. A number of musicians were thus able to sing the praises of
"Saddam Hussein" – the nickname of the son of the dictator Mobutu – who was the
patron of various bands in Kinshasa.

But the music nevertheless remained an expression of hate. The destruction taking
place was expressed artistically, to some extent, in certain instruments such as the
drums (with an acceleration in the rhythm, and a return to motifs drawn from rock
and roll and soul music), the synthesiser or even the bass guitar. In spite of this,
music espoused the sounds of suffering and social fragmentation. The spectacle of
bloodshed and dismemberment came to be musicalised. Descriptive of this social
pain are the screams, cries, moans, groans, all forms of utterance that resist language
and litter Congolese music of the end of the 20th century. Similar to melody, rhythm
and percussion, screams can therefore be read as that which bridges the gap between
pain and its expression in language.[40]

Occasionally, the music was openly wild: dancing in order not to die (or until
dying from dancing). Music was transformed into a receptacle for the emotions, for
trauma and for the repression of the everyday. Music traced the sadness and troubles
of daily life, the war and the ugliness in Congolese society. Thus, at the command
"firing positions", the instruments would produce the sound of bullets and submachine guns. The bands' clothing also borrowed increasingly from military
uniform. The response to the ugliness of life was an excess of hedonism. The lyrics of
the songs stood out for their style and language, which was characterised by a surfeit
of metaphors, parables and hyperbole. Each word could mean two or three different
things, and "quotation" became the norm.

Scene and spectacle

Moving on to the stage, let us take the case of the performance of Wenge Musica
Maison Mère by Werrason at the Stade de Bercy (Paris) in 2000. The performance
starts off with a cascade of guitars and voices. The musicians are dressed in black and

white uniforms. Werrason, wearing a leather shirt and trousers, appears in the middle of a song alternating between the lead singer and the chorus. The solo guitar is unobtrusive, leaving space for the chorus or the solo singer to take the lead. The song proceeds as if it is a Christian litany. The names of artists, both dead and alive, are called out, accompanied by faint gestures, in deep communion with a long tradition going back as far as Luambo Makiadi (Franco). The drums are almost inaudible. Now and then, the guitar seeks to take the lead, but half-heartedly, and is immediately drowned by the singing.

Suddenly a group of women appear dressed like soldiers. They sport striking hairstyles: some with red hair, some blonde. They are wearing a variety of shoe styles, from boots to Nike trainers. The choreography is formal, controlled by the screams of an *atalaku* draped in a blue Congolese flag covered with stars. Now and then, the breaks initiated by the lead guitar and by the *atalaku* introduce a spasmodic and jerky rhythm, which provokes a frenzy of movement (legs, pelvis, loins, posterior), slightly synchronised, but free enough to allow for personal style. Two *atalakus* reply to one other as if echoing each other. Then, the women begin to dance like crabs, lined up in pairs, with a leader dressed in orange uniform, like a mineworker. They open their legs, and then close them, and move their behinds, slightly off balance, not square on their feet, but on the tips of their toes, now and then with both arms on the head or around the neck, moving the two legs as if playing an accordion. At the same time they turn their heads briefly to the left, and then to the right. Suddenly, they turn their backs on the audience and rotate their hips in front of the men, their buttocks facing the audience before they withdraw.

From an aesthetic point of view, the hairstyles and the costumes are worth noting. The accoutrements include black glasses, curly hair, with coloured stripes, jewellery, and, for men, a whole variety of moustaches and beards. Each of the men dances in his personal style, with only a few coordinated movements. They break into occasional melodies, some plaintive and solitary, some heavily orchestrated.

The animator (*atalaku*) wears a blonde wig. Now everyone begins to dance. First squatting down, then forwards and backwards, to the left and to the right, arms raised. The movements are clearly choreographed, but always leaving room for individual style, depending on the shape of the body. The abrupt break in the dance comes when the dancers are kneeling down. They then turn their buttocks to the audience in movements that are simultaneously semi-erotic and semi-obscene. Gradually, the boundary between these two registers is erased, and these spasmodic and thrusting movements of the buttocks culminate in a frenzied release of energy and satisfaction. The dancers move as if penetrating and withdrawing, imitating seemingly unbridled copulation which only ends with a series of furious spasms of imaginary ejaculation.

The choreography is relatively free and informal, only broken by a duel between

89

two men, which appears as a kind of phallic collision (or a war of the penis). Each holds his scrotum, his legs slightly lifted. Suddenly, they spread their legs like an animal about to satisfy its needs, and then they start to spin furiously. The dance is centred around the hips, which the rest of the body endeavours to move to the front and then to the back, hands resting on the pelvis, which is rotated over and over again. There are fake moves of first one leg, and then the other, while the rump is thrust violently backwards before being projected forwards.

They feel for their testicles, with the athletic firmness of a black body gleaming under the effect of the lights and the vivid colours. They pretend to tickle, then to caress and then they halt, before letting out a deep sigh. The buttocks are held in a position enhanced by the plump flesh of the dancer. They pretend to introduce the penis into an imaginary vagina and then withdraw. They perform somersaults. They place their feet in imaginary stirrups and mount, before setting off at a fast trot. They wring their hands in joy. Then, they pretend to sit bolt upright, closing the legs and enjoying an intense, sensual friction. They twist and turn like satisfied grass snakes, letting out cries as they thrust and jerk, moving their loins in a simulation of masturbation, the backside clearly visible, prepared for the climax of release.

Everything, or almost everything, in this performance seeks to be seen. Here, the music is above all a language: the language of conscious and unconscious desires. It keeps all the senses on the alert. Images and scenes that concern life itself scroll past behind the spectacle. Everything with a rhythm is appropriated by the sound. This could be the song of a bird or the noise of a submachine gun. Such cadences are linked together and superimposed on one another. The tone changes constantly. Each construction is temporary.

The body remains at the centre of the performance. Certain parts of the body, more than others, play a predominant role as the turmoil of sound increases. One can see how the dancers gradually retreat further into themselves and seek to become one with the sound. At the same time, they establish a distance between themselves, who they are in real life and whom they become on the stage. The dance takes place at the very centre of this alienation from the self inspired by what Nietzsche called the disturbing power of sound.[41] It is this power that pushes the dancers to use various movements, depending on the ways in which they experience the rhythm.

Song and melody

I would like now to turn to a final dimension of the beauty of Congolese music. It involves the relationship of melody and song with the idea of joy and festivity on the one hand, and with that of tragedy on the other. To a large extent, the beauty of Congolese song can only be understood in relation to the context in which it was produced and made into the object of a listening experience. The dual dimension of *the ugly and the abject* indicated above plays a part in this.

Beautiful/Ugly

As music is, above all, *an art of time,*[42] those aspects of this ugliness most connected to the form of the melodies are primarily those related to the way in which Congolese music is used as work on time. The latter appears as *transient, unstable and ephemeral.* Congolese melodies endeavour to express this transience, this instability and this ephemeral character by skilfully assembling elongations, extensions, curtailments and violent contractions of sounds, with sudden and abrupt transitions between them.

Thus, for example, Koffi Olomide, in *Effrakata 2*, initiates the first piece with rapid guitar playing. This is quickly joined – and modified – by an *atalaku,* who produces sounds which are sometimes screams, sometimes simply noise and sometimes song, while the artist loses himself in a long litany of names. This cacophony is toned down, from time to time, by a chorus which is itself regularly interrupted by a combination of the lead guitar, bass guitar and percussion. Once in a while, the lead guitar provides the harmonic framework of the accompaniment. This interweaving of sounds paradoxically produces a strongly syncopated rhythm which is interrupted by spasmodic phrases. Nothing is stable in this composition. There are no sustained breaks. Each instrument interrupts another, taking its turn before fading or being extinguished by another instrument, by the *atalaku* or by the chorus. Then, it all ends as it began, without ever reaching a peak, and with no clear conclusion.

But an unstable, transient and ephemeral concept of time carries with it problems of length. In Congolese melodies, the idea of length is almost always combined with that of richness. The feeling of length and richness is normally achieved in two ways: by means of the superimposition, flow and synthesis of the voices, and by instrumental cycles which are intended to evoke the impression of a build-up in the depth of the polyphony. But even here, there are always breaks and ruptures. Thus, the second piece by Wenge Musica (1999) opens with what resembles an organised harmony, brought to life by a chorus in which each voice is sweeter than the other.

This chorus is sometimes accompanied by, sometimes preceded by, a lead guitar which is sharply distinguished from the other instruments. This first sequence is soon interrupted, however, and a new instrumental and vocal phase begins during which three different solo singers intervene, one low, one higher, with the chorus taking up the middle level lulled by the sound of the guitar. During the third phase, the guitar openly takes the lead. It unleashes a *sebene* and influences the chorus in a clearly audible manner. Suddenly, what was until then a relatively balanced melody is disturbed by the intoxicated voice of the *atalaku*. To the latter's screams is added a rhythm which gradually becomes more and more spasmodic. The lead guitar is soon drowned by the voice of the *atalaku* whose screams become increasingly shrill. Then this moment of "disorder" and "cacophony" is brought under control as the lead guitar re-emerges and exercises sufficient authority to discipline both the singing and the screams.

Conclusion: beauty, festivity and tragedy

These two examples clearly demonstrate how Congolese music reflects the colourful and capricious existence which I have already said is an integral part of the regime of the ugly. It is an existence comprised of sudden faintings into nothingness and of fleeting patches of light. In this heavy atmosphere which all are condemned to breathe, the *beast* exhales. The animal side of power is sometimes disguised, and sometimes mischievous. An impassive demon, it forces the subject to follow his or her dreams as if riding on the back of a tiger. This is partly what is expressed in dancing. As for the basis of voracity, insatiability, cruelty, repugnance, criminality and cannibalism, which are characteristic of the regime of the ugly and the abject, this provokes harsh screams, but also melancholy songs, in which a profound desire for duration and sensation can be found in the sombre notes of the guitar.

Faced with a world where everyone behaves like a slave, where everyone leads a life of misery and shady dealings and where "procreation, life and murder are one and the same thing", Nietzsche's statement according to which "it is impossible for a man fighting for his survival to be an artist" is contradicted by the insatiable enthusiasm for existence expressed in the music.[43] In such a torrid atmosphere, what then is jubilation? It is essentially the capacity for disguise and dissimulation. Congolese music carries with it illusion, sycophancy, lies, deception and ostentatiousness, making the dancing subject into someone who is putting on an act both for himself and for others. The obligation to lie *en masse*, distortion and the various ways of counterfeiting life find their best form of expression in dance. For to dance in a regime of the ugly and the abject is to rid oneself, in an instant, of the *labour of the slave*. Suddenly, the demon falls silent. Shaped and sculpted by sound, the subject relinquishes himself or herself and erases from his or her face the expression of destitution.

At the same time, jubilation is the expression of this mixture of sensual delight and cruelty that is so characteristic of the regime of the ugly and the abject. There is always a grotesque and brutal power to be found in jubilation. What Nietzsche called the "duplicity of the mad" can perhaps be seen in this outburst of frenetic activity and in these spaces of transfiguration: "of that sense that pain awakens joy, that the jubilation in his chest rips out cries of agony. From the most sublime joy echoes the cry of horror or the longingly plaintive lament over an irreparable loss."[44]

And perhaps in the end, beauty *is* this: that by which human beings are brought to the most profound level of their symbolic faculties. This study has dealt with those faculties that are liberated by the disturbing power of sound and the stream of the music. As I have shown, in the Congo, there is no beauty which does not relate to the body. In this case, the entire body is involved, stirred by passions, and by the language of sounds: the lips, the face, the voice, gestures, limbs all move rhythmically. But behind the sounds, there is the expression of an existence in which exuberance and the gift for suffering go hand in hand with fierce and powerful desires. Because this society, so accustomed to atrocity, is playing with death, its music is both born out of tragedy and is nurtured by it. So is beauty.

Acknowledgements
This essay is the result of sustained conversations with my late friend Tshikala Kayembe Biaya. Useful criticism has been provided by Lara Allen. Sustained encouragement was offered by Sarah Nuttall and Bogumil Jewsiewicki.

William Kentridge
Two Thoughts on Drawing Beauty

William Kentridge is a South African artist who
has, since the 1970s, traced a trajectory which
meshes the personal and the political in an
innovative use of charcoal drawing, animation, film
and theatre. His work has attracted international
critical acclaim, and has been seen in museums
throughout Europe and the US. Current projects
include work towards a production of Mozart's
Zauberflöte, which he will direct in 2005.

TWO THOUGHTS ON DRAWING
BEAUTY

Fig. 1. William Kentridge, *Untitled* (drawing for the film *Felix in Exile*) (detail), 1994, charcoal and pastel on paper

I

The dead

A heap of forensic photographs, almost impossible to look through. A man half tumbled out of bed, pyjamas pock-marked with bullet holes, blood on the floor below. A close-up of a man's head in a pool of blood, one cheek swollen – his jaw shattered. Someone – man? woman? – under newspapers, one hand sticking out. As specific photographs, it was extremely difficult to look at any of them. In the act of drawing from these images, the photos change. It is not simply that they become a series of greys, and tonal gradations and contours; but rather the horror of their origin is put on hold. Drawing is a series of equivalences and negotiations between the paper and the object. What is the shape of the open mouth? What sort of blackness is used for blood, as opposed to the shadow under the shoulder? What is line, what is smudge? At best, when the drawing is really under way and flowing smoothly, the act of drawing feels like a benevolent absence, leaving the arm, the wrist, the paper, the photo on their own. The mind appraises things as they emerge, rejects things when they go awry, but does not directly instruct the process.

Believing that there is an intelligence between eye, arm and paper that will best serve the object. "Is the image beautiful, is the image ugly?" – is not the question the hand is asking. Nor, even, I think, the question, "does the drawing keep the horror to which the original photo attested?", trying to do justice to the source image. The drawing always attests to itself, as the example of transformation. The horror of the circumstances of the original photograph regains its place only as one of the associations the image unleashes.

The set of associations shift out in radically different directions – the scale of the image, its tonality, the texture of the drawing, the group of images with which it has a familiar resemblance, images which arc back in time, all those dead Christs – Gericault's paintings of guillotined heads, photographs seen in childhood. Historical stories, riddles and awkwardnesses posed by the drawing itself (why does the hand seem so large, is that darkness on the cheek blood or just a smudge?). A mixture of common and personal associations, through which the image maps itself and locates itself and also disperses itself, scatters into fragments, to be reassembled when the image is seen again and remembered.

William Kentridge > Two Thoughts on Drawing Beauty

98

William Kentridge, *Untitled* (drawing for the film *Felix in Exile*) (detail), 1994, charcoal and pastel on paper

Fig. 2. William Kentridge, *Untitled* (East Rand) (detail), 1988, charcoal on paper

II
Germiston

There are no hills. There are no trees big enough for shade. There are no streams or lakes. In the winter glare, colour is leached away. It is not sublime, it is not awesome, it has no picturesque features. But after many years of deafness on my part, I understood it called out to be drawn. My deafness had to do with a belief in oil paint as the natural medium for representing terrain, and the conviction that the dappled light and saturated greens of 4,000 European landscape painters was where beauty lay. The call of the Germiston landscape was specific: to paper, charcoal, ruler, eraser – all materials I had been using for some years. The power lines, remnants of civil engineering projects, concrete buttresses, the flat horizon of golden mine dumps, the clarity of the winter glare between areas of light and shadow in the landscape – it seemed that half the drawing was done by the landscape itself. And with the ground grey and black with the stubble left by veld-fire, the burnt wood of charcoal itself moved between the object and the drawing. The pleasure of making the drawings had to do with the pleasure of the discovery of simple translation – power pylons constructed out of a series of ruled lines, charcoal dust rubbed into the paper with a chamois leather to echo the silver sky, short marks of crumbly charcoal to make the black and stubbled field. The excitement and the reason for doing the work (or any drawing) has to do with the engagement of being caught between the object and the sheet of paper.

I'm not sure whether I am caught between the object and paper or lost. Lost, because bearings become uncertain. I am no longer certain what constitutes a beautiful landscape. The dappled light and lush green are now all fugitive. The slime dams, reed beds and bleakness of Germiston have enormous appeal and attraction, but I'm not sure whether this is because I now feel it is all tameable or manageable or approachable, by drawing; or whether through the act of drawing this landscape many times the terrain itself has re-educated my eye.

Rita Barnard
The Place of Beauty: Reflections on
Elaine Scarry and Zakes Mda

Rita Barnard is Associate Professor of English
and Director of Women's Studies and the Alice
Paul Center for Research on Women and Gender
at the University of Pennsylvania. She is the
author of *The Great Depression and the Culture of
Abundance* (1995) and *Apartheid, Literature and the
Politics of Place* (forthcoming). Her articles on
South African literature and culture have
appeared in journals like *Contemporary Literature,
Novel, Research in African Literature, Modern
Fiction Studies and South Atlantic Quarterly*.

THE PLACE OF BEAUTY: REFLEC-TIONS ON ELAINE SCARRY AND ZAKES MDA

In this essay I would like to consider the aesthetic ideas implicit in the fiction of the South African writer Zakes Mda, and especially in his recent novel *The Heart of Redness*.[1] Mda, who is a painter as well as a novelist and dramatist, has a keen interest in visual pleasures; artists of various sorts feature prominently in his novels. He also takes a sceptical approach to the vagaries of aesthetic judgment: to the whole business of what Arjun Appadurai has called the "traffic in criteria".[2] For Mda, the word "beautiful" is always a semiotic shifter, the valence of which is always contested, always dependent on both its cultural context and on the place of the observer. This sensitivity to the geographical contingency of beauty and ugliness makes Mda an important commentator on the location of culture in post-apartheid South Africa, where the old maps of privilege and deprivation have not yet been wholly erased, but now have to be considered – and transformed – within the challenging international marketplace of global postmodernity. Mda's work also affords us a critical perspective on some of the surprisingly reactionary ways in which beauty has been discussed in recent years in the American academy. It is for this reason that I will start the journey of this essay far away from Africa – even though its aim is to make Africa not the heartland of beauty (for beauty travels and has no home), but a key site at which our understanding of the social life of "beautiful things" can be enhanced and transformed.

I

The country singer Dolly Parton (who is briefly referred to in *The Heart of Redness*) has described her trademark appearance – the sequined outfits, the extravagant wigs, the thick make-up, and the regular surgical nips and tucks – as the product of "place[s] of insecurity".[3] By this intriguing phrase she means, in the first instance, that her get-up is a compensation and cover-up for bodily flaws (mousy hair, heavy breasts, short stature, and so forth). But she is also quite conscious of the social and cultural implications of the phrase. Geographically, Parton's "place of insecurity" is, of course, hardscrabble Appalachia, where she grew up in a very large, very religious and very poor family. Her notion of glamour, she readily confesses, is a country girl's notion of glamour. In some of her more candid interviews, she describes the origins of her style with considerable comic verve: she recalls that on a visit to town with her family, back in the late 1940s, she noticed the local hooker standing on the street corner, all dolled up for trade. "Now, *that* is beautiful," Parton thought to herself, resolving to discard her own dull rags as soon as possible and to emulate the colourful *nymphe du pavé*.

I was often reminded of Parton's self-deprecating irony – an irony that in no way diminishes her pleasure in the things with which she adorns herself – as I read Elaine Scarry's *On Beauty and Being Just*,[4] originally presented as the Tanner Lectures on Human Values at Yale University. These high-minded musings make little room for

104

the likes of Parton or, more generally, for the peculiar aesthetic experiences of those who dwell in the world's many places of insecurity. Indeed, though Scarry is fascinated with the notion of an instantaneous recognition of beauty, she resolutely brackets off from consideration any visual pleasures that may bring up the spectre of class- or culture-specific discrimination, and does so quite early on in her meditation. The kind of experience Parton describes is thus placed beyond the proper scope of inquiry: it would fall under the rubric of "error[s] of overcrediting"[5] or an "imperfect version" of the impulse toward imitation that, in Scarry's view, true beauty elicits.[6] But, as always, such gestures of marginalisation reveal the most vulnerable aspects of an entire argumentative edifice: in this case they point to the parochial elitism of an argument that claims for itself a remarkable degree of universality and vast good intentions.

Now, Scarry's work on beauty (like that of other scholars eager to leap on her polemical bandwagon) is a reaction to what she describes as "the banishing of beauty from the humanities in the past two decades".[7] But her rhetoric, of course, is misleading. It is not that beauty as such has been banished (as Scarry herself admits): it is, rather, that most of us have been made appropriately aware of the fluidity of the term. "Beauty", moreover, has been discussed quite often under broader rubrics, such as "aesthetics" or (going back further in the century) "affirmative culture". In her Tanner Lectures, though, Scarry addresses this kind of critical effort in the most reductive terms possible as an "opposition to beauty." She strives to set aside the arguments of two classes of critics: those who say that "caring about beauty is bad"[8] because it distracts our attention from questions of justice (by which I assume she is gesturing towards certain strains in Marxist criticism), and those who say that "caring about beauty is bad" because the gaze of the beholder "reifies" the beautiful person or thing (by which I assume she is gesturing towards certain strains in feminist criticism).[9] The alliterative slogan that Scarry seems to want to put into the mouths of her opponents, however, is one that few, if any, who are enrolled in either of these schools would ever want to pronounce: actual "opponents of beauty"[10] are rare, if not nonexistent (as Scarry, having invented the category, is eventually forced to admit), and they would hardly use the term "beauty" in the way Scarry does – as though no debate existed about its definition. Scarry's polemic proceeds, in short, by fairly crude rhetorical tricks, despite the evident effort at stylistic elegance.

The very first sentence of the lecture is revealing of her methods: "What," she asks, "is the felt experience of cognition when one stands in the presence of a beautiful boy or flower or bird?"[11] For all her insistence that she has no interest in treating beauty as "unattached," and for all her objection to the term "reification", Scarry actually treats her subject in a radically reified manner. Her emphasis on beauty as a cognitive event – a rapt and isolated confrontation between beholder and object – ignores the fact that human beings do many things with the objects they

Rita Barnard > The Place of Beauty: Reflections on Elaine Scarry and Zakes Mda consider beautiful: they judge them, they sell them, they wear them, they display them, they court them, they collect them, they smuggle them, they forge them and so on. Most of these activities lie beyond the scope of Scarry's inquiry; but the crucial activity of judgement (since it affects the very nature of the gaze) is difficult for her to ignore entirely. Early on in her book, Scarry turns her attention to what she calls (euphemistically, in my view) "lateral disregard": the notion that one object might receive more of our "beneficial attention" than another.[12] The potentially painful matter of (aesthetic) discrimination becomes, under this rubric, no more than a mild slight, which is then easily remedied by extending the cognitive moment to include more than one beholder and more than one object: by imagining what Scarry calls a "composite event sponsored by the beautiful object itself".[13] She admits, in other words, that different beholders might find different things beautiful. But she seems to shy away from the very possibility that one person might find another's beautiful person or thing not simply "lack[ing] the perfect features that obligate us to stare," or "less endowed with those qualities of perfection which arrest our attention", but, quite simply, *ugly*.

This peculiar silence about beauty's antithesis, of course, makes Scarry seem nobler and more "fair" than disputatious scholars, like myself, who are interested in the cultural and political ramifications of taste, both "good" and "bad". She can even represent beauty as "a pacific matter": a claim which is highly disputable, not only in the colonial contexts to which I will shortly turn, but even within the European and American cultural contexts from which she tends to draw her examples. After all, the classic *casus belli* is the beautiful face that launched a thousand ships. Niceness is good and fine, as far as it goes. But it is worth bearing in mind here Jonathan Dollimore's comments on that very nice, well-meaning term "sexual preference": it is, he insists, an utterly sanitised conception and a misleading one to boot, since it serves to blind us to the complicated interplay of desire and disgust, of attraction and aversion, that makes up our sexual identities.[14] A similarly powerful and dangerous interplay of impulses, I would argue, is at work in our aesthetic experiences as well. If disgust is "the compelling expression of the terrifying mutability of desire",[15] then ugliness is, similarly, a compelling expression of the mutability of taste. And it is this mutability that Scarry's treatment of beauty as "clearly discernible" seems designed to de-emphasise. Even the state of "being in error about beauty" (the way Scarry might describe Parton's vivid childhood experience) is cast as a momentary thing, an excess or deficit in generosity, rather than a matter of systematically learned and culturally bound judgments.

Of course, these matters of taste and of learned ways of discrimination will not entirely disappear from the field Scarry surveys. The question of "cultural dif-ference", for instance, raises its head when she discusses her failure to appreciate fully the beauty of a particular palm tree, predisposed as she is by her prior experience to be more open to the beauty of sycamores, copper beeches, magnolias and the like. But this example of "an error about beauty" is a strikingly innocuous one: by dealing with trees, rather than with human faces or human products, Scarry is able to make the prejudicial effects of cultural difference and geographical contingency seem absolutely painless. And she suggests that such effects are almost automatically overcome as one becomes acclimatised to a new territory. The ability to perceive a palm tree with appreciative acuity is an effect, Scarry suggests, of being "on the same ground with a particular vegetation or animal or artwork".[16] There is no reason to believe, she posits, that our capacity for appreciating beauty is finite. But as we will see when we turn to *The Heart of Redness*, it is quite possible for people who have lived in a given locale, "on the same ground" with particular plants or animals – not to mention human beings! – to be virtually incapable of viewing them as aesthetically pleasing.[17] Such prejudice will be particularly strong and particularly enduring, or so Mda's novel suggests, when we are dealing with categories of objects or persons that have already been inscribed as signs in contested discourses. In the case of *The Heart of Redness* the contested discourse is that of modernity, a fraught one given the bloody colonial history of the South African village that serves as his novel's key chronotope. If, for instance, indigenous thorn trees, cycads and aloes (to confine myself for the moment to the realm of vegetation) appear downright ugly to the modernists of the community, it is because "the bush" has historically become associated (at least for them) with the slight of cultural backwardness and the pain of geographical isolation. Such "errors of undercrediting" (if errors they be) are unlikely to be redressed by more extensive observation, as Scarry so optimistically implies.

To bring up questions of aversion and ugliness is, of course, to seem like something of a curmudgeon, especially since Scarry – at times quite lyrically – presents the intense perception of beauty as akin to falling in love. This is a vulnerable conception, since (as Scarry herself recognises) a theory of beauty would have to account not only for truly beloved persons and objects, but for all the attractive persons and objects that one encounters in daily life. Vulnerability, however, is something of a value in this treatise: the vulnerability of the observer is, for Scarry, a way of overcoming knee-jerk arguments about the brutality of "the gaze" (and I am, in this respect, rather sympathetic with her position). Vulnerability is in fact a crucial part of her argument about the way beauty works in the interest of justice. Scarry's linkage between the aesthetic and the ethical (conjured by the dual meaning of the word "fair") relies in good measure on her conception of beauty as not merely a momentary pleasure, but as a fragile state of *ecstasis*: as a radical decentering of the observer, which ensures the disinterestedness and therefore the moral potency of the cognitive experience of beauty. It is not, Scarry announces, that "we cease to stand at the center of the world, for we never stood there. It is that we cease to stand even at the center of our own world. We willingly cede our ground to the thing that stands before us".[18]

107

But does *On Beauty and Being Just* as a whole really demonstrate any evidence of a sense of "adjacency", of standing outside oneself and one's proper domain of social power? As someone whose research interest alerts her to questions of place and spatiality, I am struck by the fact that Scarry recurrently uses the word "site", but in a completely abstract way, as referring simply to an "example" or an "instance". The term would seem to invite one to think in more concrete ways about the location – the situation – of aesthetic observation, but Scarry's universalising inclinations prevent her from doing so. Though we are given a clear sense of the place where the lectures were written (in the extremely pleasant circumstances of the Getty Research Center in California, with views of olive trees and soaring hawks and bright skies), they never hint that such a privileged "site" might in any way skew the choice of examples. There is no sense, for instance, that the beauty of gardens might not instantly strike all observers in a context (like South Africa's) where gardening has long been associated for the majority of people with domestic servitude and poor pay. While trying to cast her political opponents as people who would only permit perceptions that bring discomfort, Scarry demonstrates no awareness whatsoever of the discomfort that talk about beauty and aesthetic appreciation (the evident "beauty" of poems or paintings) might involve for people who have been made to feel that their taste is not up to standard, or people whose cultural traditions are consistently devalued. It is in this respect that Scarry's confidence in the "clear discernibility" of beauty reveals its confident cultural centrality – despite the disclaimer that "we do not stand at the centre of the world".[19]

These observations would perhaps seem like cheap shots, were it not for the fact that they do home in on a crucial issue in Scarry's lectures. Towards the end of *On Beauty and Being Just*, she does turn her attention to the problem of geographical deprivation: to the fact that, as she ever so nicely puts it, "the surfaces of the world are aesthetically uneven".[20] It is not a matter with which Scarry gets very far, in my view, since it would compel her to think more vividly than she does of the many forms of ugliness – of squalor, dreariness, ill-health – that often go along with injustice and exploitation. But her meditations on the need for equality and the impulse toward symmetrical distribution do lead Scarry to another stage in her argument: she lists, among three aspects of beauty's connections to ethical fairness, its capacity to incite a kind of preservationist solicitude. The beautiful object, she suggests, encourages the viewer to enter into its protection.[21]

But "protection" has ever been a dangerous word: one that all too easily becomes an alibi for the paternalistic exertion of power and control. Readers of South African fiction have had the benefit of Nadine Gordimer's salutary reminder in her brilliant novel, *The Conservationist,* that an impulse towards protection and preservation may serve to subtend, rather than to rectify, the old geographies of privilege and deprivation. One cannot forget the striking detail of how the rich tycoon, entranced by the subtle beauty of his highveld farm and concerned to protect its fragile marshland, erects a sign at his fence that reads, in English, Afrikaans and isiZulu:

> No thoroughfare
> Geen toegang
> Akunandlela lapha[22]

The capacity for aesthetic appreciation, the conservationist impulse and the desire to confine things in their "proper" places prove, in this fictional case and in many real ones too, to be virtually inseparable. It is in this perhaps all-too-sceptical light that we may view the moment of high enthusiasm with which *On Beauty and Being Just* concludes: a celebration of the university and of museums as sites for the preservation of culture – as institutions that, as Scarry puts it, "take such care that beautiful artifacts from people long in the past be sagely carried forward to people in the future".[23] Again the rhetoric is troubling: the emphasis on temporality ("the future" and "the past") draws our attention away from the geographical and cultural disjunctions at stake in the business of collecting, and masks the imbalance of power that is almost invariably at stake in the business of protection and conservation. Who exactly does Scarry mean when she speaks in this rather devious sentence about "people"? Can we follow her in her benign assumption of a commonality between the people in the past and the people in the future, and agree with her when she says, earlier on in her peroration, that "people" (again that universalising word) "seem to intuit that their own self-interest is served by distant people's having the benefit of beauty"?[24] How would this noble assertion sound, for instance, to the activists who have appealed to Harvard University, Scarry's own institution, to return its collection of Native American artifacts and remains to the tribal lands – and peoples – from which they were originally taken? Should they rejoice in the fact that Bostonians can have the benefit of exotic scopic pleasures, now that their own useful or sacred artifacts have been put on display as "beautiful things"? Should the Greeks, by the same token, quit complaining and rejoice at the "sage" care given to the Elgin marbles by the British Museum?

My point is not really to berate Scarry for her privileges or for her (not all that disinterested) cultural vantage point. But I do want to say that her notion of beauty's inherent connection to the impulse for preservation and conservation can only be maintained in situations where cultural conflict is minimal and identities are secure: these matters are generally much more fraught in the contact zones of colonial history. If we think about beauty from a different place, a place where the contingencies of value are less easy to ignore, a different and in many ways more social and dynamic notion of aesthetics begins to emerge. And such a notion has, I think,

109

greater relevance to the contemporary world of globalised cultural exchange: the world, one might say, of the postcolonial exotic. It is with this world in mind that we may now turn to Zakes Mda's fiction.

II

The Heart of Redness is one of the more complex novels to emerge from post-apartheid South Africa and a brief description of its plot is necessary for any comprehensible discussion of its aesthetic concerns. The novel has two time frames. A contemporary narrative involves a dispute over a proposed hotel and casino development on the Wild Coast of the Transkei (KwaXhosa) that pits village modernists against village conservationists in an urgent debate about cultural heritage and ecological preservation. The story of this dispute is undercut by a historical narrative, which is set during the infamous amaXhosa Cattle Killing of 1856-1857. Mda recounts the story of the contemporary villagers' ancestors and of their conflicting reactions to a young prophetess named Nongqawuse (and later on in the saga also another, named Nonkosi) who brought the amaXhosa the message that if everyone slaughtered all their cattle and burnt their granaries, the dead would arise from the sea, bringing with them new cattle and new grain. This prophecy, which for complex reasons was persuasive to many people, had disastrous results, as Mda's novel amply demonstrates. It meant not only starvation for thousands of amaXhosa, but also led to the opening up of Kaffraria to white settlement and the reduction of a proudly independent and fractious people to wage-slavery. In Mda's retelling, the history of the Cattle Killing also leaves a legacy of conflict between the descendants of believers and the descendants of unbelievers in Nongqawuse's prophecy, and these old divisions are re-animated in the bitter contemporary disputes over the hotel and casino.

What makes this novel so unusual in the canon of black South African fiction is that it essentially brackets off and skips over the apartheid years, which are referred to only as the "sufferings of the Middle Generations".[25] Mda thus encourages us to focus, not on the familiar drama of racial strife, but on the ongoing drama of colonial modernity. His novel is an ambitious one: its historical sections suggest comparison with Achebe's *Things Fall Apart*, with which it shares a project of ethnographic and historical self-definition, while its contemporary sections seem to invite comparison with Ngugi's *Petals of Blood*, with which it shares an interest in the dangers of postcolonial exploitation by a greedy national bourgeoisie.

Given these dramatic and politically far-ranging contents, one may well ask why questions of aesthetics are given such prominence in the novel: why "beautiful things" should be of interest from the very first page to the very last. The answer is that the novel is crucially concerned with the problems of place, belonging and cultural heritage; and it is by attending to the different sites of cultural judgement that Mda is able to trace out the multiple horizons or mediascapes in terms of which

110

post-apartheid "South African" culture must be defined. We may consider in this regard the way in which Mda indexes various female characters' physical appearance. We are told, for instance, that the village school teacher Xoliswa Ximiya, who dresses in austere, up-to-date fashions, has travelled to the US and has the looks of a supermodel. The attractive receptionist at the town's hotel, Miss Vathiswa, by contrast, dresses in elaborate but dated outfits. She has also travelled, but only to Durban, where she modelled for Mahomedy's clothing catalogue. Even a minor and unappealing character, the village trader John Dalton's wife, whose deplorable taste is made evident in the common poster she puts up in her living room, was once a (very) local beauty: we are told that in her youth she reigned as the Cherry Queen during the Free State town of Ficksburg's annual Cherry Festival. By not only describing the way the characters look, but also their sense of style, the scope of their imaginary worlds and the contexts in which they would find the greatest appreciation, Mda is able to sketch out the complex intersections of the local, the national and the international cultural landscapes.

I have already suggested that the word "beautiful" functions as a kind of semantic shifter in Mda's novel: as what James Clifford would call a "translation term".[26] Though it seldom expresses authorial sanction, it is not used ironically (since that would imply a consistent vantage), but in such a way as to emphasise the geographical contingency of aesthetic values. A similarly shifting term is "redness," which refers – significantly, given the novel's aesthetic concerns – to the amaXhosa custom of decorating the body and clothes with red ochre. This locally specific meaning, however, does not diminish in the least the novel's connection with Conrad's *Heart of Darkness*, which Mda provocatively establishes in his title. On the contrary: in the colonial discourse of the Eastern Cape, "redness" was virtually synonymous with "darkness". Even as late as the 1960s, ethnographic literature employed the term "red people" (as opposed to "school people") to refer to "uncivilised" pagans, or, to phrase it less offensively, to traditionalists with strong ties to Xhosa custom, resistant to the lure of "Western" culture. In other words, the term "redness" has historically played into what the anthropologist Steven Robins calls the "great divide" in colonial and apartheid discourse: the opposition between the urban and the rural, between the centre and the periphery and, more generally, between "progressive" modernity and traditional African custom.[27] The connection between *The Heart of Redness* and *Heart of Darkness* is therefore not entirely ironic or adversarial. Mda's novel resembles Conrad's in that its narrative also works to expose the instability of the key terms in its title: neither civilisation nor savagery prove to have a fixed centre or "heart"; otherness cannot be confined to the periphery; and value judgements ("darkness", "redness", "light", "beauty", etc.) become radically ungrounded. If there is anything at the heart of *The Heart of Redness*, it is a debate over the meaning of the novel's translation terms.

111

112

Fig. 1. *Untitled*
© B-Witched Photography, Belgium

In a crucial early scene (one which deftly evokes the post-apartheid city, violent and "swarm[ing] with restless humanity"[28]), Mda establishes Johannesburg as the centre of cultural and political power in the new South Africa. It is the place where the new national elite exert their discrimination and enforce their values in the kinds of people they hire and the kinds of objects they buy. For anyone other than the new "Aristocrats of the Revolution",[29] however, the city is not a place of belonging. It is a space of transience and insecurity, both for educated former exiles, hoping to return "home" from places like Sweden, Yugoslavia and America, and for simple migrants, hoping to escape the poverty and tedium of rural life in glamorous Egoli. Each of these groups finds themselves treated as "rejects",[30] their talents and their creativity unappreciated. To make this point Mda homes in on a single high-rise building in Hillbrow – in effect, a kind of multi-storey transit lounge – where travellers of both kinds foregather.[31] He focuses, in particular, on a funeral ceremony that takes place in a tent on the top of the building, twenty-three floors above the street. The deceased is a man called Twin: a migrant artist from the town of Qolorha, the birthplace of Nongqawuse. The "ungrateful city",[32] as his funeral orator puts it, had no use for Twin's gifts. His realistic carvings, though they were considered "wonders"[33] by the residents of his village and seemed perfectly desirable to the patrons of Dalton's trading store, where they were sold as souvenirs, have not found favour with the city's art buyers. These trendy cognoscenti prefer their black artists to be "folksy" (a trend already satirised in *Ways of Dying*) and they have a marked taste for the grotesque, for distorted figures of "people who grew heads out of their stomachs", "eyes at the back of their heads" or "twisted lips at their feet"[34]: the sort of work that Twin, devoted to crafting "beautiful people who looked like real people",[35] considered ugly and refused to produce. The unfortunate carver's fate is paralleled (at least in these early stages of the novel) by that of Camagu, the novel's protagonist: a long-time exile who decides on a whim to join the mourners at Twin's funeral and eventually ends up settling in Qolorha, as the director of a sewing collective and an ecotourism operation. If Twin's talents are too parochial to find favour in the nation's metropolis, Camagu's are too international. Having spent many years studying and working abroad, Camagu does not "dance the freedom dance"[36] that the new regime requires of its success stories. In Johannesburg's new economy of signs, the usefulness of his American PhD and his experience in international communications pales in comparison to the display value of "beautiful men and women" who are willing to be exhibited as emblems of black economic empowerment in the "glass affirmative-action offices" of corporations.[37] Both Twin and Camagu, the rural migrant and returned exile, fail to deliver the kind of product or performance the Jo'burg glitterati are likely to appreciate.

It should already be clear that more is at stake in the novel's aesthetic arguments than a binary opposition between the naïve country and the sophisticated city, or –

113

as in the grotesque allegory of *Ways of Dying* – between the "beautiful" beneficiaries
of the official economy and the "ugly" people from the informal settlements on its
fringes. Whereas the earlier novel's carnivalesque thematics required a bold visual
encoding of the gulf between the world of wealth and the world of deprivation,
The Heart of Redness is concerned with subtler and more culturally and historically
specific distinctions. It is significant, therefore, that the village of Qolorha is not at
all like the bounded village of anthropological fantasy, nostalgically sealed off from
modern influences.[38] While certainly not as restless as Hillbrow, where "[e]veryone
… comes from somewhere else",[39] Qolorha is nevertheless also a culturally porous
space. Its daily life is connected to the world beyond, whether by the traffic in
commodities or by the travels of its residents. Both as historical frontier and as
contemporary tourist destination, it is a contact zone, a place where "natives" and
colonisers, dwellers and travellers encounter each other – and where the distinction
between these categories can at times be quite blurry. Qolorha is, moreover, a
disputatious place, where certain individuals can seem as much out of place as Twin
did in the "ungrateful city". The elegant looks of Xoliswa Ximiya, for instance, are
not highly prized: her beauty is too much like that of the "hungry women … in the
fashion magazines"[40] to appeal to local men, who like their women more "plump and
juicy".[41]

The fact that Qolorha is a spectacularly scenic place is significant, of course, both
in Mda's novel and in relation to the dramatic historical events surrounding
Nongqawuse's prophecy and the fateful Cattle Killing. The historian Jeff Peires, from
whose work Mda has drawn many of his novel's details, notes that the 19th-century
amaXhosa who came to Qolorha to listen to the message of the ancestors – especially
those amaXhosa who had never seen the ocean – must have been deeply affected by
the dramatic cliffs, the pounding waves, the rising mist and the dense and variegated
vegetation.[42] Qolorha is and was a place that overwhelms the senses, a place where
some visitors might well imagine that they can hear the eerie whistling of the spirits.
But even these striking scenic qualities, as Mda makes very clear, do not mean that
the "beauty" of the place is a matter of consensus or "clear discernibility". Bhonco,
the village modernist, attributes Camagu's perception of Qolorha as "the most
beautiful place on earth" to the fact that he is a tourist and has not been "forced to
live [in the village] forever".[43] The old man's observation is worth consideration,
especially since tourism (both as a source of income and as source of scopic pleasure)
is such an important theme in the novel. A tourist is perhaps most usefully defined
as someone who is "taking a leap out of ordinary life".[44] Such a leap, as Jamaica
Kincaid has insisted, tends to yield aesthetic pleasure at the cost of other kinds of
perception. Tourists in her native Antigua, Kincaid notes, invariably find the sunny
weather to be beautiful: it means that they will enjoy the four days or so they have
come to spend on the beach without worrying about the rain. But for the person who

lives in this tourist paradise from day to day, the constant sunshine also means drought, lack of sanitation, and so forth.[45] Mda's take on the matter is not at odds with Kincaid's, but it does seem more subtle and multi-layered. The novel makes it clear that Camagu's appreciative perception of Qolorha is neither invalid nor necessarily self-serving: even Bhonco at one point lets "his eyes feast" on the "mountains of snow-white surf", the "green valleys" and the clusters of "beautiful houses painted pink, powder blue, yellow, and white".[46] Even so, Mda makes it clear that the perception of the valley as a landscape painting, "a canvas where blue and green dominate",[47] is an effect of privilege and distance. It requires a bracketing not only of utilitarian concerns, but also, more signally, of the local meanings of the beautiful thing. To apprehend the pastel-coloured rondavels as picturesque, one must not only refrain from thinking about practicalities (their vulnerability to termites, for example), but one must also be able to ignore, if only momentarily, the fact that different architectural styles (the rondavel, the hexagon, and the square *ixanga*) are signifiers in a divisive local discourse about tradition and modernity, in terms of which round houses or rondavels were considered traditional, indigenous and rural, while square houses were considered modern, imported and urban.[48]

A similar line of argument can be applied to questions of fashion and styles of dress: a pervasive theme in the novel. In one of the historical sections, Mda allows us to see the arbitrariness of this system of signs: the 19th-century amaXhosa find the idea that "the way to the white man's heaven was through trousers and dresses" to be patently absurd, and they cannot see why the convert William Goliath, dressed in a discarded suit of the missionaries, is in any way superior to them in his physical appearance.[49] In the novel's contemporary sections, however, the meaning of clothing is no longer quite so arbitrary: it is densely but differentially encoded at every level of the novel's (multiple) social hierarchies. On the village level, the key figure is the formidable NoPetticoat, Bhonco's wife and Xoliswa's mother. She is a woman who has never travelled: Centani, Butterworth, Bisho, Pretoria and America are all for her simply distant places, with no particular cultural meaning or authority. As a result she is able to enjoy fully the decorative traditions of Qolorha's *amahomba*, "those who look beautiful and who pride themselves on fashion"[50] – the red-ochred *isikhakha* skirts, the broad *iqhiya* turbans and the various kinds of traditional beadwork: the *uphlalaza*, *amatikiti*, *amacici* and *icangci*. This elaborate vocabulary is recorded in the novel for good reason. The traditional costume is for NoPetticoat "an art form": a language that she and the other *amahomba* use to "say something" about themselves.[51] Other styles of clothing are, for her, simply "soulless".[52] They are signifiers in a language that NoPetticoat cannot translate – despite what her wonderfully inappropriate name would lead one to expect. (And I should perhaps explain for international readers that "No" is the feminine prefix in isiXhosa, not the English negative.)

115

The elegant Xoliswa is also committed to "beautiful things", or, in her students' more negative view, is dismissive of people and things that do not meet her exacting aesthetic and cultural standards. Her fascination with a strange news story about Hu Pao-lin, a Taiwanese girl who stabbed her mother and mother-in-law because "they were not pretty enough to deserve to live", is expressive of a radical intolerance.[53] In contrast to NoPetticoat, Xoliswa is almost painfully aware of being in what she considers a marginal cultural location: she is prone to giving uninvited geography lessons to all and sundry, demonstrating her sense of the relative size and importance of Bisho, Pretoria and New York, which is "ten times bigger than Johannesburg",[54] or so she informs the amused Camagu. Her standards of beauty, not surprisingly, do not originate locally, but in America, which is for her a "fairytale country" and the home of "beautiful people" like Eddie Murphy and Dolly Parton.[55] As a result, Xoliswa "hates to see her mother looking so beautiful",[56] "beautiful", that is, in terms of a code that Xoliswa rejects in its entirety as shameful. But the limits to her much-vaunted cosmopolitanism are slyly revealed by her examples of beautiful people, Dolly Parton in particular. As I noted earlier, the country singer's extravagant sense of beauty arises out of her own quite marginal origins in American society. Parton's style, one might say, "talks" in a regional accent, and in this respect it is not so unlike the regional fashions of the *amahomba*. Its dimension of ironic performance, moreover, is something that Xoliswa is too parochial a cultural observer to detect.

The fashion styles of the Johannesburg elite – to return to the city – are defined by yet another set of visual and aesthetic codes. Confident in their new social power and sufficiently removed from the historic stigmas that still attach to traditional amaXhosa clothing on the local level, they are eager to buy such things as *isikhakha* skirts, shoulder bags and beadwork. Far from marking them as backward, these items denote them as particularly *au courant* and as responsive to the president's much publicised call for an "African Renaissance".[57] Mda's language, however, makes it clear that the glitterati are essentially in the position of tourists: they "conde-scendingly visit" the clothes of the *amaqaba* and only wear them as "curiosities"[58] on special occasions – especially occasions like the opening of parliament when they might be displayed on TV as visual embodiments of the nation. This sartorial leap out of the ordinary reveals the limits of the elite's cultural discrimination. Their everyday (and therefore more normative) clothing is, as Camagu observes, no less regional and considerably less authentic than the isiXhosa styles they patronisingly adopt. The embroidered Western African garments these national celebrities favour are in fact made out of fabrics imported from Java and Germany. Yet these are the clothes through which the elite signals its authentic (South) Africanness to the rest of the world.[59]

The cultural map I have just sketched out would seem to validate the most cosmo-politan character in the novel: Camagu, the expert in international communications and former denizen of New York, Rome and Paris, who often brings an illuminating comparative perspective to bear on local and national issues. Unlike Xoliswa he is able, as he puts it, to distinguish between "civilization" and "Western civilization".[60] His international cultural vantage sets him free to appreciate the amaXhosa's "beautiful artistic cultural heritage",[61] which he is also – more problematically – in a position to market in the city. It is certainly possible to view Camagu as an exemplary catalyst figure of the sort Mda describes in his academic writing on development issues, and indeed, Camagu seems to echo Mda's own views on questions like primordialist and essentialist concepts of culture and grassroots participation in community affairs.[62] Yet the novel stops short of turning Camagu into an oracle. Mda never allows us to forget that it is precisely Camagu's cultural privilege that makes him invulnerable to the stigma of being called a "barbarian" – a word that might attach to a less sophisticated man who, like Camagu, expresses an emotional attachment to his clan totem. And there is at least one small but telling scene in which a villager turns the tables on Camagu and subjects his cosmopolitan judiciousness to delightful mockery. The clever local girl Qukeswa uses the occasion of a village fundraising event – a concert at which one donates money in exchange for the right to compel any other audience member to do whatever one asks – to tease Camagu about his original purpose in coming to the village: his impulsive search for the lovely NomaRussia, a village girl he glimpsed at Twin's funeral in Johannesburg. Qukeswa essentially forces Camagu to become judge in a beauty contest: she "buys" that Camagu must decide which of the fifteen or more NomaRussias in the audience – women of all shapes, sizes, and ages – is the most beautiful. Though he wisely makes a hefty donation to release himself from the obligation, Camagu's discomfort allows the villagers a good laugh at his expense and mocks his authority as an arbiter of taste. Mda is careful, in short, not to simply repeat, albeit on a more global level, Xoliswa's assumption that judgements and standards that come from afar are necessarily the most valid.[63]

But beauty is no laughing matter in *The Heart of Redness*. Aesthetic preconceptions and practices (among which we must include the scopic pleasures of sightseeing) are not mere epiphenomena, but are enmeshed in such grave political and economic matters as the control and ownership of valuable land, the meaning and uses of tradition and the fate of a unique coastal ecosystem. There is, for instance, a clear danger in the failure of a village "progressive" like Bhonco to view the "bush" as anything other than a humiliating sign of backwardness. The old man's reluctance to appreciate anything of local origin leads him to dismiss indigenous fauna and flora – rare lizards, cycads and the like – as "ugly",[64] and to consider exotics like bluegums and pines as "civilized trees" and plantations, with their orderly rows, as "beautiful forest[s]".[65] Aesthetic judgements like these make the Qolorha vulnerable to exploitative projects like the giant resort development – especially when the

117

residents hear about these schemes from a "very handsome" black CEO in a new navy-blue suit.[66]

In Mda's satirical description of it, the two white consultants' plan for the "tourist heaven" becomes a kind of caricature of modernist aesthetics. Mr Jones's dream of a splendid crystal casino, surrounded by amusement park rides, roller coasters, cable cars and waterways filled with jet skis, captures something of the streamlined aesthetic of speed and mobility, but does so in a trivialised fashion: the "gambling city" will be a site of mechanised play. Mr Smith's vision of a retirement village for millionaires, complete with neatly landscaped English gardens, carefully surveyed roads, Olympic-size pools and new (and much more "pronouncable") names like "Willowbrook Grove" or "something ending in Close, Dell, and Downs",[67] expresses something of modernity's homogenising logic, its rage for order. But the ill-fitting English toponyms underscore the neocolonial nature of the project: Mr Smith is, one might say, the ridiculous postmodern avatar of the novel's arch-villain, Sir George Gray, the British governor of the Cape, also known by the amaXhosa as He-Who-Named-Ten-Rivers. The fact that the village progressives are blind to this recurrence, and to the fact that they would, at best, experience the glitz of the casino with its exciting rides only as spectators, would seem to emphasise the need for a new kind of aesthetic education. It is therefore no accident that the novel's very first page raises, however comically, the idea of "cry[ing] because of beautiful things",[68] or that the romantic plot ends up rewarding Qukezwa, who, as Mda puts it, is free-spirited because she is not "burdened with beauty".[69] Though Mda has no intention of banishing beauty (it is clear that he wholly endorses NoPetticoat's eventual reclamation of the traditional styles of dress that give her pleasure), he nevertheless suggests that aesthetic perceptions can be divisive and destructive, rather than pacific and protective, precisely because they are so ideologically malleable.

III

Inside the back cover of the Oxford paperback edition of *The Heart of Redness*, Zakes Mda reproduces a remarkable photograph of Nongqawuse and Nonkosi, the two young amaXhosa prophetesses of the mid-19th century. They are not smiling, nor are their eyes directed squarely at the camera; they do not return the gaze of the 21st-century viewer. They are not, in my view, pretty. But to confront this image, just after having read a narrative about the social life of exotic commodities, souvenirs and "beautiful" things, is a strangely disquieting experience: it suggests that the issues of reification and commodification (which Elaine Scarry wants so badly to put aside) are still very much with us. It is as if Mda wants to remind his readers of their own status as consumers and gazers, and also of the status of the novel itself as an aesthetic object. Like the photograph of the prophetesses, like the objects that are marketed in Camagu's collective, and like the cultural practices that are put on

119

120

display for tourists in John Dalton's "cultural village", Mda's novel has been put into circulation, put up for sale and made available for enjoyment and judgement for people in and from places far from those described in it.

Will it be considered a beautiful thing?

The judgement is hardly likely to be anything so simple. Certainly, the novel's aesthetic value will not be immediately discernible: it will be defined by any number of shifting and site-specific criteria of judgement. In South African terms, Mda is, of course, not a marginal cultural producer; but on the level of the global cultural marketplace, he shares the position of all postcolonial writers: his work, perceived as coming from the world's fascinating margins, has a market niche of a very particular kind, and one which academic readers help to create and define. His novels are not unlike the "folksy" and "kitschy" sculptures that figure prominently in *The Heart of Redness* and *Ways of Dying*: they too will be subject to classification by privileged cognoscenti. Whether Mda's shrewd awareness of what Graham Huggan has termed "the postcolonial exotic" may save his novels to some extent from such simultaneously appreciative and condescending consumption – and from the fate of being "sagely" preserved in libraries, university courses, and, yes, appreciative critical essays – is an open question. But at the very least, Mda's validation of local knowledges and tastes, of not just the city, but the village as a significant site of aesthetic judgement, forces metropolitan critics to revise the stale old notion of postcolonial literature as a matter of the "empire writing back" and encourages us (for I must include myself in this category) not to see the circulation of criteria of aesthetic judgement as necessarily unidirectional. Places of insecurity, as Mda vividly reminds us in *The Heart of Redness*, also produce ways of defining and recognising the "beautiful" thing.

Acknowledgements
This essay is dedicated to the denizens of the Vincent House in Notting Hill where it was conceptualised, and especially to Donald Shojai and Terry Saigh, who made our time there pleasant and companionable.

Rita Barnard > The Place of Beauty: Reflections on Elaine Scarry and Zakes Mda

Dominique Malaquais
Quelle Liberté: Art, Beauty and the Grammars
of Resistance in Douala

Dominique Malaquais is a historian of contemporary African culture and arts. She is Professor of Visual Culture and Africana Studies at Sarah Lawrence College (New York) and is an Associate Researcher at the Wits Institute for Social and Economic Research. She is the author of *Architecture, Pouvoir et Dissidence au Cameroun* (2002). Malaquais is Editor-at-Large of the Cape Town-based review *Chimurenga* and an editor of the French journal *Politique africaine*. She is the author of numerous articles that explore the intersection of politics, art and architecture south of the Sahara. Currently, she is at work on a book about African cities.

QUELLE LIBERTÉ: ART, BEAUTY AND THE GRAMMARS OF RESISTANCE IN DOUALA

124

Fig. 1. The Cameroonian artist Joseph Francis Sumegne
Photo: Doual'Art

i'm a poem taking form
beyond the napalm storm
a moving mosaic
a sonic volcano
while they hop till they drop
the atom bomb
cut!

Lesego Rampolokeng [1]

Of dreads and language: first words

Some time ago, in Cape Town, a Cameroonian writer gave me a book of poetry: Sandile Dikeni's *Telegraph to the Sky*.[2] Dikeni writes mostly about South Africa. His words, however, extend beyond his country, and so I shall use them to guide my remarks in the pages that follow. Another writer will guide me as well: Issa Diabaté of Côte d'Ivoire. Writing on the city, Diabaté notes the following:

> The city is born of its subjection to matter … Like all life, it rises from things rotting. Part body-part, part machine, like living beings, it creates odours and excrement and waste. From these, ideas and sensibilities are born – a language of the city.[3]

One aspect of this language, in particular, draws my attention: the vocabulary – better still, the grammar   of resistance. I write here, as I find myself doing most everywhere these days, of refusal, of empowerment born of rejecting the status quo.

Diabaté's thoughts on the city will be my starting point, along with a question Dikeni asks in a poem entitled "Lesego", penned in honour of the South African poet Lesego Rampolokeng:

> How come they make bombs out of words and dreads?[4]

The dreads in question are Lesego's, the ubiquitously unruly hair he refused to tame, just as he refused to don a suit and enter the middle class, as did, in his view, far too many of his brothers in arms after the ANC came to power – not least Dikeni himself when, in 2001, he accepted a position with the government of president Thabo Mbeki. Such waste, Lesego has been heard to say …

Dreads and language, cities, refusal, waste, resistance are what this essay is about. It is about a man notorious for his dreadlocks and about a firestorm of words born of an object he created: a sculpture made entirely of waste, of things discarded – a monument to the failings of the status quo.

The dreaded one of whom I write is Joseph Francis Sumegne, a Cameroonian artist

125

126

Fig. 2. *La nouvelle liberté* (The New Liberty) by Joseph Francis Sumegne. Photo: D. Malaquais

born in 1951 ^(fig. 1). His sculpture, sited in Douala, is entitled *La nouvelle liberté* ^(fig. 2). It depicts a man dancing, caught as if in mid-motion. The figure balances on one foot and holds an arm up. In its raised hand, crowning the piece, is a globe, a stylised image of the world. *La nouvelle liberté* is huge. It measures over ten metres in height and weighs seven tons. Set atop a solid concrete base two metres high, which is itself sunk into metres of concrete underground, it can withstand winds of 160 km/h, a matter of some concern in this the second-rainiest spot on the planet. Sumegne's massive sculpture is the brainchild of an organisation called Doual'Art, an NGO founded in the early 1990s that seeks to prompt exchanges and change within the city through art.

Never, in the colonial or in the postcolonial history of Douala, has a single object caused as much controversy as *La nouvelle liberté*. At the heart of the controversy is a knot of words, invective and threats about identity, about urban space, place, aesthetics, authorship, meaning and the grammars of resistance. The sculpture was erected in July 1996. Immediately, it prompted great interest. For weeks on end, thousands of people a day came to view it, an unusual development in a city that, until then, had seen only one work of public sculpture – a rather uninspiring piece characteristic of the French colonial project. Shortly, articles began to appear in the press. These first words about *La nouvelle liberté*, published in all manner of pro- and anti-government newspapers, were quite positive. Journalists and those whom they interviewed seemed somewhat uncertain as to the aesthetic merits of the piece, but the great majority found the sculpture interesting and were at once surprised and impressed to discover that Doual'Art had donated the statue to the city. Comparisons were made, with some pride, to New York's Statue of Liberty, which, it was pointed out, had been donated as well.[5]

Such positive reactions, however, were short-lived. Soon, the tide began to turn. This essay chronicles the response to *La nouvelle liberté* in the months following its birth and, more generally, what has happened since then. My goal is to tease out a group among the many views that emerged in response to the sculpture and to consider how these various stances have affected the sculpture itself, the production of public art in Douala and, most importantly perhaps, local conceptions of art as an expression of political resistance. Among the key concepts I explore are ideas of identity, subjectivity, order, disorder, beauty and ugliness.

Art and meaning in the city: the artist and the NGO

Multiple approaches to *La nouvelle liberté* are possible. How one begins looking at this massive sculpture is, of course, subjective and, in Douala these days, is a matter of some controversy. As I am an art historian, I propose that we begin with the artist. In doing so, however – in choosing to call Sumegne an artist – I am taking sides, making an argument that, as we shall see, the city's deeply conservative political and cultural elite derides.[6] Sumegne likes to compose himself. Ask to photograph him and he requests that you wait. He leaves the room then shortly reappears. When he leaves, he is sporting a short, tidy haircut. He comes back in full dread, beautifully crafted locks embellished with bits of metal, small stones and rich-hued pieces of cloth framing his face. The elegant coiffure he sports is a wig, which he puts on to become his public self: Sumegne the *artiste*, creator of an art form he calls *jalaa*.

The term *jalaa*, like the look of the artist, brings to mind Rastafarian concerns. Who and what is Rasta, however, is itself a matter of subjective interpretation. The label is quite elastic: Alpha Blondy, the Ivoirian reggae musician, makes one thing of it, the prophet Gad another, post-apartheid South African political movements something else still. Sumegne's *jalaa* is not explicitly Rasta, but it borrows from general notions of what constitutes Rasta philosophy: notions of universalism, communion between man and god, and the quest for freedom. As Sumegne explains it, *jalaa* is a holistic approach to the production of art.[7] It draws, he says, on several realms of artistic endeavour – painting, sculpture, weaving and architecture, among others – bringing them together in search of principles he sees as fundamental to the construction of the universe. In *jalaa*, he explains, colour patterns are chosen as by a painter (fig. 3). Structural elements are assembled as by a sculptor (figs 4 and 5) and are linked to one another – sutured – as by a weaver (fig. 6). Volumes are articulated as by an architect (fig. 7). At the heart of the whole stands the artist, whose purpose is to make manifest the work of the Creator – a goal, he proposes, in which we should all share. This approach Sumegne links in turn to notions of freedom and responsibility. Freedom – *liberté* – he suggests, is a gift of the Creator that it is our duty to nurture:

> Liberty is not something that can be imposed or be expected to last forever. It is a precarious thing, ever at risk of losing its balance, a product of constant effort, an assemblage, at times, of the most heterogeneous elements – and yet, it holds the world aloft.[8]

La nouvelle liberté, Sumegne explains, is an incarnation of *jalaa*. Like the freedom his approach to art seeks to express, the sculpture is precariously poised, it is made of the most heterogeneous materials and is shown holding the world aloft.[9]

As the foregoing suggests, the materials used to create the piece are integral to the reading Sumegne proposes. Thousands of discarded objects, some found, others collected in dumps public and private, have been welded, tied, melted to a skeleton of steel: old tires and mufflers, stopped clocks and odometers, burnt-out spark plugs and rusted conveyor belts, broken light bulbs and remnants of costume jewellery (fig. 8). The artist's stated intent is to show that from nothing – from waste (*déchets*, what has been discarded) – powerful things can rise. In this making of something from nothing, he holds, all are involved. It is the duty of all who belong to a

128

Fig. 3. Detail of a small multi-media sculpture by Joseph Francis Sunegne entitled *La chanteuse de jazz* (The Jazz Singer)
Photo: D. Malaquais

Fig.4. *Le lutteur* (The Wrestler), small multi-media sculpture by Joseph Francis Sumegne
Photo: D. Malaquais

Fig. 5. Detail of a small multi-media sculpture by Joseph Francis Sumegne entit ed *La chanteuse de jazz* (The Jazz Singer)
Photo: D. Malaquais

Fig. 6. Detail of *Le lutteur* (The Wrestler), small multi-media sculpture by Joseph Francis Sumegne
Photo: D. Malaquais

Fig. 7. Detail of a small multi-media sculpture by Joseph Francis Sumegne depicting a high-ranking man, one of seven pieces in a series

Photo: D. Malaquais

Fig. 8. Detail of *La nouvelle liberté*
Photo: D. Malaquais

community to consider its every component integral and, as he has himself, to put it to use – to refashion it – in the making of a better communal whole.

Sumegne's ideas mesh nicely with Doual'Art's vision of art, freedom and urban life.[10] The NGO's founders, Marilyn Douala-Bell and Didier Schaub, see the arts – sculpture, painting, theatre, film, music, dance, poetry – as building blocks in the construction of new, more integrated and freer cities. For both Sumegne and Doual'Art, a fundamental goal in creating *La nouvelle liberté* was to celebrate the city not as an idealised, pristine space, but as the messy, difficult place that it is. *La nouvelle liberté*, artist and NGO hold, reflects the state of Douala not as one might expect that monumental sculpture would – as an unwavering success – but as it is in its poorer neighbourhoods: awash in waste (*Doul*, its inhabitants call it, short for *douleureuse*, or painful), yet fabulously vibrant nonetheless. Both decry the city's disarray. Neither, however, is willing to dwell on the matter. It is a state, they insist, which must be resisted, combated. Through mutual effort, they hold, the city *can* be transformed; individuals and public bodies, citizens and government working together, they believe, can and will effect durable change.

For Doual'Art, the question of joint endeavour was fundamental in creating *La nouvelle liberté*. For the NGO's founders, key goals were to show: first, through funding that called on private and foundation sources only, that the government alone is not responsible for the city – that one must give to receive (a view dear to Sumegne as well); second, to draw the government's attention to the fact that it has inescapable duties, foremost among these that of making the city liveable for all of its inhabitants. The site for the sculpture was chosen with these two goals in mind. When it was first erected, Sumegne's figure stood on a disastrously rutted stretch of pavement – this despite the fact that the stretch in question was at the heart of a major artery. In choosing this particular placement, Doual'Art sought to shame the municipality into action, to make it do something – *anything* – about the abysmal state of Douala's roads. The gambit proved successful. A few months after the sculpture was raised, the city was obliged to repave the site: *La nouvelle liberté* was drawing too much attention to its disrepair.

The site, of course, was chosen for other reasons too, and here we enter the realm of controversy. Sumegne's sculpture stands on Rond-Point Deïdo, a roundabout that is the city's western gate (fig. 9). Rond-Point Deïdo is perceived as Douala's door. One must pass through it to travel to Cameroon's granary, the Western Province; to the north, whence came Ahmadou Ahidjo, Cameroon's first president; and to the north-west, home to John Fru Ndi, the most vocal political opponent of the country's present leader, Paul Biya. Given its role as a multiple gateway, the Rond-Point is a remarkably busy place. It is also one of the most multi-ethnic sites in the city. This too was of interest to Doual'Art. The NGO's goal was, in part, to erect a monument that would speak to all Cameroonians. Initially, this idea, too, was

135

Fig. 9. *La nouvelle liberté* (rear view) and the roundabout on which it stands, Rond-Point Deïdo
Photo: D. Malaquais

well received. One journalist even spoke of the statue as a tool in the building of national consensus.

Art and invective: the politics of liberty
Still, all was not well. That a journalist found himself writing of consensus and the nation in relation to *La nouvelle liberté* spoke to some rather thorny issues, issues it may not have been his intent to bring out, but which are central to the fabric of urban Cameroon and whose emergence as a part of the discourse surrounding the statue was thus probably inevitable. By mid-August 1996, one month after the statue's birth, these issues started to make their way into Sumegne's discourse about his work. Suddenly, the artist was speaking of *La nouvelle liberté* as "a gift to the Sawa people". Doual'Art, which saw the sculpture as an offering to the city and country as a whole, was dismayed.

To make sense of Sumegne's statement, a little background is required. Deïdo is one of the city's oldest neighbourhoods. It was founded by the Duala people, whose name the city bears. "Sawa" is an umbrella term. It is a label that the Duala use to refer to themselves and to other peoples of the Cameroon coast, as a group. It is also a politically loaded term. In Cameroon as elsewhere in Africa, colonial governments made extensive use of ethnic categories – categories that, to a large extent, they themselves created. First under the Germans, then under the French and, thereafter, under Ahmadou Ahidjo, an ongoing focus on ethnic categories was used to divide, conquer and rule. Since the early 1990s, when it was nearly toppled, the Biya government has been stoking the fires of ethnic division as well. In particular, it has sought to discredit citizens of one region: the Western Province. This is the place of origin of the largest ethnic group – the Bamileke people, who constitute 25 per cent of the country's population and account for over 75 per cent of Douala's 3.5 million inhabitants. Under German rule, the Duala were the local masters of Cameroon's economy. Today, they have little say in the matter. This, the growing presence of people from the Western Province among them and a 15-year economic crisis that devastated urban Cameroon, have resulted in a profound wave of anti-Bamileke sentiment within certain Duala groups. This sentiment has found its most vocal proponents in a vociferous, if relatively small, political movement that uses the label "Sawa" to articulate its identity.

If, by August, Sumegne had begun speaking of *La nouvelle liberté* as a "gift to the Sawa people", it was in part to stave off increasingly disturbing critiques of his work by self-proclaimed defenders of Sawa sovereignty. These Sawa spokespersons found their primary platform in a Douala-based newspaper called *Elimbi*.[11] Noting that Sumegne was born in the Western Province, *Elimbi* embarked upon a campaign to discredit his work on grounds that it was a monument to Bamileke expansionism. Journalists for the newspaper began peppering their columns with terms drawn from a roster of ideas developed by others to damage Bamileke interests. In pro-government political pamphlets, reference is commonly made to the Bamileke as sorcerers and as sources of infectious diseases. Such references feed on a register of images developed by the French in the 1950s to discredit a radical, pro-independence political party associated, Paris held, with Bamileke concerns. This party, the UPC or Union des Populations du Cameroun, French journalists wrote, was "an open wound", "an abscess", "a source of decomposition and rot".[12] *Elimbi* put these images of infection to its own use. In its columns, in late August and September, virulent attacks started to appear, in which people from the Western Province were explicitly compared to a metastising cancer and Sumegne's sculpture was described both as a witch involved in black magic and a cell filled to capacity with a virus preparing to burst forth (fig. 10).

La nouvelle liberté, *Elimbi* announced one day, was preparing to multiply, to bring forth clones of itself that would take over the space of the city. Ten small figures, or *balises*, it reported, were going to be arrayed around *La nouvelle liberté* (fig. 11). This had been the plan all along. Doual'Art had made a point of discussing *La nouvelle liberté* and its encircling figures long in advance with the Deïdo chief, representatives of his community and other Douala leaders, one of whom was the father of the NGO's co-founder, Marilyn Douala-Bell. For both the statue and its ten *balises*, more-over, permits had been sought and obtained from the municipality. *Elimbi* chose to disregard this. Its columnists presented the *balises* much as they had originally presented the sculpture itself: as a terrible surprise being sprung, like an epidemic, on Douala.

In its articles on this and related questions, in October and November, *Elimbi* began making use of highly sexualised language, a point underscored by Cameroonian philosopher Sindjoun Pokam in a 1997 editorial he penned on *La nouvelle liberté*. Though Sumegne's figure depicts a man, the newspaper took to speaking of it in terms typically employed to designate a female body – specifically, the body of a pregnant woman. This body, *Elimbi* stated, was about to give birth (*accoucher* was the term used), to spawn ten creatures in its image that were going to invade Douala, just as the Bamileke had invaded the city. Here again, the newspaper was drawing on a body of xenophobic ideas developed in pro-government circles. In the most virulent anti-Bamileke literature, women migrants from the Western province were presented as prostitutes who were bringing disease and unwanted children to the country's urban centres. In its articles on Sumegne's statue, *Elimbi* adopted this rhetoric. Elsewhere, the children of Bamileke migrants had been openly threatened. In one pro-government pamphlet distributed in the capital, Yaoundé, it was sugges-ted that they simply be killed off.[13] *Elimbi* argued that the poorer segments of Douala's Bamileke population should be removed, sent West along with *La nouvelle liberté*.

In its diatribes, the newspaper took specific aim at street vendors, which it

138

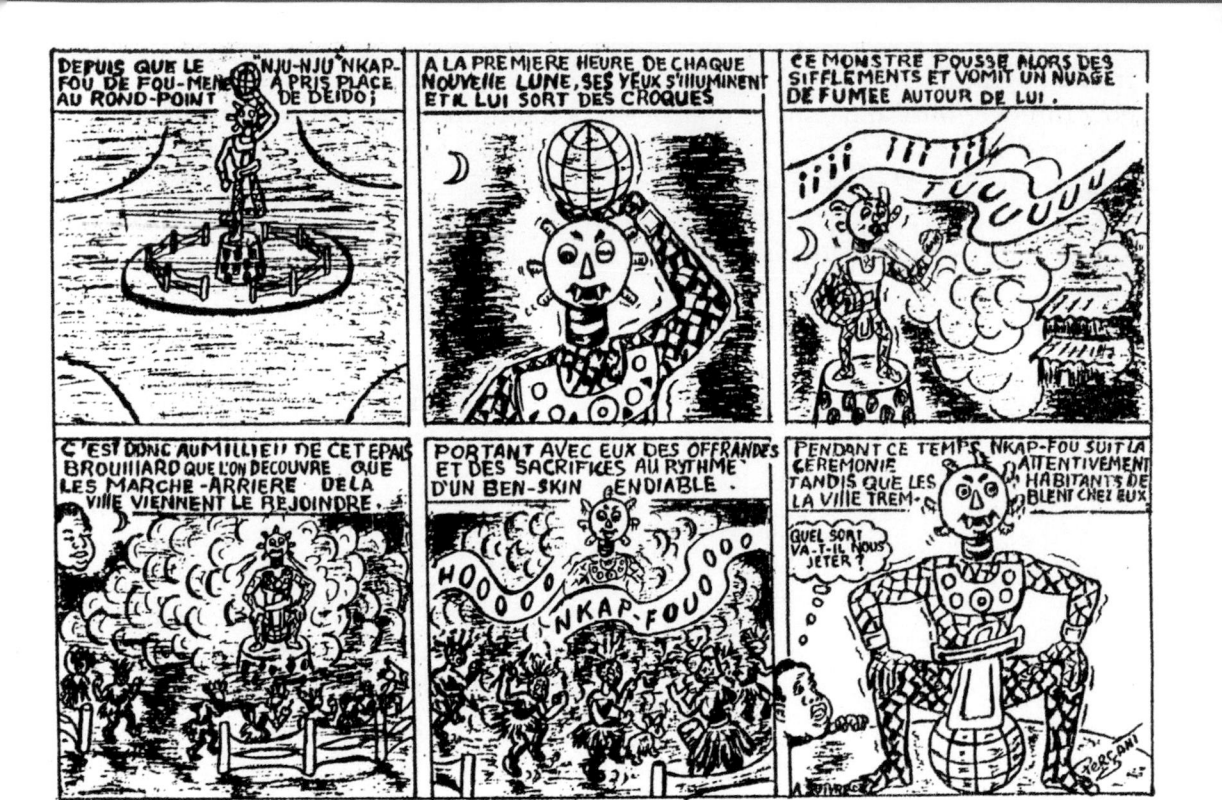

Fig. 10. Cartoon depicting *La nouvelle liberté* as an entity born of evil and involved in witchcraft, published in the newspaper *Elimbi* in 1996

Fig. 11. One of ten sculptures (*balises*), standing some seven feet high, meant to be arrayed around *La nouvelle liberté*, photographed in the courtyard of the NGO Doual'Art in the Bonanjo quarter, Douala
Photo: D. Malaquais

identified – erroneously – as for the most part Bamileke. The focus on this particular profession was not innocent. Rond-Point Deïdo is a major meeting ground for street traders, who in Douala go by the name *sauveteurs* (from *vendre à la sauvette*, "to peddle on the streets without authorisation"; also, literally, "people who save or rescue things") ^(fig. 12). Cars, vans, buses and trucks headed out of the city, laden with cargo, commonly halt here so that passengers can buy food for the road from *sauveteurs*. Incoming transport stops here as well, so that produce acquired outside the city, where it is less expensive, can begin the process of sale and re-sale that, via an intricate network of *sauveteurs*, will eventually bring it to Douala's main markets. For travellers headed to the city's outlying neighbourhoods, the Rond-Point is a key site as well. In the early 1990s, Douala's public transport company, SOCAR, declared bankruptcy. Since then, the only means available to move from one part of the city to another has been group taxis – rickety, over-burdened Toyota and Nissan *congelés* (cars rescued after nasty accidents, given a summary fix-up and paint job and shipped from European ports to sub-Saharan destinations by less-than-scrupulous business-people)[14] – and light motorcycles known as *bend-skin* in reference to a dance that, like the motorcycles on Douala's pot-holed streets, shakes the entire body, head to toe. Because petrol is prohibitively expensive and demand far outstrips supply, few drivers will agree to take a passenger all the way from Bonanjo, the colonial heart of the city, or from New Bell, home to the city's largest market, to far-flung areas such as Nylon and PK57, many kilometres and (in the rainy season) many mud-clogged roads away. As a result, commuters must take two or even three taxis, a process that calls for hour-long waits in meandering lines of prospective travellers. Typically, the first stop in this exhausting routine is Rond-Point Deïdo. In and around the lines of travellers that form here, much *sauveteur* business is done: small-scale sale and re-sale of second-hand goods and foodstuffs, from shoes and jerseys to bags of onions and tubers, grilled corn and roasted peanuts.

In Douala, as in most urban centres south of the Sahara, such business is the principal business of the city. Though Cameroon's economic capital is home to many banks local and foreign and, since 2002, to a regional stock exchange in which the government and IMF place much hope, the fact remains that for most Doualais jobs are appallingly scarce and, where extant, rarely offer enough to feed and clothe an entire household. Under the circumstances, *sauvetage* is a must. At some point in their lives, the great majority of the city's inhabitants have resorted to it as a means of ensuring the well-being of their families. For many, it is the sole means of survival.

More so even than in Yaoundé, Dakar or Abidjan, the vast gap between rich and poor, minority and majority is visible in Douala. Indeed, it is one of the most striking features of the city. The economic, social and political inequities that underpin this cleavage and explain the ubiquity of *sauvetage* in recent years have led to pitched battles between municipal authorities and ordinary folk struggling to

141

make a living. These battles have centred around the allocation of urban space: the right to define how and by whom plazas, sidewalks and roadsides will be used. On numerous occasions, colonies of *sauveteurs* have been forcibly displaced, their stalls destroyed and goods thrown into the streets by police instructed to "clean up the city". The anger born of these forced removals has been compounded by the nature of political power in Douala. The city is divided into five broad zones (Douala I-V), each of which is governed by an elected mayor. Only one of the five mayors is a member of the RDPC, the governing party of Paul Biya; the other four belong to the SDF, John Fru Ndi's powerful opposition party. To keep the upper hand in this potentially explosive political landscape, in the mid-1990s the government intro-duced a new personage to the hierarchy of local leaders: the *Délégué du gouverne-ment*. Named by Yaoundé, rather than elected, the *Délégué* supersedes the mayors: they report to him. Despite the fact that its population is overwhelmingly in the opposition's camp, Douala remains very much under the RDPC's control. This state of affairs adds insult to injury as the city's *sauveteurs*, for whom life is difficult enough, are done violence by a police force beholden to leaders most of them reject.

Targeted by municipal authorities, under threat from the city's notoriously violent police and beleaguered by an economy that suffered countless setbacks throughout the 1990s, Douala's *sauveteurs* are a powerfully discontented lot. Given few, if any, forums to express their dissatisfaction with the status quo, many have taken to thinking of *La nouvelle liberté* as an emblem: a symbol – a physical embodiment – of their plight and an acknowledgement of the role they play in the city's daily life. Just as they save, rescue, recycle and re-sell second-hand and discarded objects, many articulate, Sumegne has saved, rescued and re-used each of the components of his figure. In their eyes, *La nouvelle liberté* celebrates them.[15]

Beleaguered itself, Doual'Art celebrates the *sauveteur* celebration of *La nouvelle liberté*. Sumegne's statue, the NGO argues, has not only become a rallying point for Douala's *Système D* workers,[16] who see in it an image of themselves; it has also become an integral part of their lives. Its existence, Douala-Bell and Schaub point out, has given rise to a whole new set of mini-industries centred on the Rond-Point. Among these is photography. *Sauveteurs* sell images of the sculpture to tourists and itinerant photographers take portraits of lovers, newlyweds and families on Sunday outings, posed before Sumegne's figure. In the best tradition of *sauvetage*, *La nouvelle liberté* has itself become an object to be re-seen, recycled and re-sold.[17] In so doing, Doual'Art holds, it has become an incarnation of urban art at its most successful: a work that interacts with and, ultimately, comes to play an active role in the life of the city at whose heart it stands.

142

Voices in the quest for freedom: beyond *La nouvelle liberté*

A battle of subjectivities is at hand, in which multiple actors are seeking to define and

Fig. 12. *Sauveteurs* stand on Rond-Point Deïdo
Photo: D. Malaquais

143

appropriate *La nouvelle liberté: Elimbi*, Doual'Art, Sumegne and the *sauveteurs.*
To the ranks of these actors, still others must be added. Among them is a loose-knit
syndicate of Duala dissidents – members of the local intelligentsia – who seek
alliance neither with the government nor with *Elimbi*'s extremists. On the Rond-
Point, in 1991, members of this group organised a rally in favour of multi-party
elections. They were given a very stern rebuke by forces linked with the RDPC,
which, at the time, was engaged in a country-wide battle to retain its status as the
party of record in a one-party state. Several of the demonstrators, middle-aged and
elderly men, were publicly flogged (*fessés*, or "spanked", as the quaint local euphemism goes). These men and their supporters remember the day with considerable
emotion and look to it as a turning point in the national quest for democracy – in the
emergence of Cameroon in 1992 as (at least in theory) a multi-party state. Others
argue that change came not in response to the voice of such privileged dissidents but
as a result, rather, of student-led multi-ethnic coalitions whose members fought
with great conviction and not inconsequential bloodshed. *They*, this second group
argues, brought Cameroon its *nouvelle liberté*. Without their sacrifices, no sculpture
like Sumegne's, by this or any other name, could stand where it stands today.

These many voices, claims and counterclaims, views and counterviews result in an
immensely complex work of art, constantly acquiring new layers of meaning. This
suits Sumegne well, as does, at least in part, the fact that *La nouvelle liberté* remains
unfinished, still awaiting the addition of its ten encircling *balises. Jalaa*, he notes, is
predicated on the notion that objects created by an artist should never cease changing
and, as a result, can never be considered finished products. It is for this reason, he
adds, that he never signs his works: because they are always in a state of becoming,
because he can never think of them as final.

Surveying the contemporary arts scene in Douala, one is struck by the accuracy of
Sumegne's vision. Art here is without a doubt ever in flux, acquiring layer upon layer
of meaning, much of it political and, like *La nouvelle liberté*, linked to fundamental
questions of identity, freedom and the right to self-determination. Many young
artists at work today, however – for the most part men, two and three decades
younger than Sumegne – are more overtly concerned than he is with themes of
resistance and refusal of the status quo. While they celebrate the breakthrough that
La nouvelle liberté represents formally and thematically, many see in it a beginning
only. Art, they propose, needs to engage more directly with the city, to take it on,
head-on, speaking in ways more hard-hitting than *La nouvelle liberté* to its grime, its
pain, anger and violence.

The stance of this younger generation finds powerful expression in the materials
its members use to speak of the city. Like Sumegne, most work with found or discarded objects. Theirs, like his, is an art of *Système D*. At their hands, however, the
détournement so characteristic of *Système D* takes on a distinctive edge.[18] In the types

Fig. 13. Portrait by Hervé Youmbi, incorporating discarded, mud-splattered clothing
Photo: D. Malaquais

of objects they choose and the manner in which they assemble them, many of the younger artists seek explicitly to distance themselves from the focus on things aesthetically pleasing that characterises Sumegne's *jalaa*. The refinement and crafts-manship evident in his work make way in theirs for a grittiness that replicates rather than alludes to the state of the city.

The work of Hervé Youmbi is striking in this respect. Since 1999, he has produced a series of portraits in which the sitter's identity is expressed through two key signifiers: found objects, which act in lieu of features, and numbers, references to the national identity cards Cameroonians must carry at all times. The objects that make up the portraits are battered second- (or third-) hand clothes – shirts and shoes of the kind a *sauveteur* might sell in one of the city's poorer neighbourhoods. (*Fripperie*, the re-sale on African streets of clothes discarded by the "First World", is an important occupation for Douala's *sauveteurs*.) Often, they are stained, spattered with the mud so characteristic of the city's markets and streets during the long months of the rainy season. Playful though Youmbi's portraits are at times, the urban space they reference is invariably a hard one. There is nothing pretty here, nowhere for the eye to find respite. The inclusion of ID numbers in every portrait, these serving both as a central element in the composition and the name of the piece, brings to the fore ideas of alienation, a vision of the city as a place where one loses one's self, one's individuality. In one recent work, the sense of alienation is particularly strong. Here, exceptionally, features appear: those of five masks made for sale to tourists. Each mask has been wrapped, bandage-like, in layer upon layer of dirty white cloth (fig. 14). The eyes are completely obscured, as if the carved face has been blindfolded or, worse, its eyes gouged out. In some recent works, painted faces appear. In these eyes are visible, but are glassy, expressionless. They stare forward in a gaze that reveals nothing, tells only of emptiness (fig. 15).

In the work of Joel Mpa'a Dooh too, eyes express the city's power to alienate, to de-personify. Most often, they are hidden, shown covered – blinded – by dark glasses; in places, they become slits, akin to scars (fig. 16). Mpa'a Dooh's medium of choice is pastel. Save in collages, he rarely makes use of found objects. Still, odd juxtapositions – things depicted, colours clustered, words scrawled and scratched out – recall the *déchets* of *Système D* and the city streets from which they come. The urban landscape articulated in the process is one of both fabulous exuberance and intense violence.

In the sculptures and room-sized installations of Pascale Marthine Tayou, *déchets* and urban violence are everything. Here, any attempt at *joliesse* is cast aside. Tayou courts ugliness, things raw and appalling: a condom stretched to bursting on a shaft of splintered wood; disembodied dolls' heads, hair matted, mouths askew; surfaces thick with fur, congealed paste-like substances and scraps of filthy plastic (fig. 17). The results are haunting: few works, anywhere, have ever spoken with such force to the damage, the poetry, the insane beauty of urban spaces gone berserk.

Fig. 14. Detail of a portrait by Hervé Youmbi, one of five tourist masks wrapped in filthy bandages
Photo: D. Malaquais

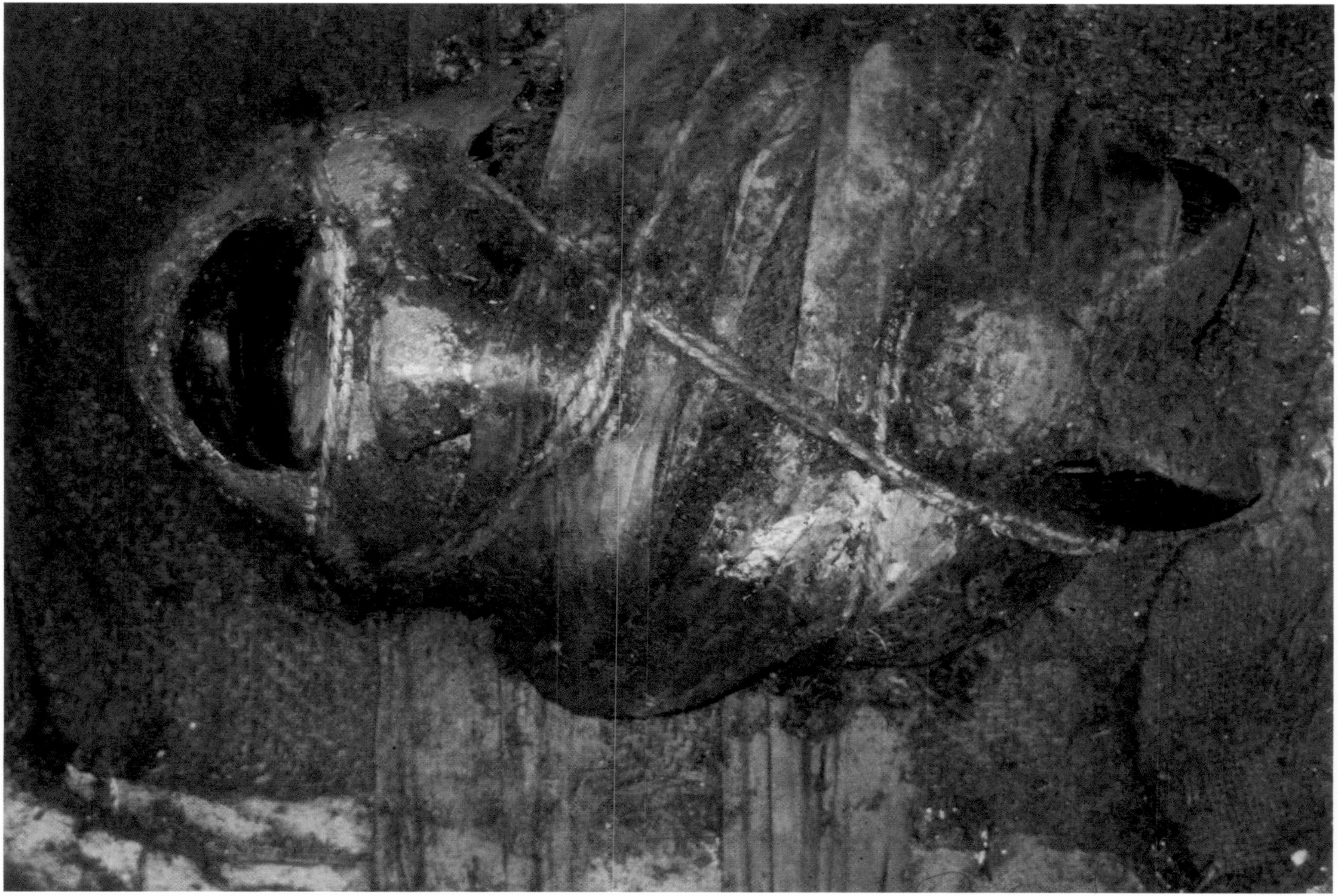

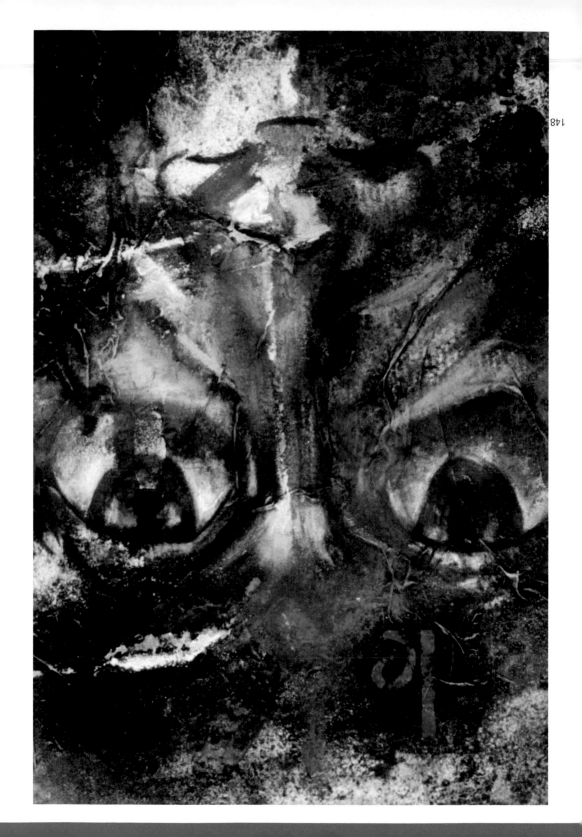

Fig. 15. Detail of a portrait by Hervé Youmbi
Photo: D. Malaquais

Fig 16. Detail of a pastel drawing by Joel Mpa'a Dooh
Photo: D. Malaquais

For one artist – Malam, the name a pseudonym – life lived in Douala at the hinge of the 21st century has proven profoundly radicalising. In his work – wall-mounted pieces and multiple-figure installations – found objects, most notably discarded pillowcases and x-rays, join forces with more conventional media, such as plaster and wood. Like Sumegne, Youmbi, Mpa'a Dooh and Tayou, Malam explores the difficulties of city life. His works, however, express in ways more direct than any of his fellow artists', the theme of violence. Several pieces in a 2001 series entitled *Confidences sur l'oreiller* (Pillow Talk) focus on rape, which the artist defines as a weapon wielded by authority figures (soldiers, European expatriates) (fig. 18). A sprawling installation is a graphic catalogue of torture techniques employed by the Commandement Opérationnel, a paramilitary force that wreaked havoc on Douala in the year the piece was completed (2001), violently reshaping the city socially and spatially and leaving in its wake over a thousand dead – victims, all, of extrajudicial executions (figs 19-21).[19]

Beast or beauty?

At the heart of the debate surrounding *La nouvelle liberté* – from the very first day – has been the matter of beauty: is Sumegne's sculpture a work of beauty or is it ugly? At first glance, the question may seem simplistic, beside the point even; it is, in fact, fundamental. "Beauty" and "ugliness", here, emerge as heavily loaded, time-, place- and class-specific terms, underscoring the parochialism of recent treatises on the subject in the American academy (see Rita Barnard, this volume). What these terms mean, how they are used, by whom and to what end all bear intimate links to the context in which *La nouvelle liberté* appears: the fraught, intricate space of the postcolonial city.

Unlike Dakar or Johannesburg, Douala lacks an arts-savvy *haute bourgeoisie*. What little there is of an "upper class" is deeply conservative, in terms of politics and taste alike. Such conservatism is not mere happenstance: it is a product of historical circumstances. Though a new bourgeoisie is fast on the rise in Cameroon – an up-and-coming class of entrepreneurs whose fortunes were built in the 1980s and 1990s – the reins of political and economic power are in the hands of a *nomenklatura* born and bred under French governance. The views this elite holds of art, of architecture and culture more generally are inherited from the colonial order: they replicate those of France's provincial bourgeoisie, of the men (and to a certain extent the women) from whom those in command today took over rule of the country. Similar circum-stances obtain elsewhere in Africa, but nowhere are the resemblances between colonial and postcolonial bourgeoisie quite as marked as they are here. This too has its historical raisons d'être: not only does the present government descend in direct line from that put in place by the French on their departure in 1960; Cameroon is also the only ex-colony, French or British, which acceded to independence with, at its

150

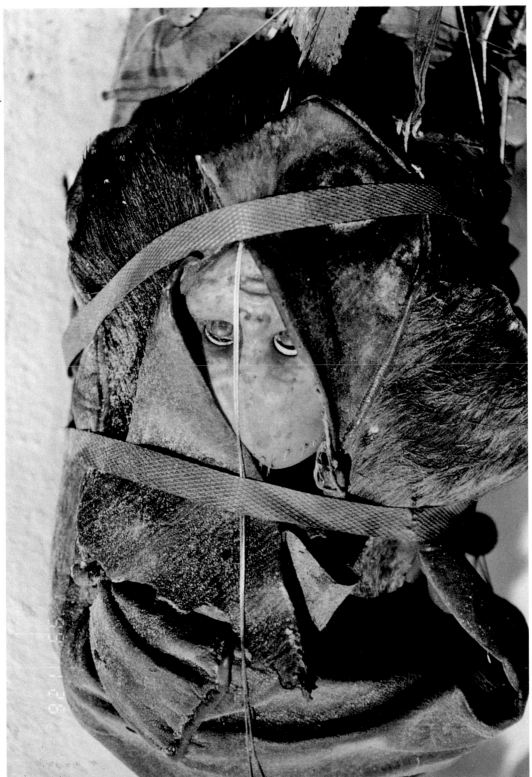

Fig. 17. Detail of a multi-media sculpture by Pascale Marthine Tayou
Photo: D. Malaquais

Fig. 18. Detail of a multi-media sculpture by Malam, the primary surface of which is a discarded pillowcase.
Part of the series entitled *Confidences sur l'oreiller* (Pillow Talk), first shown in the gallery space of the NGO Doual'Art
Photo: D. Malaquais

Fig. 19. Detail of a three-part installation by Malam, exploring the theme of violence
Photo: D. Malaquais

153

helm, a leader who had been vociferously *opposed* to independence.

For those among its audience who belong to Douala's *haute bourgeoisie, La nouvelle liberté* is little more than a heap of garbage: *laideur* – ugliness – incarnate. Underlying this view, however, is more than mere aesthetic conservatism; what most irks the city's *Délégué du gouvernement*, its bankers, hostesses and old guard, is what Sumegne's work says about the urban landscape they aspire to dominate. The Douala they see themselves as representing is a city that can only exist in the absence of those things *La nouvelle liberté* celebrates – *sauveteurs, Système D*, ultimately *liberté*. Things ugly, here, become synonymous with socio-spatial, economic and by extension political disorder, beauty with ideals of order born of the colonial era, with clear-cut (if invented) distinctions between formal and informal, use and refuse, art and junk.

Order and the ties this bears to notions of beauty are key for Sumegne as well. In his eyes, however, order is born not of disjunctures, of dividing and distinguishing, but of bridging gaps, of bringing together. He seeks to unite the city. In this, beauty is his tool. Through art, which he defines as the making of beautiful things, he seeks to unify an urban landscape he sees as increasingly atomised, physically and spiritually. The etymology of *jalaa* – a neologism of Sumegne's invention – sheds light on this approach. *Laa*, in the artist's mother tongue, Fe'e Fe'e, signifies "compound", "village", "community" and, in broader terms, "place of habitation", "home"; metaphorically, it points to ideals of unity and citizenship (Ghomala, a sister language, is "the speech" [*ghom*] "of all the people" [*laa*]). *Ja* alludes to knowledge and creation; it also refers to ideas of forward movement, of progress. Together, prefix and suffix suggest a vision of the artist's work as a means and a process of change, an alchemy of sorts whereby spaces of everyday life are transformed for the better. Beauty – balance, symmetry, harmony of colour, texture and form – in this setting is seen as a catalyst, a means of making whole a home that has been rent asunder.

In his quest for beauty and, through this, order, Sumegne is not alone. His is an approach to art shared by other creators of his generation. A case in point is the painter Koko Komegne. Komegne was among the first abstract artists to gain recognition in Cameroon, in the late 1970s and early 80s. Early on, he travelled to Europe. High modernism was all the rage then; the object's primacy, the artist's creative genius and, most importantly for our purposes, the universal nature of beauty were notions taken for granted. These and related ideas had a profound influence on Komegne, as they did on other artists of his day, throughout Europe, Africa and beyond. Influential too were commissions he received in Cameroon, requests from private patrons and later Doual'Art to "beautify" city spaces (a hotel, a restaurant, a traffic roundabout). Aesthetics, refinement – beauty – are fundamental to Komegne, a point underscored by a critique he offers of *La nouvelle liberté*. In his eyes, Sumegne's sculpture fails. This is so, however, not (as the *Délégué du gouvernement* would have it) because it is made of ugly stuff, but because the stuff it is made of has not been assembled with the

154

attention to detail, to surface and, most importantly, to form for which Sumegne has so deservedly become known.[20] In modernist terms, it is not a masterpiece – a work of true beauty.

So too, one suspects, formally, in Komegne's estimation, *La nouvelle liberté* lacks a certain sense of order. In his earlier as in his more recent work, Komegne makes extensive use of thick, linear boundaries to contain otherwise jostling planes of colour. The result is compositions that evoke movement or sound – intense, polyrhythmic – brought under the staccato control of an external, ordering force (fig. 22). Often, in Sumegne's smaller pieces, a similar effect is created by the use of sutures (stitched with copper wire or electric cords used as thread), which at once link and distinguish one section or feature from another. In *La nouvelle liberté*, such details are absent, in part because the sculpture is so large (were they present, one could in any event not "read" them, given the distance at which one stands from the figure). Not only the intricacy, but also the inherent structure characteristic of his less monumental work is sacrificed here and, in the process, the sense of order amidst chaos that one associates with many of his smaller creations.

For Douala artists who have come of age in the past decade – Youmbi, Mpa'a Dooh, Tayou – beauty is a much more complicated matter than it is for Sumegne or Komegne. So too are the city and notions of order and disorder that attach to it. At first glance, one is tempted to see in their work a rejection of all things smacking of the beautiful – of any and all things deliberately pleasing to the eye. Closer scrutiny suggests a more nuanced stance.

If Komegne and, to a somewhat lesser extent, Sumegne have been influenced by modernist approaches to art and beauty, the painters, sculptors and installation artists who follow them on the Douala scene bring a distinctively postmodern approach to these concerns. None is dogmatic in this regard. Youmbi and his colleagues are well aware of the seminal objects and texts of the postmodern period; their work, however, is refreshingly free of the era's more cumbersome formal jargon (pastiche, quotation, self-referential irony). What one finds in their work is not so much the "look" of postmodernism as its fundamental distrust of concepts taken for granted in modernist discourse: the central role of the individual as subject and creator; the need for boundaries between disciplines, genres, analytical and formal languages; the existence of absolutes.[21] Beauty, in this context, and for these artists in particular, becomes a profoundly problematic concept. Not only – as in the work of such quintessentially postmodern artists as Jane Simpson (Great Britain), Coco Fusco (US) or Chen Hui-Chiao (Taiwan) – does it prove to be wholly contingent; by virtue of place – the particular location in which it is being considered – it undergoes a radical decentring.

The sub-Saharan, postcolonial urban context in which Youmbi, Mpa'a Dooh and Tayou are at work has a very particular impact on the way these artists envisage

155

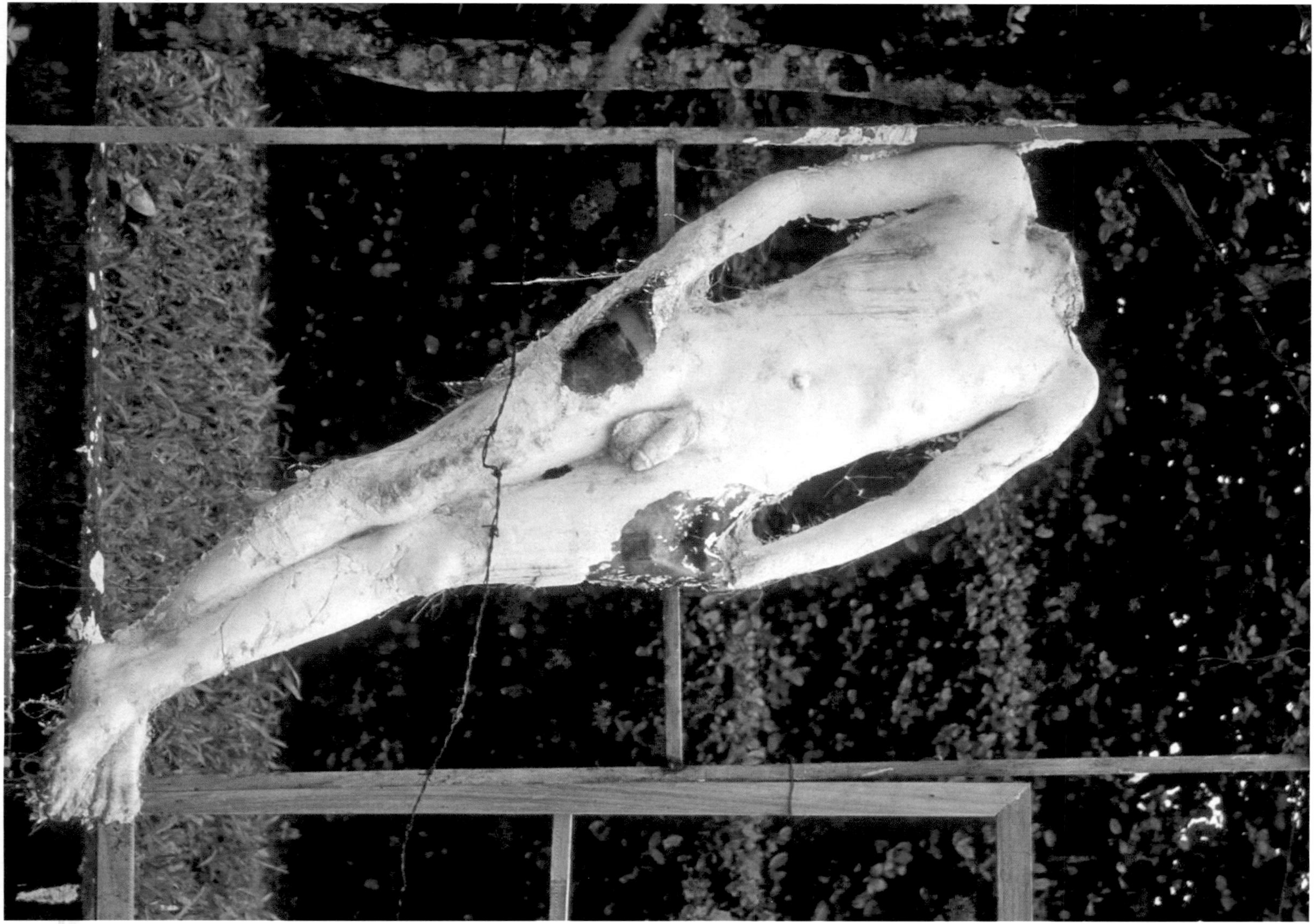

Fig. 20. Detai of a three-part installation by Malam, exploring the theme of violence
Photo: D. Ma aquais

Fig. 21. Detail of a three-part installation by Malam, exploring the theme of violence
Photo: D. Malaquais

157

beauty. This is so in several regards. To begin with, there is the fact, of which all three are (at times painfully) aware, that they are *African* artists, perceived as such even when, cloaked in postmodern garb, they seek to break loose from the moorings of cultural or historical specificity. Implicit in their approach to aesthetics is a critique of the manner in which the Northern art world deals with Africa. Countless treatises have been written and exhibitions mounted celebrating the formal perfection – the "sheer beauty" – of "traditional" African art, while at the same time denying the existence of art or beauty as concepts indigenous to Africa. "Authentic" African art, it is widely if wholly erroneously held, is ritual, cannot as such be termed "art for art's sake", and is "beautiful" in the eyes only of educated outsiders. With but a few notable exceptions (The National Museum of African Art in Washington, DC, for instance, where, thanks to the late curator Philip Ravenhill, contemporary African art is also exhibited), only such "traditional" art – exoticised, made "other", "different", "primitive" – is given a place in fine arts museums.

Though they might claim otherwise, most mainstream institutions (museums, galleries, departments of art history) have no interest whatsoever in contemporary African artists; what such artists have to say – formally, theoretically – if it is considered at all, is commonly dismissed as derivative of Euro-American sources.[22] Such approaches to what is African, what is art, and what is "good" or "important" play a capital role in the work of all three artists. Youmbi's bandaged masks – mass-produced carvings sold as "traditional" art to tourists seeking a taste of "authentic" Africa, appropriated by the artist to create a portrait in which conventional notions of visual pleasure and identity dissolve in a three-dimensional collage of wildly heterogeneous found objects; Tayou's multiple-room installations, in which the hushed space of the museum bleeds into the cacophony of a city street, the pristine walls of galleries into the sights and smells of a garbage dump; Mpa'a Dooh's scribbled words and juxtapositions of worked and reworked figures with barely delineated faces – pieces in which process, the artist's doubts, attempts and revisions are laid bare ... all are responses to the violence done the very idea of Africa by the discipline of art history.

Fundamental too to the gaze Youmbi, Mpa'a Dooh and Tayou cast on notions of art and beauty is the post-colonial city itself. AbdouMaliq Simone writes of the contemporary African city as a place of multiple, constantly changing, morphing and overlapping layers: bodies, belief systems, modes of communication, itineraries, narratives, dreams. In Abidjan's Adjamé quarter or Johannesburg's Hillbrow, he holds, the idea of maps, of charting how the urban landscape works, who goes where to do what and how is beside the point; the city cannot be ordered in such a manner, made to make such unilinear sense.[23] The portrait he draws of cities like Douala or Lagos is at once deeply pessimistic and imbued with a profound sense of hope – a sense of the poetry and possibilities of the city:

[S]ocial reproduction [is] foreclosed for increasing numbers of youth. As such, the actions, identities, and social composition through which individuals attempt to eke out daily survival are incessantly provisional, positioning them in a proliferation of seemingly diffuse and discordant times. Without structured ... certainties, the places they inhabit and the movements they undertake become instances of disjointed geographies, subsuming places into mystical, subterranean, or sorceral orders, pro-phetic or eschatological universes, highly localised myths that "capture" the allegiances of large social bodies, or daily reinvented routines that have little link to anything.[24]

Alongside the constant change and perpetual feeling of movement, such states of affairs bring into being, Simone writes, there is a sense too that, at times, nothing moves at all. The result, he suggests, is at once disorienting and energising:

African cities ... appear dynamic and static at the same time ... [T]hings can happen very fast, and where seemingly nothing has been brought to bear on a particular setting ... [S]ometimes conditions change with remarkable speed – the structures of authority, the alignments of loyalty and collaboration, the mobilisation of ... resources – where it is not apparent just what is going on and who is contributing what to these changes.[25]

Simone's words find a strong echo in the work of Youmbi, Mpa'a Dooh and Tayou and shed light on their approach to aesthetics. Youmbi belongs to a collective of young artists called *Cercle Kapsiki*, whose members entertain close ties with both Mpa'a Dooh and Tayou. In 2000, the *Cercle* – Youmbi; poet and installation artist Hervé Yamguen; sculptor Jules Wokam; painters Blaise Bang and Salifou Lindou – was invited to spend a year in France, at Strasbourg's School of Fine Arts. Some (myself included) were concerned that the artists might not make their way back to Cameroon. We were proven wrong. On its return, the group organised a round table. Yamguen, speaking for the *Cercle*, put it this way: a year spent abroad, in a city they had enjoyed because it was so unlike their own, had underscored a fundamental point for them. Douala offered immense possibilities. In many ways, it was disastrous, unconducive in the extreme to art, to creation. In this very lack of conduciveness, however, they found potential and the desire to create. Their goal, his words sug-gested, would not be, *pace* Sumegne, to beautify the city, to make it better through art or create beauty from its refuse. They would not seek to transform things rejected; they would embrace them, celebrating them in all their ugliness. The sheer intractability of the city would become their subject, the substance and the theme

159

161

Fig. 22. Two murals by Koko Komegne, commissioned by Doual' Art and positioned in a plaza in Bonanjo, Douala
Photo: D. Malaquais

of their work. From this process, beauty – Yamguen chose the word deliberately – would be born: a beauty of and about *Doul*.

Dreads again (in closing)

Dreads are a liability in Cameroon. Voguish though they may be on the streets of Durban and New York, in Douala they can get you arrested. Still, many artists choose to wear them: Tayou and Yamguen have for years; Youmbi and Lindou have adopted them more recently. The decision is not one made in the name of fashion. It is a political statement: a refusal of the status quo, its preconceptions and demands. It is a sign of resistance, symbolic but important nonetheless in the deeply conservative community Douala remains in the first decade of the 21st century.

Sumegne, most agree, was a precursor. His art paved the road, set the pace for those who now follow in his steps. Still, all say, everything remains to be done: the fight has only begun. Sumegne's dreads make for an apt metaphor. His wig gives him leave to be two men: the artist whose voice rises in discontent at the state of the city and the failures of its leaders; the ordinary man, whose countenance attracts little attention from police or persons otherwise opposed to the messages they read into his work. Tayou, Yamguen and others opt for a different stance. They are immediately recognisable for who and what they are: troublemakers, dissatisfied and ready to say their piece.

Still, Douala is nothing if not a complicated place. Simple dichotomies are hardly its forte. And so there is Malam. For many years, he donned wild dreads and a chest-length beard: "A look straight outta hell," he says with a smirk. Today, he is shorn. "I want to blend in," he says, "be as ordinary as possible."[26] Those of us who know him laugh, but see what he means. The fight, he holds, is in the ability to infiltrate, to burrow into the status quo to better expose and explode it.

In this, Malam has a fine model, an artist whose work is the most deeply politically engaged of any I have encountered on the Cameroon scene: video and installation artist Goddy Leye. No dreads greet the eye as he enters the room; with no forewarning, one might mistake Leye for an accountant, a *cadre de banque*. Pop one of his tapes into a VCR, and the situation changes dramatically. Faces crackle, then dissolve on-screen in an explosion of white light; an angry staccato beat, part machine gun, part pneumatic drill fills the air; words appear, screaming invective in print, assaulting the eye with slurs. The piece is WOL / *World On Line* (1999). It is a statement about official violence and officious hatred like none I have ever seen. *Elimbi*'s xenophobia and the alienation Youmbi's bandaged masks bespeak are here for us to experience, body and mind. The words and sounds and flashes of light make sense of the anger in Mpa'a Dooh's faces and scraps of urban landscape, give voice to the filth and the colour, the horror and the humour of Tayou's severed dolls' heads. We hear, see, feel the epithets screamed by those who, from the army camps of

Douala to the precinct houses of Brooklyn, maim, Malam tells us, because they can. To silence. To break.

The VCR clicks off. *A luta continua*, Leye says with a smile.

> I come back to you
> dung-heap
> and the anthills
> rid me of the silence
> you have fashioned inside me
> your chapel
> and the chimes of your calls
> each and every one
> and the drumbeats of your confession
> cross paths within me
> … a symphony
> of signs scrambled
>
> Hervé Yamguen[27]

Acknowledgements

For their suggestions and fine advice as I was writing these pages, I am grateful to Peter Geschiere, Steve Nelson, Ikem Okoye and my students at Sarah Lawrence College. Most importantly, I wish to thank Cameroonian historian and social scientist Yvette Monga for drawing my attention to the work of art that is the subject of this paper, and Marilyn Douala-Bell and Didier Schaub, the work's spiritual parents, with whom I have been collaborating on various projects over the past three years. Many thanks too to Victor Kouankam.

Dominique Malaquais > Quelle Liberté: Art, Beauty and the Grammars of Resistance in Douala

Pippa Stein
Fresh Stories

Pippa Stein is a researcher and teacher at the School of Literature and Language Studies at the University of the Witwatersrand, Johannesburg. She is the recipient of a Spencer Foundation Research Grant investigating the relationship between literacy and poverty in early childhood. She has written extensively on culture, education and literacy and is the author of *Deborah Bell* (2004).

FRESH STORIES

Fig. 1. Contemporary doll figure made by a child from Olifantsvlei Primary School, Eikenhof, Johannesburg
Plastic tubblewrap, plastic bag, bottle, twigs
Photo: P. Stein

In my work with children as a literacy researcher in some of Johannesburg's poorest communities, I observe children as they move in and out of the many spaces they inhabit in their everyday lives: from homes to schools to playgrounds to buses to streets to spaza shops to homes to the veld to streets to neighbours to church to home. "Fresh Stories" is a personal response to some of these lives through its focus on a collection of doll-child figures made by children from the Olifantsvlei Primary School, a semi-rural school which serves children from the nearby informal settlements of Eikenhof, Vlakfontein and Lenasia. The teachers asked the children to invent "fresh stories" about their lives and neighbourhoods as a basis for performance work, art and writing. The children thought of someone they knew who would become a main character in their story and were then asked to represent this character in sculptural form. Their teachers made a papier mâché mixture for this purpose, but according to the children, "the mixture flopped and our characters turned into puddles". At this point, the children turned to their teachers and said, "Don't worry, we'll make our own," and over the next few days, they brought into class a collection of 3D figures which they had made in their homes.

The dolls are made from that which has been discarded – used bottles, dirty scraps of cardboard, broken plastic, soiled cloths found in the veld, each of which has been transformed imaginatively. The children's doll figures show remarkable similarities to traditional fertility child figures which have been made in southern Africa for hundreds of years. Fertility dolls or "child figures" are small objects with anthropomorphic forms, traditionally made by women. At the most basic level, such doll figures are used by girl children in the same way as children play with dolls the world over. However, they have more culturally specific functions locally as "evocations of the child"[1] in fertility, puberty and marriage rituals in which the dolls function as intermediaries between the living and the dead – between women and their powers to reproduce. Such dolls have been granted magical and metaphoric powers, acting as ciphers through which a wished-for child or ancestral soul can pass through and enter into her owner's womb.

Some of the children, their mothers or grandmothers, would have seen fertility dolls. One child's grandmother, who had come from Lesotho, had taught her grandchild how to make fertility dolls. Mostly, though, fertility dolls would have been trace memories, taking their place amongst the one or two pink Barbies I came across in the course of my visits.

The neighbourhoods in which the children live are popularly known as *mkukus* or "shacks". Gogo Rosie, a Soweto grandmother who spreads the word of Jehovah in these neighbourhoods, explains:

> We call it *mkukus*, which means shacks, it's a Zulu word but it includes Sotho, it's a stand-by place, just a little place where you can put your head, a bit of shelter where you can put your children and your family.

Through my visits to families living in these neighbourhoods, I have become intrigued by the variation in shape, texture and design in the *mkukus*. In "The Air is Up to You", the final fragment in this essay, Frank Dikgale, a security guard from Pietersburg who was a *mkuku* resident for some years, throws light on this aesthetic in his detailed account of people's inventiveness in constructing shacks from waste materials found on dumps scattered around the city. In many ways, shack-making exhibits a similar creativity and sense of the aesthetic at work which is present in the children's doll figures.

In what follows below, I will work with a notion of slipping or slippability,[2] according to which deeply embedded cultural knowledges emerge – much like linguistic slips – into the hidden murk of our conceptual networks. This subconscious manufacture of subjunctive variations on a theme is also a trope that is reflected in the structure of this essay. Rather than discussing the dolls as anthropological objects, I try to allude to their fabric, their presence, by developing repertoires around the contexts from which they are made. I do this across different forms of writing and conceiving, in particular as they have to do with the aesthetics of waste. One of the questions we might also ask of the dolls is how to account for their beauty, a beauty that is rendered from the found materials of extreme poverty, what in some people's terms might be thought of as waste, the remains of the everyday, that which cannot be eaten.

That which cannot be eaten

My friend Thandi and I arrive at Tsietsi's house mid-morning. The path to his house has taken us from the centre of the city, along the Soweto highway and then along the Golden Highway, past Thandi's husband's BP garage, where we stop to pick up cold drinks and chips. We drive past Tsietsi's school, Olifantsvlei Primary School, formerly a mission school, nestling amongst fields of sunflowers, cabbages and spinach. Eikenhof farm lands, rich in soil and water, surround us as we drive along the main road looking for the slipway that will take us into the *mkukus* where we shall find him.

Tsietsi has not answered a question or spoken in class for eight months. He sits quietly watching other children so that he can work out what he needs to do. He has come from Lesotho with his mother. He is ten years old and this is his first year of school.

On the sides of the road, the lush red grasses and pink and white cosmos sway in the summer winds. We take a sharp turn off the road onto an informal path hidden in the grasses and suddenly we are in the middle of the squatter camp, winding our way over bumps and potholes into the heart of the settlement. A few shacks are visible on either side as we make our way to Tsietsi's place.

Tsietsi's home squats next to the rubbish dump. Scraps of rotting food, plastic bags,

Fig. 2. Contemporary doll figures made by children from Olifantsvlei Primary School, Eikenhof, Johannesburg, assorted fabrics, bottles, sand, stockings, twigs, koki pen, foam chips
Photo: P. Stein

Fig. 3. Contemporary doll figure made by a child from Olifantsvlei Primary School, Eikenhof, Johannesburg, fabric, mattress stuffing, sand, plastic bottle, wire
Photo: P. Stein

discarded tins and bottles from surrounding households pile up around the front door. A notice on the door reads, "I care for and love my friends with AIDS". We knock but there is no sign of anyone at home. A small boy passes and Thandi asks him if he has seen Tsietsi. He shakes his head and offers to go and look for him, disappearing into the maze of shacks. We wait and wait. A woman approaches us from the distance, a baby on her back. It is Tsietsi's mother, returning from the shebeen where she works up the road. She has no idea where her son is. She asks us to come in while we wait for him. It is hot and stuffy inside. Township jive is playing on the radio. The small TV set is covered with a cream embroidered cloth and on it sits a china cocker spaniel ornament. A curtain divides the kitchen and eating area from the sleeping area.

Tsietsi cannot be found that day.

We move on to Thandazani's house. It was Thandazani's mother's garden that first caught our eye, small pots full of flowers and some unusual varieties too. Where did you get that plant from, I ask. My husband brought it for me from Mozambique, he is a trucker. I ask myself whether evidence of order in the garden is a sign of order in the household; is a manicured garden a sign of literacy … The mother is young, she has three children and no work. She allows her son to draw on the sideboard and on the doors. Scribbled over the interior are telephone numbers, and Thandazani's name which he has practised again and again, inscribing it into the wood for all to see. Thandazani Vilakazi. That is my name. My name means "pray".

Princess, Thandazani and S'bongiseni are outside in the garden, playing *inhlomhlwane*, a "house-house" game. They have built a small house attached to their mother's house, using blocks of wood and an old carpet as a roof. Coffee tins with holes punched in them are turned into braziers for making fires. Small toy plates, cups and saucers; ice-cream sticks become spoons.

Don't worry, we'll make our own, they said.

We want to make things with our hands.

In their game, it is the men who go to work in the garden. They are building toilets, using old snuff tins to dig up the soil. Thandazani does one type of work, and that is to build toilets.

After a while they stop building the toilets, and expect the wife to bring tea. Princess takes them a small red toy teapot filled with water and some small cups. She pours them tea and waits for them to finish before she goes back into her home. Later, Thandazani comes back home and prepares the wood and coal, collecting it from his mother's yard. He gives it to Princess to make the fire.

Princess keeps a doll on her back while she is cooking, telling the doll to "*tula*"[3] all the time. She has made a small bed for her using bricks and she puts her to sleep there. When she wakes up, Princess crushes a small madeira cake, mixes it with water and feeds her. She then washes her and puts her to bed.

171

Breasts of stone

I undress Mosiuwa's doll, carefully taking off the zebra-fur coat with which she keeps herself warm against the cold. I expect to find a bottle underneath but instead I find a pair of full, enlarged breasts, breasts of stockings and cloth, tied into elaborate designs. At the heart of each breast lodges a small stone. The breasts have their partners, the fulsome buttocks, pendulent and strong. I imagine Mosiuwa's mother making these buttocks, shaping these breasts, crisscrossing the ties, her son waiting to touch them as he enfolds them in his zebra fur cloth. "My mother made the body," Mosiuwa said, "and she allowed me to dress her."

Tshidi's doll stands on the window sill, heavy and solid. If I take off her blanket, I will find an undercloth. If I take off this undercloth, I will find breasts. If I take off these breasts, I will find arms. If I take off these arms, I will find holes.

I take off her neck from the top of the Coke bottle. Her head is a ball of soft cloth. Out of the opening pours a stream of thin, fine red sand.

I remember Toni Morrison, in *The Bluest Eye:*

> It had begun with Christmas and the gift of dolls. The big, the special, the loving gift was always a big, blue-eyed Baby Doll. From the clucking sounds of the adults, I knew that the doll represented what they thought was my fondest wish. I was bemused with the thing itself and the way it looked. What was I supposed to do with it? Pretend I was its mother? I had no interest in babies or the concept of motherhood ... If, in sleep, I turned, the bone-cold head collided with my own. It was a most uncomfortable, patently aggressive sleeping companion. To hold it was no more rewarding. The starched gauze or lace on the cotton dress irritated any embrace. I had only one desire: to dismember it. To see of what it was made, to discover the dearness, to find the beauty, the desirability which had escaped me, but apparently only me. I fingered the face, wondering at the single-stroke eyebrows: picked at the pearly teeth stuck like two piano keys between red bowline lips. Traced the turned-up nose, poked the glassy blue eyeballs, twisted the yellow hair. I could not love it. But I could examine it to see what it was that all the world said was lovable. Break off the tiny fingers, bend the flat feet, loosen the hair, twist the head around, and the thing made one sound – a sound they said was the sweet and plaintive cry "Mama" but which sounded to me like the bleat of a dying lamb, or, more precisely, our icebox door opening on rusty hinges in July. Remove the cold and stupid eyeball, it would bleat still, 'Ahhhhhh,' take off the head, shake out the sawdust, crack the back against the brass bed rail, it would bleat still. The gauze back would split, and I could see the disk with six holes, the secret of the sound. A mere metal roundness.[4]

Beautiful Ugly: African and Diaspora Aesthetics

Fig. 4. Contemporary doll figure made by a child from Olifantsvlei Primary School, Eikenhof, Johannesburg
Stocking, cold drink bottle, twigs, cloth, sand, stones
Photo: P. Stein

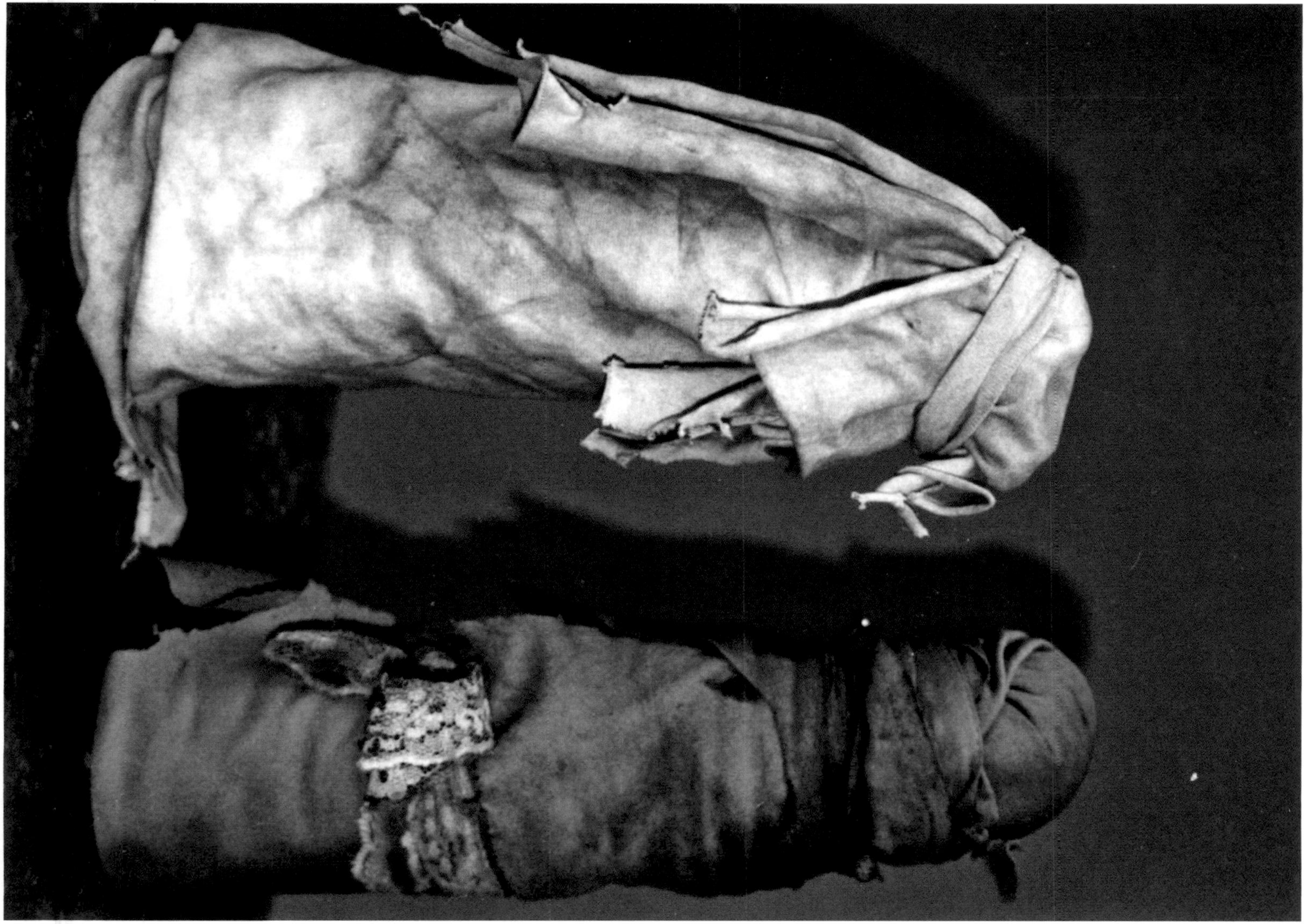

Fig. 5. Contemporary doll figures made by a child from Olifantsvlei Primary School, Eikenhof, Johannesburg, assorted fabrics, dishcloth, bottles, lace, sand, nails

Photo: P. Stein

I scoop up the pile of fine red sand, afraid to leave behind a single grain. The Coke bottle is filled to the brim, her soft cloth head wound back, her beauty restored. I have felt the secret of her heaviness and am content.

What's your dream, what's your number?
In the late afternoon we found Lerato, Sibongile and Hope outside under the trees playing a card game. They had made their own cards from old Kelloggs Cornflakes boxes, and decorated them with hearts, clubs, spades and diamonds.

> One is for King
> Two is for Monkey
> Three is for Sea Water
> Four is for Dead Man
> Five is for Tiger
> Six is for Ox
> Seven is for Skelm
> Eight is for Pig
> Nine is for Moon
> Ten is for Egg

After supper, their mother played cards with them. This time, it was called *iskuruqu*. With this one, you shuffle the cards and put them down in a circle, all cards facing down. Each child takes a card, turns it over, and puts it down again. But should a child pick up one card similar to the one card on top, she will have to pick up all the cards which have been put down, and perhaps lose the game. In this game there is only one loser, and the loser is the one who has the most cards left.

> Eleven is for Car
> Twelve is for Granny
> Thirteen is for Big Fish
> Fourteen is for Dead Woman
> Fifteen is for Slegte Vrou
> Sixteen is for Pigeon – *Amajuba*
> Seventeen is for Diamond Lady

Mother made a fire and put water on the stove. When the children had finished playing their card game, she poured the water into a dish and called Hope into the small bedroom space, separated by a curtain, where she washed her daughter and helped her put on her pyjamas.

175

Eighteen is for Small Change
Nineteen is for Small Girl
Twenty is for Cat
Twenty-one is for Elephant
Twenty-two is for Ship

"He came last week. This week, he did not come. I hear that when he finishes work, he goes to Gauteng. In town. Over there. Very far from here. He stays there with friends."

"You are left alone ..."

"I am left here ..."

"Then how do you get food?"

"Food? We ask over there, from that woman. Dineo's mother helps us. She's the one who gives us food. Even the coals she gives us, because it is chilly in the mornings. She is the one who gives us coals. Even in the afternoon we cook at her place, if we don't cook here. We have a problem, I went to a Chinese *fahfee* man, I wanted to try my luck. I asked some women for R1 to play *fahfee*. The Chinaman visits here twice a day, except on Saturday and Sunday. He flashes a number at us, what's your dream, what's your number? Then if we have dreamed that number, he pays us and if we haven't, we pay him. I use 50 cents or R1 for this game."

Twenty-three is for Long Hair
Twenty-four is for Big Mouth
Twenty-five is for Big House
Twenty-six is for Bees.

I am not relaxed (a short play by Sonti, 8)

The curtain opens and Sonti comes into view carrying her doll whom she has named Ntswaki, after her teacher. Her voice shifts from high to low as she acts out a dialogue she has made up between wife and husband.

Sonti:	*Lebitso la hae ke Ntswaki. Ntswaki o ne a rata ho bapala le bana. Jwale a itebala a fihla bosiu. Ntate a ba a mo fihlela pele. Mme ke hona a kenang ka tlung.* (Her name is Ntswaki. Ntswaki likes to play with the children. She used to be relaxed while she played and used to come back home late. Her husband would get home first and only then would Ntswaki come into the house.)
Father/husband:	(in a deep voice) *Mme o tswa kae ka nako e?* (Mother/wife, where do you come from at this time of the day?)

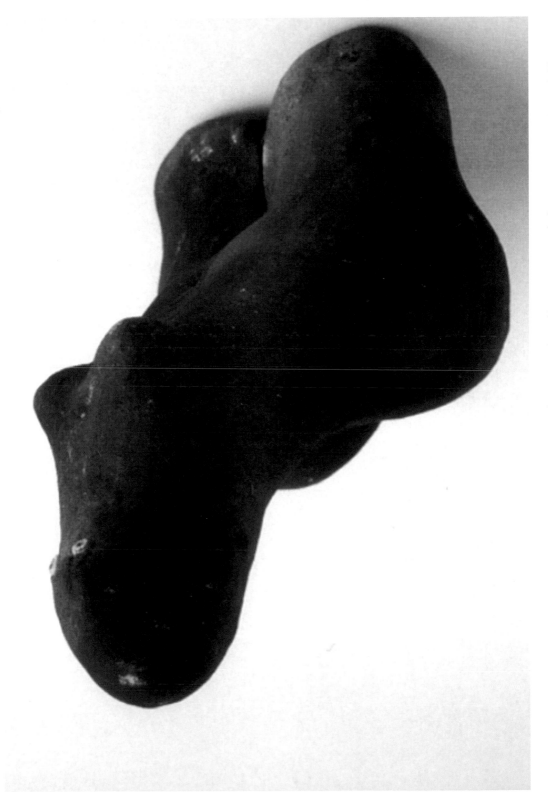

Fig. 6. Zulu doll made of clay
Collection: South African Museum, reproduced from Dell, p. 102 (see endnote 1)

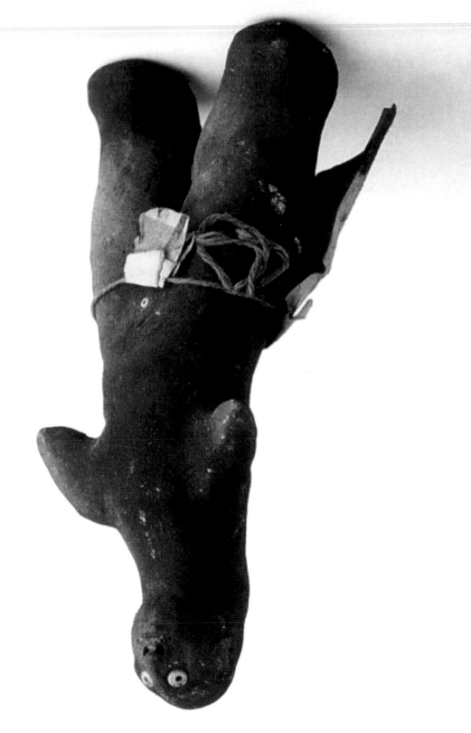

Fig. 7. Zulu doll, clay, textiles, hide, twine, beads
Collection: South African Museum, reproduced from Dell, p.100 (see endnote 1)

Ntswaki:	(trembling) *A ... a ... a ... nna ke ne ke ilo bapala le bana.* (A ... ah ... ah ... I went to play with the children.)
Father/husband:	*Why o rata ho bapala le bana?* (Why do you like to play with children?)
Ntswaki:	*Nna ke rata bana.* (I like children.)
	(A ba a setse a mo mathisa.) (He chases her out of the house.)
Father/husband:	*Mme, why o itebala hore o tlo pheha?* (Mother/wife, why do you forget that you have to cook?)
Ntswaki:	*Ha ke a itebala. Ke ne ke tlile. Ke ne ke nahana hore wena ha wa mphihlela pele. A ba a re.* (I was not relaxed. I came here earlier. I thought that you would not be home before me.)
Father/husband:	*O.* (Oh.)
Ntswaki:	*A ba a re nna ha ke sa tla hlola ke bapala le bana.* (He said that I should not play with the children, ever.)

As I lay down with the calabash child

My husband walks into the room and stares at the dolls on the windowsill. He stares at the nails which have been thrust into the torsos, at the torn women's stockings which tie a head to a neck. He won't touch them. Is it simply the embedded grime of the squatter camp on these fertile bodies? He wants to know if I am practising a form of South African voodoo. In part he is fascinated by the green doll, her shape made from a cooking oil bottle with the stumps for arms made out of two rusty nails. He vaguely remembers some talk of the seeds within and the power of these dolls as fertility icons, the ciphers through which the ancestral souls can pass and enter into their owner's womb. He wonders if disease is being brought into the house and as he says it he knows that he is falling into all the traps. And still he stares.

I wonder if fertility is being brought into the house: if I hold a doll long enough, will the ancestral souls pass through me and give me a child? Like Cawekazi, who held her doll long enough to imagine giving birth to Dineo. I recall the chant of the childless Basotho women:

> I lay down with the calabash child, and got cold,
> The calabash child makes no sound,
> The calabash child made me recite ancestral generations all night.
> How can I know this child's generations?
> I know of my own and my great-grandparents'.
> Take my place singing for I am tired.[5]

Where does their beauty lie? Is it in the creative manipulation of the leftovers, the bottles thrown into tin drums outside the disco, their contents drunk during the jive, the music still rattling in their interiors … Where have these bottles been, whose lips have enclosed these necks, their liquids emptied, their insides filled with seeds and sand? This bubblewrap which twists and folds in billowing waves, what precious object did it protect from the clumsy hands of its traders, this piece of bubblewrap, muddy and torn which now makes a sumptuous robe? And this single piece of dishcloth, muslin cloth, how many pots has it scoured, how many car seats has it wiped clean before being chucked out of the window into the veld? It has marks of oil, grease and bloodied stains. She folds it in half not round a gourd but round a bottle, in a replication of the sexual act.

When making the dolls the children consciously looked for materials to suit their needs and made careful decisions, sometimes with an adult, about how to use these materials. The child who had shaped a doll figure from folds fashioned from one large piece of discarded dishcloth told me she had gone into the veld to look for materials and had found this cloth. Another child told me he had found the bottle for the conical shaped inner core of his doll "in a rubbish bin outside the disco". No child had the means to purchase any materials for making the dolls: they had found the resources, the waste in their environments and had transformed them according to their interests. What these figures reveal is the dynamic relationship between creativity, innovation and resources: "resources" take on different values and meanings in different contexts of use, revealing the slippability of the concept of "waste". Here, waste is generative: turning the ordinary, the soiled, into the aesthetic. A discarded plastic bag on a rubbish dump becomes a *doek* adorning a head. That which cannot be eaten is fashioned into a doll. A bloodied dishcloth becomes a speckled robe, a safety pin an ear, a button an eye, a nail an arm, and a small red stone a breast.

The air is up to you

> I am sad today. My sister burnt to death in our shack.
> Lerato, 10

The generativity of waste is again present in this description by Frank Dikgale of shack building. Frank, a one-time welder, gardener and security guard, lived for many years in a *mkuku* in Zuurfontein, an informal settlement north of Johannesburg. In this detailed account of how to make a shack from scratch, Frank shows a deep knowledge of the creative principles at work in designing and building such a dwelling: the need for a constant interplay between inventiveness and the limits of possibility defined by what you can find on the streets and rubbish dumps, what other people have no use for.

Fig. 8. Swazi doll figure, beads, fine fibre, netting, textile, thread, fibre with red ochre, reeds
Collection: National Cultural History Museum, reproduced from Dell, p.168 (see endnote 1)

Fig. 9. **Ntwane** fertility dolls (left and middle), beads, grass, textile, threads, twine Ntwane/Ndebele fertility doll (right), textile, fibre, beads
Collection: Wits, reproduced from Dell, p.134 (see endnote 1)

You see, you just make a square, it depends on how much you want, then you collect the poles, the raw poles made out of wood, you have to have poles otherwise it's gonna fall. Some do cut the trees, those big long blocks of trees, and then they start to dig, perhaps four holes, with the measure of a place where a bed can stay, or a little place in there where you can cook and sit in the kitchen, it's everything that's in the kitchen you know. So you divide it up, but you make just a big block thing, you can make any size if you got enough materials. Then you make four holes, yes it's one two three four, and then it's two sides for the door, that's six holes, so you put one two three four five six then you say this, it's a door. Then you have to put the poles a little bit in the holes in the ground, then you dig the ground, you have to put the cement on the ground. Then inside for the floor, you have to make the concrete, mix it with the river sand, so the water can't come in the shack.

Now the ones who can't afford, I don't know, you see, you can't make *mkukus* with the plastic. There are some other ones who make them with the plastic, but it's not guaranteed at that point, ja, and if they don't have cement for the floor, some other ones, they just put some water on the ground, you see, you can make this soil a little bit soft, soft, then you have to stamp it, with anything, some use a spade – they hit him and they hit him and then it's a little bit stronger. Then they put the carpet on top of the soil, pieces of carpet, you can get it anywhere. They go to the dump, you can take anything there, so you have to join that piece to that piece, so that makes a little bit of carpet. Then you start to hit the zincs, nail them one two from the bottom up, two times this way and this way then you put the roof on, with the zincs. Some other ones, they haven't got money to buy those kind of zincs, they cut those old zincs from advertising things which have got rust, then they make *mkukus* out of it. You see it's cold inside the *mkuku*. To make it warm you put the cover, like a wallpaper, any paper, like hard paper, then you put it there, with masking tape so when it rains the only thing you have to do is the roof, the roof, the roof must be right. Some other ones, when it's raining, when there's no corrugated iron, they put the plastic on top and the rain doesn't come, it goes to the ground.

The electricity is up to you. With the extension you can connect it to the other friend, or to the main box. You have to cook with the prima stove, they use the paraffin stoves. They also make fires in the shacks, sometimes you see, if you forget, sometimes you cook and if you put the oil and the oil's boiling up, it's how you get burnt. Some other people are using the candles; if the candle you forget, then it's finished, then it's

183

catching the ground, it's how people get burnt, sometimes you put the carpet and the carpet it burns, the carpet starts the fire.

The air – it's up to you – there's lot of shacks they haven't got the windows. The other ones, they have windows, but it's expensive, you can get it for about 2,000 you see, it's a lot of money, those are the nice shacks; 2,500 for everything. You just call him, you say, I want the shacks, then you just pay and then they come with the floor, poles, zinc and the windows and they just put them there. The other one is making for herself, because if you make it like a box, then you just collect the pieces of wood, then the pieces of boxes, then you just join them up, it's not costing you 2,000, it's about 600.

The shacks are not safe, you see, because if you are making shacks like that, the other one is coming to join me, it's joining me like that and using my site, so if this one has got a problem, I've got the problem too. That's why when one shack's burning, it's burning all because it's one thing. I've lived with the shacks before, if you live at the shacks, you must be alone because the other one is careless, maybe he's drinking and then he's leaving the candles or the paraffin somewhere, this is how to burn the shacks, so if you alone maybe not drinking then everything's all right. The good thing is to make your own shacks not to join with another one … it looks like a street, when it's burning it burns one thing.

Conclusion

Mbembe, in his analysis of the changing forms of urban life in postcolonial cities in Africa, refers to practices of "circulation" of cultural forms brought about through global media, capital and migration. He refers to Johannesburg as a place of "circulation" in which multiple modernities converge to produce new cultural and aesthetic forms.[6] The social and cultural practices around the children's doll-making illustrate this convergence at work. In its communal and intergenerational processes of making, and in the imaginative recycling of urban waste materials found on rubbish dumps in informal settlements in this contemporary African city, signs of poverty, dirt and distress are transformed into flamboyant art objects.

Traditional boundaries around what constitutes "child fertility dolls" within ethnic and gender classifications have collapsed and in this process, the traditional in all its multiplicity of forms and materiality is redesigned into the contemporary using available contextual materials. These doll figures illustrate how individuals have many layers of representational resources available to them, not only from one culture, but from many cultures. As Hamilton has noted in her work on African women's material culture as markers of identity, the analysis of the production of material culture has the potential to change the way in which discussions about

Fig. 10. Ndebele doll, beads, textile, thread, grass
Collection: K. Nel

185

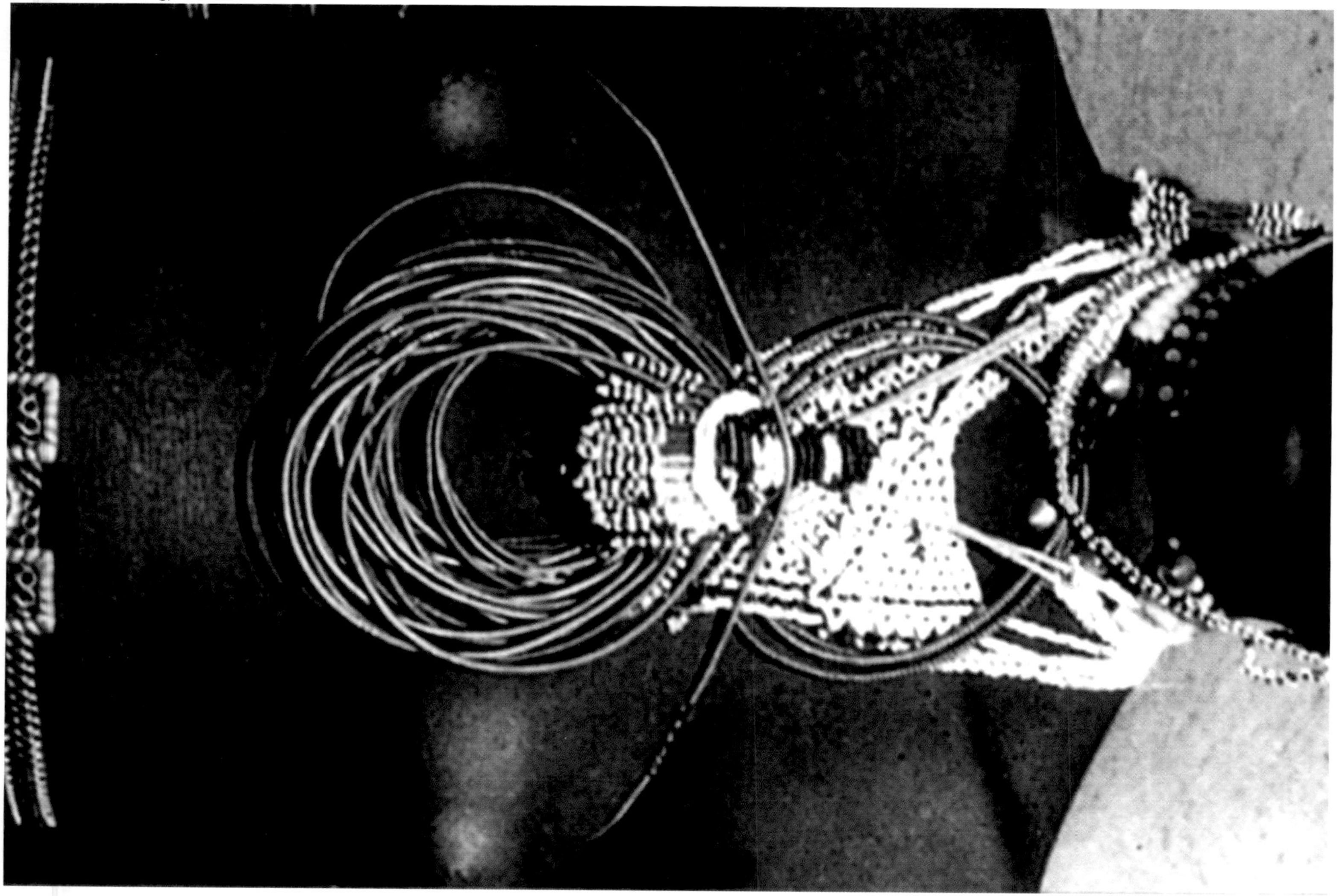

Fig. 11. Baca girl with pendant doll, detail of photograph taken in 1923 in East Griqualand Photo. Duggin-Cronin Collection, McGregor Museum, Kimberley, reproduced from Dell, p.154 (see endnote 1)

identity are framed: material culture "speaks to identity as at once conservatively continuous with the past and as creatively innovative, as bounded and as porous, as transportable and as rooted".[7]

Children's art-making is commonly analysed as a variation of play or as a form of therapy. In this essay, by contrast, children are shown to be young artists, active cultural agents and designers of meaning. In the careful choices which each child has made out of a multiplicity of modes, materials and forms, children are drawing on local cultural imaginaries in ways which are not reproductive or imitative but innovative and transformative – both of the objects which are extending the grammar of doll-making culture, and in relation to the children's identities.[8] Through making objects such as these, the children's capacity to have and cultivate their voices has been strengthened. Through forms of slippability which emerge in the delicate twists and folds of plastic bags and old cloths, the meticulous shaping of breasts, buttocks, arms, bodies and heads with sticks, stones and bottles, the children are using cultural forms to display what Appadurai calls the "capacity to aspire",[9] thereby placing futurity rather than pastness at the centre of their meaning-making.

Acknowledgements
With thanks to Tshidi Mamabolo, Ntsoaki Senja, the Principal and children of Olifantsvlei Primary School, Thandiwe Mkhabela and the Children's Early Literacy Learning Project funded by the Spencer Foundation, Sarah Nuttall, Frank Dikgale and Rosie Shabangu.

Els van der Plas
The Love of the Body: Ousmane Sow and Beauty

Els van der Plas is Director of the Prince Claus
Fund. An art historian, art critic and curator, she
was the founder and director (1987-1997) of the
Gate Foundation in Amsterdam, an organisation
for the intercultural exchange of contemporary art.
She co-edited *The Art of African Fashion* (1998),
published by the Prince Claus Fund. She writes
for several magazines and lectures at universities
worldwide. She curated the following shows,
amongst others: *Het Klimaat* (Netherlands, 1991),
Indonesian Modern Art (Indonesia/Netherlands,
1993), *Orientation* (Indonesia/Netherlands, 1996)
and *Secrets* (Netherlands, 1996).

THE LOVE OF THE BODY: OUSMANE SOW AND BEAUTY

Fig. 1. Nuba warriors, southern Sudan, photographed by George Rodger in 1949 for *Stern* magazine

In 1956, the controversial German film-maker and photographer Leni Riefenstahl visited a Nairobi bookshop, where she found a photograph by the British photographer George Rodger (1908-1995) in a back issue of *Stern* magazine. The photograph Riefenstahl found dated from 1949. It pictured two Nuba warriors from southern Sudan. One of the warriors was sitting on the other's shoulders. The victorious warrior on the top was proudly staring at the photographer. Riefenstahl, mainly known as the protégée of Adolf Hitler, discovered the photograph while she was recovering from a car crash in Kenya. She felt that the Nuba body radiated training and perfection (fig. 1).

The reason why Riefenstahl had travelled to Nairobi in 1956 was Ernest Hemingway's *Green Hills of Africa* (1935), a book that describes the writer's East African safari. The photographer was deeply impressed by Hemingway's passionate nostalgia for the continent, and she decided to visit Kenya several weeks after she finished the book. Her personal assignment for the journey was to make a film about the slave trade, which was still in existence in East Africa. While driving from Nairobi to the north, the jeep in which she and her film crew were travelling hit two large stones. The car overturned and Riefenstahl ended up in a hospital in Nairobi. She fractured the base of her skull, broke several ribs and survived four days in a coma; all in all she was to spend several weeks in this Kenyan hospital.

However, this accident did not prevent Riefenstahl from pursuing her quest for Hemingway's Africa. After discovering Rodger's photo shortly after she recovered, her new objective was to find the Nuba warriors who, she said, were "of an original beauty" and were "not civilised" in comparison with the Nuba she had encountered en route and who had mixed with the local population. In her book, she even describes them as "my Nuba" and as "people from another planet". Riefenstahl was to meet them for the first time in 1962.

After many trips to live among the Nuba, her book *Die Nuba* was published in 1973.[1] It was ten years later that the Senegalese sculptor Ousmane Sow, who was living in Paris at that time, discovered the book and her pictures. Riefenstahl's Nuba photos provided Sow, who was trained as a physiotherapist, with extra encourage-ment to become an artist. Sow used the photographer's work as a starting point for his first series of large sculptures of the Nuba.

Interestingly, his source of inspiration resembled that which had influenced Riefenstahl herself. She had also been inspired by a photograph. The beauty of Rodger's photo and its warriors persuaded her to abandon her initial intention to research East African slavery. In short, both artists, Riefenstahl and Sow, made choices after seeing an intriguing photo that was to change their lives and work. The question here is the extent to which beauty and art can inspire people. After all, it was also a literary artwork, Hemingway's *Green Hills of Africa*, that prompted Riefenstahl to travel to Africa for the first time.

Els van der Plas > The Love of the Body: Ousmane Sow and Beauty

Alongside its relationship to criteria such as quality and inventiveness, compositional construction and originality and depth, beauty is always linked to personal taste and preference. This personal aspect of beauty is shaped partly by individual experiences drawn from either the recent or distant past. The impression that the two photos made on these artists attests not only to the eloquence of these works but also to the personal interests of these two individuals at particular points in time. Riefenstahl's chance discovery of Rodger's photo and Sow's opening of her book were of great importance for these artists' development. Here, the moment itself goes beyond the anecdote, affecting each individual's current phase of development under particular circumstances. The individual's development as related to the "distributional power"[2] of art and beauty forms a leitmotif throughout this piece, as does the question that precedes it: what creates beauty?

Ousmane Sow

Ousmane Sow was born in 1935 in Dakar, the capital of Senegal. His father also came from this city and his mother was born in St. Louis. Sow grew up with a loving mother and a strict but generous father. He decided to move to Paris following the death of his father in 1956. Sow was already making sculpture in Dakar, although he had never made this his profession. Once in Paris, and without a penny to his name, he concentrated on finding work, training as a physiotherapist and starting a practice in the 20th *arrondissement.* He continued to pursue his sculptural aspirations at night.

In 1984, Sow began his *Nuba* series of sculptures, inspired by Leni Riefenstahl's book and using his expertise in both sculpture and physiotherapy. The Nuba were depicted seated, standing, fighting with sticks and having fallen on the ground. He also showed the everyday life of the people of southern Sudan: a woman tattooing another woman and two dancers, one with long hair and the other with short hair. The series consists of 12 sculpture groups.

The work of both Riefenstahl and Sow involves an admiration for the structure and strength of the human body. Riefenstahl became fascinated by the aesthetics of the "perfect body". Her appreciation of Hemingway's macho aesthetics, the Nuba warriors and the Nazi ideal of the blond, blue-eyed sportsman was decisive for her work with subjects ranging from robust male wrestlers to uniformed troops going to war and Olympic athletes.

Ousmane Sow is not seeking physical perfection. Instead he has a loving admiration for the body. As a physiotherapist, he has a vivid understanding of the body on both anatomical and instinctual levels. Sow does not precede his sculptures with sketches and maquettes. He begins by feeling his way, by creating the body in empty space. "The form already exists; it simply needs to be born," he says.[3] So he first constructs an iron skeleton that he covers with a concoction of his own making.

Fig. 2. Nuba warriors in combat practice
© Leni Riefenstahl, courtesy Leni Riefenstahl Produktion

194

Fig. 3. Leni Riefenstahl shows a group of Nuba men her last book, *Last of the Nuba*, in 1974
© Leni Reifenstahl, courtesy Leni Riefenstahl Produktion

Fig. 4. Nuba warriors Natu and Tukami, encamped. The white ashes have both holy and practical significance for the Nuba, for reasons of strength, health, cleanliness, protection against insects and bodily decoration
© Leni Riefenstahl, courtesy Leni Riefenstahl Produktion

He drapes this with jute, which he later daubs and paints. Sow refuses to reveal the precise details of this procedure. His sculptures are created from the inside out, and the skeleton ultimately defines the form. Sow admires the work of the Italian sculptor Alberto Giacometti (1902-1966), whose thin, gangly, skeleton-like sculptures are the diametric opposite of Sow's finished works. But the origins of the sculptures are the same.

In 1998 Sow commented: "There are two stages in the progress of art. You can't say that art is spiritual in the totality of its process. Art is spiritual in its conception: conceiving the sculpture and placing it in space. Also when it's finished. But between the two I think it's a physical effort. Maybe for a painter it's not the same thing. For a sculptor there's a moment when it's physical. But you also need spirituality to guide things towards the desired objective."[4] Spirituality connects Sow not only with the modernist artists he admires such as Picasso, Giacometti and the Cuban Wifredo Lam but also with the sculpture of his own country, Senegal. According to ancient tradition, sculpture is connected with spiritual powers, with ancestor veneration and with aesthetic pleasure that derives from a combination of creativity and excellent craftsmanship. This combination of expertise and the predispositions of a number of African sculptural traditions has greatly influenced Sow in the development of his own idiom. Hence, when Sow opted definitively for sculpture, it was natural for him to return to Senegal after spending 20 years in Paris.

Sow's work embodies different cultures and forms of expertise. The Dakar of his youth, the inspiration of Paris in the 1960s and 1970s, his sculptural talents and his knowledge and experience of physiotherapy have all created the artist. This has also enabled him to develop his own visual language that is distinct from the art idiom of Europe after the Second World War and separate from the visual language of Africa after independence. In fact, it remains distinct from any convention whatsoever. He has always drawn on these movements but has developed himself at a suitable distance.

Sow's sculptures are figurative. They are all larger than life, and this creates a certain distance for both the viewer and the artist himself. Yet each sculpture also has its own character. He places great emphasis on the subject's facial expression and body language, whether it be a person or an animal. His unique procedure imbues the sculptures with their own texture, colour and feeling. Whereas the *Nuba* sculptures are smooth and delicately finished, his later sculptures are increasingly raw and frayed. In his impressive and most recent series of 31 sculptures (1999) he depicts one of the final Native American victories over the settlers: the heroic battle at the Little Big Horn River in 1876. These sculptures are reddish-brown. The Native Americans and the horses are experiencing some of the most dramatic moments of their lives: a battle to the death, fighting or escaping.

Sow is guided by subjects from his history and environment. He has no preconceived plan: *The Nuba* was followed by *The Masai* (1988), *The Zulus* (1990) and *The*

Fig. 5. Ousmane Sow, *Sitting Wrestler*, part of a series of sculptures called *The Nuba*, c. 1984
© Béatrice Soulé

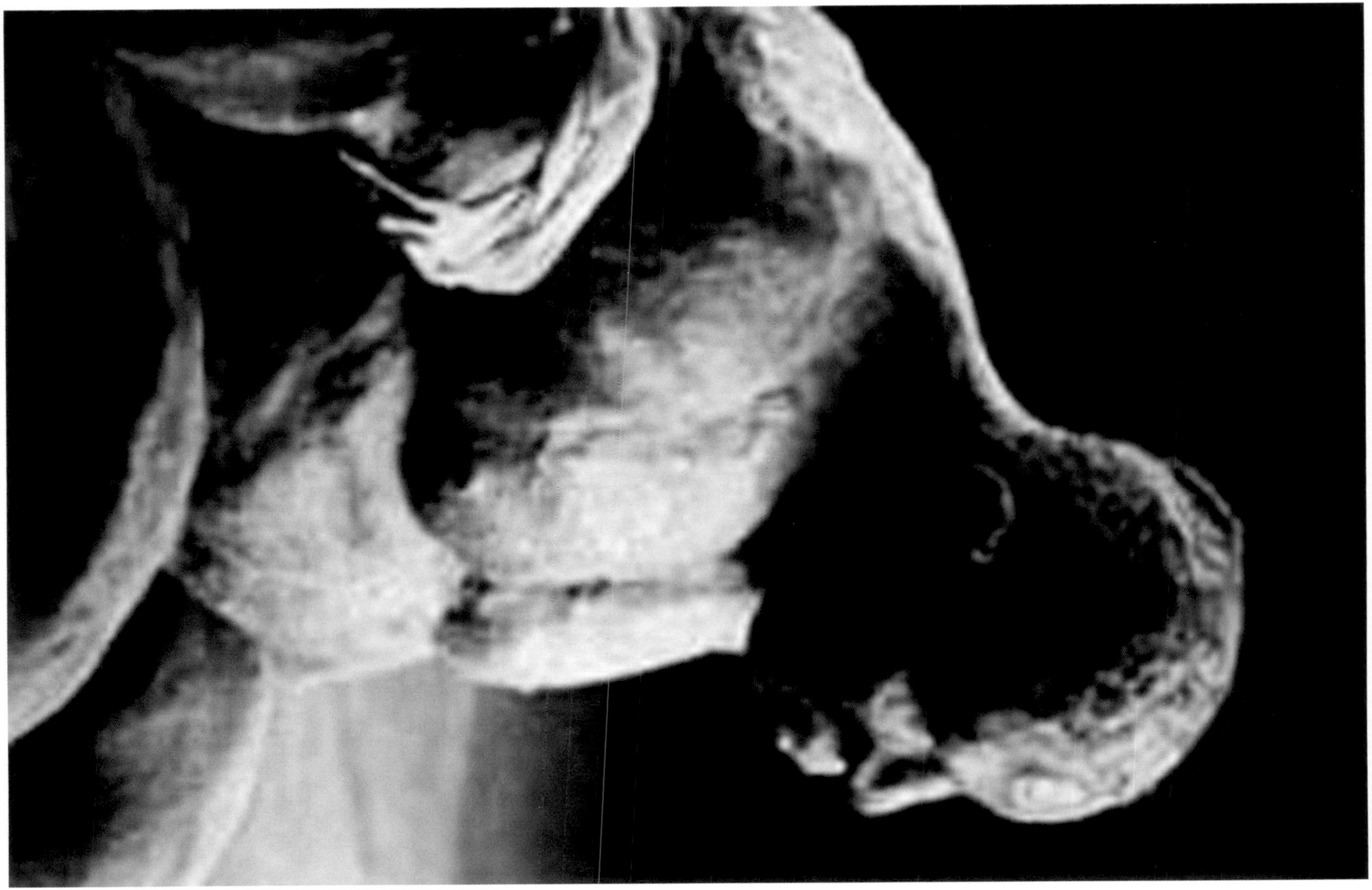

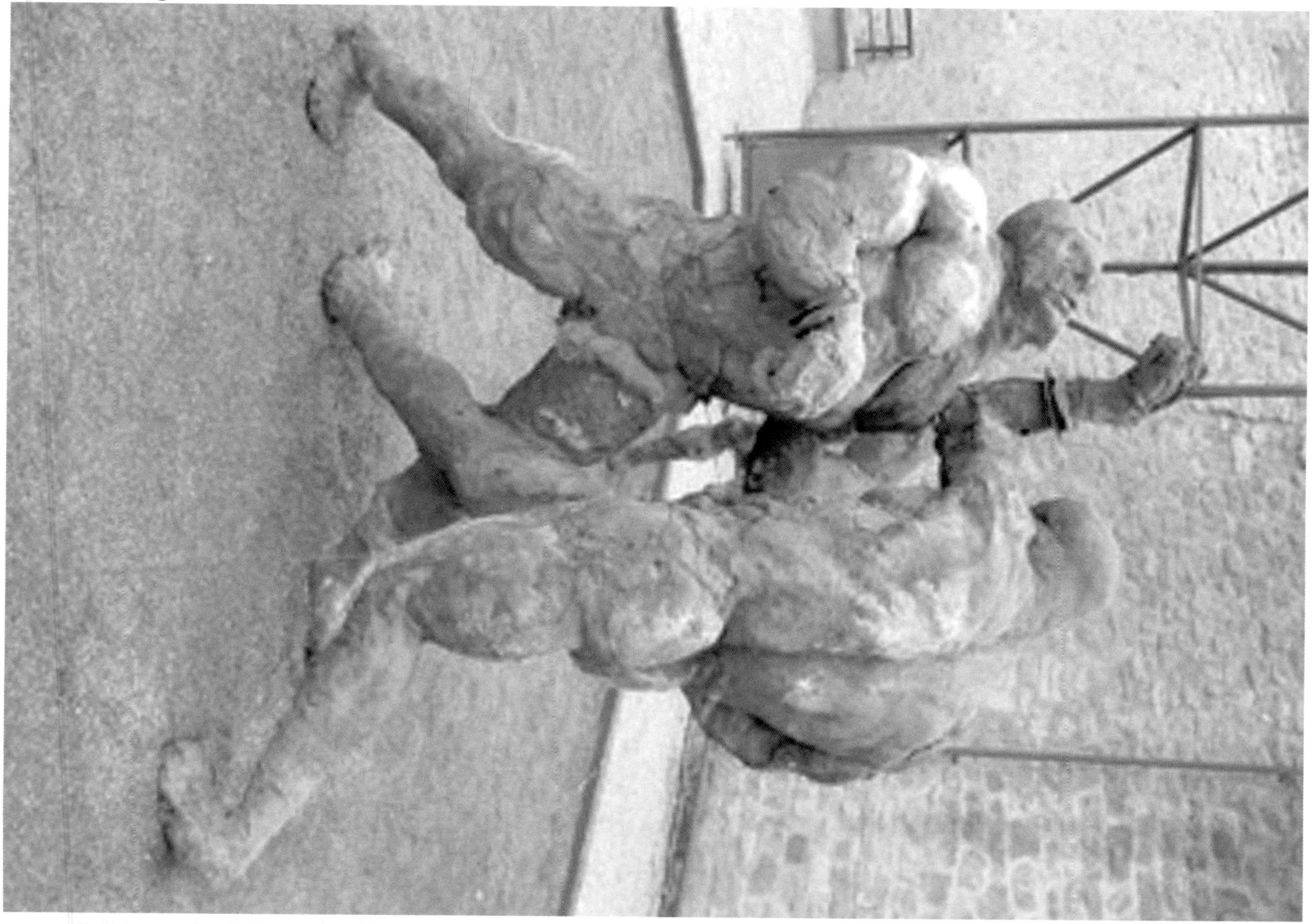

Fig. 6. Ousmane Sow, *Lutteurs aux bracelets tranchants* (Wrestlers with Sharp Bracelets), from the series *The Nuba*, c. 1984
©Thomas Loury, 2004

Peul (1993). His groups of sculptures attest to his love of Senegalese and African themes, and also to his awareness of international historical events. *Little Big Horn* can be compared with the African struggle against the colonialists or with the way in which Africans are struggling with the advance of modernism. Many artists from former colonies feel that modernism is directly linked to colonialism and outside interference. Although many recognise the modernist movement's positive aspects, the latter is also associated with contentious Western values such as individualism, originality and a linear concept of development. Inevitably, these criteria raise questions about beauty when applied to communal and multi-directional societies.

Modernism

Sow has a complex attitude to modernism. He works on his oeuvre in a singular way although he both understands and respects the modernist masterworks. His figurative work clearly distances itself from the modernist idiom and relates more closely to African sculptural tradition in terms of its form. The immediate and craft-like way in which Sow constructs his figures – a process which involves neither sketches nor studies – and his figurative and monumental style relate directly to African sculptural tradition. Technically he opts for the best of both worlds. The final result is that his work has been embraced both by the Western art world and by African art lovers, while also achieving widespread public recognition.

In 1999 Sow showed his sculptures in that most public of Parisian spaces: the bridge of Pont des Arts. Sitting Bull and Crazy Horse fought their battle against General Custer in the presence of an audience of millions who crossed the bridge. This presentation was a resounding success. Jan Hoet, who is now retiring as the director of Ghent's Museum of Contemporary Art (SMAK), commented in 1992 that "art must not be hidden away in museums, it should be brought to the people".[5] And this is what Sow achieved, not only in Paris but also previously in Senegal in 1998, where his Native American battle was shown facing the Atlantic Ocean on the Corniche. The work is well-suited to outdoor presentations because the nature of the material, and the size and volume of the work mean that it will never be swamped by its environment. In addition, it appeals to a great many people.

Beauty

Hoet wrote in the preface of the catalogue to the "Documenta IX" international exhibition in Kassel (1992), of which he was the artistic director: "I might for example write about beauty: the physical experience of the secret of art. Artists do not investigate the aesthetics of things: they reveal the hidden beauty, the essence, the ecstasy."[6] It was in this exhibition that Sow's work was first shown on an international scale. A Nuba warrior, with a red painted triangle on his face, sat between the white museum walls and the conceptual works by artists ranging from Richard

Els van der Plas > The Love of the Body: Ousmane Sow and Beauty

Artschwager to Gilberto Zorro. The warrior looked up obliquely towards the viewer, proud and with a strong physical presence. In his text, Hoet refers to the physical experience of art. In fact, he had fought as a professional boxer before he became involved with the arts, which in part explains his love for Sow's work. The love of the body and the recognition of the fight's beauty form similar points of departure for both men's work. Hoet opened his "Documenta IX" with a live boxing match, an unusual action for the art world but a logical one for Hoet.

The Nuba also have a long sporting tradition (fig. 2). The fight is an annual event and the warriors are community heroes. They have an athletic appearance, and accentuate the shape of their bodies with ash. These silver-white bodies resemble living sculptures in the reddish-yellow landscape. Riefenstahl documented this in her photographs (fig. 4), Sow visually expressed it in his three-dimensional sculptures (figs 5,6) and Hoet, who exhibited Sow's work, dramatised it with a boxing competition. For each of them, beauty is a physical experience that is intricately connected with the body, physical movement and the arts.

But beauty is a complex notion. Ultimately it not only imbues reality with form, it also concerns the maker's attitude and character, the sublimated, subjective relation to reality and the quality of the creation. It is about the strength of interpretation. Sow's work embodies these characteristics. This, in combination with his modest attitude towards his artistic profession and his respect for his subjects, has resulted in his creations. He says: "Creation covers a lot of things. For me, creation is when you achieve something that others can't. That's my definition, whatever it is you do. But it's a bit like a child trying to wear his father's shoes. I think God must smile when he sees us jumping about, when he sees us imitating. It's more imitation than creation. We imitate because it gives us pleasure, because we penetrate the mystery a little."[7]

Riefenstahl and Sow have approached the concept of beauty in different ways, yet both artists have made choices that were based on the same inspiration. Both of them have been guided by a recognition and appreciation of the impressive beauty of the Nuba, although they have radically different backgrounds and present different arguments. For Sow, the Nuba stimulated the development of his work, and his *Nuba* sculptures were the forerunners of his apotheosis-like work about Little Big Horn. The content of Sow's work, which also directs his life, partly contributes to its strength. *Little Big Horn* is not simply about depicting the Native Americans' struggle, it is also about oppression, about standing up for yourself and the drama of history. Sow's strength lies in his personal engagement in combination with his expertise in expressing this. Each aspect reinforces the other, so that the depicted surpasses the personal. Here, eloquence and meaning are important criteria for beauty alongside complex concepts such as originality and quality.

Riefenstahl's images remain on the surface of beauty. Their clever imaging and technical fireworks get in the way of analysing their contents. "Her Nuba" are "people from another planet". This exotic admiration does not lead to in-depth analysis. It is the attitude of a consumer. She, like George Rodger, lived with the Nuba on a number of occasions. Like an anthropologist and an admirer of "primitive life", she had moved away from the trauma of the Second World War, a war which she helped to create. She looked for a utopian world. After her controversial work for Hitler and the Third Reich, which culminated in the film *Triumpf des Willens* (1934) and her two-part documentary about the Olympic Games, *Fest der Völker* and *Fest der Schönheit* (1937), she became known as a propaganda film-maker of Nazi Germany and never lost that stigma. The discovery of Rodger's photo provided her with a way out.

Interestingly, after the end of the war, George Rodger was one of the first British photographers to enter the German concentration camp of Bergen Belsen and to photograph the corpses that he found there. This experience made him decide to avoid war photography and to search for a more peaceful world, which he found amongst the Nuba and in other locations. Both Riefenstahl and Rodger shared this ideal, which the Nuba and their culture literally embodied. Both needed to get away and to break with their past activities – past activities that were totally in contrast to each other.

Sow does not strive for a perfect world. Instead he takes life as it is. He walks in his father's shoes in a world of tragedy and happiness, and makes reality a little bit more beautiful. Jan Hoet was one of the first museum directors to recognise this quality. He perceived, through the opposite of a form of exoticism, "the hidden beauty, the essence and the ecstasy" of Sow's Nuba. It is the unique position that Sow has taken within both the African and European art worlds which makes him stand out, both as a person and as an artist.

Acknowledgements
With thanks to Malu Halasa for her comments
and Annie Wright for her translation.

203

Mark Gevisser
Inheritance

Mark Gevisser is a writer, journalist and heritage consultant. He was born in Johannesburg in 1964 and educated at Yale University in the US. He co-edited *Defiant Desire: Gay and Lesbian Lives in South Africa* (1994), and an anthology of his Mail & Guardian columns was published as *Portraits of Power: Profiles in a Changing South Africa* (1996). He wrote the documentary feature *The Man Who Drove With Mandela* (1998) and scripts for the drama series *Zero Tolerance*. He is currently Content Advisor to the Heritage, Education and Tourism program of Constitution Hill, and is completing his biography of Thabo Mbeki, which will be published in 2007.

INHERITANCE

I

In May 1962, as South Africa descended into the darkness that was the 1960s in this country, a beautiful young teacher was introduced, by one of her colleagues at Barnato Park High School, to a successful young businessman, a bachelor in his early thirties. Theirs was a passionate love, and in August that year he proposed marriage to her. When she became pregnant, they bought a suburban ranch house in the new suburb of Atholl, north of Johannesburg. The man was a follower of Alan Paton and had been involved in the production of Todd Matshikiza's *King Kong*.[1] The woman's father, a furniture manufacturer, had been a self-taught intellectual of the 1930s and a member of the Left Book Club, and had bequeathed a voluminous orange-bound library to his only daughter: *The Road to Wigan Pier*; *Red Star over China*; *The Mind and Face of Bolshevism*.

By November 1964, when the woman was about to give birth to her child, Nelson Mandela and his Rivonia co-accused had been sentenced to life imprisonment on Robben Island. South Africa had become intolerable and many in the young couple's circle of white liberals were emigrating. On the brink of starting a family, the couple feared for the future but did not want to leave. A close friend was apprehended by the police; he had typed a "subversive" letter, but had managed to throw the incriminating typewriter into the Hartebeespoort Dam and so was not charged. A handyman working for the young couple turned out to be a moonlighting police-man, and they feared a raid. And so on one balmy summer's night, they lit a fire in the living room and fed her father's library, book by book, to the flames.

A few days later I was born. In 1964, the year of my birth:
- Nelson Mandela and seven others were sentenced to life imprisonment for sabotage and Communism.
- 48 people were placed under house arrest, 11 of whom fled the country.
- 173 people were placed under 90-day detention.
- 671 people were found guilty of political offences, five of whom were sentenced to death.
- 303 South Africans were banned, 22 of whom left the country.
- 175,099 "Bantus" were admitted to the main urban areas under Influx Control regulations, and 98,241 were endorsed out of them.
- 141 white men and 110 "Bantu" women were convicted of inter-racial carnal intercourse, as were one white woman and four "Bantu" men.
- 56 men were convicted of bigamy, 42 of them "Bantu".
- 21 women were found guilty of illegal abortions, 12 of them "Bantu".
- 13 people were convicted of keeping a brothel, five of them coloured women.
- 643 men were convicted of "public indecency", 309 of them "Bantu".
- 41 people were convicted of being in possession of "indecent publications", and
- 504 publications were banned.

Beautiful Ugly: African and Diaspora Aesthetics

- 216 people were convicted of "other indecent, immoral or sexual offences".
- 57 people were convicted of bestiality, 42 of whom were "Bantu" men.
- 20 white men were convicted of the "unnatural act" of committing sodomy with other white men.
- 186 "non-white" men were convicted of committing sodomy with other "non-white" men.
- Two white men and two "Bantu" men were convicted of committing sodomy with each other.

II

There is a cupboard in my parents' study, at the home in which I grew up, filled with the story of my family. It is a very South African record, a record of gardens and swimming pools, and of the growing white suburban family that filled them. There is a particularly lucent quality to the family photographs of white middle-class suburban South Africans in the 1960s and 1970s, not just because of the excess of Johannesburg's sunlight but because of the ease of childhood too: that perfect balance between containment and freedom that comes, when you are a child, from being in a garden; the promise in so much firm, tan skin; the trays of lemon-barley squash and tennis biscuits; the unthinking certainty that there will always be people to look after you.

My entire childhood is documented in the garden, culminating in my Bar Mitzvah speech, delivered Juliet-like from a balcony to the appreciative masses on the grass below: I am wearing an inexplicable brown suit, silver teardrop spectacles and a hairstyle that my partner, looking at the photos now, calls a "Jew-fro". Here are my first baby shots, in a dazzling white smock; here a later series, more playful, naked on a mohair rug clutching a carnation. Here I am, staring with palpable alarm at the future on my way to my first day at school, with a tiny brown case (empty) in one hand and an unthreading fluffy toy in the other. And there is my brother Antony done up for a fancy-dress party as Cupid, threaded with cardboard hearts and a bow and arrow spray-painted gold, while I am draped in my mother's clunky 1960s jewelry and swathed in layers of her Indian-print scarves, bearing a bejewelled turban on my head. The caption beneath the photo notes that I was "The Maharajah". Was it my idea, or hers, to raid her wardrobe?

The photographs are stuck, with a somewhat insouciant hand, into the adhesive pages of mass-produced albums with garish plastic covers. One album, however, is different. Bound in red leather with a leather bow, and embossed in the bottom right-hand corner with a gold springbok, it has black cardboard pages onto which its holdings are secured with silver photo corners. It is, in the grammar of my child-hood, the past perfect: before-I-came. It contains my parents' wedding photographs, from January 1963, and the record of their first few years together.

207

208

Fig. 1

The photo that compels me is not from the wedding collection, but rather a bit further on in the red leather album – from their first holiday alone, after my birth, to what was then the Portuguese colony of Mozambique, and the favoured weekend getaway for people of their class and station. They are in Xai-Xai, suspended in the tepid and translucent tropical water, their legs entwined, clearly visible beneath the surface as they hold each other. They are a human conch; a heart drawn in the water: so beautiful are they that their son forgives them, immediately, their solipsism, as he imagines how he must have been abandoned to facilitate this moment (fig. 1).

III

It is 1999. I am 35, exactly the age my father was when he met my mother. To find the Johannesburg into which I was born I drive northwards, out of the city, through the endless boomed suburbs and cluster-home developments and neoclassical office parks, along thoroughfares named for Afrikaner leaders through suburbs that evoke bucolic idylls. I pass the obscenity of a gargantuan casino housed in a Hollywood impression of a Tuscan hillside village, its ramparts leering over Johannesburg in a nightmarish reincarnation of the mining town's bawdy-house past, and drive through the peri-urban sprawl of light industry and squatter camps, out onto what is known as the mink-and-murder belt, where the descendants of the mining magnates build their follies, keep their horses, hoard their treasures.

At Lanseria aerodrome I bump down a crenellated dirt road, past cows and gum-trees and labourers' children coming home from school in their gymslips until, my car encased in the fine ochre dust of the Highveld, I arrive at the Bailey's African Photographic Archives, on the eccentric country estate of the recently deceased founder-publisher of the *Drum*[2] empire, Jim Bailey. Here, in rooms filled in equal measure with dust and whimsy, are housed those images that have come to define black urban Johannesburg life: Nelson Mandela sparring with Jerry Moloi on a city rooftop; Dolly Rathebe in a bikini up a minedump; Hugh Masekela and Satchmo's trumpet.

Buried deep in the filing cabinets, I come across a folder entitled "No Colour Bar: 1961". I pour its contents out onto a table, and they are a genie unbottled, the stardust of what might have been: dozens of prints of blacks and whites boxing together, playing tennis together, acting on stage together, swimming together, helping each other across the street, arguing at art openings together, jamming together in late-nite jazz clubs. Cross-referencing the photographs to a bound volume of *Drum*, I see that they were collected for a six-page pullout, written by the magazine's *enfant terrible,* Nat Nakasa, in the March 1961 issue, entitled "Fringe Country, Where There is No Colour Bar". Fringe Country, declares Nakasa, is "that social no-man's-land, where energetic, defiant, young people of all races live and play together as humans … where anybody meets anybody, to hell with the price of their false teeth, or any-

thing else ... Some people call it 'crossing the colour line'. You may call it jumping the line or wiping it clean off. Whatever you please. Those who live on the fringe have no special labels. They see it simply as LIVING. Dating a girl. Inviting a friend to lunch. Arranging a party for people who are interested in writing or painting, jazz or boxing, or even apartheid, for that matter."

One of the photographs accompanying the text is that of a white woman and a black man horsing around in a swimming pool, above the caption, "Where's this? Surely not South Africa, with white and black in the same swimming pool? If that's what you thought, you are wrong, this picture was taken in one of [the] smartest suburbs of white Johannesburg." The eyes of both man and woman are closed: as in the photograph of my parents at Xai-Xai, they are in a whirlpool of their own making, utterly contained, held by the corruscations of the late-afternoon sun on the rippling water. What makes this photograph so brilliant an analogue of its subject material is that – unlike that photograph of my parents – there is no visible physical contact between the man and the woman and yet we *know*, by the positions of their bodies and the expressions on their faces, that beneath the surface of the water they are intertwined (fig. 2).

In the folder of photographs there is another image of the same scene taken from a wider angle, shot just moments before the above clinch. Standing in the shallow end is a coloured man, locked in intimacy with a white woman who is sitting at the pool's edge dangling her feet in the water. Behind them, receding back to a house and a row of old sun-dappled trees, are untidy clusters of seminaked white families, doing what white families do on a Sunday afternoon in suburban Johannesburg. All form a halo of human activity around the focal point of the photograph: a powerfully built, strikingly handsome black man, wading through the pool at nipple-level towards the white woman who will – we know, from the following photo – pull him down into the water with her (fig. 3).

I am a child of suburban Johannesburg. I look at this photo and I feel unutterable loss. I feel a hunger that ripples down the sides of my tongue and gathers in my throat, for the sycamore berries and the bluegum pods beneath bare feet, caught in the grooves between the slasto paving; for that tray of lemon-barley squash and tennis biscuits on a glass-topped iron table; for the sun reflected off a zinc roof onto beds of Namaqualand daisies; for the insane, prehistoric shriek of hadeda ibises piercing the sky, the purple violence of a cloudburst, the lengthening shadows, the inevitable nightfall quick as a gangster's knife. I was born three years after these photographs were taken, just as the Rivonia Trialists were beginning their life sentences on Robben Island. There were no such poolside gatherings any more. I look at these photographs and see my childhood, blanched, with the focal point – that black man advancing through the water – removed. I see what might have been.

213

Fig. 3

IV

My friend Pam was a denizen of "Fringe Country", one of its poster girls. And so I take the poolside photographs from the "No Colour Bar: 1961" file to show her, in the hope that she will be able to identify some of the people. She does, immediately: "That's me," she says, pointing to the white woman sitting on the edge of the pool, flirting with the coloured man. "And that's Joe."

My parents were already courting, in May 1962, when the Johannesburg newspapers blared the headline, "19-Year-Old Typist in Skin-Tight Red Jeans Held on Morals Charge With Coloured!" Pam – Pamela Beira – was the typist in question, and her lover was Joe Louw, a photo-journalist who told their story in *Drum.* Joe worked for *New Age* and had captured the first photographs of the slave-labour potato farms in Bethel; Pam, a rebellious Jewish teenager, had found a way out of suburbia by striking up friendships with the musicians who would play at venues like the Nightbeat or the Barclay Hotel in town. "First we white girls met the musicians," she tells me, "and through them the journalists, and through them the activists." She left home, in mid-1961, to move in with Joe. In November of that year they were staying at an acquaintance's flat in Hillbrow when the police, informed by the caretaker's wife, burst down their door. They found a woman draped in a red towel, in bed behind a beaded curtain, and a man sitting at the table, fully clothed, his arm in a sling. She threw on some bright red jeans and a red, green and white top, and the two were taken down to Hillbrow police station, where she was subjected to a complete medical examination.

The police medical officer found, as he was later to testify, that "one would tend to think there was no intercourse", and so the couple was finally found guilty of having "conspired to commit immorality" rather than the perpetuation of the act itself. This verdict hinged on two key items missing from Pam's person at the time of the arrest: her hymen and her underwear. The magistrate asked: why would a woman, no longer a virgin, be wearing nothing but a red towel in the presence of a coloured man at 15 minutes to midnight if she didn't have immoral intentions? The arresting officer testified that he watched her "put on panties … She looked half asleep, but I couldn't say with accused number two because he is a Coloured and it is more difficult."

Pam fled into exile before sentencing, and Joe spent six months in jail, where he underwent severe harassment from the wardens for having sullied the honour of a white woman. After his release, he joined her in exile, and wrote "My Flight To Love" for *Drum* in June 1962, alongside a photograph of the two of them walking along the palm-fringed shore of Dar-es-Salaam, in Julius Nyerere's newly liberated Tanganyika. Even by *Drum*'s standards, Mohammed Amin's rear-view photograph of them on the beach at Dar is racy: a black man and a white woman, on a beach, together, holding hands. The straps of Beira's bathing suit have fallen suggestively off her shoulders, and her hand assertively clasps that of Louw, who is clad in a scant

214

pair of bathing trunks. There is something unmistakeably victorious about it all: their clasped, outstretched arms actually form a triumphant "V" at the centre of the image, beneath the headline, "Journey's End in Lovers' Meeting" (fig. 4).

V

I am sitting in the home of Mrs Norah Moerane, high up on the Inanda Hills over Durban. When she and her husband moved here in the 1950s, there was no better address for a black South African. Elsewhere, people were being forcibly removed from land their families had owned for generations and were only allowed to rent property in the new townships, but the missionaries who had founded Inanda managed to prevail over the new apartheid authorities, and this was one of the only places outside of the Bantustans where you could buy your own stand and build your own house.

Mrs Moerane had class and she had style: when her husband was appointed principal of the famous Ohlange Training Institute at Inanda, she chose a plot that looked down, through the sugar cane fields, to the port of Durban below, glistening alongside the Indian Ocean. She built and furnished the home she built in perfect 1950s style – pastel walls, modular furniture, a funky lounge suite with wooden coasters that slide out from beneath the chair arms for you to put your cocktail glass on. Now, at the turn of the 21st century, the hills that roll down from Inanda to the sea are covered in shanties, and, from the *stoep* of Mrs Moerane's home, you see corrugated iron, rather than sugar cane, glinting in the sunlight. A widow now, she lives alone, slap-bang in the middle of one of South Africa's largest squatter communities. There might be a layer of urban dust over everything now, and the doilies on the dining-room table might be a little frayed, and she might need to fetch water from the pump outside when you need the toilet because her water supply has been cut off, but the walls are still pastel, and she still slides out those coasters from under the chair arms when she serves you a High Tea of little cucumber sandwiches with the crusts cut off, at four o'clock sharp.

I am visiting Mrs Norah Moerane because I am writing a biography of Thabo Mbeki, and she is his aunt. Her husband, Manasseh "MT" Moerane, was the brother of Mbeki's mother, Epainette Mbeki; after he died and her children left, she filled the rooms of her home with memories. She has become the custodian of the family history. She pulls out dozens of photo albums, but while I am supposed to be looking at the images of the prosperous Moerane gentry gathered around their schoolmaster-farmer patriarch at the family seat in the Transkei in their Edwardian finery, I find myself drawn to another image, a photograph taken on the beach at Durban in the late 1960s, at about the time my own family albums reveal boisterous and crowded seaside holidays at Clifton or Plettenberg Bay.

To an eye not lidded with the colour filter that comes of growing up in apartheid

215

..JOURNEY'S END IN

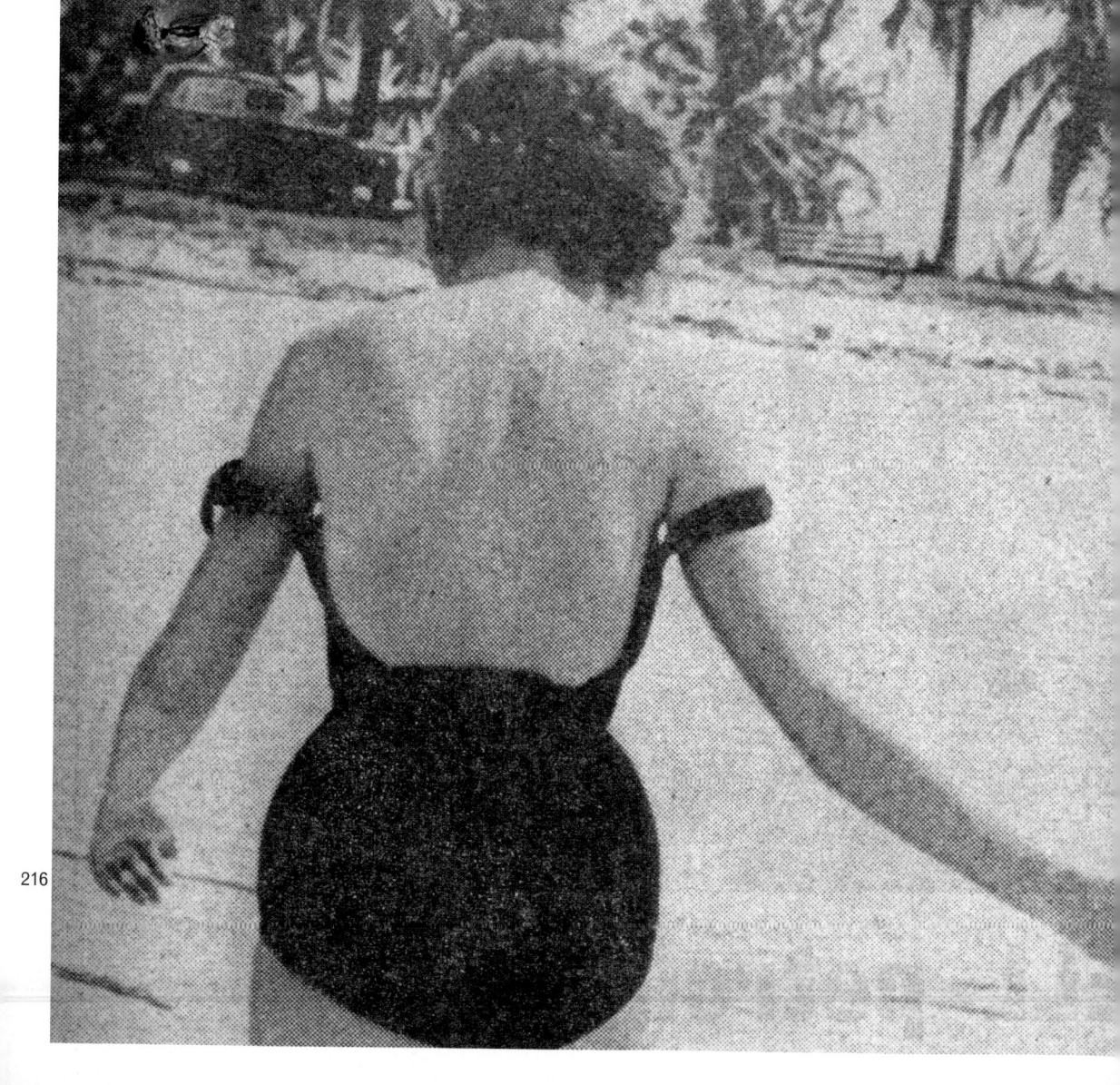

LOVERS' MEETING

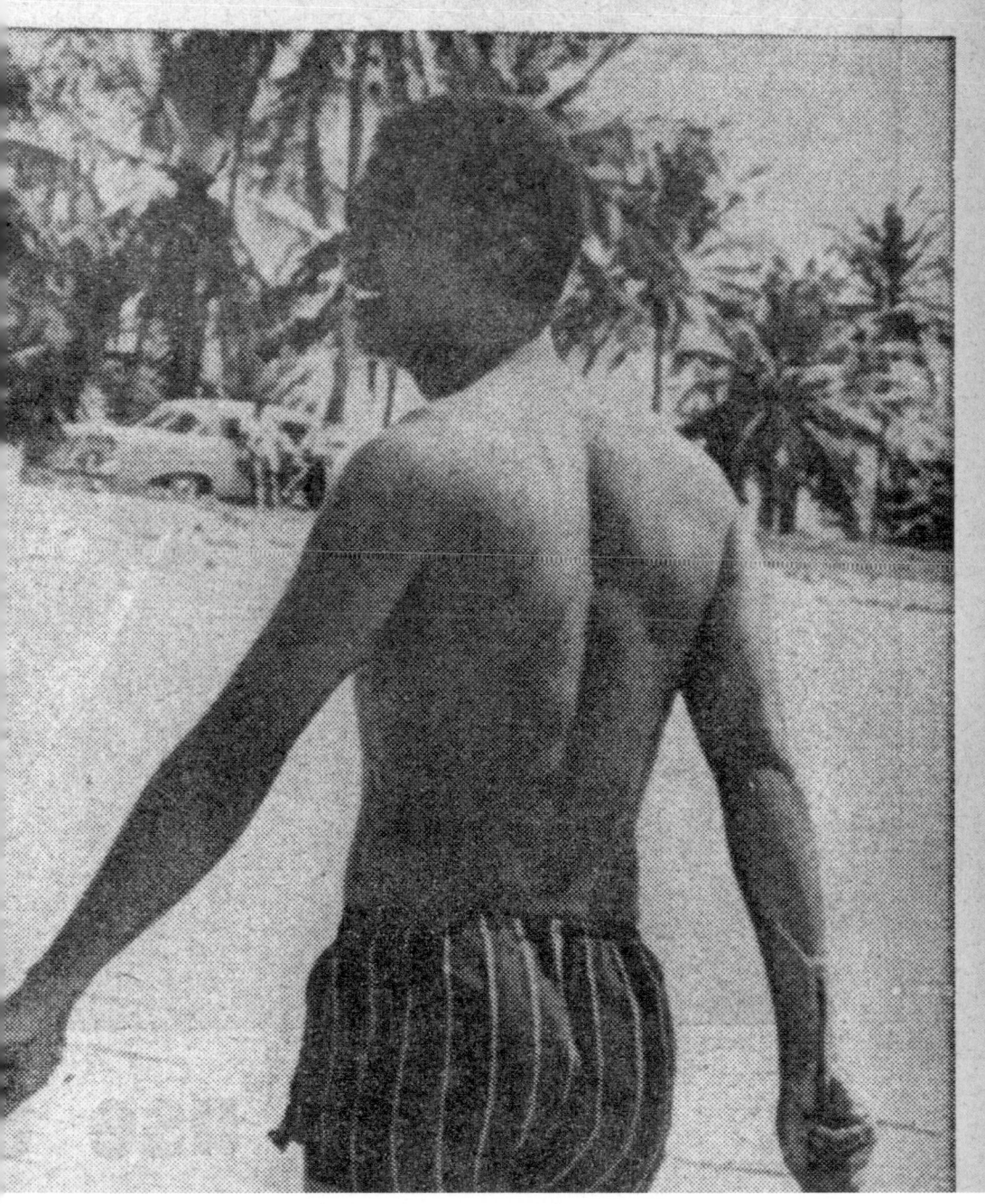

South Africa, the photograph would appear mundane, barely worthy of comment. A party consisting of two women, a teenage girl and a child pose on the beach for the photographer. Their shadows – elongated eastwards away from the setting sun – tell us this is at the end of a long and lovely beach day. One of the women sports a rather stylish psychedelic bathing suit; the other is more homely in a chequered housedress. The women have gathered in their arms the paraphernalia of a day on the beach: blankets, shoes, lunch box, transistor radio. The stylish woman is Norah Moerane; the other is Thabo Mbeki's sister Linda; the child is Linda's daughter and the teenage girl her minder. The photographer, Mrs Moerane tells me, is her husband, "a real shutterbug". I look at the photograph and imagine Mrs Moerane piling her family in the car and motoring down through the canefields to take the waters, during a time when blacks were being thrown off beaches and corralled into "non-whites only" enclosures, usually where the swimming was most dangerous ^(fig. 5).

VI

In the early 1990s, while I was writing a history of gay and lesbian life in South Africa, I came across a huge scrapbook, with the hand-printed title "Special Projects" across its cover, in Johannesburg's small Gay Lending Library. The euphemistic title reflected beautifully what was within it: a decade's worth of meticulous clipping and pasting of newspaper articles, from the mid-1950s to the mid-1960s, without anything in common save that the maker of the scrapbook had collected them together. Some of the articles are explicitly about homosexuality – particularly those dealing with police raids on parks or "cottages" – but a great many can only be identifiable as "gay" because of their context in the scrapbook: society page photos, articles about suicides, even a clip of a young man winning a prize at a local supermarket.

The scrapbook is an obsessive endeavour; its author's "Special Project" a determined attempt to find the homosexual subtext in South Africa's mass media. I spent hours poring over it, and eventually tracked down its creator: his name was Joe Garmeson; he was a great fulsome bear of a man, a banker and a toastmaster, given to grand proclamations and florid stories. Like Mrs Norah Moerane he was a hoarder, a historian's dream, with cupboards full of photographs, notebooks and journals. These items are now the foundation collection of the Gay and Lesbian Archives at Wits University; an extraordinarily detailed account of white male homosexual life in South Africa through the 20th century.

In one of Joe Garmeson's albums is a series of young men on the beach, some time in the 1950s. The photographs are taken at Bachelors Cove in Cape Town – a pile of smooth rocks at the extreme west end of Clifton Beach which was the gathering point for "queer society" in the city. According to Joe and other regulars, men would gather on the rocks at the end of the day to swim, talk, cruise, bathe naked beneath the dying sun. In one of his photographs, we see him at Bachelors Cove, looking with

Mark Gevisser > Inheritance

220

Fig. 6

Fig. 7

his matinee-idol smile directly at the camera, as he poses with four friends. Their bodies fold into each other as they sit on the rocks, as if they were sirens, or beached sylphs from a water ballet. Such is their intimacy that you would not need to find their photo in a big scrapbook labelled "Special Projects" to know they were homosexuals (fig. 6).

In another photograph we see the matinee idol sitting on the rocks and looking, once more, straight at the camera. But this time he has composed an almost classical triptych: his arm is around a blonde friend, and both of them have a hand on the shoulder of a mixed-race or Malay man who sits beneath them, caressing their legs. In the background, oblivious to this flagrant transgression of the laws forbidding both racial mixing and public indecency, three coloured fishermen carry on their task of catching dinner (fig. 7).

The photograph is taken on the rocky promontory between Bachelors Cove and Maidens Cove, one of the only coloured beaches on the entire Atlantic seaboard, and one of those gaps in the stitching of apartheid. Here white and coloured men cruised and courted; here, between Bachelors and Maidens, they developed networks of desire, affection and even just friendship.

VII

On the 22nd of January 1966, when I was one year old, the *Rand Daily Mail* that landed on the door of our Atholl home had an unusually large banner headline: "350 IN MASS SEX ORGY!" A "queer" party had been raided in Wychwood Rd, in the Johannesburg suburb of Forest Town; nine men had been arrested for "masquerading as women" and one for "indecent assault on a minor". It was, of course, a garden party; it took place, of course, around a swimming pool. Although my parents do not recall the incident, they must have pored over the article, for they had several homosexual friends, and many names were printed.

The raid provoked a massive public outcry, and a Parliamentary Commission of Inquiry was launched. According to the official police report, officers had found "a party in progress, the like of which has never been seen in this country. Males were dancing with males to the strains of music, kissing and cuddling each other in the most vulgar fashion imaginable". In Parliament the following year, the Minister of Justice proclaimed that "we should not allow ourselves to be deceived into thinking that we may casually dispose of this viper in our midst by regarding it as innocent fun. It is a proven fact that sooner or later homosexual instincts make their effects felt on a community if they are permitted to run riot."

"Queers" were as threatening to the white civilisation as Communists or miscegenating heterosexuals, and the state proposed legislation that would make it illegal to be homosexual. A spirited defence by a "Law Reform" movement grew within the gay community; one of its leaders was Joe Garmeson. The current South

African Chief Justice, Arthur Chaskalson, was then just setting out in his legal career, and he was hired to represent the movement, whose meticulous submissions managed to temper this legislation. Nonetheless, three amendments were finally made to the very same Immorality Act under which Pam Beira and Joe Louw had been arrested: the first was to raise the age of consent for male homosexual acts from 16 to 19; the second was to outlaw dildoes (which, police reported, were the primary tools of the trade of lesbianism), and the third was the infamous "men at a party clause", which criminalised any "male person who commits with another male person at a party any act which is calculated to stimulate sexual passion or give sexual gratification". Most absurd was the definition of a "party": "any occasion where more than two persons are present".

But it wasn't only this new legislation that broke up the "party" on that rocky promontory between Bachelors and Maidens. In the early 1970s, at about the same time our family was taking summer holidays at Clifton, there were complaints about housebreaking from white householders, and so the authorities erected a ten-foot-high fence right across the promontory. So determined were the authorities to prevent the coloureds from Maidens from crossing Bachelors into Clifton that the fence was actually extended, for about 20 feet, into the icy Atlantic Ocean. The stated reason was to stop vagrancy and crime, but the net effect was to shut down one of Cape Town's last and most enduring spaces for cross-racial intimacy.

Now, at the turn of the millenium, I have full constitutional rights to equality. I am involved in a long-term relationship with a man of a different race group to my own; we live together, sleep together, holiday together, socialise together with other mixed-race couples, gay and straight, with none of the strictures that homosexuals or mixed-race couples experienced at the time I was born, nearly 40 years ago. I have held my partner in the water just as my parents held each other in the water in that beautiful Xai-Xai shot, our legs intertwined.

But after hearing the stories of Bachelors Cove and Maidens Cove, I went there for the first time a short while ago and saw that ten-foot-high barrier for myself. It was a summer evening, and the astonishing Atlantic sun, all fiery and swaggering, was bisected by the diamond mesh. I felt, like a blow to the stomach, the history of pain in beauty, and I reflected that while I might have been denied the bequest of my grandfather's handsome orange-bound Left Book Club library, I – like all South Africans – am the beneficiary of another inheritance: a fence, between Bachelors and Maidens, that still stands.

Célestin Monga
Let's Eat: Banquet Aesthetics and Social Epicurism

Célestin Monga is an economist from Douala,
Cameroon, who works for the World Bank in
Washington DC. He is the author of *The Anthro-
pology of Anger – Civil Society and Democracy in
Africa* (1997). He is regarded as one of Cameroon's
leading intellectuals, and his critical writing about
Cameroonian politics has been widely published.
In 1991 he was arrested for criticising the president
as the result of a piece he wrote for *Le Messager*.
His arrest sparked protests throughout the country.

LET'S EAT: BANQUET AESTHETICS AND SOCIAL EPICURISM

"Antou!" This song was immensely successful throughout Africa for a number of years and allowed the Ivorian group, Magic System, to establish itself firmly in the world of African variety music. It tells the story of Antou, an ambitious and materialistic young woman who chooses her victims on the basis of their purchasing power. However, she commits errors of judgement, as when she drops a young man to set herself up with an apparently wealthier man. The story tells of Antou's desperate comeback attempt when she learns that the young man she had jilted has become a famous singer – and probably therefore wealthy. The latter, no fool, shows a certain elegance of spirit. Having agreed to invite her to dinner, he promises to serve braised cayman as well as *kedjénou* of elephant, thus ironically mocking the eating habits of his lady love, and drawing a parallel between them and her desire to appear to be something that she is not. The well-known refrain of the song, taken up in the chorus by children from the popular quarters of the large sub-Saharan cities, is as follows:

> *Je dis chérie Côco qu'est-ce que tu veux manger*
> *Sans même hésiter, elle me dit poulet braisé*
> *Je dis chérie Côco, c'est poulet tu veux manger,*
> *Poulet est trop petit, ça ne peut pas te rassasier,*
> *C'est caïman braisé, tu vas manger*
> *Kédjénou d'éléphant, je vais te donner*
> *Elle est fâchée, elle dit s'en va à la maison …*[1]

> I say dear Côco what do you feel like eating
> Without hesitation, braised chicken she says
> I say dear Côco, it is chicken that you want,
> Chicken is too small, it cannot satisfy you,
> It is braised cayman that you will have
> Kédjénou of elephant, I shall give you
> She is cross, she says she is going home …

Civilising through enjoyment

Eating has never been a trivial matter or an activity without significance. In every time and in every place, people have attributed symbolic importance and aesthetic significance to this physiological and biological imperative. Eating has provided an opportunity for families and social groups to exchange complicit signals, ways of deciphering power relations in the existing social order.

In Africa, as elsewhere, the act of eating can assume myriad forms: it can be an intimate and private activity which accompanies dialogue and helps to structure relations within the family; it can be a semi-public activity affording members of a social group the opportunity to discuss frivolous or serious and sensitive subjects in a friendly atmosphere, easing tensions by having the discussion organised around the ritual of specially prepared food and drink; or it can be an entirely public activity where what one actually consumes during the meal is less important than the symbolism of these meals, the quality of the menu, the calibre of guest, the formality of the venue, the solemnity of the ambience, the type of music which accompanies these moments.

In his contribution to *L'histoire de la vie privée en Occident* (The History of Private Life in the West), Paul Veyne informs us that in the times of the Roman Empire, the banquet was regarded as a ceremony of civility:

> As soon as Horace is on his lands, in his dear retreat, he invites a friend to dine, no doubt a famous emancipated singer or actress. For the banquet, customarily, provides the occasion for the private man to savour who he is and to reveal himself as he is to his peers ... The banquet was much more than simply a banquet. It was expected to reveal the general opinions, exalted subjects and recapitulations of the self; if the master of the house had a philosophy on music (with song and dance executed by hired professionals), this raised the tone of the feast. The banquet was a social event as much as, and more so than, the enjoyment of drinking ...[2]

The banquet thus served both to affirm oneself in private, in one's familial or personal space, and to provide the opportunity for the public man or woman to define him- or herself in the eyes of their fellows. But the ritual of eating does not always have the same meaning in different places, including those cultural spaces that one would think to be *a priori* homogenous. The Romanian philosopher Cioran, for example, recounts his discovery of the importance of eating on his arrival in France in the 1950s as one of the major cultural shocks in his life:

> Before coming to France, I ate like an animal. Because my mother had never explained to us: at lunchtime we will eat this or that. I never heard any comment like: this is good or this is bad. We ate, that's all. My family was not exceptionally poor, far from it, but we did not consider the act of eating to be part of civilisation ... When I arrived in Paris, I landed up in a small hotel in the Latin Quarter. Every morning I went downstairs to telephone, and I remember, right at the beginning, hearing the proprietor, her husband and their son discussing: "Maman, what will we have for lunch?" It's true; they would carry on like this for half an hour. I thought they were having guests. This happened twice or three times,

Fig. 1. Place settings for an opulent dinner
© Owen Franken/Corbis

and then every day, so eventually I said to myself: "So, eating is an intellectual activity. It really does form part of civilisation."[3]

Recounting the same story in another text, Cioran explains:

> The organisation of meals, the succession of dishes were the subject of an exchange of opinions, as if they were the most signal event of the day, which was indeed the case. Eating – I discovered – did not simply correspond to a need for food but to something deeper, an act which, strange as it may seem, dissociated itself from hunger to acquire the sense of a veritable ritual. I therefore learned only at the age of twenty-seven what eating actually meant, what was remarkable and unique about this everyday demeaning activity. And so I ceased to be an animal.[4]

Eating is a powerful French tradition, going as far back, according to Martin-Fuguier, as the 19th century. "To have a meal is not simply to eat, it is to be with the family. Manuals on etiquette emphasise the role of the mistress of the house who knows how to create happiness around the table."[5] To cite Madame Celnart who wrote, in her *Manuel des dames* (Ladies' Manual) of 1833, a kind of "how-to" on managing domestic life:

> It is not only when we have visitors that we must pay attention to the honours of the table, we must do so for one's spouse, to civilise the inside. I use this word for good reason; for what distinguishes civilisation is the ability to impart, to the satisfaction of all our needs, a character of enjoyment and dignity.[6]

In the individualistic tradition of the Enlightenment, the family meal is an intimate affair with which strangers are only rarely associated, especially on Sundays, when lunch and dinner assume the quality of veritable family rituals. This contrasts with African traditions, where it is impossible to conceive of a stranger being excluded from a family meal. But with the industrialisation of Europe, the tradition of the intimate family meal has been progressively lost: too concerned with their affairs, and having to work far from their place of residence, men and women no longer return home for the midday meal.

South of the Sahara, eating has become a powerful means of identification and a symbol of the aesthetics of power. Power is associated with metaphors of eating ("*la bouffe*" or "grub" as it is crudely referred to).[7] The Cameroonians have even invented a now-famous expression to refer to the perception, in the collective subconscious, of the loci of power as first and foremost the privileged loci of pleasure where one eats and consumes to one's heart's content: "the politics of the stomach". According to J.F. Bayart:

> The very term "politics of the stomach" is rich in meanings that should not be overlooked. It refers in the first place to situations where there is a dearth of food, and which continue to prevail in Africa. Feeding oneself continues to be a problem, a difficulty, a concern. More often, however, the term "to eat" … refers to desires and practices other than those related to food. Above all, activities of accumulation which open the way to social advancement and which allow the holder of positions of power to "stand upright" … The "politics of the stomach" are also the politics of sophisticated banter, what the Congolese term the "second office", and mistresses are one of the cogs of the post-colonial State. The "stomach" refers both to the corpulence, which it is good to display when one becomes powerful, and the lineage which remains an ever-present social reality which is not without political effects at the national level.[8]

Eating therefore participates in a culture of power at the same time as it expresses a ritual of belonging to a network of relations: the ethos of munificence, which certain writers speak of, is enunciated with the same force, whether by a citizen of the town or of the country. Even the Pygmy populations of the forests in south Cameroon attribute these same kinds of meaning to it. According to D.V. Joiris, who has studied the Kola and Baka Pygmies, except in times of scarcity, meals are systematically shared among the families of the same encampment, even if they are not eaten together. Thus, at nightfall, the children move up and down the village with dishes that are distributed to parents and friends. Each family therefore consumes several dishes from different kitchens and practically no one is forced to be content with only one family dish. The fact of "being integrated into a network of exchange is supplemented by the relations of harmony specific to the representation of the individual".[9] The food consumed and the manner in which it is distributed within the group therefore constitute important aesthetic rituals of "civilisation".

   The collective infatuation with positions of power in which one can "eat" under-lines the importance of eating in societies experiencing want. Whether shortage exists or not, it is appropriate to remember first of all that cooking, and more general-ly habits of consumption, take place within a cultural, sometimes secular, but always dynamic, context. Rice, which today has emerged as the basic foodstuff of a large part of Sahelian Africa, was introduced there less than a century ago. Bread, which the Bantu populations of central Africa consume every day as if it were part of their most distant imagination, only dates back to the colonial period. As for whisky or champagne, which today are used to validate certain of the most important rituals

230

of African cosmogony,[10] their origins can easily be traced. The culinary identity of African societies, all of this shows, is as changeable as the societies themselves.

It is, moreover, possible to state that African societies have always afforded great importance to the art of enjoyment, deemed to be an essential component of the art of living. And just as they almost always strive to define themselves in relation to a certain kind of solidarity – even if this is merely a façade – it is logical that the picture of privileged consumption within these societies is one of celebrating life in the community and enabling each individual, if not to maintain a certain social status, at least to claim a specific position in the social order. "To eat well" and "to drink well" have always been at the heart of an aesthetic of pleasure and social epicurism found equally among the Sudanese as among the Bantu.

The aesthetics of the pleasure of the stomach is dependent both on the place and the moment of eating, as these are rarely fortuitous. Certainly, the poor and disadvantaged eat what they can, when they can – sometimes from public waste bins. But those who consider themselves neither poor nor disadvantaged tend to attribute increasing importance to the loci and rituals of food. As was the case with the French families of the 11th and 12th centuries studied by Duby,[11] table manners are taught in wealthy African families. In these families it is not appropriate to eat just anywhere in the family home, nor under just any conditions. For eating has much to say about the image that the family wishes to project of itself. The dining room is the most important room in the house because it is there that family identity is most completely expressed, and it is there that the dynamics of parent-child relations, nuclear and extended family, inhabitants and guests are brought out into the open. Human relations are *cruder* and more real there than in any other space.

Obviously, things are not the same in other societies. If we are to believe Borges, for example, the Japanese do not accord great importance to the place where meals are taken. Commenting on some errors of analysis in his own work *Historia universel de la infamia* (A Universal History of Infamy), Borges states: "I knew nothing about Japan and wrote, for example, about the dining room, the bedroom, curtains, all concepts alien to Japanese culture since, in Japan, the table is laid and the bed made anywhere."[12]

In other regions of the world, food communalism has sometimes been imposed because of harsh historic conditions. In Japan, for example, in the days following the defeat of the country in the Second World War, the authorities attempted to regulate the food market and food habits, not only by regulating the supply of food but by recommending that the population eat an "emergency diet" that would provide them with their daily ration of calories without lapsing into wastage. According to J. Dower:

231

Based on a research report by local army officials, the emperor's loyal subjects were encouraged to supplement their starch intake by introducing such items as acorns, grain husks, peanut shells, and sawdust to their household larder. For minerals, people were encouraged to introduce used tea-leaves and the seeds, blossoms, and leaves of roses to their diet. Protein deficiencies could be remedied by eating silkworm cocoons, worms, grasshoppers, mice, rats, moles, snails, snakes, or a powder made by drying the blood of cows, horses, and pigs.[13]

In the China of Mao Tse-tung, by contrast, the grand communal feasts imposed by the political authorities at the end of the 1950s, and served daily in the large communal dining halls, led to an unprecedented waste of the country's food resources, contributing to the great famine of 1959-1961 and resulting in the death of 15 to 43 million people, according to some sources.[14]

Today in Africa, communal meals have different meanings depending on the context in which they are organised. Those organised by charity organisations in refugee camps to fight against famine or against the consequences of civil war can obviously not be compared to those organised periodically by the inhabitants of a village or district in response to a customary ritual. The actors, the ceremony, the ingredients and the mystique of these meetings are not the same. In the very "ordinary" circumstances of everyday life in large African cities, a style of fraternisation and socialisation around the table is developing and warrants more attention. Wedding feasts, which are becoming increasingly ritualised in African urban elite circles, are aesthetic phenomena that deserve to be analysed.

Wedding feasts and the principle of pleasure

You have to have attended a banquet organised for one of the "grand" marriages in Douala, Cameroon, in recent years to understand eating as being symbolic of having and being. These marriages, which regularly monopolise the attention of all who are counted among the upper echelons of the private sector, of administration and of government, are generally held on Saturday evening and constitute the apotheosis of a celebration that sometimes lasts for several weeks. At the heart of the ritual is the grand wedding dinner, whose splendour, pomp and luxuriousness not only define the "success" or "failure" of the ceremony, but also the position that the married couple and their families mean to occupy in society.

When they do not invest most of their savings in these events, the families generally incur debts in order to organise these dinners, where one comes as much to see as to be seen and admired. Both the organisers and the guests thus prepare themselves well in advance. The venue is meticulously chosen to reflect the importance that the families concerned would like to attribute to themselves. The largest banquet halls

232

Fig. 2. Food from a banquet in Cameroon. Dishes include roast fish, salads, fried plantains, cassava, French bread and couscous.

in the country are booked – in Yaoundé, a wedding feast among the jet set is not considered "successful" unless it is held in a grandiose venue such as the Palais de Congrès or the Hilton Hotel, the most luxurious hotel in the country.

A detailed programme is generally planned for the evening, printed and distributed with the invitations to the marriage feast. As with official ceremonies, the programme generally gives the precise time of arrival of the different categories of guests and the sequence of events in respect of interventions to be made by invited personalities. The most prestigious guests are usually seated in an area specially reserved for them around the main table, where the married couple and their families will be seated. These guests usually consist of Minister So-and-So, General X, the local businessman or the most popular *feyman*[15] of the moment. Obviously, the prestige associated with each personality is solely dependent on his power of influence and his supposed financial wealth, and not on any recognised moral or social leadership.

Bridesmaids and pageboys, dressed in outfits specially designed for the occasion, receive the guests and lead them to the tables reserved for them. Each table may include a dozen or so Limoges porcelain place settings, Christofle cutlery for the classier weddings (for the guests to keep) as well as a selection of the best apéritifs. The banquet hall is often decorated in the colours of the family of the bride or bridegroom. Primacy is accorded to the family that is financially more comfortable, regardless of the usual considerations associated with tradition or lineage. In fact, in the preparations leading up to the grand ceremony, acrimonious negotiations take place between representatives of the two families to determine who will have the longest guest list and who will finance the principal events of the evening.

To imbue the event with the greatest possible weight, professional MCs (TV presenters, comedians and well-known artists) are sometimes recruited to enhance the splendour of the evening. The dinner is then accompanied by shows and playlets designed to entertain and relax the guests and extol the merits of the families involved in the marriage. Quite often, games of chance, like a lottery and other types of draws, are played during the course of the dinner to provide an opportunity for the distribution of gifts to some lucky guests.

The organisation of the meal is particularly rigorous and draws on the customs of French high society of yore. When the guests are seated – which generally takes several hours because they are always so numerous,[16] and arrive at various times between eight o'clock in the evening and one o'clock in the morning, regardless of the time indicated on the invitation – they are served an apéritif: beer, whisky or wine. Frequently, one of the families will have obtained a special order of French red wine or champagne, and have the family name printed on the labels. Thus you will find bottles of wine from Bordeaux bearing the name Château "Family X" and the date of the marriage.

234

The meal is a ritual with the stamp of solemnity. It starts with an *hors d'œuvre*, which bears no relation to local culinary customs or to the most popular culinary tastes, but which is eaten simply because of its prestige: smoked salmon, caviar and *pâté de foie gras* among high society; French salad with the most refined dressings. This is followed by the main course, of which there is always a great variety and quantity. French, Dutch or Swiss cheeses and desserts follow, the apotheosis being the famous wedding cake, specially created by the best *pâtissier* in the area, which is eaten with good French champagne.

Toasts and speeches form part of the ritual of the wedding dinner. At various times during the course of the evening, someone will take the floor, make a short speech, generally lauding the couple and their families, and not forgetting to crack jokes to relax the atmosphere. This unusual "dinner ballet" unfolds to the accompaniment of music. The choice of songs and other musical compositions at intervals during the meal is not fortuitous, having been the subject of particular attention. Often meetings are organised beforehand to plan the order in which musical compositions are to accompany the meal.

Very few of the guests invited to the wedding actually have any real affinity for classical music. But each of them recognises the importance attached to such a culture by those who believe themselves to have succeeded. They religiously allow themselves to be soothed by Mozart's adagios or Beethoven's concertos – Beethoven's ninth symphony is very popular since everyone knows that it is called "Ode to Joy". But these moments do not last very long: like intermittent and slightly tedious interludes that one is forced to tolerate because they are part of the accepted ritual, the classical music is interrupted at regular intervals by local songs. Without any transition, one moves from the sharpest *makossa,* to the most forceful *ndombolo,* to sophisticated classical music. Koffi Olomide cohabits peaceably with Beethoven. Like the character of Luis de Funès who cries out in the midst of a meal in the film *L'aile ou la cuisse* (*Wing or Thigh*): "No, not Wagner! Wagner is for dessert!", it is not unusual to hear the master of ceremonies calling out to the disc jockey: "Play some music for us to eat by! Something to give us appetite."

These organised wedding feasts are certainly the privilege of the urban jet set. But even if it is true that not everyone has the financial means for such extravagances, there are many in middle-class society who attempt to reproduce the same grand designs. This is why the Congolese novelist Sony Labou Tansi has so often caricatured the ferocious manner and propensity for orgies which characterise the African elite. In his posthumous work *L'autre monde* (The Other World), he depicts, in ferocious and jarring style, the collective need for social affirmation through what one consumes. This leads him to make extravagant extrapolations:

235

Fig. 3. Sarah Porter, *Market Day*, 2002, acrylic on canvas, 102cm x 76cm
Private Collection/Bridgeman Art Library

Someone entered the room, serving, on an immense silver platter, huge toads which continued to move under the mayonnaise; on the back of each toad were three red balls which had to be Djobanis peppers. The back legs were tied with the leaves of leeks; their mouths were stuffed with small bunches of parsley. You could see that the toads were still alive, but people were crunching them with evident pleasure [...] The waiter reached Bonnévaranchio. He presented the platter to him.

Bonnévaranchio saw in the red eyes of the toad before him what seemed to be a plea for mercy. He turned his head away and all the masks began to laugh. When the laughter had quietened down, a woman's voice invited him to eat. Bonnévaranchio shook his head. The voice insisted. He shook his head again.
– Then why did you come?

The others had already emptied three platters of toads; some were now licking their fingers. The waitresses (now Bonnévaranchio knew) were carrying immense platters of 'ladjina', eels, cat-snakes, which the people were eating.
– Eat, said the woman's voice.
– I'm not hungry, Bonnévaranchio said.
– Here we eat with pleasure and for pleasure.[17]

Obviously not all meals have the intensity and significance of a wedding dinner. But even when they are sober and banal, even when the menu is lacking in extravagance and the guests modest, feasts are often occasions to celebrate familiarity and friendliness, and to exalt the collective self. It is not only the middle levels of society which seize on the slightest excuse for a celebration and to organise generous meals to just within the limits of their means. The most disadvantaged families will not deprive themselves of rice or meat on feast days, nor of Flag, Cravattée, or 33 Export.[18]

Aesthetics and the social significance of taste

As with civilisations everywhere, in Africa certain flavours and tastes are associated with ethics and with moral sentiments. Whereas in the West what is "sweet", for example, has evoked moral judgements since the middle of the 17th century, south of the Sahara sweetness tends to evoke a certain form of candour and immaturity, even weakness and naïvety. These tastes and flavours are therefore "naturally" reserved for women or children. Generally, throughout sub-Saharan Africa, a woman worthy of the name may only consume alcohol in public if the drink is sweet. This is why, in the major African cities, women generally imbibe imported liqueur wines. Similarly, a well-brought-up minor would scandalise sensitive souls if he or she were to order liquor in a public place.

The taste for "strong" drinks (which is to be understood as the taste for "bitter" or "alcoholic" drinks, which include traditional or imported beer as well as local or exotic liquor such as whisky), is an expression of adherence to the positive values of solidity, virility, courage and stamina. "Strong" drink is generally consumed together with very spicy (hot) meals, for their part symbolic of strength and virility. This combination of "strong" and "hot" is a ritual which marks the transition to adulthood, the affirmation of indisputable virility, admission to the hall of the greats. When a woman shows too great a propensity to consume liquors and spicy foods, she is admired at the same time as she is feared and the virility of her companion questioned. In Cameroon, such a woman would be teased and her companion asked: "Who wears the pants in your house?"

Sparkling alcoholic drinks such as champagne disturb this social order because the sense of ceremony associated with them transcends these social categorisations and etiquettes. Everyone seems entitled to food and drink that celebrate the joy of living. By virtue of the principle of the democratisation of happiness, everyone is entitled, for example, to enjoy the good taste of champagne, which embodies this appetite for life – the cardinal value shared by all African societies. The sparkling bubbles seem to carry within them the pomp and splendour of a life that people would like to be as gay and dynamic as possible. The impetuous noise of the cork as it pops; the round of applause that greets it; the pure transparency of this refined alcohol – strong enough not to be drunk in one mouthful, mild enough not to make the guests tipsy after the first glass; the need to keep it at the appropriate temperature (for champagne has, of necessity, to be drunk well chilled): all of this forms part of an aesthetic and of a new ritualisation of taste.

This collective infatuation with the orgy of luxury does not prevent many citizens from cultivating another form of distinction by opting for atypical forms of behaviour. There are increasing numbers of vegetarians among the African executive classes – notably among those who have studied abroad. This is related to the fact that certain young executives embrace religious beliefs and practices that advocate this mode of life. Others, more ambitious, conform to these practices out of a desire to cultivate a pure and sober public image that will distinguish them from the masses. If being a vegetarian in Calcutta is nothing out of the ordinary, since it is customary among a large number of people there, in Dakar or Douala it represents an unusual chic, allowing a person to position him or herself in the collective imagination as the same category of mythical, vegetarian personality as Malcolm X or Mahatma Gandhi.

Conclusion

Eating in times of scarcity, in the bloody context of African countries, assumes a profoundly aesthetic significance. Certainly one eats to satisfy one's biological needs, but one also eats to respond to the demands of everyday survival, to express one's commitment to the struggle of life, to hold on to existence, to proclaim one's courage, to mark a small victory – provisional, yes, but victory nonetheless – against death, which prowls in the vicinity with the frenzy and patience of an angry debtor. Seen from this perspective, the *a priori* inconceivable attitude of the head of a poor family who spends most of his or her monthly savings in order to give his or her family a kilogram of meat, or of the young executive who celebrates with champagne, is easily explained: it is not simply the generalised desire for distinction as articulated by Bourdieu.[19] Over and above the principle of pleasure, which is an essential dimension of the art of living in sub-Saharan Africa, such choices are also the expression of the struggle against failure, against scarcity, against misery. By supplying the kilogram of meat not normally covered by his income, by "downing"[20] a bottle of Dom Perignon champagne when one does not, in principle, have the means for it, the ordinary citizen is heroically hoisting himself into the ranks of people he respects and admires. This apparently unreasonable act – if one is to judge according to the standards of financial rationalism – commands respect and admiration, not contempt. For beyond the apparent superficiality of the act, there is essentially a desire for self-affirmation and a need for the recognition of one's humanity. The message is clear: misery will not frustrate our dreams, nor our unquenchable quest for dignity and respect.

Françoise Vergès
Let's Cook!

Françoise Vergès is a lecturer at the Centre for Cultural
Studies, Goldsmiths College, London, and has written
extensively on slavery, Frantz Fanon, processes of creolisation, the formation of the Indian Ocean diaspora and the
politics of reparation and post-colonial theory. She is the
author of, amongst others, *Monsters and Revolutionaries –
Colonial Family Romance and Métissage* (1999). She is
currently completing research on Chinese restaurants in
African port cities. Her most recent work is on post-colonial
museography.

LET'S COOK!

Fig. 1. Cook, Beijing Restaurant, Dar-es-Salaam, Tanzania, August 2002
Photo: F. Vergès

It was summer in Réunion Island, the hot, tropical summer months. On the sidewalk, in front of the primary school, every afternoon, six to eight women set up small wobbling tables. They sat on stools in the shade. They were selling *jamblons* – small fruit with a dark, shiny skin which, when you eat them, give a dark purple colour to your tongue – with dry chilli drizzled on top. They also offered green mangoes which they cut on each side along the pip; they put salt and dry red chilli in the cuts with a knife, then closed the mango up again. After two minutes, the salt-chilli mix had dissolved into the mango's juice, giving the fruit a delicious taste. We could also choose coconut cakes, *bonbons piments* (fried purée of white beans mixed with saffron and green chillies) or bread with *achards* (vegetables cooked with saffron, onions and chillies). Going to school after the lunch break meant a stop at one of these women's tables. We always bought something because we loved this food. When we ate mangoes, we arrived in the classroom, our mouths dribbling, our eyes watery with the strength of the chilli. Our French teacher was appalled. She could not understand our pleasure: our lips and tongues burning with salt and chilli, unable to close our mouths for a bit, waiting for the burn to disappear.

Taste in food is a difficult thing to define. There is the influence of the culture into which we were born, of what we ate at the family table. There is the impact of the economy, since we do not eat exactly the same food if we are poor or wealthy. Add to this history and politics (slavery bringing sugar to Europe, colonialism bringing bananas, rice and corn to Europe), the expansion of commerce and the introduction of certain ingredients onto the shelves of supermarkets (tropical fruits in the West; wines outside of Europe), fashion (what is chic at a given moment), the development of take-aways, fads, the popularity of cookbooks, of chefs, of TV programmes, of travel (tasting new food), of immigration (bringing with it new recipes and ways of preparing food), of religious taboos and regulations. Add the idea of *haute cuisine*, of cuisine as a national characteristic, as a regional characteristic, as the sign of "*haute culture*," of "higher civilisation". Add the taste that we acquire through an education of the senses, the domain of the Eros of taste. These are the bits and pieces that reveal, like a recipe, the complexity of food and taste.

Eggplant: according to the dictionary, this vegetable's first name was *vatin-ganah* in Ancient Hindi, transformed into *badin-gan* in Persian, then *al-badinjan* in Arabic, *alberginia* in Catalán and *bringelle* in the Creole of Réunion. In Europe in the Middle Ages eggplant was known as *malum insanum,* or apple of the mad, because it was said to be dangerous to mental health. The Chinese had included it in their cuisine by 500 AD. It was cultivated and eaten in North Africa around the 9th century and was introduced in Europe quite late, at the end of the 17th century. To me, it is a vegetable invented by the gods of cooking. It can be sweet or bitter, its skin a yellow white or a deep purple. It can be cooked in so many different ways that entire books have been devoted to it.

243

244

Fig. 2. Beijing Restaurant, Dar-es-Salaam, Tanzania, August 2002
Photo: F. Vergès

Food is a territory in which we move throughout our lives, and one which we never leave. We might discover new regions beyond the borders we draw, though we like to return to our native territories of taste, names and memories. Even when people are fluent in a foreign language, they usually continue to name fruits and vegetables in their native language. For instance, I continue to use Creole terms for vegetables and fruit despite the fact that I know their names in French or English. When I see fruit such as *goyaviers*, mangoes, pineapples, I want to eat them as I ate them when I was a child, unripe and with salt and chilli.

You take two mangoes that are not ripe (but not too unripe either. They must be firm under the thumb), a pineapple (the kind called "Victoria" is the best of the best. It is cultivated in Mauritius and Réunion), two limes, a piece of fresh ginger (big as your thumb), fresh coriander, sugar (a tablespoon), salt (a teaspoon) and a small green chilli. You cut the fruits and the ginger in very, very thin slices. You press the limes on the slices of fruit and ginger, you mix in the sugar and the salt, then add the sliced green chilli and the leaves of the coriander. Mix well, put in the fridge for two hours and serve. You can serve it in the afternoon as a refreshment, or with rice and meat, or rice and fish.

A recipe reads like a sheet of music: the musician hears the melody when she reads the notes, the notes acquire a materiality, the processes are simultaneous – reading and hearing a melody that has not yet been played. The cook reads a recipe and smells, tastes the dish that is not yet done. The cook is like a musician, she works out a melody and, like the musician, adds a bit of collage and bricolage when she cooks.

Food is a marker of events in our lives. We remember the food we had at the first dinner with a soon-to-be lover (more so if we did not eat because we were *filled* with desire). We remember the taste that the body of our lover left on our tongue. We like to reminisce about the food of childhood. We grew up loving some food, yet we are often unable to convince our friends that that thing is just "great". At breakfast in Cape Town, a friend was delighted to find "Marmite" while the others thought it was an insult to taste. The moment we see that "thing" – Marmite, bread, mustard, rice, chutney – our senses are mobilised. We want it, regardless of what other people think. We do not think we *need* to share. My addiction to chilli is something I do not dream of sharing. I do not even want to exhibit my addiction. When I travel with my bottle of chilli, I sometimes hide it under the table and add chilli as discreetly as possible to my plate. I hate it when people want to try it and then spoil it because they get burned. Taste is tied to a complex blend of memories of family cooking, of forbidden food, of food discovered with friends, lovers. Our sentimental education of taste never ends.

246

Claude Lévi-Strauss, in his *Mythologies*, has argued that cooking is about putting an end to a natural process which transforms something raw (whether vegetable, fruit or meat) into something rotten. Cooking stops that natural process, intervenes

Cooking utensils, Reunion Island

Fig. 3. Street market, Maputo, Mozambique, July 2002
Photo: F. Vergès

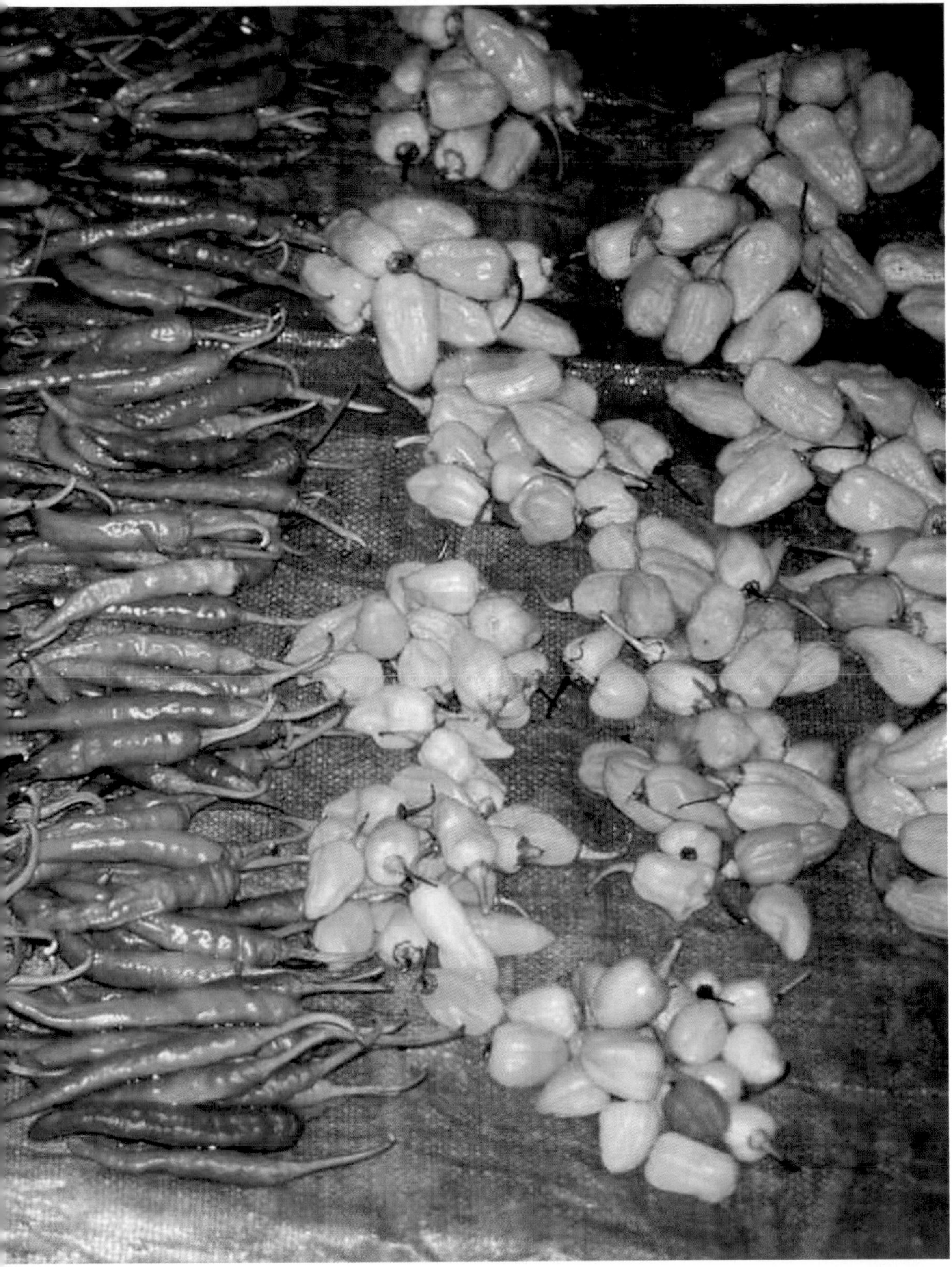

in nature. To clarify his point, Lévi-Strauss drew a triangle, the sides of which connect the three states of food, raw/cooked/rotten. Raw is the upper corner of the triangle and cooked and rotten at its base. In this culinary triangle, cooked is the *cultural* transformation of the raw, rotten the *natural* transformation of the raw. The culinary triangle is a semantic field which can be described only by the external observer. Indeed, it is the external observer who is able to situate the food of a group within the triangle, what is perceived as "raw", "cooked", "rotten". For the observed group, food is what it considers edible and tasty. For instance: to me, raw fish or cooked fish is not a "cultural" question but a question related to the kind of fish that is best when it's raw, of its freshness, of the availability of ingredients (lime, coconut milk, ginger, soy sauce, coriander) that I want to add. It will depend on my menu, on my guests (do they eat raw fish?). If it is a cooked dish, vegetables, meat, fish, it is not simply "cooked". I think about the entire process: how will I cook it? With what? How long? Cooking is about putting together a puzzle in which colours and ingredients construct a whole and complex picture. Cooking is a deeply aesthetic act.

Food is a territory on which history and politics fight their battles. Food has always been used as a weapon in wars, whether commercial or political wars. Man-made famines, prohibitive taxes on basic foodstuffs, destruction of crops, the imposition of a single crop, the conquest of land, the unequal distribution of land: one could write the history of a people, of a country, of a continent by writing the history of its culinary habits. Wars, migrations, commerce deeply affect what people eat and how they eat. One can write recipes of the age of embargoes and wars – people eating pets, rats, barely cooked food – or of the age of plenty – tables covered with sweets, fruit and spices. One can also observe the relation of food and the politics of water and land distribution. I remember crossing the border between Mexico and the state of New Mexico in the 1980s. In the mid-20th century, the US had diverted the Colorado River from its route (it no longer ended in the Sea of Cortèz but watered the states of New Mexico and California). On the US side, we saw green fields, while on the Mexico side, barren land. There is also the relation between food and the politics of gender – girls with no access to meat because it is reserved for young boys; women who cook but are the last to eat. So it is that we might map the world around territories of food and eating, economies of plenty and shortage. In particular, we might remap the cartographies of colonialism, particularly for Africa, with a vocabulary of cooking.

At the beginning of every year, sugar cane that had been harvested was brought to the factory to be processed. The smell of crushed burning canes was very strong. It was because of sugar that the island was colonised by the French. It was because of sugar that slaves were brought to Réunion Island. It was because of sugar that the island remained a colony. It is because of sugar that the soil has been impoverished, that lagoons today are polluted (pesticides are carried to the lagoons by the rivers).

Beautiful Ugly: African and Diaspora Aesthetics

Sugar put the island on the map. Now, it threatens to put the island on the margins of history. What do you do when sugar is your only source of revenue in a world in which so many other countries produce sugar with lower costs of production, in which other sources of sweetening food have been discovered? You eat food sweetened with the bitter sugar of your oppression.

The relationship between Africa and food brings forth a series of stereotypes and icons. One icon is the representation of the African continent as a body to be dismembered, swallowed, digested and discarded as waste. Another is that of a barren land. It is a continent of peasants, but there are few representations of the countryside as a cultivated space. In Europe, Asia and the Americas by contrast, images of fields, of rice paddies, of an "order", are constantly evoked. We could say that there exists no aesthetics of the African countryside, neither pastoral nor exotic.

A third icon is of a mother and her child dying of hunger. In Africa, it seems that there is no food, there is hunger and famine. It is a continent of deprivation and want. Africa becomes a continent on which cuisine is about the kind of food distributed by NGOs, bland and full of vitamins. We could write an NGO cookbook for Africa: an endless series of nutritive, dull recipes. Baby food for a continent represented as a hungry child, unable to feed itself and which must be force-fed by the West. The morbid side of such cooking cannot escape us. True, there was a famine, there is a famine, there will be a famine in Africa. States are unable or unwilling to stop the famine. The West must intervene with humanitarian aid and who are you to protest? I want simply to point to the deprivation of taste that the gesture of feeding "humanitarian" food entails. It is not just a detail. It participates in the exclusion of the African continent from the arts of cooking.

In the mid-18th century, a European travelling in Mozambique asked a group of slaves waiting to be taken aboard the slave ships what they thought awaited them. The slaves said: "They have bought us and they are taking us to the ship so they can eat us." The European asked them why they thought the whites would eat them and they answered: "Why would they hide us below the deck? This is where they cook us."

The encounter between Europe and Africa has been expressed in metaphors related to the process of cooking. Slaves were convinced that whites were cannibals. That belief, which was found along the coasts of Africa and Madagascar, said something about the imaginary relationship between enslavement and the culinary triangle of Lévi-Strauss. Cannibalism was a cooking process, made from slavery and colonialism. Being a slave was to be eaten as a human being below the deck and to be rejected as a thing on the shore of a colony. Enslaved Africans understood this. They understood that slavery was a process whereby they would no longer be humans. Whites were thought to be cannibals because what other impulse than the desire to devour would explain the act of capturing, branding, selling, buying a human being? The mouth of the cannibal was in Africa, its stomach was the ship, its anus the plan-

251

Fig. 4. Street market, Maputo, Mozambique, July 2002
Photo: F. Vergès

252

tation. The cuisine of European cannibalism was about the smell of burning flesh, the noise of the whip, the taste of bitter sugar. The colours of its dishes were the red of the blood, the black of the skin, the green of the sugar cane.

When the colonial conquest proper started in Africa, the metaphor of cannibalism was seized by the Europeans and turned against the Africans. Africans became the cannibals, eating the missionaries. The reversal of the metaphor of cannibalism spoke of the aggressivity, the violence of the Europeans projected onto the Africans. To return to the culinary triangle, the cook kills the animal and transforms what has been killed into food to be eaten. The cook transforms what is not edible into what is edible in an act of creativity. In the colonial culinary, the coloniser "cooks" the native to colonise her, to transform her into matter to be exploited.

Two kinds of "cooks" appear in colonial literature: the European cook transforming the native into a colonised person, the "raw" material into a "civilised" subject, and the native cook, always suspected of dealing in sorcery, of mixing food for evil purposes. The native cook had access to tools that kill (knives, hatchets), she knew about plants and she could poison the master. She was needed and feared. The cuisine was a territory over which the native had some control. It was a contested terrain of power on which battles around the rules of "good taste" and the purity of recipes were fought. The master wanted to replicate in the colony the "taste of Europe", to impose his ideas about the preparation of food. The native invented a cuisine, neither entirely native nor European. On the master's table, pale imitations of European food were served while, back in the cooking room, a new cuisine was invented.

On the islands of the Indian Ocean where Africa meets Asia, Islam and Europe to create a Creole society, the cuisine embodies trans-ethnic, trans-cultural processes and practices of creolisation. Creole cuisine forsakes purity. It is the cuisine of a society built on destruction and erasure. On the islands, not a single inhabitant was a native. Slavery and colonialism meant that languages, cultures, traditions had to survive as traces, palimpsests of what existed in the ancestors' country. Creativity was a matter of survival.

Creole cuisine is a hybrid. It has borrowed from every cuisine. It is not fusion food, which sounds like baby food, but a highly elaborated and sophisticated practice in which recipes from China, India, Europe, Africa and Madagascar are reworked and translated into a Creole way of cooking. What is Creole cooking then, if not fusion food? It is about an incredible attention to detail. It is not so much about putting together fruit and meat, fish and sauces. I often shudder when I read the translation of Creole recipes in French women's magazines. It seems that it is enough to mix coconut milk with tomatoes and chilli to make a curry! Creole cooking requires time and, as such, it can be compared to other cuisines; it is a cuisine that demands long preparation. It has been affected, as other cuisines, by the lack of time for preparation, by the need to eat fast, as well as by a certain "Americanisation" (for instance,

254

an "American" sandwich in Réunion is a piece of baguette with *bouchons* – a kind of Chinese dim sum – covered with mayonnaise and cheese and grilled. No comment). Meat or fish is always served with rice and vegetables, a *rougaïe* – cooked or raw vegetables or fresh fruit mixed with chilli and onions, and chilli with *combava*. There can be rice *and* potatoes. The food is served in a particular order which never changes: first the rice, then the meat or fish, then vegetables and on the side, *rougaïe* and chilli. It is a cuisine open to new ways of cooking, to new recipes. Creole cuisine is a practice of creolisation: imitation, appropriation, translation.

During the Réunion Island summer, fruit abounds: litchis, pineapples, mangoes, *coeur de boeuf*... Yet, what people await all year long is the arrival of *bichiques*, small alevins[1] that arrive from the sea and try to go up the rivers. Réunion people are crazy about *bichiques*, ready to pay extraordinary amounts of money to have a kilo of these beloved alevins. Sometimes, you run into huge traffic jams, cars stopped in the middle of the road, abandoned by their drivers because *bichiques* are sold along the road. It is known that people have braved hurricanes to fish for *bichiques*. One always knows someone who knows someone who can get you a kilo of *bichiques* when you are desperate. *Bichiques* awaken passion amongst Réunionnais. Food is about desire.

Cheryl-Ann Michael
On the Slipperiness of Food

Cheryl-Ann Michael is a lecturer in the Department of English at the University of the Western Cape, South Africa. She has studied at the universities of Natal and Cambridge. Her fields of interest are 19th- and 20th-century literature, including children's literature and the history and philosophy of language. She is co-editor, with Sarah Nuttall, of *Senses of Culture: South African Culture Studies* (2000).

ON THE SLIPPERINESS OF FOOD

The truth of the matter is that the cookery of every nation has borrowed freely, often with unblushing audacity, from that of every other nation, and that only where it has succeeded in impressing its own stamp on its cooking technique, by the practice of local methods and the employment of local foodstuffs, can it be said to have reached the level that merits a distinct territorial adjective.

C. Louis Leipoldt[1]

The essays in this collection variously point to, celebrate and reaffirm the making of African identities as an inevitably eclectic process. Célestin Monga reminds us that:

> ... it is appropriate to remember ... that cooking, and more generally habits of consumption take place within a cultural, sometimes secular, but always dynamic, context. Rice, which today has emerged as the basic foodstuff of a large part of Sahelian Africa, was introduced less than a century ago. Bread, which the Bantu populations of central Africa consume every day as if it were part of their most distant imagination, only dates back to the colonial period. ... The culinary identity of African societies, all of this shows, is as changeable as the societies themselves.

Françoise Vergès delights with a passionate celebration of the hybridity of Creole cooking. Some, like Pinho and Clarke, point to the problem of attempting to fix African identity into an identifiable "Africanness". Food, as a subject, presents a tricky problem. Rampant nationalists may claim it as symbolic, at the same time as it is celebrated as embodying cultural fusion. The danger of celebrating such fusions as triumphantly refusing the rigid construction of homogeneous identities, is that it is possible to overlook the ways in which such hybridities often mask the inequities of their own making. In C. Louis Leipoldt's *Cape Cookery,* we find the following anecdote: The Duke of Wellington, during a visit to the Cape, was frequently entertained by a wealthy Cape Town family whose cook "was a Coloured woman, the daughter of a Malay slave, who had been trained by a Mozambique cook. Her pastries, curries, *boboties*, *sosaties*, and fish dishes were renowned, and there is a legend that on occasion she was invited to show her skill at Government House, which had a white cook and stuck to French cookery".[2]

In Hildagonda Duckitt's *Hilda's Diary of a Cape Housekeeper* (first published in 1902), she describes the servants of relatives as "... emancipated slaves and their descendants. One charming Malay woman had been the nurse and was devoted to the family".[3] She occasionally refers to a recipe as "an old Malay speciality", but mostly the recipes are presented as "Cape food".[4] Both instances may be read in

Household cabinet, Durban, South Africa

terms of an emerging "Cape nationalism", which ambivalently insists on the acknowledgement from the metropole of the value of a distinct Cape culture. Here we have, seemingly, the centrality of Malay cuisine as a marker of this distinction. People of Malay descent, however, are curiously vague figures, scarcely visible despite, or perhaps because of, their food. Their food is, of course, not "theirs" here, since its hybrid transformations allow it to be invoked in early colonial bids for recognition – and by implication, the right to self-government in one instance – and as an element in the forging of a united "nation" of British and Afrikaner in the other. Duckitt's anxieties to this end are apparent: "We ... have always lived in a most cordial and happy way with both our English and Dutch relatives."[5] Learning the art of Cape cookery becomes a means of training "for those (both South African and colonist) who may one day have to direct others".[6] Yet the food itself eludes any simple regional labelling, insisting on many stories, like that of the daughter of a Malay slave, trained by a Mozambique cook ...

In this slipperiness of food as a cultural referent lies its value. Achille Mbembe (in this volume) notes that "In the Congo, words themselves always refer to a plurality of references. The things they designate are multiple and their significations structurally ambivalent." One might make the same claim for food. The word "slipperiness" itself is fitting, offering a slippage between literal and symbolic meanings. We need food to be "slippery" before we may comfortably digest and assimilate it as part of ourselves. Its symbolic slipperiness both allows and disavows fixity – any claim to a single referent, or to ownership.[7]

For me, food and food memories offer simultaneously a means of connection to particular places and people, and a refusal to limit these meanings to these particularities. In this slipperiness is beauty.

As a child I sometimes accompanied my grandmother on her monthly food shopping expeditions. In what used to be the old Indian business quarter of Durban, South Africa, there were, and still are, a number of old-fashioned (even then) grocers. Their shops, dark and musty, invited one away from the noisy streets and the glare of the sun. They were tiny spaces, crowded with sacks of rice from India with strange curly writing curving across the hessian, and tin bins of maroon, white and speckled beans. Scooping up a small handful and letting them trickle slowly back released a slightly dusty beany smell that mingled with the scent of other goods – camphor and incense for prayers, oils (sunflower, mustard and coconut), tea leaves, soaps and candles – and with the smell of the sunlit streets outside. The world had come to the local. The rice and beans, with every mouthful, were both satisfyingly here (Durban), and not here – the promise and allure of elsewhere. The blending of tea, Indian and Chinese, strong and delicate, was peculiarly my grandmother's, but also webbed out into the wider world. We drank travel.

My grandmother's *samp* (*mielies* or corn) and beans were cooked in a sauce with chillies, cumin, mustard seeds and curry leaves. We did not think of this as fusion

Cheryl-Ann Michael > On the Slipperiness of Food

between African and Indian food. It was simply *samp* and beans, unthinkable without the spices. She made *patha*, a savoury roll of the large leaves of the *madumbi* plant (whose roots when boiled are like knobbly, sticky potatoes), layered with spices and deep fried, to be served with *puri* (small, white, unleavened, flat bread) and lemon juice. The recipe is Indian, but I don't know what leaves would have been used originally. I know it only in its local version. *Patha* for me means both grandmother and Durban, yet India lurks on the margins of this association, refusing a plain Durbanness. In *Indian Delights*, a fascinating record of South African Indian food, the editors emphasise "thrift". The "thrifty housewife" adapts and improvises, using local ingredients.[8] "Thrift", like Scrooge, seems a death knell to exuberant hybridities. Another memory intervenes: of standing on a chair at the kitchen table helping to prepare pumpkin flowers. The flowers, a sunny orange-yellow, are wiped with a damp cloth, the pollen-dusty stamens carefully removed. Rolled in a light, spicy batter, they are quickly fried in hot oil, till the batter crisps and the flower inside melts slightly. Light, fragrant, with the surprising bite of chilli, pumpkin flowers seem far away from the workaday world of thrift. Yes, we have used all of the plant (the leaves stir-fried with mustard seeds are delicious), but thrift is too dour a word to encompass the richness of the idea of eating flowers. More fittingly, it becomes a tribute, a celebration of the pleasure and beauty of food and place.

I say Durban, and not South Africa, because these food memories are tied to a particular place, the local, and cannot be extended to include the national. In his essay "The Road to Brixton Market", Gabriel Gbadamosi notes that it is through food that local identities resonate beyond the national: "I love walking in a London street market because it's full of Londoners: Irish, West Indian, Indian, African and, among others, some English, too."[9] To insist on Durban in this regard does not speak of any simple regional allegiance. I have chosen to live in the Western Cape in preference to Durban. Yet in reflecting on food memories, it is clear that my notions of beauty in food are shaped by Durban. My horror at the thin, ashy grey soil of the Western Cape has to do with memories of my grandmother's garden in Durban, where vegetables grew in lush black soil. Is it possible, I wonder, with a strong inclination to the negative, to grow beautiful vegetables here? Will this soil not produce anaemic tomatoes and pale transparent coriander, so unlike the intense reds and vigourous, pungent greens of childhood memory? Beauty in food is intensity – it is subtropical. The Mediterranean falls short. A clear association of food with place? Only partly – since food memories accumulate associations, linking places through imagination or experience. I have cooked my grandmother's fish curry, with variations, on three continents. There is no authentic recipe any more than an original memory. Food memories are not neatly adjacent. Françoise Vergès writes of eating mangoes with chilli. Here we share a similar childhood food memory. Now, my memories of a Durban childhood where summers meant dipping slivers of green or ripe mangoes

262

in a mixture of chilli powder and salt, are tantalisingly linked to faraway Réunion, a strange and distant place made partially known. A new, composite, elusive beauty is made ... It is often through food that other places are made knowing-worthy. Wole Soyinka's *Aké*, his wonderfully food-saturated memoir of his childhood, has made Nigeria a beguiling place for me. He describes

> ... that rarest of delicacies – *leki* – made of crushed and skinned black-eyed beans and melon-seed oil, a teaspoonful of which, in the sharing, could cause week-long hostilities in the household.[10]

A people who flavour their beans with the fragrant oil made of melon seeds are worth knowing. Here beauty indulges the senses, with scent and the slow unfolding of the pleasures of taste and texture in a visual feast. I read with approving pleasure of Soyinka's mother's careful choice of a delicate and beautiful dish in which to serve the *leki*. Such a dish embodies finesse. It unsettles tedious stereotypes of Nigerian tricksters and Nigerian chaos, refusing them primacy. It traces a connection between my end of Africa and theirs through beauty, making their world both known and yet-to-be-known.

I am tempted by the idea of food as sharing, as an intimate means of connection between people, yet food memories slip the net of comfort, pointing to more disturbing possibilities. I remember my uncles and their friends chaffing in a colourful, hybrid slang about *roti ous*, and *porridge ous. Ou* is Afrikaans, here meaning "fellow", but carrying too the sense of the old, the familiar, the affectionately known. Linguistic divisions between Hindi and Tamil speakers are given food associations. People who speak Hindi supposedly eat *roti* (unleavened bread), while Tamil speakers are supposedly known for their propensity for a porridge made from fermented mealie meal, sometimes cooked with fresh chives. The linguistic divisions had largely fallen away. Most people we knew spoke English as their "home" language, yet the idea of difference remained, wrapped in food. I remember how these terms of affection sometimes slipped, in an instant, into contempt. The foods we all enjoyed could suddenly become markers of an irreducible difference. In the child's world, alarm lurks constantly. Where did I fit, in this world of *roti ous* and *porridge ous*, since I loved *roti*, warm and elastic with the addition of ghee (clarified butter), and never did acquire a taste for the sour fermented porridge? Was I a *porridge ou* by birth, if not by inclination, and possibly, treacherously, a *roti ou* by association? I hoped never to be asked to choose.

Food divisions feel wrong, yet they linger insistently. I thoroughly enjoy the nostalgic weaving of genres in J.K. Rowling's Harry Potter books. Why then, when I am amused by the harking back to old-fashioned school stories, am I irritated and disappointed by her food apartheid? In *Harry Potter and the Goblet of Fire*, we find the following scene in which Hogwarts (Harry's school) hosts two foreign wizarding schools:

263

… there was a greater variety of dishes … than Harry had ever seen, including several that were definitely foreign.

"What's *that*?" said Ron, pointing at a large dish of some sort of shell-fish stew that stood beside a large steak-and-kidney pudding.

"Bouillabaisse," said Hermione.

"Bless you," said Ron.

"It's *French*," said Hermione. "I had it on holiday, summer before last, it's very nice."

"I'll take your word for it," said Ron, helping himself to black pudding.[11]

If I accept that the Harry Potter books are not meant to reflect contemporary Britain with its vibrant mix of food cultures, why does this insistence on "English" food continue to annoy me? It is, of course, partly because this food segregation (its tongue-in-cheek gesturing to food-laden Anglo-French rivalries notwithstanding) is at odds with the eclectic cast of characters Rowling assembles. Perhaps more so, it is because it harks back to a tradition of food in books that made England strange. In Enid Blyton and *The Wind in the Willows*, and countless other books in that vein, I would read of an England of picnics with sandwiches made of cold tongue and spam. What was spam, and what could one make of a people who would willingly eat tongue, and perfidiously, on occasion, rabbit? Places are not simply *known about* through books, they are *known*, as intimately as the places one inhabits physically. English landscapes were as confidently mine as was the subtropical garden in which I played and read. The landscapes merged, the one calling up the other, twinned. Yet the problem of food remained. My father's explanation of post-war austerity soothed only partially. Entry to a culture is negotiated unquestionably through food. In the first of the Paddington Bear stories, the Browns meet the bear they will call Paddington in Paddington Station ("I haven't really got a name," he said. "Only a Peruvian one which no one can understand."). Paddington's strangeness is negotiated, mitigated, by his ability to speak English and his love of marmalade. The Browns invite him to live with them:

"Well, that's settled then," said Mrs Brown, before her husband could change his mind. "And you can have marmalade for breakfast every morning, and …" she tried hard to think of something else that bears might like.

"Every morning?" The bear looked as if it could hardly believe its ears. "I only had it on special occasions at home. Marmalade's very expensive in Darkest Peru."[12]

The world of books and the world of food are inextricably and deliciously linked. The best books are food-laden. My favourite passages in books are often those which include food. Characters become people when we want to share with them their experience of food. If England was the world of books, since this was where my books came from, was I shutting myself out of this world, or did it shut me out, through the food I found distasteful?

I was to find later that it was more than possible to live in England unpursued by spam, cold tongue or marmalade. My food memories of England are of sitting in warm kitchens, eating West African food for the first time – plantains, and chokingly spicy stews sticky with okra, and at last the many bean delicacies I had read about. They include learning to cook Chinese food (dumplings, most suited to the English climate) with new friends from Beijing, and eating a bewildering array of Sri Lankan food at an exuberant Christmas dinner. There are, it seems, foods that travel well, and then foods that come to mean a certain place, travelling uncomfortably, with resistance. I found some English foods to like. Puddings, uninteresting to me in books read in the heat of Durban, are now loved for their association with winter cold, when it is dark by three in the afternoon, and sticky treacle pudding offers a new kind of "home". Mangoes, on the other hand, eaten in England are not the same – they lack "mangoness", the scent of a certain kind of place. Perhaps, then, food divisions are only pernicious when they are other people's food divisions!

Nonetheless, it is the coming together of place and people through food that entices. One of my favourite restaurants in Cambridge, my local, was an Indian restaurant on Castle Hill. Legend has it that the ghost of Cromwell still gallops furiously down the hill, uncompromisingly bent on subduing Cambridge to his will. I have never met the ghost of Cromwell myself. I wonder whether this is because he has been routed by the strong smell of spices pervading Castle Hill, and has retreated to his secret corner of Sidney Sussex's garden where his skull lies buried safe from Royalist desecrators, to curse (with Puritanical restraint, of course) the advent of this new kind of Commonwealth, so different from the one he envisioned. I prefer, though, to think of him still galloping down Castle Hill, cloak flying, having grudgingly learnt to live with the whiff of elsewhere *here*.

Cheryl-Ann Michael > On the Slipperiness of Food

Patricia Pinho
Afro-Aesthetics in Brazil

Patricia Pinho is a Brazilian sociologist whose work deals with the themes of blackness, identities, racism and anti-racism. She is currently Visiting Assistant Professor of Black Studies at Amherst College (US), having spent 2002-2003 as a Visiting Lecturer at the Department of African American Studies and the Council on Latin American Studies at Yale University. Her most recent work focuses on African-American tourism in Brazil, analysing its impact on transnational black connections and the position of Brazil in the Black Atlantic world. Her PhD dissertation has been published as *Reinventions of Africa in Bahia* (2004).

AFRO-AESTHETICS IN BRAZIL

Fig. 1. An advertisement presenting a new trend in products for "treatment and maintenance" of hair. A good examp e of the vast variety of hair products that bear the term "Afro" in their label.

> The word [diaspora] comes closely associated with the idea of sowing seed. This etymological inheritance is a disputed legacy and a mixed blessing. It demands that we attempt to evaluate the significance of the scattering process against the supposed uniformity of that which has been scattered. Diaspora posits important tensions between here and there, then and now, between seed in the bag, the packet or the pocket and seed in the ground, the fruit or the body.[1]

This chapter examines the growing trend among Brazilian blacks who search for references to beauty in idealised images of African aesthetics as a way of confronting the continuous association of blackness with repulsiveness. The dominance of Eurocentric standards of beauty in the Brazilian media, and the cruel forms of racism that associate black bodies with ugliness, stench and criminality, have contributed to an ongoing stigma and sense of low self-esteem, especially among black youth. Afro-Brazilians, however, have defied such nefarious notions of blackness through a rich cultural production of aesthetic elements that refer to Africa, or to what Africa is believed to be. Plastic braids, synthetic dreadlocks, fabrics from India and Bali, together with locally produced jewelry and clothes, are just some of the elements used to invent an "Afro-aesthetics" in Brazil. This analysis addresses the issues of the visual, the tactile and the senses of smell and colour of the black body in a diasporic context, focusing on the ways through which Africanness and therefore "Africa" itself have been imagined in order to produce beauty and restore dignity. This process, while liberating, also carries its own risks and contradictions.

Inventing blackness and its inappropriateness

Observed from the outside, through the common images of carnival, samba and football that are divulged worldwide, Brazil is usually perceived as a black country. And in fact that's what we are. Besides having the largest black population outside of Africa, second only to Nigeria, Brazil is also known for its vibrant black culture, from which, in addition, the main symbols of our nationality are drawn: the spicy food with *dendê* oil, the frenetic musical rhythms guided by drums and the black bodies playing *capoeira* and dancing in the tropical landscapes of the postcards that divulge Brazil's image internationally. However, in spite of statistics that prove, and icons that celebrate, our blackness, a powerful and persistent Eurocentrism also permeates Brazilian society, determining and classifying, among other things, categories of beauty and ugliness.

The negative representations of blackness in Brazil can be traced back to the period of slavery. Brazil was the last country in the Western hemisphere to abolish slavery and one of the largest buyers of African slave labour in the world. Approximately 3.6 million African slaves were brought to Brazil between the second half of the 16th century and 1850, when the slave trade was officially (but not effectively) abolished. The legacy of slavery is evident, on the one hand, in the African presence that undeniably formed Brazil's rich hybrid culture, and on the other hand in a stock of striking racial inequalities and the perpetuation of vicious forms of racism.

The deterministic ideologies of the Portuguese colonisers, which associated characteristics of people to those of the land, contributed to the formation of current Brazilian racism. Later, 19th-century eugenicists maintained that each "race" occupied a different position on the scale of evolution, and that the characteristics of the body, such as skin colour, hair texture and facial features, corresponded to characteristics of the soul. In other words, bodily appearance determined one's personality. Black bodies were then associated with the evil of darkness or at least to a state of backwardness, and thick noses and lips were/are considered in Brazil as *grosseiros.* Significantly, the term refers at the same time to a "rough" physical appearance and to "rude" behaviour. Arthur de Gobineau, a French diplomat who spent 15 months in Rio de Janeiro in the late 19th century, commented on the appearance and behaviour of the local population: "It is a population that is absolutely mulatto, of vicious blood and vicious spirit, and horrifyingly ugly."[2]

The negative images historically associated with blackness weigh heavily on black people in a country like Brazil. In spite of its founding myth as a racial democracy, where cultural and racial miscegenation is celebrated as one of the main pillars of our national identity, there co-exists the notion that "interracial" breeding is a way of "improving the race" of the darker partner. Contrary to the concept of the "one-drop rule" that determines "hypo-descent" in the United States, in Brazil there is a belief that "white blood" can "whiten" the children of "interracial" couples, not only by making their skin lighter but, if nothing else, by offering them the possibility of having "less kinky" hair and finer facial features.[3]

But there are other ways of "whitening" the body in Brazil or, at least, of "taming" its black characteristics. The most common is to alter one's appearance, especially through straightening hair, a habit practised by large numbers of black women until the 1970s, when fundamental changes in black aesthetics started to occur. The desire for whitening the body, or "controlling" its blackness, is indicative of a need for acceptance in a society dominated by Eurocentric values. The term Eurocentrism refers here to the supremacy of white standards as "universal", the idea that "whiteness" is the norm, from which all other representations deviate. In the context of Brazil, Eurocentrism defines not only notions of beauty, but also how people of "deviant" phenotypes should be represented. Magazines, soap operas and commercial advertisements openly make different use of actors with white or black phenotypes, constantly counterposing white standards of beauty with negative and derogatory black images. Eurocentrism also shapes formal education in Brazil, still favouring the models inherited by Portuguese colonisation. Explicit examples include the celebration of the exoticism of blacks and Indians in the schools' calendars of festivities,[4] while they rarely appear as part of the everyday representations of life or of history.

In spite of the constant attempts to deny the existence of racism in Brazil, official census statistics continuously reveal the extent of our racial inequalities. The information on which groups are doing well in the job market, which have greater access to education, rates of unemployment and child mortality and other relevant figures, leave no doubt about the existence of racism in Brazil. There is also the less explicit, or, at least, less measurable dimension in which racism operates. The representations of blackness are overwhelmingly negative, and there are a significant number of stereotypes about blacks present in the everyday life, thoughts and actions of Brazilians.

The negative images of blackness that permeate Western popular culture originated in the 16th century, during the first encounters between the Europeans and the peoples they subjugated and colonised. In Europe, colonists represented Africa as a nebulous land, replete with magic and fetishism, and its inhabitants as monstrous and primitive creatures. The views of the continent and the representation of its people became inextricably linked. The enslavement of Africans, carried out in the colonies of both exploitation and settlement, fed Europe's imagination of Africa and its dwellers and, in fact, determined the emergence of what today we call "Africa", and of the heterogeneous groups since then labelled as "Africans".[5] Although the term "blackness" did not yet exist, its meanings originated within that historical context, indicating that "race" is originally a product of racism. This explains the inappropriateness attributed to the "black race", and as a result to blackness itself, as opposed to white standards of normalcy and appropriateness.

More than 300 years of slavery in Brazil was more than enough to reinforce and expand the negative images of blackness. Besides being considered ugly and rough, the black bodies of the slaves were associated with filth and stench. The expansion of soap production in the 19th century established new standards of personal hygiene among the upper classes, which further augmented the association of blackness with dirt and body odour. "Soap and cleaning rituals became central to the demarcation of body boundaries and the policing of social hierarchies."[6] If the new standards of body hygiene served class divides among whites, they defined degrees of humanity between masters and slaves. The smell of the slaves' bodies became a factor for classifying them closer to animals than to humans. In Brazil, the indigenous Tupi word "*catinga*"[7] became the main category to describe the body odour attributed to animals, Indians and blacks alike. A century after the abolition of slavery, this word lives on in present vocabulary and is still employed along with other negative categories to classify black bodies.

The need to dissociate blackness from filth and stench was one of the main concerns of the most important Brazilian black association of the 1930s, the *Frente Negra*

Brasileira. Struggling to create a new and more positive image for blacks, the leaders of the *Frente* maintained that it was the duty of blacks themselves to overcome their "tendency" towards alcoholism and laziness, and to make an effort to look suitable for the job market. Based on the ideal of integration, the *Frentenegrinos* encouraged their peers to take on a "good appearance", which included dressing in "social clothes" – a Brazilian denomination for formal dress – and looking tidy and clean. The new look also required very short hair for men and iron-straightened hair for women, giving the impression of tidiness and hygiene. Caring about one's body odour played an essential role in maintaining a clean appearance, by controlling the supposed "natural tendency" of the black body to smell bad.

Although many decades have passed since then, the expression "*boa aparência*" is still used in Brazil in job ads that seek candidates with a "good appearance", usually a euphemism for the preference for hiring whites. For the jobs in which blacks are more numerous, such as maids, a position mainly occupied by black women, the employers require body hygiene (*asseio*) as the key criteria for hiring. For the *patroas* – the female employers of the maids – it is indispensable that they have a "clean appearance", which usually entails straightened hair and an "adequate" body odour. Sometimes even teeth and fingernails are discreetly examined before the candidate is "approved".

The prejudice towards the supposed smell of the black body has resulted in a constant feeling of discomfort and vigilance by many black people who struggle daily with the need to keep their bodies "clean" (*asseado*) and "smelling good" in order to counteract the stereotype that blacks have *catinga*. Responding to this fear, many black people take excessive care of their bodies, making diligent efforts to keep a tidy appearance and a constant smell of cleanliness. This personal patrolling includes avoiding the appearance of sweat marks, especially close to the underarms, and obliges many people to wear an extra T-shirt under the clothes in spite of the discomfort of doing so in a hot climate. Racism operates in this context in such a perverse manner that it obliges its victims to adapt their bodies to standards of cleanliness that are humanly unfeasible, and therefore inhuman. Underneath the vigilant control of one's smell and appearance lies a strategy to avoid the repugnance that other people may express towards one's body. Commenting on this, a young Brazilian black woman stated: "I try not to give an impression of untidiness, because, for me, the worst kind of racism is in the gaze. It is in the gaze that you realise that someone is staring at you with disgust."[8]

The act of staring can have a demeaning effect on those whose appearance is deemed inappropriate. It can reveal an expression of reproach towards something or someone considered repulsive. Contrary to Elaine Scarry's argument, staring is not necessarily an expression of awe towards the encounter with beauty. The gaze can indeed reify, and turn people – who are marked by specific phenotype – into objects of repulsiveness. Instead of a mere "wish to create" and reproduce the beautiful

Beautiful Ugly: African and Diaspora Aesthetics

AFRO BELA

O único permanente com extrato de frutas tropicais

Porque o seu cabelo merece mais suavidade...

273

Rossini Heine Ind. Com. Ltda.
Rua Juliana, 626 CEP 26226-080 Rio de Janeiro
PABX (021) 796 0752 TELEFAX (021) 796 2517
Representantes em todo o Brasil

displays hair products on a straw mat, probably to strengthen the notion of a "tropical" hairstyle

object of the gaze, the act of staring can be an expression of disgust. There are many ways of, and many reasons for, staring. And it is an act loaded with power. Of course there is a dialectical relation between the person who stares and she or he who is stared at. But finding someone beautiful, or rebuking someone's ugliness, is much more a consequence of the cultural classification of the person who stares, than of that who is stared at. Besides, the person who is stared at does not have the choice of doing so, as has the person who stares.

The need to maintain a tidy appearance is a strategy, especially amongst black males, to avoid being "stared at" by the police, that is, to prevent racial profiling. Like many other countries of the African diaspora, Brazil is no exception when it comes to correlating the dark phenotype with suspicion. Due to striking racial and social inequalities, and to strong doses of racism, the black body in Brazil became a cipher of dishonesty, obliging many people to minimise the threat that their appearance represents. Commenting on racial profiling, a young black man from Bahia explained how he avoided police harassment by adopting a tidy appearance: "I always try to look neat, and I keep telling my younger brother to do the same. As blacks we are already discriminated [against]. So why should we make that worse by walking around in flip-flops, or with no T-shirt on?"[9] Again, racism operates in a way that requires the victims to adjust to the imposed standards of normalcy.

These instances of racism, many with more severe consequences, can be found in other places of the black diaspora. In the US, for example, the figure of the *Bad Buck* is constantly represented in the movies, reinforcing the stereotype of the strong, violent black man who is always a potential rapist.[10] The commercial media in most countries is one the biggest culprits when it comes to the diffusion of negative images of blackness. If nothing else, television shows and magazine commercials contribute greatly to the absence or under-representation of blacks. Brazil's popular soap operas are filled with blue-eyed white actors who play the protagonists and represent the ideals of Eurocentric beauty, while the black actors usually play the secondary and undervalued roles of maids, slaves, subservient employees or threatening thieves and murderers. As a response to the demands of black organisations, Rede Globo, Brazil's main TV network, broadcast a soap opera that had black actors playing the key roles.[11] However, the show did not initiate a deeper transformation in Brazilian media as many expected. Instead, it became an exception to the rule. The percentage of black actors on television continues to be strikingly small, especially if compared to the proportion of blacks in the Brazilian population.

Within standards of white beauty, there is also a hierarchy that places blond hair and blue eyes at the top, as very rare and valued features. The three main TV shows for children in Brazil have blonde women with very thin features as hosts. Xuxa, Angelica and Eliana, three young, physically fit, blonde women, dressed in provocative clothes, host their shows at almost the same time, competing for child audiences.

Besides setting the new trends in clothes, make-up, hairstyling and even music and dance, these shows continuously establish the standards of feminine beauty in Brazil. All three of them commercialise their own names on brands that sell dolls, perfumes, lipsticks and other objects "for girls". But, most of all, these women are icons of beauty for the children and teenagers that watch them, especially the girls who buy their products in an effort to imitate their clothes and hairstyle, and possibly their beauty. Girls with dark skin and kinky hair make an extraordinary effort to replicate an unachievable ideal of beauty, which commonly leads to frustration and self-rejection. As a way of avoiding the accusation that her program doesn't hire black artists, Xuxa's production staff ascribed a secondary, but very visible role, to a young black dancer named Adriana Bombom. As her name suggests, Bombom is supposed to be as "appetising" as a chocolate candy, which explains her erotic dancing, and the miniscule shorts and tops that (un)cover her sculpted black body. It is certainly questionable whether this is a better reference for black girls. But it's undeniable that her presence in the program has helped to sell the products of Xuxa's most recently explored niche: cosmetics for "ethnic hair". These products are advertised during one of the most popular parts of her show, in which a stylist "transforms" one of the girls in the audience into a "beauty princess". Not surprisingly, this is called *momento transformação*", and, predictably, girls with kinky hair are transformed into girls with straightened hair in order to "become beautiful".

In very contradictory terms, the standard of white beauty is hegemonic even in the moment of Brazilian Carnival, nowadays considered the "reign of black culture", and therefore of black bodies believed to be the repositories of that culture. Racism acts in paradoxical ways in the carnival of Salvador, capital of Bahia, which is regarded as "the most African piece of Brazil". In spite of its predominantly black population and the exhilarating black musical rhythms that prevail in Bahia's street carnival, strong racial discrimination takes place, and its defenders use aesthetic grounds to justify it. Arguing that they are seeking to have only *gente bonita*" (beautiful people) amongst their members, the directors of many carnival groups, the so-called *"blocos de trio"*,[12] discriminate against those they describe as "ugly people", which includes the majority of blacks, and to a lesser extent, overweight women. In order to participate in such a group it is necessary to fill out an application form and attach a personal colour photograph. Because of this requirement, the *blocos* have been denounced for "racial, aesthetical and geographical discrimination", according to the reports of the Parliamentary Commission of Inquiry established in 1999 by a Green Party council to investigate racism in the carnival of Bahia.[13]

The attempts to ban the participation of blacks in the carnival of Bahia have a long history that can be traced back to the late 19th century. The first black groups to parade in the streets of Bahia during Carnival, which portrayed elements referring to Africa, suffered an aggressive campaign from the local press and were victims of brutal

276

Fig. 3. This advertisement emphasises the "brightness" and "lightness" of hair treated with these products. The undulating heading, which follows the shape of hair in movement, implies the possibility of having wavy, weightless hair.

police repression, on the grounds that they were threatening "civilised" European standards through an "Africanisation" of Bahia. The repression towards groups such as Pandegos d'Africa, Embaixada Africana, and all forms of Afro-Brazilian cultural expression was justified on the basis of their "ugly", "savage" and inappropriate appearance, which presented a hazard to the attempts to create a "refined" and "elegant" celebration modelled on the carnivals of Paris and Venice.

Reinventing blackness and its beauty

As a response to the racial-aesthetic discrimination that has historically permeated Bahia's carnival, in 1974 a group of blacks whose participation had been rejected by one of the carnival groups founded their own *bloco*, one in which only people with very dark skin would be allowed to participate. The group was called Ilê Aiyê, and it was the first *bloco afro* created within a context marked by the arrival in Brazil of new and intense aesthetic references set by the *Black is Beautiful* movement, and by the soul music that since the 1960s had served as a powerful soundtrack for the civil rights movement.

In his influential book, *The Black Atlantic*, Paul Gilroy elucidated the ways in which elements of black politics and aesthetics constantly travel amongst black communities, and are detached from their local origins and re-elaborated in the new contexts. The adaptation of the styles, rhetoric and moral authority of black objects, rhythms and symbols are facilitated by common backgrounds marked by the shared experiences of slavery, similar, although not identical, forms of racial discrimination and by a general legacy of Africanisms. Disconnected from their original conditions, the elements of this African-American culture nurtured a new metaphysics of blackness elaborated in public spaces through an expressive culture dominated by music. The political language of citizenship, racial justice and equality became one of the narratives of transference of political and cultural forms throughout the Black Atlantic, contributing to the formation of black cultures that are much more the result of vibrant diasporic interchanges than a mere consequence of static African cultural survivals.[14]

Many other *blocos afro* were founded in the 1970s leading to the "re-Africanisation" of Bahia's carnival by divulging a wide range of diasporic Afro-aesthetic elements, such as braids, dreadlocks, colourful clothes and jewellery made of seashells and woven straws/fibres. This production of black symbols belongs to a wider context that can be traced back to the 1970s when the African revival in African-American culture, inspired by the publishing of Alex Haley's *Roots*, and a general feeling of the need to build an ethnic past, disseminated symbols of Africanness throughout many other black communities around the Atlantic. African maps were drawn on clothes and ornaments, and new hairstyles, inspired by an imaginary African aesthetics, became important elements in the public demonstration of identity and pride.

277

Following the ideals of beauty initiated by Stokely Carmichael and other mentors of the *Black is Beautiful* movement, the transformation of previously negative attributes of the black body such as dark skin and kinky hair into positive ones was certainly one of the main characteristics inaugurated by this movement that also sought to elevate self-esteem and confer pride on racially oppressed people.

As happened with their peers from the late 19th century, the *blocos afro* were initially condemned by the local press for portraying an image of exclusive blackness, although this time the justification for its censure was based on the argument that these groups were taking a separatist attitude that could threaten Brazil's racial democracy. However, the original unease caused by the *blocos afro* was converted into quiet complacency as they became an important part of the cultural landscape of "black Bahia". The boom of the samba-reggae rhythm created by *bloco afro* Olodum,[15] coupled with the clientelist relationship established between these *afro* groups and the state government, helped attract an even bigger number of tourists and consolidated the image of Bahia as a place where blackness is tirelessly celebrated.

Nevertheless, the impact of this movement was extremely important among blacks in Brazil, and added to local cultural creations in the struggle against the hegemonic, excluding standards of beauty. Although at first black cultural organisations sought to defeat racism within the sphere of Carnival, the results of their cultural production surpassed the boundaries of entertainment, producing a new Afro-aesthetics that was adopted by many black people in Brazil as part of their daily lives. This brought significant changes in the bigger cities. People started wearing more colourful clothes, matching bright yellow with vibrant red and green, composing colors in a way previously considered tacky. Many women stopped ironing their hair, assuming sophisticated "Afro-looking" hairstyles, while a large number of men adopted dreadlocks. Because they were associated with an ideal of how Africans dress and style their hair, these elements were used to confer *Africanness* in Brazil, and therefore became essential for the composition of an Afro-aesthetics in a diasporic context.

Black activists and cultural producers employ the term "Afro-aesthetics" to describe a wide range of elements that are created to produce beauty, in particular to bring into existence a very specific kind of *black beauty* based on an ideal of Africanness. I take Afro-aesthetics as both constituent and constitutive of Africanness, and engendered within the continuous process of imagining and reinventing "Africa" itself. The prefix "Afro" has gained a growing importance among blacks in Brazil. Notably, it is employed as an adjective to describe objects that are believed to be loaded with Africanness. Thus one can speak of *roupa afro* (Afro clothes), *maquiagem afro* (Afro make-up), *cabelo afro* (Afro hairstyle in general), *permanente afro* (a curly hairstyle achieved through a chemical process), *artesanato afro* (Afro handicraft) and *bijuteria afro* (Afro jewellery); more recently, it is possible to speak even of Afro-nails, which are artificial nails made of plastic that can be glued to one's natural nails. What makes these nails "Afro" is the fact that they are very colourful and have geometrical patterns that "seem" African.

The Africanness of the objects that are considered "Afro" in Brazil is conferred on the basis of impression and intuition, independent of *where* or *how* these objects were produced. What matters is the meaning of Africanness that is attributed to these objects. The term "Afro" is therefore used to determine those things that, in spite of being created outside of the African continent, have the purpose of referring to Africa, or to what Africa is believed to be. If Africanness is defined on the grounds of impression, the same can be said of how Africa is imagined and recreated for the purpose of creating Africanness and the elements that compose its beauty.

In the same way, plastic braids, synthetic dreadlocks and fabrics imported from India and Bali may seem very African-looking and can therefore be used as symbols of Africanness, composing, together with locally produced ornaments, the elements that form and inform Brazil's "Afro-aesthetics". Amongst all the objects that compose this aesthetics the most popular are those used to style the hair. Besides the artificial extensions that can be weaved into the natural hair, a substantial number of creams carrying the word "Afro" on their labels are sold in the Brazilian market (figs 1-4). As a result of the success of Afro-aesthetics, the market has invested in labelling shampoos, conditioners, humidifiers, moisturisers and even more aggressive chemical treatments under the term "Afro".[16] An important channel of publicity of these products is *Revista Raça*, one of the rare magazines geared to a young black public in Brazil. Besides advertising the products, the magazine carries frequent features on Afro-hairstyling.

A curious fact within the tendency of labelling everything with the term "Afro" is that the so-called "Afro" hairstyle that represented the main symbol of the newly born Afro-aesthetics of the 1960s in the US did not gain the same designation in Brazil, where it is called "Black Power hair", certainly a homage to that historical moment. The lyrics of the first of Ilê Aiyê's songs to become well known in Brazil go like this: "*Somos criolos doidos, somos bem legal. Temos cabelo duro, somos black pau.*" (We're crazy blacks, we're really great. We've got kinky hair, we're Black Power.) Commenting on how history can be intentionally inscribed on the hair, Mariane Ferme describes how plaiting is associated with historical moments in Mende culture in Sierra Leone: "Hair weaving was more responsive to changes in style and technology (synthetic extensions, chemical products and other hair-straightening gadgets, and decorative additions such as beads) than the other forms of weaving. It inscribed the history of the moment on women's bodies, as styles took on the name of events or popular icons on the national or even global scene."[17]

Undoubtedly, the importance of hair as a signal of beauty or ugliness is not exclusive to Brazil, nor is the association of blackness with repulsiveness. The

279

280

Fig.4. This advertisement affirms that "Afro" products are for women who "place a lot of value in their hair". The pictures indicate that an "Afro-perm" hairstyle is suitable for both formal and informal settings

conflation of blackness with ugliness was to be found in most colonies in which Africans were enslaved. Besides attributing negative meaning to the dark colour of the skin, Eurocentric standards counterposed the kinky "bad hair" to the "good hair" of whites. Significantly, the expressions "bad hair" and "good hair" can be found in the African continent and in many other places of the diaspora, such as Jamaica and the US. In an article that discusses hair politics in South Africa, Zimitri Erasmus explains that in most coloured communities, "good hair" means straight hair, either naturally straight or straightened by iron or chemical processes.[18] So, in South Africa, it is possible to turn "bad hair" into "good hair". In Brazil, on the contrary, the act of straightening the hair does not turn it into "good hair", but instead, is proof that one's hair is "bad", or "hard" (*duro*), exactly because it needs straightening. As opposed to South Africa, the process in Brazil does not have the power of making the hair "good", but – like in South Africa – makes the hair "done". Straightening reveals the effort to achieve a more "appropriate appearance" by looking tidy through "taming" the blackness of the hair.

The appearance of dreadlocks in Jamaica is one of the most famous examples of the creation of a new aesthetic reference for inverting the negative meanings of the kinky hair. Rastafarians defied the dominant system through cultivating long and "dreadful" locks, challenging at once the idea that men's hair and "bad hair" should be cut short, and expressing that what is ugly for the Babylon system is beautiful for Rastafarian philosophy. In Brazil, dreadlocks became an important component of Afro-aesthetics. Together with other Jamaican symbols, such as the national colours and Bob Marley's face stamped on a great number of T-shirts, dreadlocks became a symbol of Africanness. Although they did not originate in the African continent, these Jamaican signs of blackness are perceived to be filled with Africanness, therefore confirming the Afro-Atlantic composition disseminated to imagine and invent "Africa".

The Black Power movement in the US also used hairstyling as a powerful symbol of rebelliousness, inaugurating big round-shaped hair known as "Afros". Displayed by men and women alike, these hairstyles created a whole new aesthetics of black beauty that surpassed the country and travelled through the routes of the Black Atlantic, arriving on new shores. In Brazil, these aesthetic elements intermixed, in the late 1960s and early 1970s, with a local tendency amongst black activists and cultural producers to seek in the emergent African nations elements that would represent pride and dignity for Afro-descendants. The difficulty in determining which African nations or ethnicities should serve as cultural references for the creation of a new Afro-aesthetics dissolved into creative doses of selection, blending and invention of the elements that could produce beauty.

As a product of exchanges of thoughts, objects and symbols across the Black Atlantic, Afro-aesthetics in Brazil is constantly recreated. While elements originating in Jamaica, the US and the African continent feed Brazilian Afro-aesthetics,

Brazil simultaneously feeds the black production of beauty for some African-Americans. In addition to its legacy of old "Africanisms", Brazil has been exporting newer forms of blackness, especially represented through its Afro-aesthetics. Due to its famous African cultural inheritance, Bahia has been receiving a growing number of African-American tourists who travel to Brazil, amongst other places of the African diaspora, aiming to find what they believe to be their African roots. The movement of people contributes to the movement of objects and ideas. When African-American tourists arrive in Brazil, seeking to enhance their blackness through the "Africanness" of Brazilian blacks, they are also exposing their own forms of "Africanness" to local people. Therefore, African-American "roots tourism" also informs the creation of Afro-aesthetics in Brazil, representing a very updated source of reference for the exchange and production of black objects. On the one hand, the presence of African-American tourists serves as a "shop window" for "Afro" clothes, jewellery and hairstyles for Brazilian blacks. On the other hand, local artisans produce clothes and jewellery (bracelets, earrings, necklaces, etc.) inspired by an "Afro" theme, since they have observed the willingness of these tourists to search and pay for all forms of Africanness.

Although initiated by activists, Afro-aesthetics in Brazil surpassed the boundaries of the black social movement, becoming a major reference point for many blacks. Of course, it is not possible to make generalised assumptions: not all blacks in Brazil have adopted these new elements in their dress or hairstyle. The adoption of Afro-aesthetics varies according to factors such as age, region and political engagement with the black social movement. While elderly black people feel more comfortable dressing in more conservative ways, black teenagers commonly combine elements of Afro-aesthetics – inaugurated by a previous generation now in their fifties – with updated and globalised fashion trends. Dreadlocked boys use recent hip-hop style baggy pants, while girls wearing long plastic braids match their low-waist boot-cut pants with Afro-style colourful blouses.

Blacks in Bahia are much more likely to embrace Afro-aesthetics than they are, for example, in São Paulo. Recent governmental efforts have led to the establishment of a black official image for the state of Bahia. Although this was done much more for the sake of tourism and for electoral purposes than to combat racism effectively, the resulting association of "Bahian-ness" with blackness plays a role in the acceptance of Afro-aesthetics. In contrast, the image of São Paulo is not so favourable for the dissemination of Afro-aesthetics, since it is commonly associated with work and seriousness, and is frequently opposed to the playful conception of black Bahia, which, not coincidently, is a mixture of leisure, pleasure and laziness.[19]

However, it is important to point out that even in Bahia there are different levels of acceptance in relation to Afro-aesthetics. It is acceptable to have braids or dread-locks and to wear colourful Afro-clothes and handcrafted jewellery in the sphere of leisure, or if one works in the realms of culture and tourism, or maybe in the more liberal atmospheres of some NGOs. But for those who work in banks, schools and official institutions, the norms of "good appearance" require a more conservative look, making the braids, the colours and the big earrings seem "out of place". Therefore, the "appropriateness" of Afro aesthetics in Brazil is determined by its connection with exoticism and leisure, within a hierarchy of standards that places work and "normalcy" at the top.

Another important factor leading to the adoption of Afro-aesthetics, but one that does not depend on region, is black political activism. Those who are more concerned with reinforcing their racial/ethnic identity are more likely to take on the diacritical characteristics offered by the wide range of elements making up Afro-aesthetics. In this sense, besides creating beauty, Afro-aesthetics is also a realm for protesting racism and displaying "black consciousness". In Brazil, the slogan "to become black" ("*tornar-se negro*") represents the need to gain awareness of one's black identity by assuming an attitude of pride towards an African inheritance, and refuting the dishonour associated with blackness. The creation of an Afro-aesthetics in Brazil, as well as in other communities within the black Atlantic, is a major component of the movement through which blacks took control of the production of blackness.

The beauty in producing blackness

The pejorative concepts associated with blackness, and the definition of standards of beauty and normalcy that are unachievable for those of the black phenotype, cause great psychological and emotional damage, especially in children and youth. Recent research has demonstrated the harm these racist standards have on the self-image of black people in Brazil.[20] As shown in the work of Ronilda Ribeiro, the unfeasibility of achieving an impossible "white" beauty affects more than one's self-esteem, and has negative social effects as well. "The obligations of defining an impossible ideal for the reality of one's own body and one's personal and ethnic history, leads to an unfavourable self-image and a humiliated self-esteem ... If this relationship is conflicting, rigid and stereotyped, it will tend to build a distorted self-image that will seek refuge from its physical reality and stimulate mechanisms of negation and compensation that are incompatible with projects of personal and social fulfilment."[21]

In response to a "universal" white standard of beauty, a transnational black aesthetics emerged, feeding the production of counter-discourses of blackness elaborated by blacks themselves. This became a political position for confronting collective imaginaries that had confined blacks to stereotypes and by creating new narratives to be told in the public sphere. The production of an Afro-aesthetics in Brazil, therefore, arose within a wider movement of self-affirmation by blacks in many other parts of the world. Adopting a new Afro-referenced look plays an important role in

POR CARLA NASCIMEN

Cuidando dos cachos

Formulada especificamente para o tratamento de cabelos crespos, a linha Hidrasil é composta por xampu, condicionador, creme sem enxágüe e hidratante capilar. Todos à base de silicone e com preços bem populares. Além de reduzir o volume, eles proporcionam mais brilho aos fios.

O vitaminado

Sabe aquele brilho e vivacidade da cor dignos de quem faz tintura no salão? Pois é, agora você pode mantê-los com Powerdose, da L'Oréal. À base de vitamina E, ele prolonga os efeitos obtidos nos cabelos tinturados. Uma aplicação dura até quinze dias ou seis lavagens e a ampola custa R$ 3,20 cada uma.

Você sabia que...

Para controlar o volume dos penteados estilo rastafári basta usar pomadas à base de água ou fazer manutenção no salão a cada dois meses?

Festival de estilos

A linha de styling, da Redken, traz opções para você dar o efeito que quiser em seu penteado.

EFEITO	PRODUTO	PREÇO
Brilho instantâneo	Complexo Suavizante Glass	R$ 28
Desestruturado	Creme de Definição Suave Undone	R$ 39
Mechas e cachos	Pomada à Base de Água Water Wax	R$ 30
	Mousse de Modelagem Touch Control	R$ 30
	Loção de Modelagem Contour	R$ 27

Brilho, Volume & Maciez

Inspirada nos elementos da natureza, Universal, a nova linha de xampus e condicionadores de O Boticário, é indicada para uso freqüente e todos os tipos de cabelo. Quem quer fios mais fortes e brilhantes deve usar xampu e condicionador à base de algas marinhas e aloe vera. Os que buscam mais volume devem lançar mão dos produtos à base de extrato de ginseng e D-pantenol. Para os fios macios e soltinhos o ideal são as embalagens com extratos de algodão e proteínas da seda.

FOTOS: DINIS GAÇÃO

CONSULTORIA: ANA PAULA CATARINA, CABELEIREIRA DO ETNIA E BELEZA: TEL. (011) 214-1082
ERON ARAÚJO, CABELEIREIRO DO SPETTACOLO SALLONE TEL. (011) 535-5757

284

Fig. 5. "Good Hair" ("Cabelo Bom"): a column from the magazine Revista Raça. The feature explains how to take good care of locks "in the Rastafarian style" in order to maintain their "neat appearance" (this evidently alters the original significance the rebellious "dreadful locks" had for Rastafarians)

the process of producing beauty and dignity. Although the changes in self-image may seem superficial, their meaning goes beyond the mere external transformation of an individual's appearance, as they have the power to recover self-respect for people who learned to feel ashamed of their bodies. To become black, therefore, is a means of elevating self-esteem and restoring dignity. But it also carries the dynamics that blackness itself is produced rather than inscribed. Commenting on the dynamics involved within the processes of the production of identities, Vron Ware explains that the expression "what makes you black?" opens the possibility of discussing and questioning the contents of blackness. The term "to make", although imbued with connotations of obligation and authenticity, points to the importance of the political choices involved in the production of racial identities, therefore serving to complicate more essentialist notions of blackness.[23]

However, if blackness is not inscribed, neither is beauty. Contrary to what scholars such as Elaine Scarry argue, beauty does not exist autonomously as a metaphysical entity that emanates from objects, places or people. Instead, the values of beauty are projected by the observer, and are immersed within classificatory systems. Just like everything else, beauty, and its counterpart ugliness, only exist within the production of meanings and their attributes. Beauty is relational and does not exist separately from a cultural context. Although briefly recognising that beauty is produced within culture, Scarry uses the term as if no debate existed about its definition, and exempts it from the processes that impose the hegemonic ideals of beauty.

Scarry also links beauty with perfection: "perfect features that obligate us to stare".[24] But, then, isn't "perfection" – especially "aesthetic perfection" – also defined within one's cultural understandings of the world? Doesn't it change according to place and time? Certainly the current anorexic standards of feminine beauty would be considered abnormal in the Europe of Charlie Chaplin, as in present-day Brazil, where "fleshy" women are still considered the most beautiful according to common standards, in spite of the images of thinness continuously imposed by the media. The ideal of "perfection" not only establishes white beauty as universal, but even determines the election of "beautiful people" amongst non-whites, based on how close they come to the "perfect white beauty". This tendency can be seen in the trendy magazines in which black and brown models of varied geographical origins have "caucasian-like" features – thin noses, lips that are not too thick, straightened hair – that "alleviate" their aesthetic otherness and turn their phenotypes into ones more "palatable" and sanitised, while simultaneously being "inclusive", "multi-cultural" and "politically correct".

Scarry fails to consider the production of power embedded in the establishment of beauty. Standards of beauty go far beyond the frivolity of fashion shows, window displays and magazines. If "beauty", understood as this metaphysical, autonomous entity, dignifies, elevates and promotes on the one hand, it excludes, humiliates and

285

harshly subjugates those who do not fit its parameters on the other. If we agree with Scarry that "beauty" leads us to copy and reproduce, and therefore that beauty leads to preservation, will that mean that beauty's opposite, ugliness, leads us to destruction or, if nothing else, to the expulsion of what is considered ugly? No, says Scarry. To the "unfair accusation" of lateral disregard commonly attributed to beauty, she responds by stating that the attention and regard given to the beautiful objects and people are extended laterally, even if by "charity".[25]

The problem then is not that beauty has been "banished from the Humanities", as Scarry complains, but that in fact it hasn't received the attention it deserves. Together with issues of self-image and self-esteem, beauty has been dealt with in the Brazilian academy much more as an object of psychology than of sociology or even anthropology. Not much importance has been given to the analysis of beauty in relation to power, especially within the production of a specifically black kind of beauty, created to invert the dominant negative images of blackness. By creating new forms of beauty, Afro-aesthetics has contested the mainstream values and the prevailing Eurocentric standards of beauty, confirming that "beauty" itself is always being created and transformed through the production of new representations. In that sense, the study of beauty should consider how it works, both internally, in the self-esteem of individuals, and externally, in terms of social transformations.

However, it is important to take into account *how* the terms "self-esteem" and "beauty" have been used, and for what purposes. In Brazil, both terms have become easy slogans for commercial ends and also in governmental campaigns with electoral aims. If the meaning of self-esteem is confined to surmount stigmas within isolated groups in a fragmented humanity, the term will continue to be co-opted by the market as an easy slogan, or become just a therapeutic solution, limited to individuals or segregated groups. As Gilroy has written, the recurrence of pain, humiliation and loss of dignity should contribute to the formation of a sense of universal humanity, and this idea should be powerful enough to make solidarities based in cultural particularities seem insignificant.[26] Then, more than merely elevating the esteem of individuals or seeking fulfilment through temporary comforts, we should seek to regain the human dignity that has been violated through the histories of colonialism and racism. The elevation of self-esteem and the promotion of black beauty will only be truly liberating for the individual if they can bring about transformations in the collective realm, both by disobeying the racist standards imposed as "universal" and by liberating it from the duties imposed on the black body.

The risks of producing blackness

Certainly there have been fundamental changes in the ways blackness has been understood and felt. The struggles of black movements and organisations all over the world have led to significant gains, and have inverted negative images into more positive ones. The production of new representations of blackness has played a significant role in this inversion, stimulating feelings and attitudes, and mobilising fears and anxieties. Afro-aesthetics has been one of the major realms for the production of new representations of blackness, reversing the nefarious meanings previously attributed to skin colour, hair texture and facial features into signifiers of beauty and pride. Nevertheless, the inversions of the meanings of blackness have not been able to surpass the boundaries imposed by binary oppositions. As pointed out by Stuart Hall, binary oppositions are still a cruel and reductive way of representing blacks. "They seem to be represented through sharply opposed, polarised, binary extremes – good/bad, civilised/primitive, ugly/excessively attractive, repelling because different/compelling because strange and exotic. *And they are often required to be both things at the same time!*"[27]

Based on an idealised and, many times, exotic ideal of "Africa", the production of Afro-aesthetics carries within it the danger of reproducing the exoticism often attributed to blackness. Keeping in mind that blackness was first of all a product of slavery and colonisation, it was initially imagined as "exotic", in as many ways as possible: interesting, mysterious, but also foreign, bizarre, alien, unusual and strange. However, the narratives produced by black cultural movements, to invert the pejorative meanings of blackness, frequently contribute to reinforcing the exoticism associated with blackness and Africanness. One way of doing this is by expecting that all blacks will feel compatibility with the "ideals of blackness", therefore fitting into the new "positive" categories established to elevate the meanings of blackness. These categories include the stereotypes of *body skills*, that is, the belief that blacks are great dancers, musicians and athletes, which are at once *frustrating* for those who lack these gifts, and also *disregard* those who work hard to develop these abilities, by not acknowledging the effort and training put into this.

The "ideals of blackness" also include *the need to correspond to Afro-aesthetics*, requiring that blacks should "dress as blacks", leaving little freedom for those who desire non-prescribed forms of appearance. Some forms of dressing, for example, are considered too formal and therefore unsuitable for a "black setting", defining once again the "right" and "wrong" ways of how to look as a black person. To some, Afro-aesthetics, created as a way of recovering pride and conferring beauty, and considered a "liberating" form of appearing black, can end up becoming an obligation. However, if Afro-aesthetics can function as an obligation for those of dark skin, it can also be a prohibition for those of light skin. Or at least, it may seem "unsuitable", since many believe that braids, dreadlocks and colourful clothes don't "match" whites or light-skinned *mestiços*.

Many black women in Brazil, especially if linked to a black group or organisation, feel patrolled if they decide to straighten their hair once in a while, and are frequently accused of denying their "natural blackness", or of desiring to whiten themselves.

Patricia Pinho > Afro-Aesthetics in Brazil

Commenting on the patrolling of hair straightening in South Africa and the US, Zimitri Erasmus contends that, by opposing natural/authentically black hair to artificial/whitening forms of hair, we are again limiting blacks to binary oppositions: "One cannot deny that hair-straightening as a practice has been shaped by colonial-racist notions of beauty. However, the notion that straightening one's hair is a mark of aspiring towards whiteness and that we should thus abandon it misses the complexity of black cultural practice. It also represents a simple and fictitious binary: black women who straighten their hair are reactionary/ black women who do not are progressive."[28]

It is important to consider that all hair is worked on, even those who take on a more "natural" appearance. Dreadlocks, in Brazil considered the most "natural" of black hairstyles, require the (hard) work of twisting the locks with beeswax or other "natural" substances for quite a few hours. Besides, nowadays there are all sorts of dreadlocks, ranging from the "messier" look of the Rastafarians, to those that have a more tidy appearance because they are constantly retouched either in hair salons and/or with special products. Those who defend "black naturalness" contend that the use of manufactured products on dreadlocks is a betrayal of its original meaning.

The "Afros", another emblematic example of "natural" black hair, also require a lot of work and dedication. The time spent first disentangling and then combing the hair upwards with a metal fork to give it a perfectly round shape confirms how much this "natural" look is a result of constant effort and attendance. Using specific products, such as hairspray, and knowing certain tricks, such as trimming the hair every two weeks to keep its round shape, are also constitutive parts of this "natural" black hair.

Social practices enacted on the body play a fundamental role in the perpetuation of identities and the maintaining of traditions, no matter how invented these may be.[29] It is therefore necessary to take into consideration not only inscribed traditions, but most of all traditions that have been literally embodied in the process of the formation of a collective identity. In that sense, people are induced to perform an "appropriate" identity, having to learn how to be, become and behave black. They should be trained so that their bodies automatically reproduce whatever is believed to be inscribed in their cells: the habits of dancing and playing music, or "black" ways of dressing and styling the hair, as if recovering once-lost traditions. When tradition is understood as a set of rigid rules that should be applied repetitively, it becomes more than a sign of ethnicity, turning into an alibi for authoritarianism. The invention of traditions can turn into an imposition of traditions, allowing for conservative and imprisoning forms of culture and social regulation. Gilroy has remarked:

> When identity refers to an indelible mark or code somehow written into the bodies of its carriers, otherness can only be a threat. Identity is latent destiny. Seen or unseen, on the surface of the body or buried deep in its

cells, identity forever sets one group apart from others who lack the particular, chosen traits that become the basis of typology and comparative evaluation. No longer a site for the affirmation of subjectivity and autonomy, identity mutates … Rather than communicating and making choices, individuals are seen as obedient, silent passengers moving across a flattened moral landscape toward the fixed destinies to which their essential identities, their genes, and the closed cultures they create have consigned them once and for all.[30]

Adopting an Afro-aesthetics in Brazil means more than just confronting the supremacy of white standards of beauty. It is also a way of reinforcing a separate racial identity in a society that celebrates miscegenation. Adorning the body with elements of Afro-aesthetics is a way of becoming *blacker*, through emphasising the blackness considered inscribed in the skin colour. But as we have discussed above, blackness is not inscribed. If we recall the role played by colonisation and slavery in inventing the "races" and moulding what we today designate as "blackness", the horrors implicated in this process may lead us to do more than turn blackness into a positive sign. We can then seek the humanness that has been fragmented and suppressed among those who are defined as blacks.

We should recall that what unifies blacks transnationally is the experience of racism and oppression. But even this experience occurs in different forms, distinctly influencing the construction of local black identities. To forge a common African or Afro-referenced identity for all blacks in the world requires disregarding the different historical trajectories carried out from slavery to the present, and above all, dismissing the rich and dynamic exchanges that have influenced black transnational cultural production among blacks, and between blacks and their "others".

By understanding diaspora as dynamic webs of circulation, communication and interaction, we will refuse to accept the ethnic absolutisms imposed by uniform creations of blackness molded by unicentrist conceptions of Africanness. The compelling epigraph should inspire us to opt for open-ended and creative routes through which the African diaspora can work as a seed on the body. In this way, we can conceive of the Afro-aesthetics created in Brazil as one among many fruits or flowers originated from that seed. We can then discover how scattered seeds, spread throughout fertile grounds of the imagination obey no predeterminations, and flourish in infinite colours, smells and forms.

289

Kamari Maxine Clarke
Yorùbá Aesthetics and Trans-Atlantic Imaginaries

Kamari Maxine Clarke is Associate Professor of Anthropology at Yale University. She received a BA in Political Science from Concordia University, an MA in Anthropology from the New School for Social Research, an MA in the Study of Law from Yale University and a PhD in Socio-cultural Anthropology from the University of California, Santa Cruz. Her research focuses on religious and legal movements, and recently on the cultural politics of international treaties and non-governmental organisations. Clarke is the author of *Mapping Yoruba Networks: Power and Agency in the Making of Transnational Networks* (2004) and, with Deborah Thomas, she is a co-editor of *Globalization and Race: Transformations in the Cultural Production of Blackness* (2006).

YORÙBÁ AESTHETICS AND TRANS-ATLANTIC IMAGINARIES

Any legitimately "new" world economic order carries a seed of the old that invariably suggests the familiar hegemonic attitudes severely under attack today. It would appear that one can't endorse globalisation without borrowing from the antecedent rhetorics of colonial exploitation.
Okwui Enwezor[1]

The dynamic changes in the world order in the late 20th to the early 21st century have given rise to transnational networks which shift people's ties from territorially rooted alliances towards those which take place across nations. This shift has not only led citizens in one country to reconceptualise their national allegiances to other places, but has also reinforced features of citizenship which are tied to heritage alliances which, though superficial, continue to undergird meanings of belonging and alliance. For while new archaeologies of governance are influencing changes in approaches to understanding rights, democracy, and citizenship, alongside these forms of expansionism are shadow alliances that continue to order transnational belonging along antecedent social organisations.

Thus, even as changes in the structure of citizenship and civil participation in the polity have had the impact of destabilising the workings of state authorities world-wide, analyses of global changes that have charted shifts in political governance, economic institutions, technological mechanisms and the movement of people must inform how we understand substantive social and cultural transformations within fundamentally modern ideological scales of organisation. These forms of ordering reflect the ways in which colonial inscriptions of governance map onto post-colonial futures. The history of trans-Atlantic slavery led to the exportation of various West African traditional practices, and in this essay I will focus on one particular religious linkage, that of Òrìṣà worshippers in the US, who practice Yorùbá religious traditions in transnational contexts. The dispersal of these age-old practices beyond the African continent plays a significant role in the transnational imaginary and is central to the globalisation of Òrìṣà practices in the Americas.

Over the past 400 years, as the offspring of African captives were eventually freed, they participated in the parallel development of traditional Òrìṣà practices and the building of nation-states. In this essay, I examine the ways in which racial discourses deployed by black nationalist practitioners in the US – who are part of a transnational network of Yorùbá Òrìṣà revivalist practitioners[2] – further strengthen their linkages to American citizenship by producing a black aesthetics of African belonging. I consider how participants in this movement undertake this through the re-signification of citizenship in racial terms and the reclamation of what they see as their historical roots prior to the trans-Atlantic enslavement of African captives. This process of reclassifying and reaffirming discourses of national geography is enacted through the blackening of "light-skinned symbols": that is, the use of signs of dark-brown and black skin, broad features and kinky black hair as the sign and texture of black authenticity.

As self-consciously evident as this form of sign reclassification is, it is not without a long and related history of identity- and nation-making. It is also part of the larger machinery of national regulation of citizens in the mid-18th to 19th centuries in Cuba and Brazil, in which practitioners lightened black female iconic representations in Yorùbá shrines, transforming them into Catholic saints with parallel characteristics. References to their African origins were driven underground by colonial legislation during Cuban slavery and post-slavery. As such, the aesthetics of blackening was fundamentally organised in relation to blood and territory, which were linked to modern foundations of early European colonial regimes as they intersected with new settlements in the Americas.

Within these configurations of descent and place, the language of racial and gendered lineage developed alongside the formation of property and paternity. These forms of classification evolved within status hierarchies constituted in particular through historical and economic fields of power. As I highlight, these fields penetrate the ways that new global relations and practices are created, ordered and sustained, and therefore reinforce the ideological centrality of the complex geographies of belonging. My argument is that particular framings of racial aesthetics of black beauty must be fundamentally understood in relation to an aesthetics of *black moral geography* which is historically inscribed and ideologically territorial. That is, an approach to understanding the production of black racial difference which is deeply embedded in articulations of blackness is complexly routed through both a modernity of national origins and vectors of economic and territorial networks. Its power lies in historical discourses of post-slavery suffering and through the narrating of such suffering as the basis on which authentic rights are claimed.

Approaching the racial production of difference through an *aesthetics of racial signification*, which is understood in relation to moral geographies, highlights how, in the face of hegemonic notions of black inferiority, there exist counter-hegemonic narratives of blackness as Africanness, which are also fuelled by forms of exclusions.[3] I end by concluding that particular Òrìṣà-based black nationalist revivalist movements employ the tools of racial politics to re-inscribe autochthonous mappings onto otherwise fluid articulations of personhood.

Yorùbá networks

The connections of Yorùbá Òrìṣà practices between Nigeria and the Americas are critical to the proliferation of contemporary Yorùbá networks globally. The contemporary US Òrìṣà and Cuban Santería movements have their history in the importation of a majority of Yorùbá captives who arrived in Cuba between 1760 and 1886 from the Benin region of the Òyó Empire, and who were forcibly enslaved and

293

transported to the Caribbean and South America. This period was characterised by the collapse of the Òyó kingdom in what was to become Nigeria, the civil wars in the Bight of Benin and the interventions of the British, which eventually succeeded in overthrowing monarchy governance and establishing a British colony in the new Nigeria. These conditions set the stage for the conditions of slave raids and slave trading along the West African coast and, eventually, the influx of captives to Cuba.

The historical development of networks of social and religious Òrìsà organisations led to the spread of related worship in Cuba, especially in the urban regions where there existed strong networks for religious practice. In Cuba today, Òrìsà worship exists as part of a larger continuum of religious change in the Americas in which religious practices, now known as Santería – but also referred to as Lucumi and Regla De Ocha – have transformed the shape of Òrìsà worship outside of Nigeria. Cuba and Santería are critical components of how Òrìsà revivalism is shaped among Yorùbá revivalists. For even as Santería has developed into a distinctive practice that combines the syncretisation of Òrìsà and Catholic religious practices, there continue to be critical tensions between those who advocate for the return of Santería to its Òyó-Nigerian roots (otherwise known as the Africanisation of Òrìsà practices) and others who insist on the legitimacy of the development and survival of Santería within necessary conditions of regulation. One such advocate of the Africanisation of Santería is a group from a larger network of Yorùbá revivalists who hail from Òyótúnjí African Village.

Understanding the global spread of the Yorùbá imaginary in the Americas as a widespread blackening of the post-slavery descendants of Yorùbáland calls into question the ways in which agents borrow from dominant meanings of the past while also re-signifying them for their purposes.

Òyótúnjí African Village

Situated on the outer perimeter of Beaufort, US, approximately 100 kilometres southwest of Charleston, South Carolina, Òyótúnjí is 8,000 kilometres from the westernmost tip of West Africa. The development of religious revivalist movements as part of a counterculture is not new and often reflects people's attempts to respond to particular social conditions. For a period of over 300 years, the US became the home to millions of black Americans, many of whose ancestors were enslaved, sold to traders, and transported to the Americas as slaves. As captives in slave ships, hundreds of thousands settled in small and large plantations in places such as Mississippi, Alabama, South Carolina, Texas, Georgia, Florida and North Carolina.

When the Declaration of Independence was written in the 1770s and adopted by the Congress on July 4, 1776, slavery was still permitted to remain legal. In 1807, Congress passed a law prohibiting the importation of slaves and by January 1808 it went into effect. As more states entered the Union and more laws were enforced to

294

enable the spread of the growing economy of pioneer settlers and their slaves, slavery became more entrenched by both the establishment of cotton and sugar plantations as well as the ideological forms of classification which defended human bondage.[4] In the US, the politics of enforced racial segregation, known as Jim Crow, led to the development of racialised spaces that enforced legal racial segregation. In spite of slave rebellions and uprisings, as well as the growing formation of anti-slavery societies over the first 250 years (1600-1850) of the formation of the Union, it was not until the drafting of the 13th amendment to the American constitution by Abraham Lincoln, and its signing in 1865, that slavery was outlawed with the end of the Civil War – the war that led to the incorporation of the South into the Union.

After the 1865 abolition of slavery, large waves of black migrants moved to northern urban cities such as Chicago, New York, Philadelphia, Buffalo, Boston and Detroit in search of employment and educational opportunities. Yet, despite the eradication of segregation laws, the ideological and cultural practice of race shaped the terrain on which the development of American democracy took shape. Thus, it was in this historical context that the racial tensions of the 20th century took shape, and that the institutionalisation of black nationalism and black American African-centrism produced new mechanisms by which to understand the ways that culture became marked as a vindicative and moral process of racial reclamation possible through deterritorialised imaginaries. Given the politics of racialisation that have dominated black Atlantic zones of exchange, agents reproduce typologies of racial continuities in order to debunk the cultural logics of white racial superiority. These politics of racism, and, by extension, their indexical references to territorial origins, continue to shape the imperatives of Yorùbá revivalism as an ideologically black social movement. Ultimately, that is what makes this form of revivalism a culturally American, rather than West African, movement.

Though born in America and therefore legally classified as citizens of the US, the vast majority of practitioners within and outside Òyótúnjí have philosophically rejected US citizenship and instead have created a deterritorialised kingdom in a modern nation. As such, they claim belonging to African cultural citizenship as their national identity and the Yorùbá Òyó Empire as their ancestral heritage. Òyótúnjí is both a physical and conceptual space for making history through cultural practices that carry within these spaces a heritage denied them in the United States. It is a place for making and maintaining an imaginary Africa denied as a result of the history of American slavery and continually thwarted in contemporary processes of US daily life.

As a site of Yorùbá transnational movements, Òyótúnjí is increasingly intercon-nected with international urban and rural networks of ritual, revival and knowledge production. With the work of the imagination, the conceptualisation of Òyótúnjí as a home away from an African home operates within the limits of reality, enabling

295

subjects to become someone else, somewhere else. In this realm of the imaginary, Òyótúnjí practitioners trace their origins to those of the descendants of the men and women taken from West African communities and exported to the Americas as slaves. As a result of the belief that they have a right to control the African territory that was their homeland prior to European colonisation, residents of Òyótúnjí Village, claiming diasporic connections to the ancestral history of the Great Òyó Empire of the Yorùbá people, have reclassified their community as an African kingdom outside of the territoriality of the Nigerian post-colonial state.

This act of reclassifying national belonging is an act of legitimising the basis for the return to African cultural origins. As such, Òyótúnjí Yorùbá practitioners inscribe a racial politics of difference onto historically divergent genealogies of trans-Atlantic slavery, through which they produce an African cultural community outside the boundaries of Africa. However, it is clear that the techniques of personal transformation, ritual and aesthetic acts that link them to their ancestral home in Òyó, Nigeria, are not simply achieved through semiotic and representational distinctions. These cultural practices are both products of culturally active processes of building reality,[5] and are also remnants of particular imprints that the circulation of commodities and cultural products leave in various geographical locations.

Yorùbá history and identity, therefore, as well as the globalisation of Yorùbá transnational practices, should not simply be understood in terms of the spread of Yorùbá slaves and cultural practices throughout the world. The use of Africa as the symbolic home of black people is fundamentally central to the imaginary conflation of race and culture in the making of the modern world. Therefore, the use of origins narratives and the moral authority of race as the basis for linkage is itself part of a larger machinery of nation building. To understand contemporary Yorùbá movements is to understand both the work of state classificatory ideologies as well as the ways that transnational identities must be mapped both within and outside of the nation state. Yorùbá revivalists who engage in the work of transnational linkage as a form of racial legitimisation do so within the power of state alliances and institutions of power.

Aesthetics of race and space

As the dusk cloaks daylight's distractions, night rituals begin. White candles along the community's private road lead participants towards syncopated drum sounds and the smell of incense. In the mystic aura of the moonlight, Yorùbá practitioners walk in and out of the palace courtyard, transposing themselves from Americans into Yorùbá voodoo practitioners in sync with the mysteries of the occult from ancient times.

With the power of religious ritual, Òyótúnjí awakens at night. Ritual initiations and rhythmic beats echo in the endless hours of the night. Possessed dancers are consumed by the power of trance (fig. 1). Bare-breasted women and men with white cloths draped around their lower bodies invoke the ancestors through prayer,

Fig.1. *Parading Egun gun* (ancestral masquerade)
Photo: K. Clarke

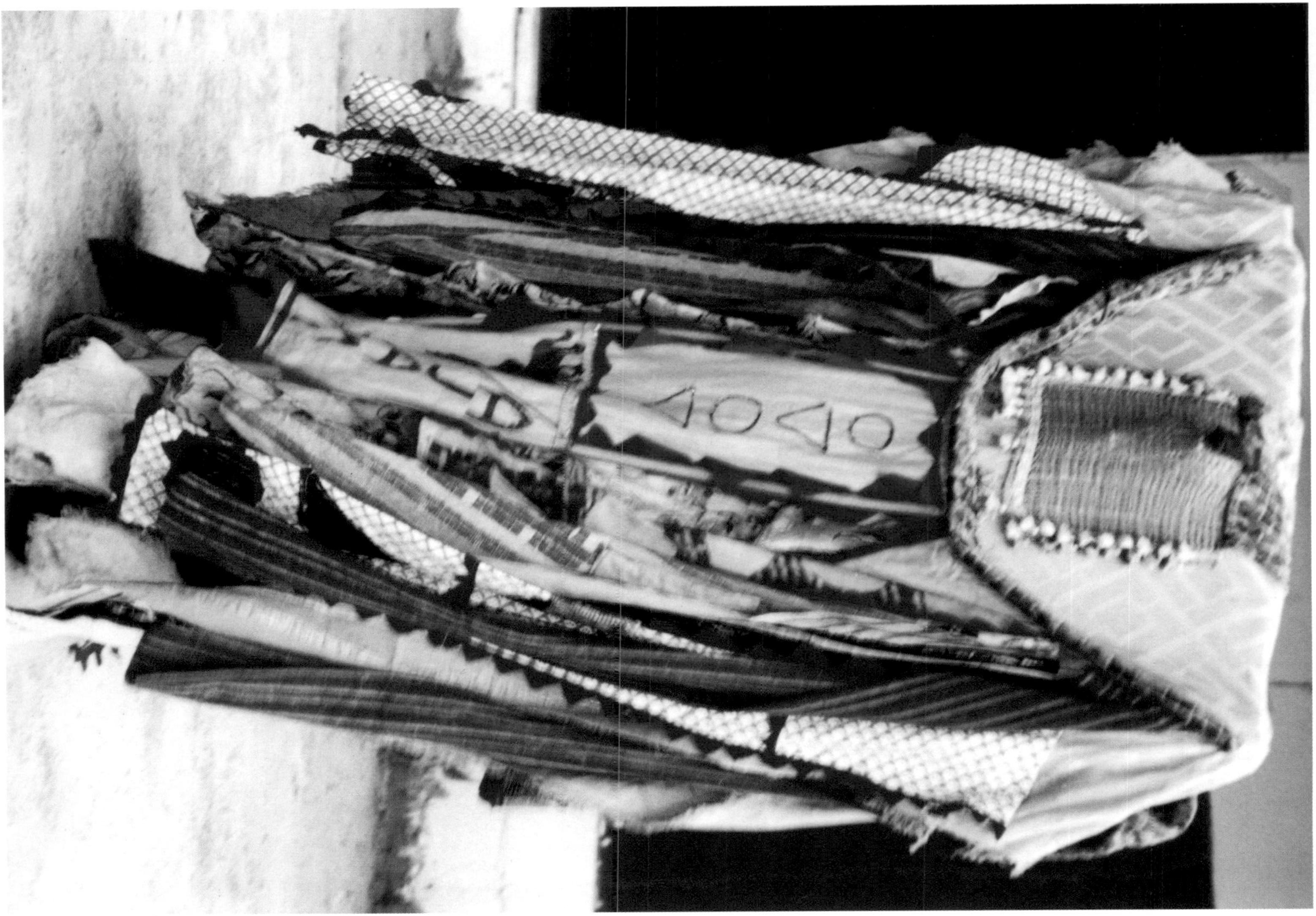

transforming death into ancestral communion. Bodily possession fully appeases the ancestors as the trembling figures announce the presence of the dead. Here in the darkness of the moment lies ritual ecstasy. The celebrations have begun.

The mysteries of midnight are held in tension with the promise of sunlight. The practitioners' willingness to believe makes everything and anything possible. The degree to which various Òyótúnjí revivalists are able to innovate efficacious Yorùbá rituals in America is the degree to which they have successfully formed symbolic alliances with hegemonic technologies of knowledge.

The day after

At the start of a standard workday, residents, some of whom live in polygamous groups of two-family compounds, propitiate the gods and ask for blessings of good health, money, peace and guidance (fig. 2). Rancid bloodstains and old feather remains from animal sacrifices decorate enduring ritual objects in ancestral shrines. During mid-morning, the usual cacophony of men hammering, old engines and acorns falling onto zinc roofs blends with the sound of people conversing, with both Yorùbá and English words in every sentence(fig. 3). The daily speech practices of Òyótúnjí villagers suggest that language is an aesthetic and ideological site for the reclamation of African ancestry. Mothers call out for their children, "Àgò Yétúndé, Adémíwá, Yétúndééééé, WOLÉ, come for lunch!" And children respond in Yorùbá, "Oóò!" These sounds may indeed transport the listener to a place seemingly far away, yet conveniently attainable. In the mind, they create a norm of "African life" in a South Carolina landscape. The blended smells of livestock feed, fresh paint and southern fried chicken refresh the community with the comforting banality of everyday life.

In the heat of the day, while men in workgroups artfully decorate two-storey buildings in the palace courtyard, and children sit in classrooms learning African-centred humanities, sciences and social sciences, clients pull up in the parking lot, here to seek out spiritual guidance or healing. They are stopped by a young man on guard at the gate.

In announcing regular clients, new visitors in tour buses or simply local service repairmen, one of the boys beats a drum rhythmically, spelling out the message: "Àlejò mbò wá, Àlejò mbò wá, Àlejò mbò" (visitors are here, visitors are here, visitors are here).

> Welcome to Òyótúnjí. You are now leaving the United States of America and about to enter the Yorùbá Kingdom of Òyótúnjí African Village.

This sign, posted outside the front gates of the entrance to Òyótúnjí, introduces a community that resembles the popular American image of a quintessentially "African village", somewhere on a faraway shore, whose aesthetic articulations lie in enactment of the imaginary. For many visitors, its artistic presentation, coupled with the mementoes of ritual, evoke nostalgic desires to see and experience ancient African village life. On a standard tour the onlooker may see Òyótúnjí children in school uniforms – untucked and oversized – selling home-made jewellery to impressionable young tourists and referring to various historical texts published by colonial enterprises over 100 years ago. Tour guides often insist that "it is the ancestral powers that make Òyótúnjí what it is today". As one said, "The ancestors, what you guys call the dead, are our guides." Depending on whether a guide thinks he or she needs to further explain that point, he or she might add, as I heard one do for a group of white tourists, "Europeans also worship the dead. Yes, your ancestors are Abraham Lincoln and Thomas Jefferson. Ours are the Òyó kings and millions of Africans sold into slavery."

However, despite the successes of Òyótúnjí revivalists in re-signifying the efficacy of their rituals and aesthetics as African, there are also obvious failures. As the object of practitioner desire, ritual in Òyótúnjí Village is the means through which the Yorùbá ideal is held in tension with its distant origins, yet reconstituted within Americanised spheres of sociality. Upon recognising the patterns of cultural production which reflect things American, tourists who visit Òyótúnjí are often disappointed by what they regard as Òyótúnjí's inauthenticity. And although poverty and village conditions contribute to the appearance of African village "primitivity", young teenagers of the community are often unabashedly engaged in hybridising Africanness. For example, rather than playing one of the old tourist standards – West African rhythmic greats such as Felá or King Sunny Adé – they groove to American rap songs by Tupac Shakur or Snoop Doggy Dog, wearing African garb and holding African idols.

As they trudge in the summer heat behind tour guides, going in and out of public shrines and buildings, tourists smirk endlessly with disbelief. With a tone of chagrin, some visitors ask questions that make their judgements clear: "But they were born in America." "Are they into voodoo?" "But they don't believe in God." Yet, Òyótúnjí Village comes alive with the dreams and doubts of those who enter. The hegemony of racial ideologies that tie blackness to Africa is held in tension with the realities of American citizenship.

If the tourists' looks of disapproval as they walk by and hear American rap in the young men's compound is an indicator of Òyótúnjí's failed attempts to maintain Yorùbá "authenticity", the ritual knowledge and spatial organisation of a homeland long ago are all reminders of the other ways in which Africanness is legitimised through different modes of knowing. These alternate approaches to producing knowledge through the deterritorialised production of African aesthetics and nationhood in America, and the use of different temporalities through which to understand racial and national continuities, are both critical mechanisms through which race and

299

Fig. 3. Ọ̀yọ́túnjí Village marketplace
Photo: K. Clarke

302

religion are played out in this intentional community. That is, Yorùbá belonging in Òyótúnjí is in itself a process of producing the terms of temporal and spatial legitimacy – modern institutional legitimacy – through which one becomes Yorùbá. The ability to re-signify daily meanings and reproduce others is a complex process: "truth" is negotiated through the production of ongoing acts of remembering and forgetting, which are closely aligned with state and scientific institutions which endow legitimacy on what gets to count as viable. As such, it is no surprise that the majority of disbelieving tourists impatiently question the ethics of voodoo, the efficacy of ancestral worship or the authenticity of black Americans as Yorùbá practitioners.[6] Thus, Òyótúnjí practitioners use an aesthetics of moral geography to legitimise their transnational alliances to West Africa, and depend on the historical power of scientific classifications of racial difference and origins to attend to their deterritorialised practices outside of Africa.

Three national flags wave in the Òyótúnjí palace courtyard, representing black American emancipation from slavery, black nationalism and the establishment of an ancient Yorùbá Empire in South Carolina.[7] (fig. 5) Lying outside the geographic boundaries of African nation-states, Òyótúnjí was born out of complex controversies over both the conditions of slavery that brought Africans to the Americas and the contestations between African American converts and Afro-Cuban Catholics over the legitimacy of their adaptations of West African practices. (fig. 4)

Founded in 1970 and by the late 1970s boasting a residential population of 191 residents, Òyótúnjí is part of a network of hundreds and thousands of Òrìsà practitioners throughout the US. Though a small community on its own – built to accommodate only up to 25 housing compounds with a potential capacity of only 500 people – the institutional format of the community shifted in the 1980s and the average population plummeted to 70 residents. Compared with past numbers, fewer revivalists than ever resided in Òyótúnjí in the 1990s.[8]

Between the early 1980s to the late 1990s, increasing numbers of practitioners left the community for urban centres.[9] However, it was this outward migration and a new moment of post-Black-Power institutionalisation of African roots that laid the seeds for the spread of new institutional forms of urban Yorùbá practices. Thus it was through the creation of Òyótúnjí rural and urban nodes throughout the US that new Yorùbá revivalist networks were forged. Because of this added level of deterritorialised networking between Òyótúnjí and its satellite communities in urban centres, Òyótúnjí became more important than ever for practitioners to claim a shared network of Yorùbá revivalists. Through the regulation and standardisation of revivalist rituals, dress codes and routinised daily practices, a normative form of Yorùbá practice took shape in the late 20th century. Texts as well as computer technologies were used as tools for the teaching of traditionalist Yorùbá doctrine. These tenets of practice, formerly communicated and circulated within the once-separatist

304

Fig. 4. Large image of the Olukun òrìṣà in Ọ̀yọ́túnjí Village
Photo: K. Clarke

306

Fig. 5. The Òyótúnjí Village militia awaiting the final march to the palace of their *Oba* (king)
Photo: K. Clarke

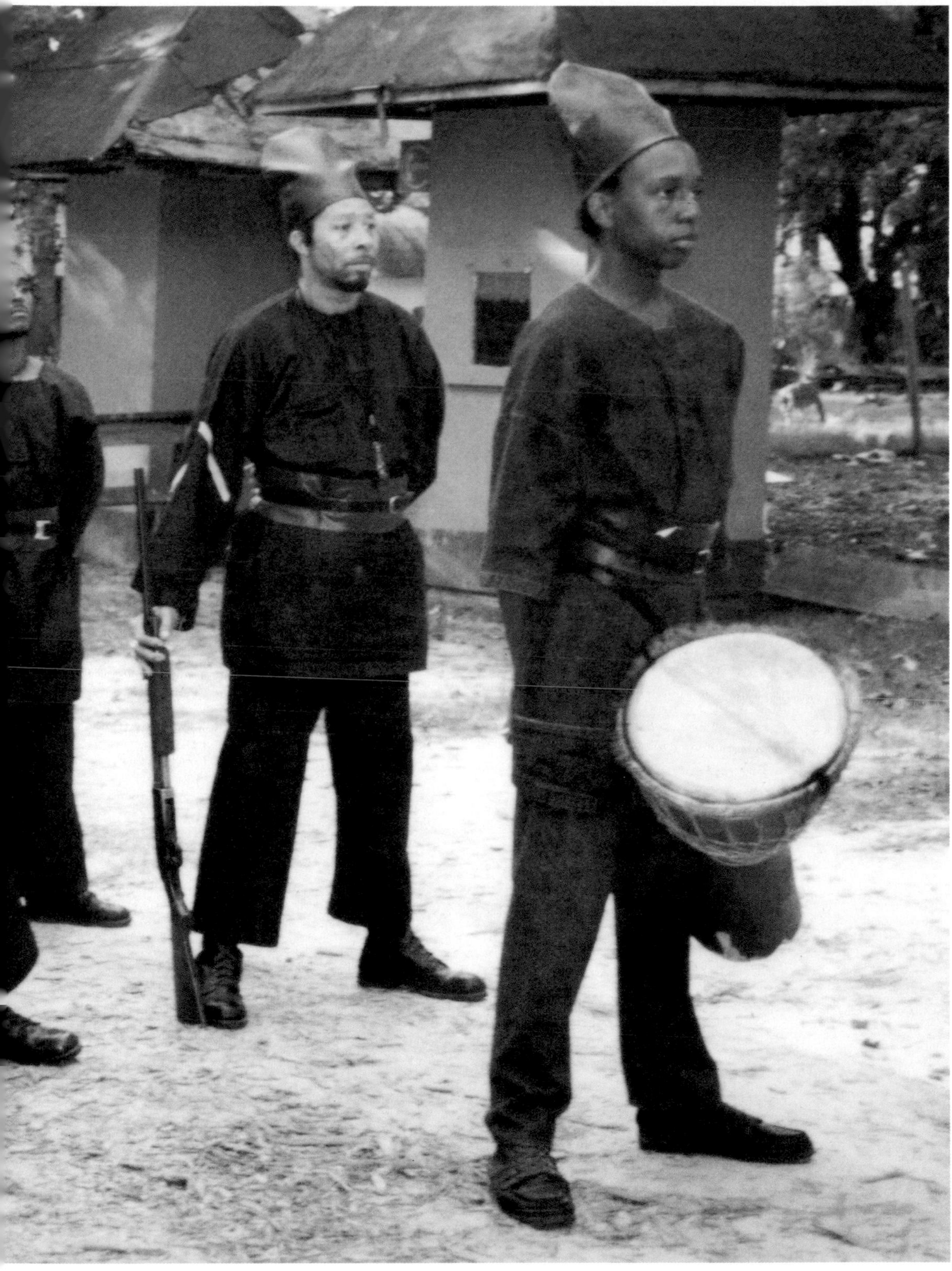

Òyótúnjí community, were, in the 1980s and 1990s, reconstituted through the spread of new forms of knowledge. Within these circuits, the movement, estimated to exceed six to ten thousand adherents – spanning major urban and rural centres throughout the US – reconstituted itself as a black nationalist one, drawing its power from the symbolic prestige of the African past.

In thinking through the reclassification of racial aesthetics as symbolic of how the African homeland is imagined in the US, I am also suggesting an analytic shift from the language of "invention" or the "imagination" as an individual process that is not real or that is without boundaries, to a return to Althusser's insistence that it is "only imaginary communities which are real",[10] or Emile Durkheim's[11] intervention into understanding the existence of religious truth by insisting that the empirical basis for truth is secondary to the social conditions under which particular interpretations are internalised as real. Seen in this way, it is the aesthetic production of a particular racial imaginary that makes historical connections between black Americans and Yorùbá West Africans. Thus, it is the practice of transnational norm-making and the creation of new geographic maps that are critical for understanding how and why some internalise particular practices and others do not.

Performing nobility

The Yorùbá movement from which Òyótúnjí Village was institutionalised originated as an ideologically separatist black enclave that separated from the larger Spanish Catholic-influenced Santería movement. Many Yorùbá revivalists who live either inside or outside of Òyótúnjí advocate that black Americans should adopt pan-African religious nationalism as the basis for their identity and focus their worldly desires on their black ancestral solidarity, rather than the state, as the basis for political equity. Maintaining the goal of eventually converting all black Americans to African religious practices, the prevailing belief is that through conversion and broad-based outreach, revivalist practitioners can subvert the legacy of slavery that has oppressed and historically impoverished black Americans. It is through the rendering of slavery and the adaptations of slave practices as abjectly "inauthentic" that nationalist practitioners reinforce the importance of purity and, therefore, the importance of recasting their cultural descent through West Africa and not Cuba.

For Òyótúnjí practitioners, the symbolic significance of a Yorùbá homeland is both based on the prestige of the past and the demise and dispersal of the Òyó Empire. The image of a grand and noble black empire, as well as enslaved Yorùbá practitioners being captured and taken away to the Americas, are at the centre of Yorùbá revivalist imagery. This abjection of mixture and whiteness underlies the popular representation of blackness as ancestrally African and noble and makes the reformulation of Yorùbá identities a distinctly American, rather than a predominantly African process.

The materiality of Òyó as an African homeland deeply embedded in the geographical designations of pre-colonial empire status is hierarchical and divided into various levels ranging from the leader (the _Oba_) to the chiefs, the priests and the non-priest practitioners. The _Oba_, sophisticated and learned, is more commonly known by his followers both in- and outside of Òyótúnjí as Oba Adéfúnmi I, the Yorùbá father of dispersed Africans. He claims a constituency of thousands of African Americans in the US, hundreds of whom lived and trained in Òyótúnjí.

Clearly setting the terms for the use of racial continuity to forge pre-statehood claims to African nobility – empires and rulers – Òyótúnjí governance in South Carolina is organised into four central spheres of social life – political, religious, cultural and economic. These domains are not only territorially construed, but they are aesthetically racialised within particular scales of value. Nevertheless, as I will demonstrate, this act of "blackening" is deeply embedded in the institutionalisation of particular imaginaries of Africa as the legitimate home of dark-skinned people.

The making of blackness

Plantation slavery in the Americas followed diverse but related racial typologies, and, using legal regulations that prohibited the mixing of Europeans with colonial subjects or slaves, anti-miscegenation laws were passed. Blood represented what was being passed on from generation to generation and the act of procreation involved the transmission of the ancestral line of one race to another, ultimately constituting the nation. And, although different classes of European traders in varied regions intermixed differently with slaves on plantations, the flow of ideas about civilisation and purity further intensified the taboo of racial intermixing as well as the practice of African-based religious practices, eventually rendering illegal and non-Christian the intermixing between whites and blacks on American plantations. In Cuba, for example, there also existed class distinctions and prohibitive notions of miscegenation. The existence of differential contact among white colonial settlers with African slaves created different relations of intimacy between indigenous populations, working-class whites and African populations. Over time, however, with the increasing regimentation of state standardisation, bans on spaces of social exchange between Africans and non-Africans as well as bans on the overt practice of African-derived practices were enforced and led to increasing racial regimentation.

Given these histories of the regulation of African practices by European colonisers, the development of Òrìṣà voodoo Yorùbá revivalism was self-consciously driven by the growing tide of black nationalism in the 1960s, in which black Americans reconceptualised Santería in order to disentangle it from its Spanish and Christian influences. Ultimately, these changes meant symbolically "blackening" Santería and referentially indexing the West African empires and kingdoms that preceded the colonisation of Nigeria by the British Empire.

On a basic level of signification, therefore, Òyótúnjí practitioners argued for the

309

Fig. 5. Lïe-size carving bordering the king's palace
Photo: K. Clarke

need to Africanise Santería as fundamentally Yorùbá and visibly "African". There-fore, spurred by ideological clashes over the "whitening" of Yorùbá ritual practices in Cuba, Yorùbá revivalists in the US – black American nationalists – renamed their version of Yorùbá-Santería "Òrìsà voodoo", substituting Spanish-language words and pronunciations with African words. Using representations that incorporated the mythic visual imagery of the old empire from which Yorùbá people are known to have descended, the founders created landscapes that resembled Nigerian Yorùbá religious and political institutions thought to be more "authentically" African. They substituted their Anglophone names with Yorùbá names, producing performative cartographies of Yorùbá membership.

These reformulations of Africanness shaped the terms of contestations between early black nationalists and new Cuban immigrants to the US that developed in that country. By the late 1970s, the membership of the growing Yorùbá movement, an outgrowth of Santería, comprised hundreds of US voodoo practitioners spread throughout the US and Canada. This form of Yorùbá transnational religious nationalism, as well as the proliferation of Afro-centricity and African American cultural movements, can also be seen as a sort of culture industry in which the production of local aesthetic forms is itself a part of the globalisation process.[12] As such, it is within various zones of production that we need to understand the channels and circuits for the global circulation of commodities of various kinds,[13] as well as the ways that particular events contribute to particular imprints.[14]

Òyótúnjí revivalists often highlight the bringing of Òrìsà voodoo to the US as the event in which Afro-Cubans were called on by the gods to give their secrets back to black people. According to the narrative told to me by the *Oba* of Òyótúnjí, this moment took place in 1959 when the first two Americans were to be initiated into the Afro-Cuban priesthood cult of Sàngó in Matanzas, Cuba. They were the soon-to-be-founder of Òyótúnjí Village, then named Serge King, and his friend, a Cuban American man named Chris Oliana. This ritual moment is seen as critical because the diviner identified King as being protected by the patron Òrìsà Obàtálá, but in a negative configuration (Òsé Méjì in osobo). He told King that he should not assume positions of leadership. So rather than initiating King into the Obàtálá cult, the diviner told him that the gods prohibited him from initiating others into the Sàngó secret society and warned that he was to be careful not to share the secrets of Africa's gods with not only noninitiates but also non-Cubans. The story told to me by King, the now Oba of Òyótúnjí, to explain the sources of tension was that Santeros did not want black Americans to participate in African rituals for fear of radical changes to their practice. Relegating the divinatory interpretation of the Odù to white Cuban racism, he noted that "white Cubans are afraid that black Americans will enter the Santería priesthood and Africanise it".

Although black Americans were outside of the parameters of African cultural

311

knowledge in the past, he repeatedly emphasised that the reason he entered the Santería priesthood was so that he could gain the necessary ritual training in order to return Santería practices to their "purest African form". For this reason, King remained loyal to his Santería alliances in New York City and tried to abide by the basic cultural and political rules of secrecy and discretion – legacies retained from the disguising of Yorùbá religion during conditions of slavery.[15]

King and Oliana together established an Òrìsà religious organisation and named it the Sàngó Temple. During this period increasing numbers of Santería networks began to proliferate. These new networks not only involved the movement of people to urban areas and the institutionalisation of networks of Santería worship houses, but also the creation of ritual products for sale and consumption. The products ranged from candles with pictures of light-skinned saints to fresh and processed herbs and remedies, Òrìsà objects, witchcraft protection, and lucky charms that often referenced the iconic imagery of Catholicism. However, by the mid-1960s, King had incorporated into his practice the fundamental principles of black nationalism that had been circulating within artistic and political circles of the time. He renamed his new version of Santería Òrìsà voodoo, naming the new temple the "Yorùbá Temple", and emphasised the African origins of Santería and not the conditions of slavery that led to the creation of Santería from Yorùbá-Lucumi. The consequence of developing an African-centric orientation was that over time he lost his constituency and his potential economic power, as most of the Santería consultants refused to support his increasingly race-centred approach and severed ties with him.

Through routinised practices that emphasised the African origins of Yorùbá practices – from Africa to the Americas – Yorùbá revivalists recast Santería through the signs of African grandeur and performative nobility. Adéfúnmi and other prominent Òrìsà voodoo leaders changed the Santería saint-like representations of deities, replacing them with symbolic objects from the earth. In an attempt to Africanise symbolically what are popularly referred to as the European features of Catholic saints, they substituted the white faces of the saints with brown faces. They painted pictures that emphasised thick lips and broad noses. The membership officially adopted the principles of black nationalism and began wearing West African *dashikis* and *bubas*, afros, and adopting what they saw as either African names in general, or Yorùbá names in particular. They changed the spelling and pronunciation of Spanish/Lucumi ritual words, and King changed his last name to Adéfúnmi, discarding "King" as a slave name. Arguing that such vestiges needed to be shed, he emphasised the aesthetic return to African forms, even while he underlined the need to pursue such goals in the Americas. These aesthetic interventions into religious representation were embedded in values connected to differences between whiteness and blackness and Christianity and Lucumi, and reflected King's attempts to resignify the meaning of Santería through a temporal return to a pre-colonial period in referentially African spatial and aesthetic terms.

Geographies of race

With the increasingly transnational cultural relations between practitioners of various nations and the increasing affordability of travel for middle-class Americans interested in experiencing life elsewhere, thousands of black nationalists embarked on pilgrimages to the Middle East and heritage tours to various parts of Africa. In 1972, to strengthen their ties to Nigerian Yorùbá clan groups and to gain the ritual legitimacy of Nigerian rituals, Adéfúnmi joined many of those voyagers by travelling to Nigeria. While there, he embarked on a ritual initiation and returned to South Carolina with the symbolic power of having undergone West African rituals. With the goal of studying and learning about Yorùbá ritual processes, Adéfúnmi lived amongst families for a four-month period and learned the Yorùbá language in order to study the organisation and history of Nigerian Yorùbá practices. There, he was initiated into the cult of Ifá (a ritual cult group) in Abẹ̀òkúta – which provided him with the legitimacy that he sought. The ritual process clarified for him the 1959 Santería interpretation of his initiation *Odù*, *Òsé Méjì*. In responding to his request that they clarify the symbolic meaning of *Òsé Méjì* in osobo, his new Nigerian advisors told him that his configuration of *Òsé Méjì* did not represent someone who would be a dangerous leader. Rather, the Abẹ̀òkúta-based Yorùbá priest who initiated him explained that the *Odù* represented a highly powerful leader who would do many things that could have great consequences for his family.

When Adéfúnmi completed his travels at the end of 1972, he returned to Òyótúnjí, where his constituency crowned him as *Oba* (king), endowing him with the official Yorùbá title, Kábíyèsí. "Kábíyèsí" – often translated as "Long Live the King" or "Your/His Royal Highness" – signalled the temporal and spatial power of Yorùbá governance, establishing symbolic codes which set the terms of particular social relations. With his ascent to the throne, Kábíyèsí became the leader of Òyótúnjí, a democratic dictatorship governing Yorùbá revivalists in the United States. With symbolic as well as ultimate power, his leadership set the terms for particular assertions of Yorùbá social memory that worked within the historical workings of race.

Joined by the arrival of over a hundred residents throughout 1974 and 1975, the growing members of Òyótúnjí had to contend with implementing their visions of Yorùbá social organisation. They set up a traditional decision-making council referred to in Yorùbá as the Ògbóni society, a council of landholders and chiefs. With the Ògbóni, designed to replicate the organisation of Yorùbá customary towns, establishing continuities in ancestral governance and contemporary governance, village leaders were able to implement practical decision-making rules and procedures.

As community leaders established political structures, legal codes, Yorùbá

313

language training and physical spatial design in such a way that represented Yorùbá social life, members interested in developing ancestral and Òrìsà worship created social and religious cult groups, and constructed a physical plant that was organised around a large palace courtyard called the Àafin (palace) – replicating images of African kingdoms. Unlike the social organisation of Santería as a covert practice incorporated in the structure of the nuclear family, the founders of Òyótúnjí decentralised Òrìsà worship and initiation, creating a universe of governance organised to incorporate distinct Yorùbáland towns as a means of drawing a parallel between towns and their accompanying patron Òrìsà. They created landscapes of pre-colonial African village life and recreated ancestral symbols such as disembodied Òrìsà shrines.

At the apex of the village's zones of governance is the palace, a signifier of ancient ancestral leadership. In keeping with the nobility of empire, Òyótúnjí is politically structured according to hierarchies of grandeur and social status. Embracing these symbols, embedded in the pride of African nobility – signs of Yorùbá institutional power – the formation of Òyótúnjí governance marked the development of a new kind of black nationalist governance in the 1970s that required an ideological framework from which to determine what counts as Yorùbá.

Notions of biological succession from one black ancestor to another have shaped the parameters for legitimising racial ideologies[16] about African identities as constitutive of shared origins. For, ultimately, Yorùbá revivalism stands at the imaginary crossroads of the enslaved African body, which reinforces the forced migration of enslaved Africans from Africa to the Americas, and the redemptive hope of an ideological return to black governance.

These reconfigurations were organised to indexically reference key regions in West Africa from which nine of the most popular Yorùbá-American Òrìsà were known to emerge, and employed Yorùbá names and terminology. The Àafin, the centre for noble governance, was configured as a large compound to house the Oba, his four wives and his children, as well as the royal ancestral shrines. One such shrine represents an offering to the Oba's royal ancestors as well as to the unknown ancestors, also known as Domballahwedo. Other shrines housed in the Àafin include the Òrìsà Onílé, the Oba's Òrìsà of Ifá and the patron Òrìsà of the community, Obàtálá, dressed in white signifying purity, leadership, the creation of all things and grand nobility.

On the outer northern, southern and western end of the Àafin are the large schoolhouse, museum and guest houses for new residents, indentured workers and unmarried women who are betrothed or otherwise accountable to the Oba. The centre of the community is located in the outer courtyard and is divided into four main areas: three formal temple districts and one sacred forested district – the Ìká gbó, the Igbóòsà, the Ànàgó and the Ìgbàlè, respectively. Each of these Òyótúnjí districts is governed by a series of town chiefs who are responsible for either one of the Òrìsà society temples or a political or town society within that town.

At the base of the temple districts, popularly referred to by the young people in Òyótúnjí as Temple Row, is the Òrìsà temple of Oya. Extending westward, in the Ìká gbó district (translated in English as the "place of the stickers"), is the temple of Òsun. The Ìká gbó region begins where the Òsun temple ends and extends to the sacred grove area. Its name was taken from the odù Ìká, a divinatory verse that describes the road for that region and houses the Òsun, Ògún, and Òsóòsì temples. The Ànàgó district, named to honour the Dahomean people or Nàgó, is located behind and to the eastern side of the Àáfin. Finally, the place of ancestral veneration for the community is known as the Ìgbàlè area. Ìgbàlè represents the official grove of the sacred egúngún (ancestors). Housing the shrine for the Òrìsà Obalúayé, it is located near the Àáfin and behind the Ìká gbó district on the outer periphery of the settlement.

These configurations of community were developed to produce a sense of connection to Africa that was not only represented as ancestrally legitimate but also indexical. They indexically reference, that is, parallel Nigerian Yorùbá towns. The indexical signs of African ancestry are re-signified by black nationalists to mark certain aesthetic features about being "Yorùbá", thus "African". These signs of deterritorialised belonging link the territoriality of African ancestry to the figure of the black imaginary.

Conclusion

As we have seen, the formation of Yorùbá revivalist aesthetic values are connected to the formation of modern capitalist development in the circum-Atlantic world. The variables central to how belonging and membership are imagined are as much factors of the history of trans-Atlantic slavery as they are factors of the power of histories of exclusion in shaping aesthetic signs of belonging in racial terms.

Ultimately, there are ideological boundaries to the imagination that must be acknowledged if we are to understand the production and persistence of racial distinctions as historically contingent. However, racial distinctions are not simply distinctions between black and white. Understanding the cultural politics of racial difference involves charting the ways in which particular types of moral geographies are incorporated to authenticate some practices over others, as well as the ways in which the particularities of aesthetic geographies of race play into the moral economy of lightening and blackening in time and space.

Acknowledgement
Special thanks to Duke University Press for permission to reproduce part of this text.

Rodney Place interviewed by Sarah Nuttall
Urban Imaging: The *Friche* Waiting to Happen

Rodney Place is an artist living and working in
Johannesburg and Warsaw. He studied architecture
in London in the 1970s and worked and taught for
15 years in the US. He returned to South Africa in
1996. He has exhibited internationally, concentrating
on large multi-disciplinary and multi-media projects
that engage art with conditions of urbanism.
RETREKS (1999-2002) explored emerging Johannesburg through four social viewpoints and *Infections
of the Void* (begun 2002) bridges the two post-terri-
tories of South Africa and Central Europe.

URBAN IMAGING: THE FRICHE WAITING TO HAPPEN

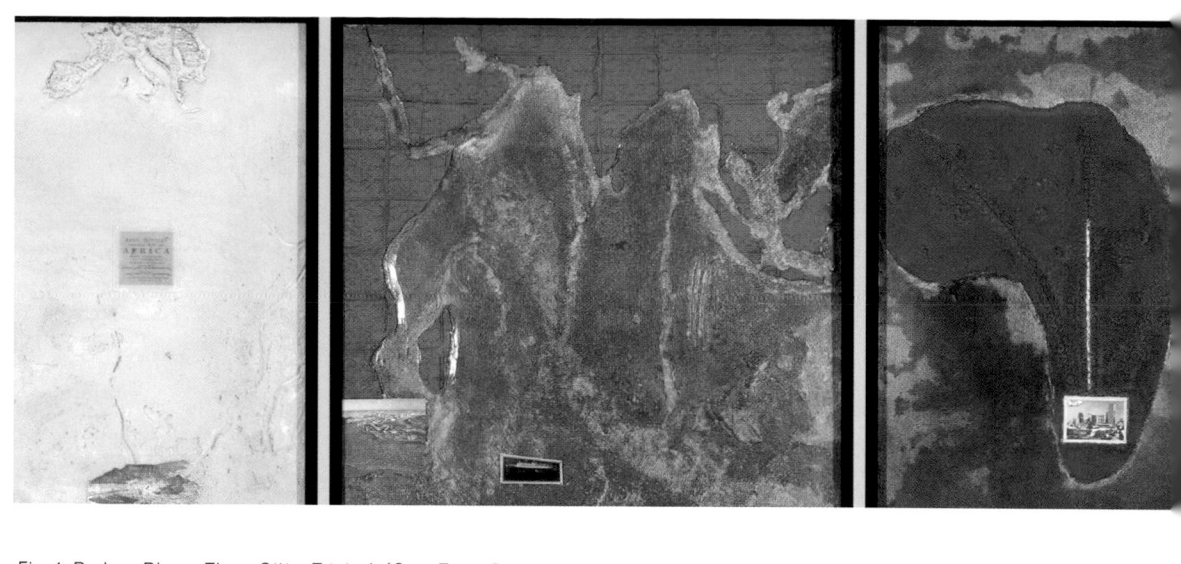

Fig. 1. Rodney Place, *Three Cities Triptych (Cape Town, Durban, Johannesburg)*, 2002, mixed media and resin, 3 parts, 123.5 x 287 cm

SN: I want to start by asking you about the images of maps ^(fig. 1) you made, because they are about spaces mapped onto other spaces, the aesthetics of African connections and, within this, they approach an idea of Johannesburg as a city in formation. What kinds of acts of topographic and artistic decipherment did you intend these to be?

First, I'd like to say something about work in general, about making things "imaginary". According to Ernst Cassirer, imagination has as much to do with recall as it does with a projection [into the future]. Flannery O'Connor was once asked by her agent to give an outline of her next novel and she said that she was like the little old lady who said, "I don't know what I think, 'til I see what I said."[1] I like language as something of an agitator of things whose visual meaning is "set" – a conversation or joke that reinterprets and often disrupts things, particularly clichés. I'm not looking to language as the final solution to the visual world.

In the early 1980s I set a project for [architecture] students in the Midwest. It was called "Use, Misuse, Abuse". The US, under Reagan, was then entering its current period of acceptable, consuming certainty, having lost any sense of the interesting doubts of the 1960s and early 1970s. I asked students to choose particular spaces and objects and take up different viewpoints, in which they neither accepted the meaning, nor the function of what they were looking at. The most successful projects involved creating longish narratives – where students displaced themselves thoroughly into characters with lives and viewpoints other than their own. The less successful were those that professed to define a "new" aesthetic. After that I began to work, along with a writer, more explicitly with fiction writing in conjunction with visual work, through a studio we dubbed *The Laboratory of Uncertainty*. It was a way, as well, of trying to resist the academic pretensions implicit in contemporary visual production. Fiction writing manages, for the most part, to resist academia. What if you created a character who didn't care much about visual work, or found it boring, or slept through dissertations? It is a form that best celebrates the "ordinary", where the writer has to wait while his characters finish dinner.

This is something that has always interested me and I think it probably comes from growing up in South Africa and thinking a lot about it – even at a distance – in all its dualities and absurdities, and rejecting the usefulness of ideology in trying to imagine something. The dance piece I made on Sigmund Freud[2] was ostensibly about masturbation, not in its pejorative sense, but rather in its amazing sense of combining a physical act with an act of imagination, in a way that is difficult to grasp exactly.

After I graduated in 1978 in London, I was given a residency at the British School in Rome to look at parts of the city in the period just after the sack of Rome. Those parts, near the Forum, that were reconstructed by inhabitants who had little respect for the meanings and symbols established by Imperial Rome. Emperors' heads ended

319

up as bricks in houses. It is a very beautiful part of Rome, where you can see changes of mind and priorities through habitation. I think this is an aesthetic that arises from a dynamic, rather than a stable, position – more like thinking than Thought.

So, yes, I've been doing mental/physical maps of South African cities having to face their new continental inclusion – at first unearthing spatial and territorial clichés, if you want, and agitating them with language. These are the beginnings of narratives from Johannesburg, my preferred site for making work about this new "African" inclusion – the excitement and the terror. It is probably in these conflicting narratives that any idea of an aesthetic might lie.

In Dakar, recently, an Egyptian artist told me it was the first time he'd been in Africa. Then he laughed. So I suspect this is a rather complicated undertaking anywhere on this continent. Unfortunately, Africa is more often characterised sentimentally by its ethnic "identities", rather than its dynamic cultural potential. The latter, after all, is incredibly resilient; it has not only resisted annihilation, but spread throughout the world and in large measure makes up that global thing we call American culture. No wonder the West has "problems" with Africa; it's too powerful culturally. If a 10 per cent population of slaves influenced Elvis Presley and got his hips banned on the Ed Sullivan show, imagine what disaster a majority population might visit on a country like the US.

SN: Johannesburg is now attached more than ever before to the rest of the continent. You have said elsewhere that we should ignore South Africa's old habits, xenophobia and petty delusions and celebrate instead the primacy of this city as a continental destination – much as New York was to 19th- and early 20th-century Europe and the world. But how might we animate the lines of connection, the process of remapping and the frictions which make for such a reinvention?

Because of the apartheid gap that turned the Limpopo into an ocean, Johannesburg is probably as much of a cliché in Africa, as Africa is in Johannesburg – a misguided machine, waiting to be put to more useful continental purpose. The machine still seems content to churn out theme parks, whether Euro, or Afro, or whatever, as the fruits of its frenetic labour. In this, it's more like a capitalist annex of the US – a consuming everywhere-and-nowhere kind of place. Somerset Maugham once said of Henry James that he was equipped with all the literary skills to climb Mount Everest, but climbed Primrose Hill instead.[3] Johannesburg is similar. This is probably, historically/mentally, the result of paying more heed to what was under the ground than on the surface. Like a dog obsessed with digging, it seldom pays much attention to the stuff it unearths. So, relative to "Africa", it is a chicken-and-egg situation. Should the machine now be let loose to dig up Africa, or should it first try to develop a little

320

Fig. 2. Rodney Place, The Johannesburg skyline (with Ponte City, home to hundreds of African immigrants, visible on the left and the Hillbrow Tower elevated on the right), 2003
Photo R. Place

322

Fig. 3. Rodney Place, *Modernism Revisited*, 2001,
digital photomontage, 50 x 50 cm

more self-consciousness about its own situation, as both a place and a destination?

My sense is to concentrate on the latter, so that immigrants from the rest of Africa might help Johannesburg develop a mind on top of its over-developed body. The dynamic of its "progress" might not be seen then as separate from so-called African identity, as it is now, but a part of it. Although I admit this is an optimistic idea for a city where culture and intellect are considered marginal, compared with the real work of acquiring as much money as possible.

SN: What we could call the aesthetics of industria (fig. 2) seems to be another theme in your work, in contrast to, say, the rural spaces of Africa. What can we make – what do you make – of Johannesburg's landscape of commercialism and industria, of its display of infrastructure, industrial skeletons and deposits? What territorial frames do they offer and what material and imaginary topographies?

It's funny – going back to Rome – I remember thinking how incredibly boring and ugly Rome must have been during those periods of Imperial Singularity. They have postcards all over Rome, reconstructing the city in all its clean, imperial glory. In 20th-century Rome, you think, thank god for ruins, late arrivals and changes of mind.

Similarly, flying over this continent, you cross the Limpopo into South Africa and are suddenly confronted with an industrial agricultural landscape – that culminates in Johannesburg's industrial urban landscape – very American in fact, especially driving in from the airport on the highway. Industrialism, like Roman imperialism, constructed singular landscapes very quickly, a political act of appropriating the landscape by structuring it. Jefferson's grid did the same for the US, creating exact addresses long before they were occupied. It seemed as if they wanted first to locate everyone and everything, a bit like Bill Gates with Windows. I once drove for miles at the equinox, taking pictures of the sun gradually setting at the western ends of Midwestern roads. Even the sun had its place fixed on the grid, as if the grid were there first.

I quite like the idea of South Africa's rural and urban landscapes then as inherited machines – up-for-grabs territorial frames now waiting for waves of (cultural) occupation. It's why I keep resorting to images of grounded ocean liners (fig. 3). Having served the purpose of carrying new middle-class immigrants from Europe after the Second World War, these ships became, in their local, grounded conditions, everything from sunken artificial reefs in Australia, to housing projects in Malaysia, to luxury restaurants in California. The French would call them the *friche* waiting to happen. Johannesburg is also a *friche* waiting to happen. To me, it suggests a potent beauty, where the idea of an African aesthetic might lie as much in the power of (re)interpreting these structures, as it would in making things "African".

323

SN: Several of your postcards in the metro-allegory series take up this idea. In *Jo'burg – An African Metropolis* (fig. 4) you depict the city built from gold, beer, plastic sandals and paper planes. It reminds me of Ivan Vladislavić's recent novel *The Restless Supermarket*⁴ in which the Hillbrow tower, symbol of the Jo'burg city skyline, is described as a vacuum cleaner attachment and an enormous parking meter; in which women's names at the Café Europa in Hillbrow – Raylene, Maylene – sound like "household cleaners" and the commercial detritus of the city is reflected in shop names: Mr Exhaust, Mr Cash and Carry and Mr Spare Parts. Best of all is the Restless Supermarket itself, intended by the owner to mean "never rests" rather than "fidgety", two different metaphors for the city itself.

I don't think that these images of the aesthetics of industria, as you put it, are as "innocent" here as similar images associated with the growth of commerce and consumption in the US. Jefferson's grid created a landscape of addresses for the now mostly middle-class US population; but it also left, in the unseen folds of the Appalachian Mountains or the dusty deserts of Arizona, the non-addresses, the marginalised-in-perpetuity, or the quaint drunks.

In South Africa, these landscape "margins" represent over 80 per cent of the population, who are now the political majority, pausing for the time being in places, neither rural nor urban, where they were dumped during apartheid. Although our country has blind faith in the social glue of US-style consumption and its delusions of trickle down, these landscapes and their imagery are evidence here of the now global apartheid, the condition of 80 per cent developed space for 20 per cent of the population. They still seem almost like a tease, or propaganda, or an "urban civilising device", as if you need a qualification to enter them, with all the signs along the highway telling you how to acquire this qualification. I'm more interested in them as "future-perfect" and speculating, often in images, about the time when consumption doesn't crack up to all that it promised and we have to face the pressing questions of cultures, urbanisation and a nation in the making (and what it all might be like). Actually, only then would new identities and aesthetics become possible, as traces of this process begin to show – a little like the hundreds of plastic bags blown by the wind onto fences when the shopping is done.

SN: In *Stealth* (fig. 5) you seem to depict two kinds of city stealth, both born out of the old order but creating new circuits of their own. Here's one reading, anyway: at the top the old army vehicle is appropriated by the small-business inner-city entrepreneur, turning the old structures into a site from which to reinvent him- or herself in the city. Behind are the

Fig. 4. Rodney Place, *RETREKS post-CARDS: Jo'burg — An African Metropolis*,
1999, digital photomontage, 60 x 42 cm (postcard)

Fig. 5. Rodney Place, *RETREKS post-CARDS: Stealth,* 1999,
digital photomontage, 60 x 42 cm (postcard)

trappings of the city – the Wembley building, a car, another building. Every small space is used – even the wheels. In the other picture below, superimposed on the old order, even built into it, is the car – of the hijacker, perhaps, or the rich man, or both. This practice, too, is born into and out of a culture of surveillance. The people who police society now, you suggest perhaps, are those who drive expensive cars, politicians, businessmen and women, hijackers, gangsters. Here the background has nothing to do with the real city, but with a fantasia, dreams of wealth, money, success. Both images seem to emphasise the travelling circuits of power and violence.

That's nice about using every small space, including the wheels. At the time, I hadn't consciously thought of it that way – it's been a while since I made these images. It was more like an observation about the rather sudden and comical efforts of civil (and private) security authorities to quickly create a user-friendly presence after 1994 in our mind-bogglingly uneven urban spread, and trying, at the same time, to get on with their usual job of policing this unruly city. To me, these images reflect, almost literally like chameleons, the context in which they operate. So stealth is an old habit, turned to new marketing purposes.

SN: In *Hot Pursuit* (fig. 6) you depict erotic circuits of fear and desire, where the pursuer and the pursued is the city itself. The halo and electrical lines given a prominent place overhead suggest two different charges, the ritualised energies of the urban itself, and of multiple narratives firing off each other, in a network of violations and frissons. Who is the bike rider?

The image you mention is another of the viewpoints of *RETREKS*.[5] It is of the motorised cowboy and the city, one of the notions I have of the urban Calvinist in the post-1994 period. It is what I like to call the after-life of apartheid operatives who carried out the "ordinary" work of power during apartheid.

  I must say that I like your interpretation of his lasso as a halo very much. It seems like a way of transferring Catholic icons into Calvinism, a religion sorely lacking in exuberant things to look at, and where even looking can be a sin, as Jimmy Carter once pointed out.

  It reminds me of a song by the Texas musician, Butch A. Hancock: "Saints and sinners all agree that Spanish is the loving tongue, but she never spoke Spanish to me" – another fell-in-love-with-a-Spanish-whore, trans-border song, with a Protestant Texas boy yearning for a Catholic Mexican girl across the Rio Grande. You have to keep the border, it seems, as the glowing coals of the hate-romance, to rekindle the flame: "I don't ever want to be Catholic, except for one night."

Rodney Place > Urban Imaging: The *Friche* Waiting to Happen

This may well explain why the Truth and Reconciliation Commission in South Africa did not work well for Calvinists. To paraphrase another song from Texas, forgiveness is a bitter apple at the root of a bitter tree. Life is a line that cannot be erased, only elongated; it is the trace of the belief that there is no other place to go, except by trekking onward, this time perhaps on motorcycles and in 4x4s.

It is interesting to me that what seems like a very site-specific religion like Calvinism – probably born of an immense social discipline to do with the daily task of keeping back the sea in the low countries – for better or for worse, transferred itself suddenly onto the African continent. At first the sense of moving forward in lonely and disciplined survival served it well, as its congregation trekked into the vast and alien African interior. However, having settled down, it became a problem, because survivalist religions need something against which to survive and South Africa was far too elevated, temperate and easy. So, it seems, they had to create a monster against which to reinforce their survival imperative. In image terms, the monster had to be equal to the dark and threatening winter days of the North Sea, a truly fearful sight.

To put it mildly, Calvinism is not an ideal religion on which to base a broad civil society. Apartheid was constructed like a landscape of dykes, social containments in which there was little space to move and everything had its place. It was far too terse a territory. Pleasures and fascinations were forced to wrestle constantly with denial, as if happiness were a condition that had to be distrusted, as both temporary and vicarious. Like passing a tree while walking along a hot road, shade is just another temptation in a biblical landscape where everyone had become a Jesus Christ.

So, yes, urban conditions after 1994 have presented Calvinism with new vigour. The city, as you say, represents a new, alien territory for this dynamic of fascination and denial and unsettled movement. Calvinist heaven was wrestled down to earth for nearly 50 years – apparently as a gift – but the unconverted found it lifeless and boring, so now heaven is back to being a signpost along the road, a direction for Calvinists, rather than a definition of space. It is better that way.

SN: Some of what you have said about Johannesburg before would suggest a reading of the city as a kind of anthropology of the senses. I am interested especially in your comment that "Most of Johannesburg was constructed around the visual middle-distance bubble demanded by us, where trees were deployed to hide the neighbours. In Diagonal Street one used one's body, not only one's eyes, in urban space … In the lexicon of apartheid this was, of course, unacceptable. The physicality of being touched was also unacceptable in the Anglo-Saxon urban paradigm that still lingers in our idea and design of cities."
        Rem Koolhaas has said that you can't build "visions of the social" into

Fig. 6. Rodney Place, *RETREKS post-CARDS: Hot Pursuit*, 1999, digital photomontage, 60 x 40 cm (postcard)

329

Fig. 7. Rodney Place, carved African heads lining Mary Fitzgerald Square in central Johannesburg, 2001
Photo: R. Place

being. What he seems to mean is that there is no transparent relationship between space and the movement of bodies in space. For Koolhaas, a "post-architectural" style of intervention is governmental rather than aesthetic, eschewing finally the "dream city" of le Corbusier and others.[6] But surely the relationship between cities and people, buildings and bodies, has to be left as question. The notion of architectural interventional as "governmental", at least in the way that Koolhaas uses it, is still tied, for instance, to a language of visuality. What kind of city culture do we see and understand if we filter it via the other senses? This seems to be a challenge implicit in your ideas above. How might these other senses lead us closer to what the non-metropolitan city, in particular, is? Japanese architect Sasaki has observed that tactility may be the language of inhabitants, visuality the language of visitors. How does the principle of contact versus good form provide us with a different understanding of Johannesburg in your view?

This is a complicated question. I don't mean too complicated to answer, but I don't want to indulge in a long argument with a Rem Koolhaas "position" by over-claiming a counter-position. Actually, Rem's book written in the 1970s, *Delirious New York*,[7] is a wonderful and, for me, important (re)affirmation of allegory in urban thinking. I was a student at the school in London, the Architectural Association, where he taught as a "young Turk", to use an extant colonial English expression. Urban thinking in the West had become terribly dry and pseudo-scientific by the early 1960s, presumably to protect the old blokes who thought it. Rem set about to disrupt it (and them), with wit and ingenuity. Nowadays, it seems a bit like having been in Kubrick's movie *Paths of Glory,* where Rem doesn't seem as disillusioned as Kirk Douglas in venturing into the cynical framework of power. But all this is personal and largely uninteresting, like glossy gossip magazines that are nice to read at dentists.

I'd rather say, in response, that urbanism, especially in Africa, is now a complex field of situations in which one learns to act "creatively" according to circumstances and occasions, at different scales and in different forms, and sometimes by trying very hard to do nothing, as an ethical position gleaned from social participation, rather than from a helicopter. Urbanism is no longer fully embraced by the positions, habits and techniques of traditional Western architects. Traditional Western architects tend to be too nostalgic and heroically motivated to participate effectively in this developing and largely "ordinary" urbanism, indeed in an African urbanism that probably reverberates around the developing world. They often seem to want to control things from above, or at a distance, through proclaiming a "new" (really?) idea of government intervention, which would, of course, manifest itself visually,

Rodney Place > Urban Imaging: The *Friche* Waiting to Happen

as you say. We all know by now that politicians thrive on opening hard copy, even if it remains empty afterwards, and there will always be architects willing to oblige them with something to smash a bottle of champagne against. Architecture is, after all, a job with Western bourgeois strings attached, rather than the voice of God.

One could say that architecture as a profession is probably coming to the end of a historical Western cycle that first manifested itself during the Renaissance. This had as much to do with the spatial predictions of perspective-as-drawing as it did with buildings and craft. There was tremendous power in the collusion between a vision and political strategy that could become "future real". As these "drawn" strategies were ambitiously extended, you could eventually plop "society" into them – whether you wanted society to believe more fervently in God, or wash itself more often. In fact many architectural projections remained military secrets into the 18th century because, of course, these drawings could also determine the trajectory of a missile.

To a certain extent this powerful collusion between the professional visualiser and the source of power has remained endemic to the field of Western architecture ever since. The desire for a marriage partner in architecture remains; it is only the partner that changes, from Popes, to Kings, to Emperors, to Conservative, Liberal, Socialist, Communist and Nationalist Governments, to Corporations, until lately – having apparently grown bored with vicarious power attachments – the architect has now emerged as power itself, a late 20th-century media star. By and large the profession consistently follows the 19th-century creed of Carlyle, that Great Heroes make Great History (or, in this case, Great Heroes Design Great Cities and Architecture). I'm inclined to agree, in this context, with Tolstoy's comment that Carlyle seemed like a deaf man replying to questions that nobody had asked.

I think the geographer, the late J.B. Jackson, is far more relevant to our situation here. He drew a distinction between political and vernacular landscapes. This distinction was not to do with urban and rural landscapes, but rather a distinction in how landscapes are conceived and occupied, or occupied and conceived – as pre-visualised and organised space having much to do with representations of power, or in the organic, quirky practicalities of "ordinary" social lives, responding to all manner of forces and circumstances not deterministically realised as "social vision". In sub-Saharan Africa, the political landscape is usually a relatively small, leftover colonial centre or under-realised infrastructure, and so, in Jackson's terms, urbanism on this continent resides largely in the more everyday forces of the vernacular.

Even with Johannesburg's well-developed infrastructure, its spatial emptiness suggests an enormous future change that will be vernacular and close at hand, despite feverish architectural attempts to quickly update our modernist space – for instance, the hundreds of little "African" wooden sculptures in Johannesburg's Mary Fitzgerald Square – presumably hoping these representations might stem the social

Fig. 8. Rodney Place, *Bread City Streetwear – Bambara Bonkari (Burkina Faso)*, 2002, mixed media, screen-and stencil-printed garments, 200 x 70cm

Fig. 9. Rodney Place, *Bread City Streetwear – Unnamed Immigrant (with mirror),* 2002, mixed media, screen-and stencil-printed garments, 200 x 70cm

tide. "KEEP OUT, this space has already been occupied by Africa" kind of thing (fig. 7).

I went to a competition of bands in Alexandra Township near Sandton. It was held in a space edged on one side by a large dormitory building built for "migrant" women during apartheid, and on the other by a proliferation of shacks. There was an enormous performance space of red earth between. What held this space intact throughout the afternoon was no visible marking or structure, nor marshals, but simply a social agreement amongst the hundreds of spectators to make and hold this space for the performers and then refill it when the bands had finished. One has to reckon with urbanism here, not through a Western notion of training a population through built structure, but rather through an idea of urbanism that is already social, already cultured, already structured and already densely populated. It is a kind of social movement that one inherits; one is not an individual trying desperately to find one's place in this movement, because one already belongs.

I think the modernist structures of Johannesburg have become far more beautiful, now they are detached from their original ideological aims and meanings. They can now exist in pure physicality, since their instructional intentions are redundant to people already social and urban in their habits.

I visited St Louis in Senegal in 2001 and walked down a street that, by UN standards, would probably be called destitute. Down the middle of this street, stepping over muddy puddles and goat shit, and around children and fish skeletons, two men dressed in beautiful, embossed white gowns talked as they walked. It is from this image that I decided to make clothes, men's city clothes, based on a simple, traditional West African gown, but patterned with the modernist buildings of Johannesburg, maps of its highways and markings from its streets, as if the whole space of the Western city could be held in a suit and carried around with the wearer (fig. 8).

African cities are probably very good for your eyes. In search of interest, familiarity or even beauty, you have to keep changing your focus – sometimes far, sometimes close – and keep turning your head. The city is not held in the collusion that arose from perspective where everything, including social behaviour, is designed and compels your eyes to fixate on what is, hopefully, the stable point. In these cities and slowly in Johannesburg, your eyes are watching movements and little things all the time and your body, negotiating with them and often for them, pushes you past people to an occasional view. It is an urban space that is forming socially and, yes, I think this needs to be a matter left entirely open. In being social, it is also, of course, a space that carries all the senses with it.

SN: In *The Reef – Divers' Paradise* (fig. 9) you seem to be emphasising the role of the imagination in creating public space. The Reef was not always an urban void created by apartheid policies, but a place of gold attracting a global network of interest and capital at the beginning of the century, and a world which was cosmopolitan, a site of racial cohabitation. What does it take to reinvent this urban magnet?

I hope I responded to this in answering some of your other questions. On the other hand, I should say that I don't think there is necessarily a convergence of the four viewpoints in RETREKS towards a singular idea of public space in Johannesburg. Each viewpoint has a particular sense and narrative of what that space might be. Perhaps some are dying slowly and others are growing fast, but all of them, and not definitively, make up what might be termed our current urban "reality". Sandton, for instance, seems to have an idea of public space based on the individual's virtual belonging to the world of global capital, although this view of "virtual belonging" has certainly been disrupted recently and has proved shockingly vulnerable and real. A fact Johannesburg knows already by its less spectacular but daily experience of "crime". The Manhattan boys, wearing mirrored glasses, got sand kicked in their faces and sent shock waves throughout the electronic world. Perhaps this serves to remind the one-way mirror of global capital – where the individual can see, but is not meant to be seen – of other pressing physical adjacencies and of other co-inhabitants of the beach we call the planet, or, more locally, South Africa.

Central Johannesburg is certainly not a void. In its recent social reoccupations, both local and continental, it is almost as if it is rediscovering its origins as a Gold Rush mining town. An intense horizontal city is being staked out, like claims, along its pavements. The vertical 20 stories hover overhead like the original empty highveld sky. It's fine, there's no pressing need to yearn for and try to usher in again the old concentrations of wealth that led to the clean modernist Johannesburg of the mid-1960s, occupied on all floors by heavenly bodies. The Five South African Families had their chance and grew rich and withdrew north; it's surely time for more grassroots continental capitalists to settle themselves into the city and make of the city what they will.

In *The Reef-Diver's Paradise*, yes, there is an idea of the imaginative social agglomerations that make for public space. On the other hand, in temporal terms, the hulks of ocean liners sunk to make reefs first appear as alien and colourless frames on the ocean floor, in stark contrast to what surrounds them and the fish that sniff around. Very slowly adjacencies begin to invade and appropriate their structures and surfaces and engulf them in the culture of vivid colour and peculiar growths. All this takes time and my fear is that Johannesburg has no time for these natural (historical) social agglomerations and the frictions that form urban relationships and new hybrid urban cultures. Instead it is pressured both by apartheid habit from within, and the World Bank, or more likely "African" American capital, from without, to prove that time doesn't matter, only the development of space, when time is in fact the more important element of a lasting urbanism that arises from local conditions.

The languid and bloody social drifts into democracy in the West are not tolerated in history any more. Instead we, the rest, are forced to respect that most futile and anti-urban "benchmark" of democracy that emanates from the US, the suburban individual and his nuclear family, designed quite recently and deliberately for the industrial revolution and now fastened to the internet for news. This is a completely irrelevant model for our urban situations, although, of course, it can be found here as anywhere. After all, this individual has become engulfed in an experience-free paranoia that articulates sophomoric feeling, but resists actual experience. This is the cost of putting one's democratic money on such a tiny social unit, connected to public space like a vacuum cleaner plugged into an electrical grid.

We need to have time to define, more like Europe perhaps, our democracy as primarily social in its ambition, with our cities at that defining edge of sociability. We should try to ignore the confused ideas of the US, where "democracy" often seems like an empty slogan for individuals who have lost their social place in the world and have grown bitter. One could read US foreign policy as the simple transference of its domestic anxieties – its antisocial realities – whether as the Jewish anxiety to Israel, the working-class anxiety to the Soviet Evil Empire or the African-American anxiety, first to Liberia and now to South Africa. The list continues to grow, as of course it has to, during the course of this colonisation by a power trapped in intense social denial.

SN: One way, as your postcards suggest, is to try to catch in "reflective frames" a sense of the cultural spaces that could become available in the cacophony of the city. What they also suggest is that, as you have said, it is impossible to have a view on art without having a view of the city. Can you say more about this and what it might imply for a non-metropolitan notion of an urban aesthetic?

To answer this, it seems one has to take on the idea of both "contemporary" and "individual". Both of these terms seem to me to have developed into tyrannies by now, not only in art, but also, as I said before, in relation to the development of democracy and of cultures. The terms are meant to be the benchmark, or high point, of where our idea of development in the global village is aimed. But they have both become entirely suspect, neo-colonial terms.

Democracy is a little big to take on, so art might, in its usual way, frame the question in a smaller, graspable way.

Contemporary is, by now, a clearly and largely academically defined market in the West – fed by various outreach programmes like *biennales* – and the idea of the individual is one now firmly based on critical alienation – the artist detached from his social being, acting merely as a pseudo-witness or judge, an emblem of the market, if you want.

337

Rodney Place > Urban Imaging: The *Friche* Waiting to Happen

The "death of the author" is nonsense, or, if dead, it is because the author has been redeployed as a motionless icon. The icon-author, particularly in the visual arts, is by now so dominant, so intrinsic to the Market of Contemporary that, as the South African critic Ivor Powell once wrote, meaning has become just another art material. One is no longer permitted to try to penetrate subject matter, in order to participate. Subject matter is simply something to hang on one's sleeve, like a bracelet, to establish a kind of dog-tag of identity in the marketplace. It is a little like those plastic bracelets they give you that show you paid to be in a club.

To me the imaginative focus on the city, particularly in Africa – where the questions are so open and rich – suggests a way of overcoming this tyranny. The city-information offers a field and course of action that resists the alienated Western ideas of Contemporary and the Individual, and allows artists to keep finding a place for their work, because they already have a (social) place for themselves. This is a more complex and multi-layered notion of time that does not centralise "contemporary" into simple actions designed for a singular marketplace. The city on this continent allows artists to keep contact – socially and productively – across a much wider terrain that demands much of their skills. The notion of contemporary is rooted in and fuelled by changing conditions, rather than stabilised and emptied into a marketing slogan.

338   Acknowledgements
This interview was first published in the journal *Public Culture*, no.16 (3), 2004, pp.533-547 under the title 'The Laboratory of Uncertainty'. Permission to republish kindly granted by Duke University Press.

339

Fig. 9. Rodney Place, *RETREKS post-CARDS: The Reef-Divers' Paradise*, 1999,
digital photomontage, 60 x 42 cm (postcard)

Michelle Gilbert
Things Ugly: Ghanaian Popular Painting

Michelle Gilbert received a PhD in Anthropology at the School of Oriental and African Studies, University of London. She teaches in the Department of Fine Arts and the International Studies Program at Trinity College, Hartford (US). She has made many research trips to southern Ghana between 1976 and the present and has published extensively in *Africa, The Journal of Religion in Africa,* and *The Journal of the Royal Anthropological Institute.* She is currently writing a monograph on the kingship of Akuapem, southern Ghana.

Acknowledgements
An earlier version of this essay was presented at the 12th Triennial Symposium on African Art, ACASA, 2001, and published as "Shocking Images: Ghanaian Painted Posters / *Images choc: peintures affiches du Ghana*" in *Ghana: hier et aujourd'hui / Ghana: Yesterday and Today,* Musée Dapper, 2003. For stimulating comments on earlier versions I would like to thank Bennetta Jules-Rosette, Rosalind Shaw, Isak Niehaus; I am particularly grateful to Sarah Nuttall and Cheryl-Ann Michael who pressed me to rewrite and rethink. Dominique Malaquais, Joe Banson, Ohenewaa Larbi and Angela Adjua-Oforiwaa Mensah assisted in numerous ways. I thank especially Bossman Murrey, without whose help, encouragement and good humour this research could not have been done.

THINGS UGLY: GHANAIAN POPULAR PAINTING

Huge colourful paintings on plywood boards are displayed during the dry season on the main streets of Accra and favoured byways of rural market towns. Vivid images of voracious animals, hooded executioners and white-skinned angels flogging black-tailed devils are depicted with consummate skill alongside film imagery that can be traced to *Kung Fu, Dracula* and *Splash,* with Daryl Hannah transformed into a mermaid-like Mami Wata.[1] The paintings (in sets of three to five) are advertising posters, two and a half metres square. Like trailers for a film, they portray the highlights of morality plays performed by travelling bands of actors and musicians. These plays, part of all-night open-air theatre events locally called concerts, or concert parties, begin with high-life music, dancing and a comedy sketch.[2] This is fusion art with a vengeance. In the captivating patchwork of what are at first sight wildly improbable juxtapositions, the past is used to address the present and future, and the global to address the local. The performances, lyrics and paintings inform one another and articulate parallel discourses that draw on events from everyday life, folkloric and biblical tales and violent and disturbing fantasies. This is urban art,[3] and a form of popular culture,[4] in which local perceptions of what is "exotic" are appropriated and in the process transformed and re-interpreted[5] (fig. 1).

Concert paintings are much like the thresholds of palaces or temples in that they are the things that people see first. Leach argues that for those who enter North Indian temples at Khajuraho, the ornate, condensed and complicated sculptural scenes comprise confusions of the natural and the supernatural worlds, and "the jumble is the message".[6] In Ghana, on the day a concert comes to town, the paintings are displayed at the busy crossroads and in the market. Just before the evening performance they are moved to the "theatre" entrance, a place of encounter with a heterogeneous and prospective audience. The paintings entice prospective viewers, and warn them of the dramas they are about to encounter. The images reveal complex layerings of meaning, only some of which refer mimetically to what will happen in the plays they announce. The paintings depict the confusing complexity of the natural and spiritual worlds, of men and women, animals and spirits, of the strange and the strangely familiar, in ways that take on a life of their own. While everyone knows that by the end of the play all is resolved and good triumphs over evil, it is the complexity which emerges from the poster images that is particularly compelling.

Ghanaian concerts are woven from richly varied elements, such as Akan tales (*anansesem*) about the trickster spider Ananse, which are told at night and incorporate mime, proverbs and an emphatic moral message structured with musical interludes. Other ingredients include church nativity plays, Hollywood movies, vaudeville comedians and "black-face" minstrel shows mixing song, drama and dancing. Nineteenth-century American minstrelsy featured white actors enacting stereotyped southern slaves, the tenacious cliché of blacks caricatured as clowns.[7] Black-face was adopted in Ghanaian concerts – a case of Africans imitating whites

343

Fig. 1. Concert painting by Mark Anthony displayed on street in southern Ghana to advertise an evening performance of a play for A.B. Crentsil's Band entitled *Ayen Nye Wo Hoo* (You are a Witch), 1999, acrylic on plywood. 2.4 metres square
Photo: M. Gilbert

imitating blacks – apparently without any racial overtones,[8] and this fused with the trickster Ananse into a joker/servant character called the "Bob", after the Ghanaian actor Bob Johnson, who created the role in the 1930s.

The first concerts, in the 1920s, were short comic plays performed in English at the end of the school year for the English-speaking Ghanaian elite. The all-male cast had three characters: the Gentleman, the Lady Impersonator[9] and the "Bob". The characters were, and still are, painted broadly as stereotypes. With time the plays became longer, the number of actors increased (from three to more than 40), the vernacular came to be used throughout and the audience became less wealthy. By the 1960s and 1970s, concerts were at their height and between 50 and 60 groups toured the country. They dwindled in popularity in the late 1970s and early 1980s due to drought and famine, economic hardship and government curfews.

By the 1990s more than 12 per cent of the Ghanaian population was living abroad sending remittances home; structural adjustment had been implemented and with the socioeconomic decline came a huge appetite for the Pentecostal "gospel of prosperity".[10] Concert attendance was affected by the disapproval of the charismatic churches: "born agains" said that concerts were associated with evil deeds and *juju*; they regarded the painted depictions of a traditional god as the portrayal of a devil, a monster, God's opposite. To counter this, bands began to take Christian titles for their plays, included crosses and angels in their paintings and incorporated Christian sermons into the evening entertainment; some even used taped American Pentecostal sermons as play outlines.[11] The 1990s was also a decade in which electricity spread to the rural areas, and one result of this was that concerts now had to compete with low-cost videos, television dramas and films. Chiefs and the elite also stopped attending, looking down on concerts as being "bush". In an attempt to reinvigorate concerts as a cultural tradition, short 45-minute concerts were performed once a week at the National Theatre in Accra and rebroadcast on television. The plan to reinvigorate live performances backfired, as people of all ages and most incomes now could watch in the comfort of their homes theatrically more realistic televised plays.[12] By 2001 only six concert groups were still touring Ghana. The cost of transportation, instruments and paintings is so high that despite the publicity gained for the bandleader and the sale of the band's tapes and CDs, the days of all-night outdoor touring concert events are clearly numbered. When they disappear, so too will the genre of painted concert posters that advertise them.

The bad, the ugly and the strange

Mary Douglas has asserted that "the discourse about dislike and ugliness is more revealing than the discourse about aesthetic beauty"; if so, then Ghanaian concert paintings and video posters are an ideal place to start exploring contextual meanings and psychological nuances. Concert and video audiences today are primarily semi-literate young men, rural or first-generation city dwellers; but everyone sees the paintings on the street and their responses reflect their personal experiences. The artists incorporate Western, Chinese and Hindu imagery in the service of local fantasy and the imaginary. The objects of their imagery are not neutral: the images are seen as seductive, violent and shocking, and evoke powerful responses in their viewers. The evils of witchcraft, in the traditional form of co-wife rivalry and in the sense of acquiring new wealth allegedly by the exchange or sacrifice of one's fertility – or a close relative – are also considered to be "shocking".

Akan speakers say that strange and shocking images are internalised and experienced physically in the *yam* (from *yafunu mu*, literally "stomach inside"), the inner cavity that includes the belly, the womb and the bowels, though *yam* is also used to express the realms of the psyche and stands figuratively for emotions and feelings. Viewers laugh and are "shocked" when they see torture, violence and obscenity portrayed in the concert paintings: such practices (whether real or fantastical) are supposed to be hidden, and their public depictions cause intense unease. Viewers are also "shocked" to see supernatural monsters that are portrayed as half man/half beast, or as composites of different animals. These ambiguous creatures capture the viewer's interest; their anomalous character generates anxiety and feelings of disquiet.[13] This is related to the fact that the categories of human and animal ought to remain separate,[14] but here are merged. The ability of Akan witches (like English ones)[15] to assume animal form is believed to be evidence of their alleged supernatural powers. Other anomalous beings include mythical *mmoatia* who are very small and *sasabonsam* who are very large: both are hairy in contrast to human beings. Real-life dwarves (or others with physical deformities), while normally prohibited from entering a palace in an Akan kingdom in Ghana, were on occasion employed as court heralds (*esen, nsaneafo*): in body and costume they were thought to represent the non-ancestral powers of the forest and savannah and thus to be able to create order in the animal world. In their disfigured bodies and provocative and offensive language, they are the opposite of the king, and like jesters they are privileged to say what they like about their master.[16]

In the Akan language, beauty (*eye fe*: it is beautiful, nice, amusing) is distinguished from ugly (*eye tan*: it is ugly, disgusting, irritating, nasty) and, as in many other languages, "good" is never "ugly". But while viewers recognise that Mark Anthony, the acknowledged master of the concert painting genre,[17] is a good and skilled artist, his paintings are never described as being either beautiful or ugly. Instead they are discussed in terms of their content, which is said to be scary or frightening (*huhuuhu; eye hu; me suro*) – a scariness that is associated with evil, the devil (*obonsam*),[18] or the witch (*obeyifo*). In other words, that which is ugly is related to that which shocks: the "shocking" supersedes the ugly – although the distortion which produces the shock is related to the sheer ugliness of what is being portrayed.

In the reception of these images, one could also say that it is the "strangeness" (*hu*) in the portrayal that supersedes its ugliness (*eye tan*) as such. Further, when people see these images, they associate them with madness or foolishness (*nkwasea sem*), and with witches (*abayisem*): they say they are ridiculous, frightful, dreadful (*nsem hu*). The paintings take your breath away (*eye hu ebo wo hu*); they are frightening (*wo yam hye wo*, literally "stomach is burning"), and associated with cruelty or brutality (*atirimoden*, literally "head is strong"; or *ne ho popo*, "his body shakes"). This is neither a negation of beauty, a reaction to disorder (*basa basa*) nor a stylistic counteraesthetic – rather it is a response to a subject matter that is fearful, raw and powerful. And doubtless because of the mystery and obscurity, implied and unconscious confrontations and forceful vulgarity, these shocking images convey a powerful emotional energy.[19]

It might be worth reflecting here on the emphasis in the reception of these images on their content and symbolism, more than, say, their form. In my work in the Akan kingdom of Akuapem, I would hear carvers discussing the relative merits of pieces of traditional regalia with their patrons, for instance, while in terms of actual use of the pieces, viewers commented exclusively on the symbolism. As Biebuyck has written in relation to the Bwami association of the Lega (DRC), all pieces were good in that they fulfilled their function.[20] Horton has written too that in Nigeria, Kalabari Ijaw sculpture was not intended to convey "beauty", but was seen as handwriting would be to those from more literate traditions: "so long as the minimum test of legibility (i.e. recognisability of signs) is passed, one piece of handwriting was as good as another, and there is no point in making a critical comparison between the two".[21] For the Ibibio of Nigeria, a damaged mask loses its functional value: for a mask to please the ancestors and be effective, it must be pristine, though the Ibibio do make purposefully ugly masks. The reversibility of the beautiful into an aesthetic of the ugly is manifest in the paired appearances of the beautiful *sowei* and the damaged, old or crudely made *gonde* masks of the Mende in Sierra Leone.[22]

The monstrous and fantastic portrayed in concert and video paintings are not necessarily the same as the ugly, and powerful things (which have a double valance) are not necessarily beautiful or ugly. Participants in Akan rites involving dangerous protective deities (*asuman* and *abosom*) would not describe the sometimes rather shapeless forms that contain these powers[23] as "beautiful" or "ugly". Nor would black stools, the ancestral shrines whose forms become softened over time with accumulated encrustations of sacrificial matter and libations of blood and schnapps, be described in this way. This is not a case of an "aesthetics of the ugly" as *might* be argued for Bamana *boliw*.[24]

346

To understand the aesthetics of ugliness in Ghana, the concept must be broadened, as Ebong notes when analysing Ibibio theatre in Nigeria,[25] to include what is distasteful and disagreeable in areas of the vulgar, obscene and pornographic. Ghanaian concert events begin with music and dancing followed by an interlude of broad and robustly farcical comedy full of male chauvinist derisive attacks on women, pornographic gestures and scenes of mimed copulation. All this vulgarity, aesthetically appealing and inoffensive in performance situations but repugnant to good taste and decency in actual everyday interaction,[26] evokes boisterous laughter from the audience. These midnight cathartic thrills form another "gateway": they are structurally oppositional to the morality play that follows and continues until dawn, the goal of which is for the audience to be uplifted emotionally and instructed in proper behaviour and social responsibility.

Imagining evil

Evangelical and charismatic churches, found throughout southern and central Ghana, have transformed popular culture. Many of the imported-from-America Pentecostal churches[27] especially popular among upwardly mobile would-be middle-class men and women are based on a theology of the Faith Gospel of success, health and wealth. Meyer[28] argues that members of these churches and prayer groups "share a popular Christian culture", one of whose features is "the imagination of evil, in which witchcraft, money and family problems are recurrent features". She suggests that Christianity demonises traditional gods and the temptations of "uninhibited consumption", proclaiming witches (who try to destroy the lives of family members they envy) to be agents of the devil from whom one gains protection only through prayer.[29] The crux of stories about satanic riches is that money is gained either in exchange for a living human being, preferably a close relative or spouse, or by sacrificing one's fertility – in other words, one's future offspring. Thus people are exchanged for money.[30] Depending on whether money is acquired with the help of God (a miracle) or of the devil, riches may be either a blessing or a curse.[31]

In Ghana today, increased poverty exists alongside unprecedented displays of new wealth. Money, sent home by relatives working "abroad", sustains the former middle class and mitigates, for many, the harsh economic realities of life.[32] Akyeampong dryly remarks that "Going 'abroad' is linked with the notion of going to 'hustle' or seek one's fortune – preferably in a country where one's efforts are not witnessed or supervised by one's kin."[33] Wealth, once acquired, is flaunted. Many of the new mansions surrounded by two-storey protective walls topped with razor wire in the Accra suburbs, in Akuapem and in the Central Region have been built by Ghanaian emigrants and "been-tos" (*akwantufo*). "The nightmare of Ghanaian migrants is to return home empty-handed. Such a migrant is denied a hero's welcome."[34]

Those Ghanaians who achieve great wealth or political power too quickly are commonly accused of entertaining occult forces. Fast money is desirable, but suspect. The popular collective imagination in Ghana[35] views the successful trader, politician or rich person through images of sorcery, cannibalism, Mami Wata or

347

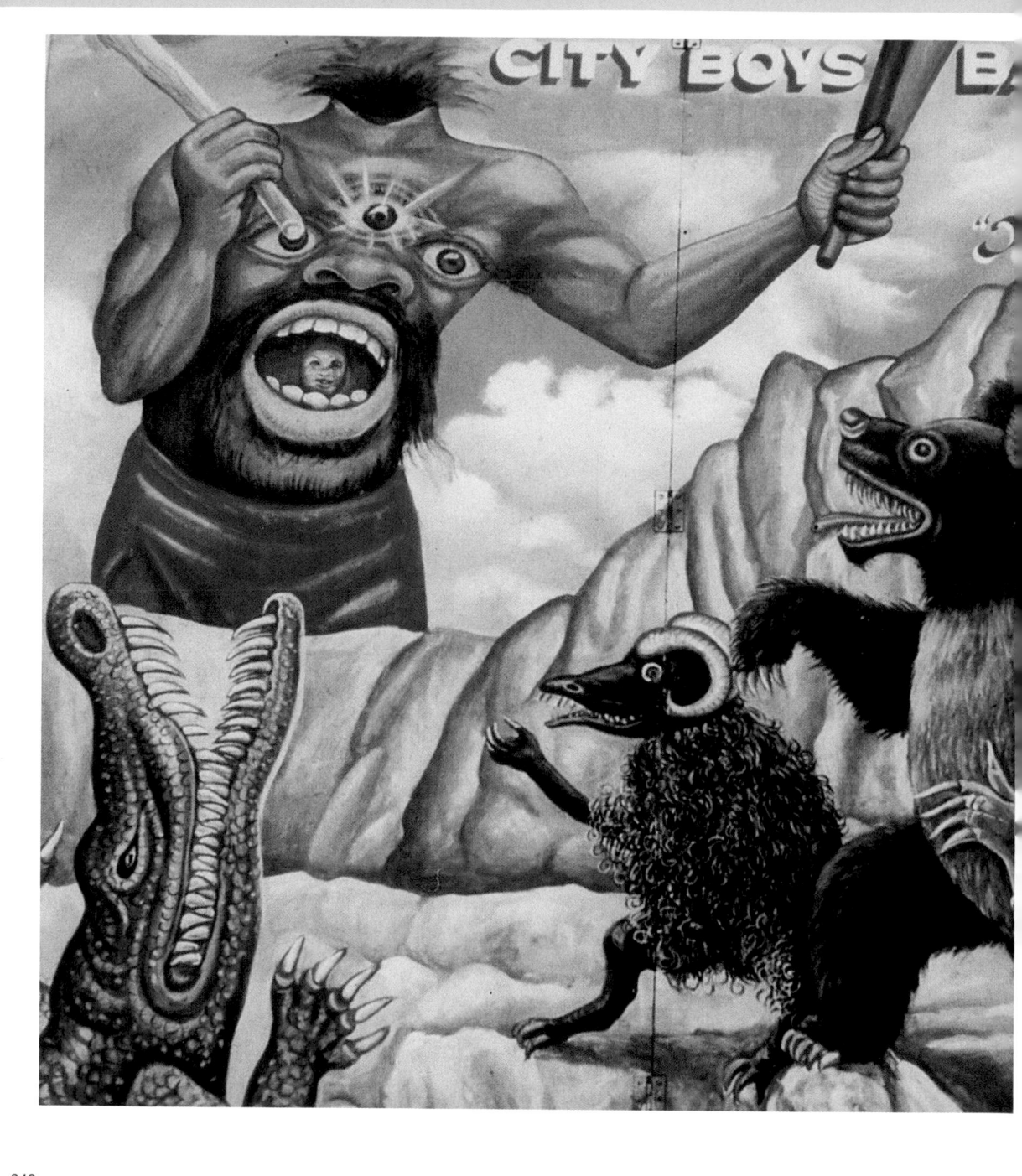

Fig. 2. Concert painting by Mark Anthony of voracious animals representing greedy witches for the play *Head of Medusa* performed by the City Boys Band in 1999, crylic on plywood. 2.4 metres square
Photo: B. Murrey

Satan. Popular Ghanaian tabloids[36] and even ghanaweb on the internet are full of witchcraft accusations and stories about *sika duro* (literally "money-medicine" rites) in which vampires suck the blood of innocent relatives in order to get rich. Concert plays, such as *The Judgement Day*, similarly focus on false prophets who gain wealth and followers from *juju* instead of from Christ. Video films on television address the same concerns.[37] Most of the popular Nigerian films shown in Ghana are about witchcraft or cheating to make money.[38] The exchange of human blood for money is a common theme connoting witchcraft. Witches, a*bayifo*, a*bonsamfo* (male and female plural), suck human blood. Huge monsters of the forest, *sasabonsam*,[39] also live on blood. Blood in "traditional" Ghanaian cosmology is a highly charged multivalent symbol linked to lineage and life, to purification and to pacification. Blood (*mogya*) is inherited from the mother among the Akan and defines membership in the matriclan (*abusua*). Shedding blood, whether by execution or menstruation, is hedged with rites. Powerful ancestral shrines (black stools) and some shrines for deities (*abosom*) were created with and renewed by human sacrifice or substitute offerings of fowl or sheep.[40] The blood of Jesus is a powerful image that has captured the Ghanaian Christian imagination because of its promise of salvation, association with the cleansing of sins and protection from hell, and ability to rebuke the devil (*obonsam*). People say *"Yesu mogya nka w'anim"* (literally, "the blood of Jesus should splash your face").[41]

In the 1990s, to discourage their members from leaving to join the Pentecostals, Catholic and Presbyterian churches began to perform "deliverance" services for those who believed themselves to be witches or thought they had been bewitched. In what follows I discuss several images from concert posters which depict and elaborate on some of the contexts I have alluded to above. As we have seen, while the urban elite view witchcraft among the rural masses as a barrier to development and innovation,[42] and many prosperous Ghanaians refuse to go back to their hometowns for fear that they will lose their money and be bewitched by those left behind in the villages,[43] the complementary accusation from below is that the newly rich have become so by witchcraft. These malevolent practices are often personalised in concert paintings in the form of threatening, jealous and greedy witches about to devour their rivals' children. They may be shown as voracious animals that resemble images from children's school books, daytime television shows or films: a crocodile from the Nigerian film *Jewel*; a black bear from *Goldilocks* or the cartoon *Cedric the Crow*; a blue-skinned, fanged, snake-nosed creature from Hindu tracts, Indian films or cartoons like *Head of Medusa* (fig. 2). The owl, too, is readily identified as a night-travelling, shape-shifting witch – as are crows, vultures and parrots (that eat carrion or talk). These ambiguous animals and "monsters" play on viewers' fear of death. The idea that Europeans use "their" witchcraft for development and technology – the "witchcraft of the whites"[44] –

Michelle Gilbert > Things Ugly: Ghanaian Popular Painting

is seen in the grimly playful depiction of an anthropomorphic airplane with a snake entwined around its tail manned by witches that resemble creatures from outer space (fig. 3). A more subtle but related belief in Ghana and the Côte d'Ivoire is that witchcraft has a double valence – positive, tied to development and innovation; and negative, associated with destruction and malice.[45]

Bold and vivid images of violence on concert paintings dramatise the moral lesson of the play and grab the attention of passers-by, even though they may not illustrate actual scenes from the play. A white-winged angel flogs a black-tailed devil (fig. 4); a pale, winged angel, golden sword in hand, whose volume suggests Mark Anthony's familiarity with Piero della Francesco reproductions, points imperiously as a horned furry black Satan drags a sinning prophet off to hell in the *The Judgement Day* (fig. 5); a white angel reaches a helping hand through a window as a hooded black man (a tunic-clad figure probably derived from a Bible illustration) murders a white baby with a large knife, observed by two protagonists and a small Mallam seated on a mat in the rear (fig. 6); a berobed prophet holds a large white cross to ward off a white and black, half-human, half-feline monster as a man and his child run towards the saving outstretched arms of a winged angel, and so on.[46]

In all of these paintings the appeal is to the passion of Christian religious fervor, to ideas about the Devil's witchcraft and fear of damnation. The prophet protecting himself with a cross suggests the victim in a *Dracula* film in which Count Dracula, as the fanged representation of the Devil in human guise, feeds on the blood of women at night in order to have human form but is repulsed by the sight of a cross.[47] Violence is used to suggest everlasting suffering in hell and to imply that one may escape such torments through salvation. Christianity is read into the paintings even before viewers have seen the play and even when the pictorial image is (at least superficially) Muslim. The Mallam, as his light brown skin indicates, is not a local. He is a mediator who can resolve moral contradictions, just as formerly Muslim clerics, outsiders, with knowledge of writing, medicines and amulets, were employed as intermediaries by Asante kings. Viewers associate the image of a bearded Mallam in robe and *kaffiyeh* head scarf (fig. 7), with Bible illustrations of Old Testament prophets (who also were intermediaries) and with scenes from Ghanaian biblical films, such as *The Death of Christ*.

Haunting and violent images appeal to the fantasies and fears of the youthful semi-literate concert audience – youngsters, mostly boys, who are aficionados of Hollywood horror and action films. Paintings of seven-headed cobras in a cave or of attacks by lions in the forest and hippopotamuses in the river, which announce Kaakyire Kwame Appiah's play *Agya Nyame* (God the Father), tap the vicarious pleasure of watching a protagonist win a fight. Everyone wants to see whether the hero will escape or be devoured by the monster.

Grotesque images of a woman giving birth to snakes and a sheep giving birth to

Fig. 3. Concert painting by Mark Anthony of an anthropomorphic airplane for a play
by the Original Sibo Bros Band. 1995, acrylic on plywood. 2.4 metres square
Photo: M. Gilbert

Fig. 4. Concert painting by Mark Anthony for the Sika ne Abrantee Band's play titled *Wo Yefuru Ba Mpo Ni*
(If you treat your own child this way, how about someone else's?), 1998, acrylic on plywood. 2.4 metres square
Photo: M. Gilbert

Fig. 5. Concert painting by Mark Anthony for the play *The Last Judgement* (*Atemoda no*), painted for the Dadwen Professionals in the 1990s, later rented to Jackson Volta and the Wailers Band. The play is about a false prophet whose powers unbeknown to the congregation came from *juju*, acrylic on plywood. 2 x 2.4 metres
Collection of the William Benton Museum of Art, University of Connecticut, Storrs

a human baby while a preacher stands by with a large cross to ward off harm, advertise a 1999 A.B. Crentsil concert called *Ayen Nye Wo Hoo* (You are a Witch). These images, in turn, suggest a poster for the Nigerian video *Opportunity* in which a human brings forth an ape. A concert painting depicting three carrion-eating vultures with human heads and legs for Original 32 and his Super Concert Party might be influenced by the video poster for *The Vulture Men*, of which the subtitle "... the quest for riches unknown" suggests that a sacrifice is necessary to attain such riches. An alternative source might be a video poster for the film *False Witch*[48] that shows a vulture with a beautiful woman's head waiting predatorily on a high cliff. In their anomalous confusion of animal and human, both suggest Mami Wata, half woman, half water-spirit (with a fish tail), whose relation to her devotees is that of a lover: she demands sexual abstinence in return for riches. She gives money in exchange for the sacrifice of a human or one's own fertility. She represents the *femme fatale*/prostitute and the "modern" woman who doesn't submit to man's authority. Her image as a white-skinned voluptuous mermaid with wristwatch, mirror and snake, probably derives from 19th-century lithographs of mermaids and snake-charmers popular in Ghana from the 1950s to 1970s and elsewhere in West and Central Africa somewhat earlier.[49]

A video poster (fig. 8) that at first glance seems to advertise the romantic comedy *Splash*[50] shows Daryl Hannah as a fish-tailed mermaid lounging on a rock in the water gazing at her real life, earthbound Indian-looking boyfriend, based on Tom Hanks. A closer examination reveals that the subtitle of the poster for this modern fairy-tale is *Indian Mummy Water,* and that the artist has transposed the mermaid (a.k.a. Daryl Hannah) into Mami Wata (pidgin for "Mother of the Water"), and this, in turn, has been translated into English as "Mummy Water". The poster in fact advertises a Hindu romance fantasy, a popular genre with women in Ghana,[51] called *Laal Paree;* and the Bollywood imagery has been transfigured and translated into a new image bewilderingly inseparable from that in the Hollywood film *Splash*. And the meaning of *Laal Paree*? Ghanaians say "Here we do not mind if we do not understand the title of a film; it is the action in the film that matters." In fact the capital "*L*" in *Laal,* composed of the mermaid's back, is ambiguously suggestive of a *J*. In Hindi, *pari* means "fairy" and *jal* means "water". Both words put together mean "mermaid" in both Hindi and Urdu. But *laal* means "red"; so *Laal Pari* means "red fairy" (and indeed Daryl Hannah is shown with a red fish-tail).[52]

More fantastical is a series of headless monsters painted over the years for a variety of different concerts. In one, the headless figure emerges from the ocean with a face on his chest and webbed hands;[53] in another, a huge monster wades in a river with a snake wrapped around his headless body as a man in the foreground runs away in fear;[54] yet another headless figure in a leopard-skin wrap, with blue skin[55] to show he is a spirit, holds his head in his hands as blood spouts from his neck.[56] Well-muscled

354

Fig. 6. Concert painting by Mark Anthony for the Kristo Asafo Band led by Nkomode, 1998, acrylic on plywood. 2.4 metres square
Photo: M. Gilbert

Fig. 7. Concert painting by Mark Anthony depicting an owl (witch) carrying a baby in a basket as an offering for the play *Different Kinds of Love* (*Odo mu gu ahodoo*) performed by the City Boys Band in 1999. Acrylic on plywood, 2.4 metres square
Author's collection
Photo: M. Gilbert

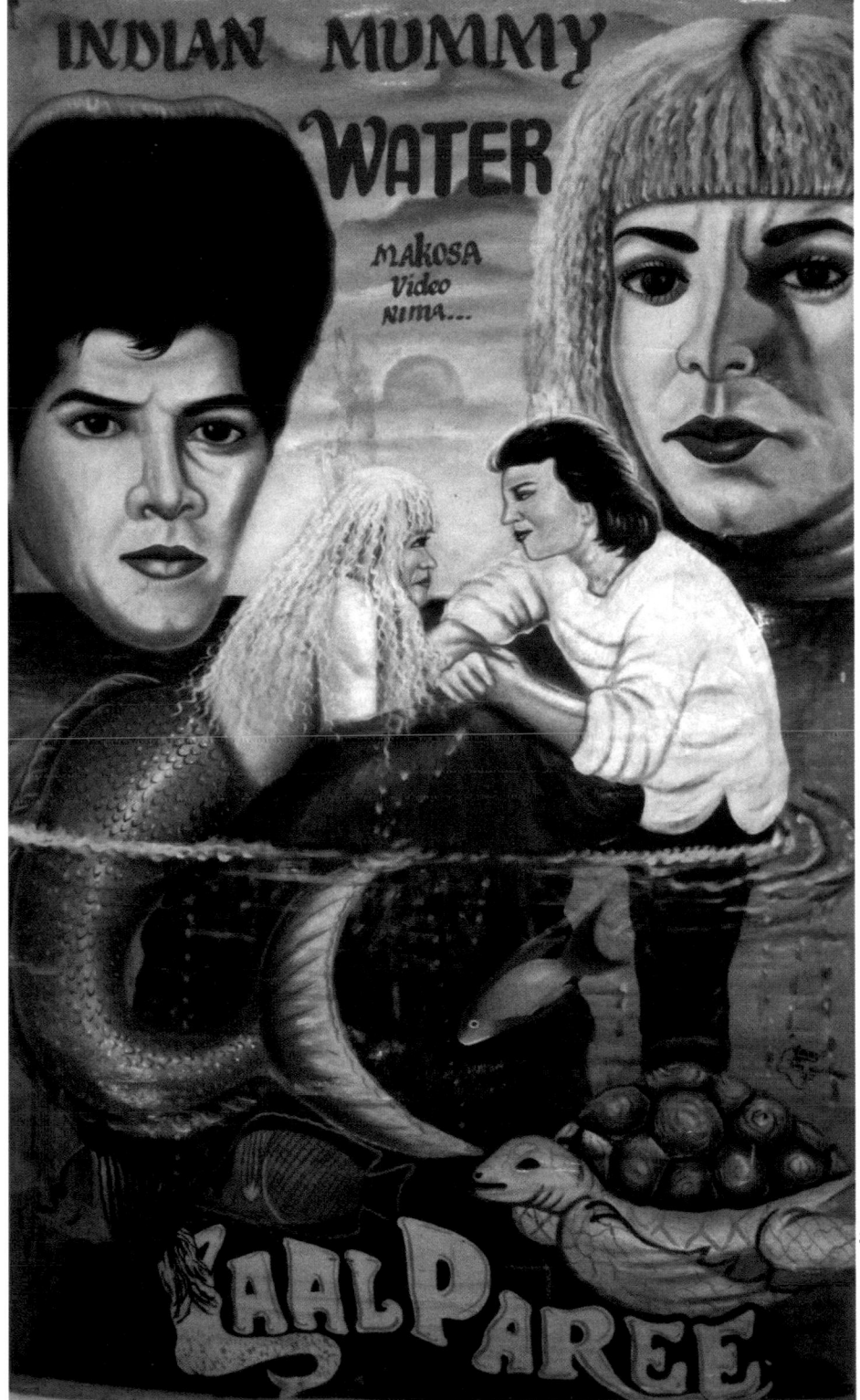

Fig. 8. Poster by "Sowwy's Art" for a film entitled *Indian Mummy Water.* I: depicts Daryl Hannah in the film *Splash* as the well-known West African water-spirit goddess Mami Wata, 1997, oil on canvas. 206 x 120 cm

Photo: M. Gilbert

(*macho*), headless figures with blood spouting from their necks doubtless suggest human sacrifice and were frequently depicted throughout the 1990s on small posters for *The Serpent and the Rainbow* and other horror films. Human sacrifice, the ultimate violence, elicits fear but also a feeling of pride (in the sense of association with former royal power). It is difficult for Ghanaians to discuss, and yet paradoxically a common topic of discourse that is reinvigorated in the public imagination through proverbs, everyday threats, mimed dance gestures and royal regalia.[57]

Foreign video cassettes became popular in Ghana in the mid-1980s and throughout the 1990s big city distributors provided rural and urban theatres with "unofficial" pirated dubs of action, fantasy and horror films and with hand-painted video posters (one and a half metres tall) to advertise them.[58] Some concert painting imagery has been influenced by these one-of-a-kind posters for one-night, one-place viewing.[59] The many young commercial artists who paint these posters on recycled flour sacks say that they are refiguring and enhancing the images on the video box or on the off-set printed paper poster to make them "more interesting". They may add violent or playful fantasies, oppositions to Christian powers or threatening warnings, as in the hand-painted film poster for *Child of Destiny*, where a large skull has been added with the subtitles "born to kill" and "born to destroy". The paper poster for the film *Spiritual Husband* shows a man in a European suit standing before a spear-holding spirit husband wearing a leopard-skin garment like Tarzan. In the hand-painted version of this collage of incongruities, a clerical collar has been added and a Bible placed in the hand of the now-recognisable priest, and a weird horned and feathered monster (resembling something from *Star Wars*) with blood dripping from his Dracula-like fanged teeth has been added in the foreground (figs 9 and 10). This gruesome and startling image (however tongue-in-cheek the artist's conception) is both alluring and repelling; it suggests violence and death and has erotic connotations as well.[60]

In the off-set printed poster for *The Rise and Fall of the Prophet 2*, the hero grabs the prophet by his shoulder and stands guard, holding a gun. In the hand-painted poster for the same film, the subtitle "the final battle" is added along with strokes of lightning, the prophet has lost his head and in the foreground a man and woman are pounding a baby with pestles in a mortar, as if it were *fufuu*,[61] a disjointed arm and leg displayed on the ground outside the mortar at their feet (figs 11 and 12). Grisly anecdotes of babies being pounded in a mortar were recorded in the 19th century from the Galinhas River islands in Sierra Leone,[62] and illustrated in a 17th-century manuscript from the Kongo.[63] In early 19th-century Kumase, some prisoners were allegedly pounded to death in a mortar, and others presumably put to death by other means.[64] Depictions of cannibalism – of converting a person into food to thus degrade him – tap a fundamental fear. Myths of cannibalism – of humans who are like animals because they eat humans – are also nearly universal stereotypes about outsiders.[65] To pound a baby in a mortar is a fairly common, if lurid, trope in Ghanaian folklore, where it is generally associated with witchcraft. It is alleged that those who have extra eyes, i.e. witches, see babies pounded in "chop bars", that human blood is used to fry *kelewele* [66] and that human flesh is served as bush meat. These are among the stories told at concert parties and in videos about what happens in the spirit world. So if a baby is born mentally retarded, it means his/her head was pounded in the spirit world, and if born with a deformity of a limb, it is from being used in a game of tug of war, etc. Or the opposite, as in a Dagaba rite,[67] where a malformed or otherwise imperfect child is pounded in a mortar, the flesh thrown into a room and the child then walking out whole and healed. Here, too, the pounding is symbolic "cooking".

Concert and video posters provide insight into the complex layering of traditional symbols and transnational media. They may be shocking, enticing, fearful, haunting, vicariously pleasurable. A lion-headed man (fig.13), seemingly influenced by *The Wizard of Oz,* with a cobra headdress and a body out of a Hindu romance clad in a draped and folded waist-cloth resembling an Indian *dhoti,* is seamlessly juxtaposed with a huge menacing creature from *Jurassic Park* or some children's picture book on dinosaurs.[68] Both depict "traditional" gods, their power and importance suggested by their large size in contrast to that of the play's tiny human protagonist. Another painting (fig.14)[69] features a tree god, the trunk animated with a human face, the branches laden with golden human-faced fruit. Was this inspired by Bosch, or by illustrations of popular German folktales about tree-gods? Rivers, trees, the sea are all regarded as spiritually powerful, and those with power to do harm are often propitiated. In the foreground, the losing contestant for a chieftaincy position has been bound tightly with ropes and is being tortured at the end of an ordeal. Danger, insecurity, disempowerment, a helplessness evoking fear are all suggested in this image of an enslaved prisoner. The executioners, portrayed as men with animal heads, are spirit beings who mediate between life and death. Miraculous and horrifying, they perform their deeds with conviction and energy. The caves or anthills from which they have emerged suggest shrines or sacred homes for deities.[70]

Sometimes icons of traditional religion and Christianity are conflated as in the image of a tree trunk surmounted by a hand from which an angel emerges (fig.15) – an image that is pictorially balanced by a heavily muscled giant in a leopard-skin loincloth straight out of a boy-meets-girl Indian film. Here, too, we see the pre-occupation in the 1990s among urban youth to transform their bodies by "pumping iron" and thereby become *macho* (*macho*: a well-built person who is strong, a bully; *slim macho*: someone who is slim and strong as Bruce Lee in Chinese films).[71] Again, both images depict "traditional" gods. Because there is no traditionally established way of portraying gods, the artist continuously varies his creations. The artist's

Michelle Gilbert > Things Ugly: Ghanaian Popular Painting

Fig. 9. Poster for the film *Spiritual Husband*, 2001, four-colour off-set print on paper
Photo: B.Mur'ey

Fig. 10. Poster by E.A. "Heavy" Jeaurs for the film *Spiritual Husband*, 2001, oil on flour sacks. 155 x 104 cm

Photo: B. Murrey

361

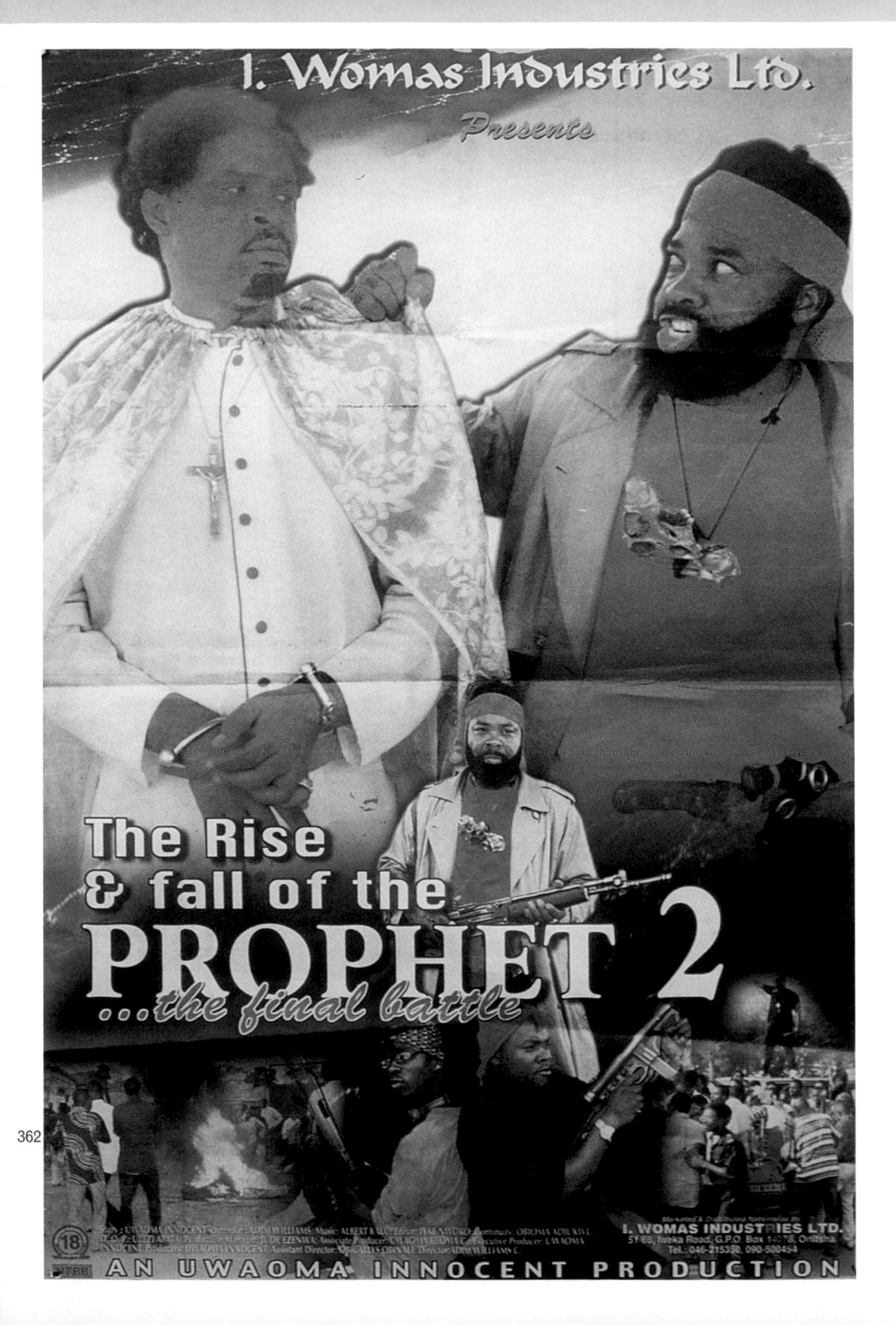

362

Fig. 11. Poster for the film *Prophet 2*, 2001, [Four-colour off-set print on paper.

Photo: B. Murrey

Fig. 12. Poster by E.A. "Heavy" Jeaurs for the film *Prophet 2*, 2001, oil on canvas. 155 x 104 cm
Photo: B. Murrey

364

Fig. 13. Concert painting by Mark Anthony influenced by the *Wizard of Oz and Jurassic Park* for Kaakyire Kwame Appiah and his Golden Boys Band. The title of the play is *Nnipa trim wo sum* (People have evil thoughts; literally, There is darkness in people's head). 1995, acrylic on plywood. 2.4 metres
Photo: M. Gilbert

creation is not the result of an isolated personal conviction,
but the outcome of interactive contributions from the artist and his patron(s) – the
bandleader, along with the musicians, playwright and actors. In the end, the
meanings of these starkly new, vividly conceived and exuberant forms are unstable.

Ad hoc shock

The recombinations of images, shocking in themselves, force the viewer to make
sense of what he or she sees in an *ad hoc* way. The viewer recreates just as the artist
does. While the plots of concert plays are fairly formulaic and repetitive,[72] there may
be considerable discrepancy between the plot and the images that advertise it, and
so the viewer is free to create and recreate meanings. Concert paintings, furthermore,
are not permanent. If the large plywood boards haven't disintegrated after a few
years' exposure to the sun and rain, they are cut up and recycled as storage boxes,
"chop boxes" and kiosks. A painting by Mark Anthony for a Kaakyire Kwame Appiah
concert shows a man bound and apparently about to be tortured. Three years later at
the end of the concert tour, a fragment of the same painting has been turned into the
door of the bandleader's room (fig.16). Sometimes a new band with very little money
will create a painting out of a patchwork of previously used fragments. Any
semblance of internal narrative disappears in such a collage. Recycling images as pure
form trivialises the content; but the separate images are still "readable", they still
make sense and whet the appetite of the passing viewer: the message is "Concert is
here; the 'supernatural' has come to town. Come to the show."

Videos are also places for active and creative audience interpretation. Horror,
action or biblical films; Ghanaian, Nigerian, Hollywood, Chinese or Hindu films –
the children don't care what language the film is in. Indian films shown on daytime
television on Sundays are in Hindi with English subtitles. The children enjoy them
even if they can't read, and at the end they can tell you the story, because those who
can read pick up a few lines and guess the rest. At the video theatres where films are
shown day and night, two or three in succession, the youngsters discuss the film
during intermission and explain the parts their friends have not understood. For this
reason it does not matter if they are literate or not. Generally it is only boys between
the ages of eight and eighteen who hang around the video theatres.[73] Some are school
children on holidays. Many are "street children": truck pushers or shoeshine boys
who sleep in kiosks and go to watch videos after they have made a little money. Most
do not know English and do not care what language the film is in. This explains the
popularity of action, horror and romance films, which are self-explanatory. This also
means the poor audio and blurred images, due to frequent repair of the dubs, don't
matter as they would for more verbally nuanced "art" films (which are not available in
any case).[74] Video centres are small; most hold around 150 viewers seated on the floor or
on benches or standing crammed together. The young boys get scared and scream; they

365

Fig. 14. Concert painting by Mark Anthony of a tree god for a play by the C ty Boys Band called *When a Royal Dies We Take Him Home* (*Odehyee wu a yede o ko fie*). 1998, acrylic on plywood, 2.4 metres square. Author's collection Photo: B. Murrey

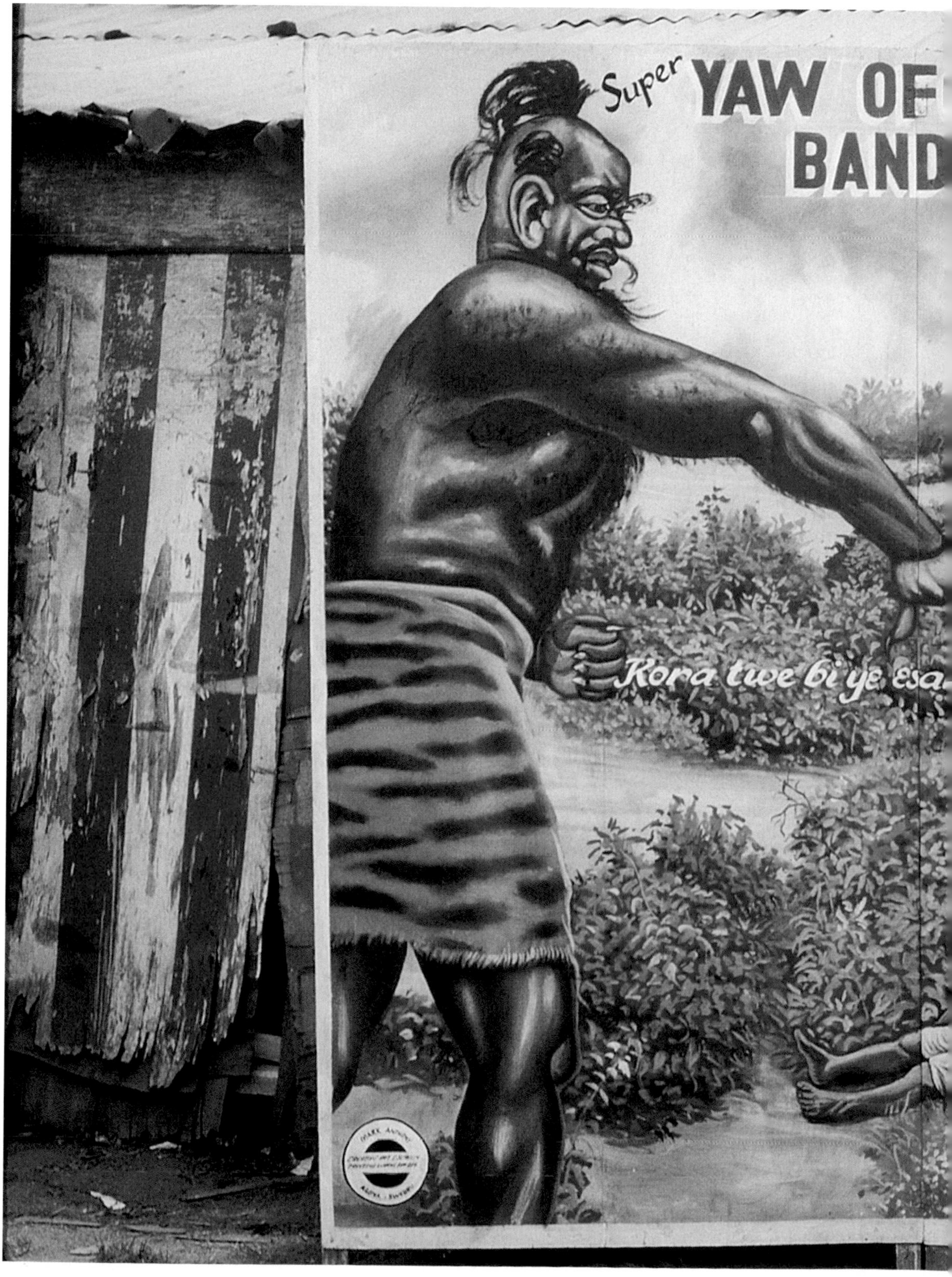
Super YAW OF
BAND
Kora twe bi ye esa

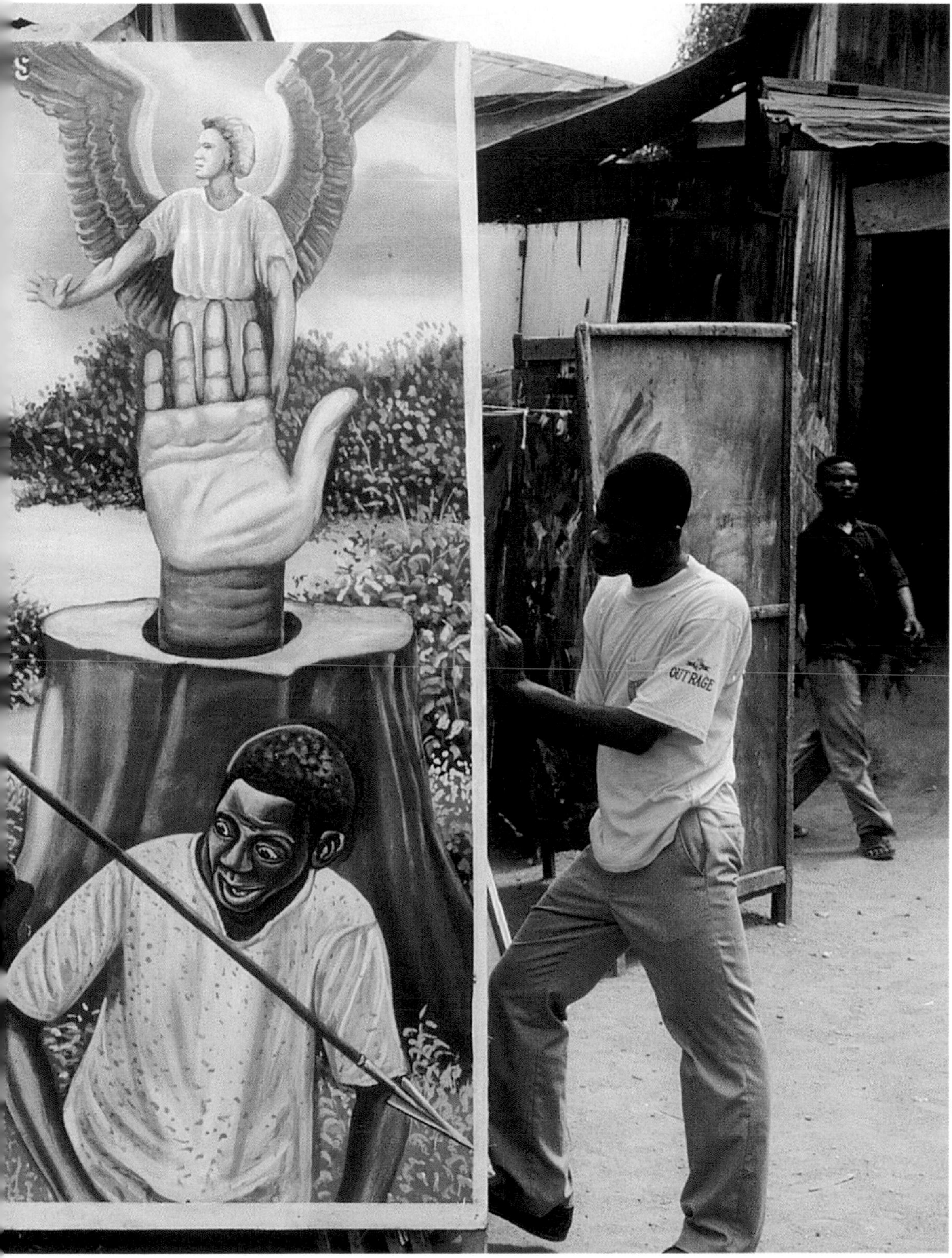
OUT RAGE

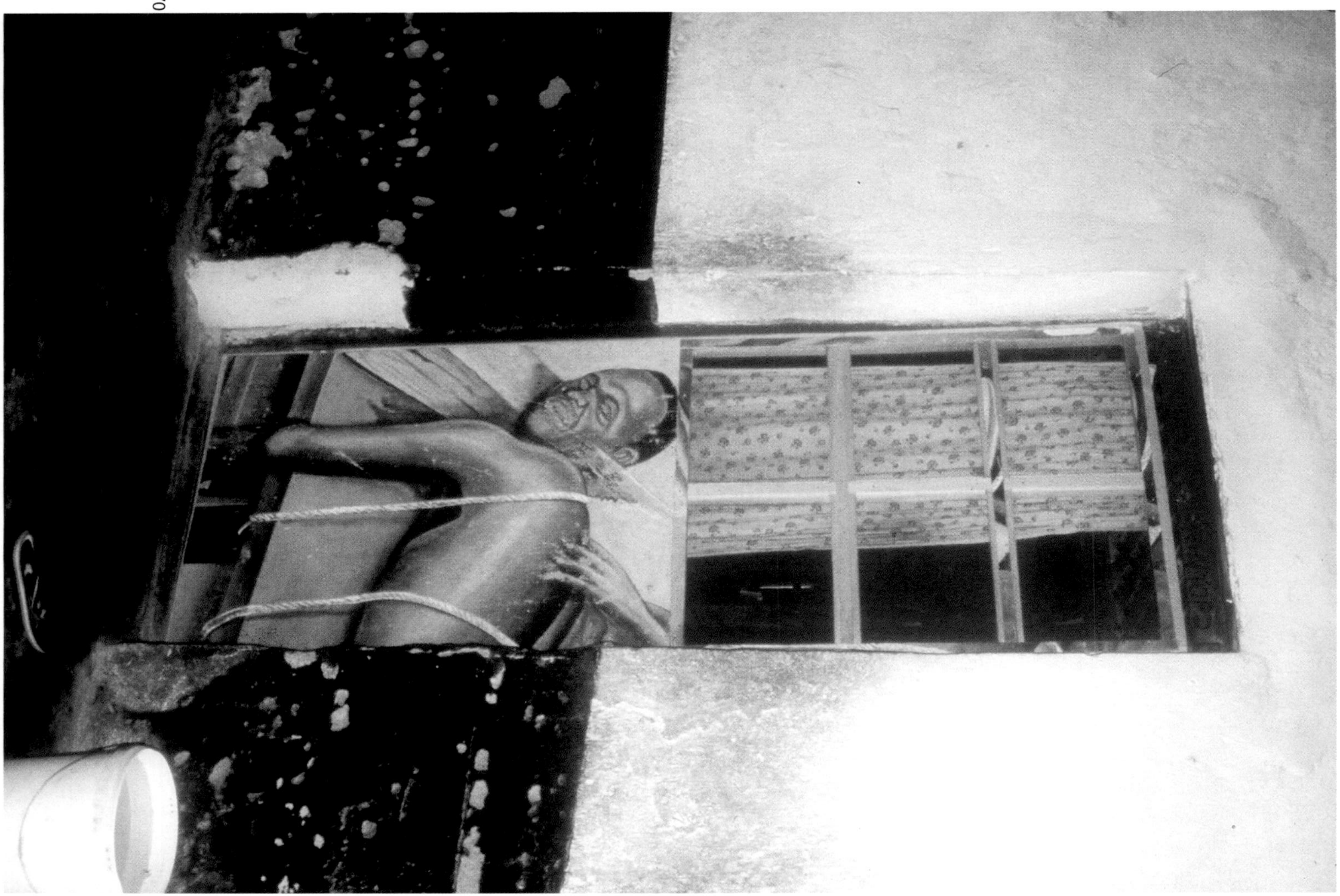

Fig. 16. Concert painting by Mark Anthony for the play *Nnipa trim wo sum* (*People have evil thoughts*), painted in 1995 in acrylic on plywood, and cut up and recycled as the door to the band-leader's room in his house in Central Region, southern Ghana, 1997
Photo: M. Gilbert

compete to see who can bear to watch the horror films, the hero with no fear, the evil with no cure, the larger-than-life heroes and villains. Can they manage to endure to the end, when the world will feel safe again?

Conclusion

Because people see the paintings before they've seen the play, they draw on their own experience and on images they have seen in videos, television dramas, other concerts and illustrated books in order to interpret the meanings. The paintings are similar in style and represent familiar themes concerned with moral and supernatural issues. The paintings are direct, devoid of details to detract from the narrative. Basic primary colours are used and handled intuitively, and the figures include just those details necessary to contribute to the story. Fact and fantasy are brought to life in the paintings, but there is a tension in that some of these notions are not meant to be understood – they are meant to be obscure and enigmatic, to horrify as well as to entice. Such painted images tap the personal psychology of the individual viewer, and are tied to the innermost thoughts and temptations, the dreams and nightmares, the fears and fantasies of the mostly youthful viewers. They are the thresholds to the "sacred" or otherworldly place that they will see when the play begins and when the "jumble" will be made clear to them.

All concerts, like Ananse folktales, conclude with a strong moral message concerning everyday life. The inclusion, however indirect, of traditional spirits, Muslim holy men and Christian evangelists constructs a present in which the individual parts only have meaning when united in a new morality. This goes beyond religious pluralism. Although there is no complete break with the "traditional" as promulgated by the charismatic churches, the focus is on what lies elsewhere, in the future.

In concerts and the paintings that advertise them, Ghanaians wed the commercial and the aesthetic. They create representations of themselves and bring together ideas and images from diverse sources to explain and entertain – what Jewsiewicki appositely calls "Africa's cultural and intellectual cannibalisation of the West".[75] The shocking and sensational images, naïve and powerful, honest and direct, lure the viewers into confronting otherwise incomprehensible aspects of their pasts and present. They transfix and haunt. They testify to a universal fear of death and torture, to emotions of terror and horror, to the pleasure of escape and triumph. And, as with theatre everywhere, concerts and films also provide viewers with a sense of catharsis, a way to confront and perhaps control their fears, and the surety of future safety and happiness.

371

Mia Couto
Two Stories: Old Man with Garden at the Rear End of Time
and
The Fat Indian Girl

Mia Couto is an award-winning Mozambican poet, short-story
writer and novelist. He was involved in the independence struggle
in Mozambique, and after independence became Director of the
Mozambique Information Agency (AIM). He later left government
service to pursue a career in environmental biology and to write.
Vozes Anoitecidas (Voices Made Night) was first published in
Mozambique in 1986. *Cada homem e uma raça* (Every Man Is a
Race) was published in Portugal in 1991. Other notable works by
Couto include *Cronicando* (1991), *Terra Sonâmbula* (1992) and
Estórias Abensonhadas (1994).

TWO STORIES

374

Balcony living on Avenida Julius Nyerere, Maputo
Photo: J. Fox

The weathered façades of apartment blocks on Avenida 24 de Julho, Maputo
Photo: J. Fox

Old Man with Garden at the Rear End of Time

In the Dona Berta garden, there's a bench. The only one left. All the others have been torn up, turned into loose planks bound for firewood. On this last remaining bench there lives an old man. Every night, seat and man, wood and flesh, cuddle up together. It's said the old man's got stripes on his skin, patterned by the shape of the planks, his outer skeleton. The elderly gentleman has been given a name: Vladimiro. He's been named after the avenue that passes by there, brushing against his solitude: Vladimir Lenin Avenue.

Today I was told the bench is to be removed because they are going to build a new branch of a bank on the site. I was knocked sideways by the news: that little garden was the only world my friend had left, his last refuge. I decided to pay Vladimiro a visit, a mission of the heart.

Sad? Who said I was sad?

I couldn't believe my ears: the man was overjoyed with the news. A branch of a bank, one of those financial ones, all firm and concreted, was worth much more than a branch of a tree. They'd already told him how big it was going to be, there'd be plenty of room for him to sleep along with his pet animal. And who knows, maybe he'd get a job there too? Even if it was only looking after the flowerbeds round about. So he was moving from a garden full of branches to a branch full of garden.

I'm going from branch to Branch.

His was a sad laugh, devoid of tincture. It would soon grow dark. When night fell, Vladimiro would wallow in drink, emptying the dregs left in bottles. When he was drunk, he would cross the night, crablike. On the other side of the avenue stand the prostitutes. The proxitutes, as he calls them. He knows them all by name. When they don't have any clients they venture into the garden and sit down next to him. Vladimiro tells them his tall stories and they take his nonsense for lullabies. Sometimes, he listens to these girls of the night shouting and screaming. Someone's beating them. The old man buries himself impotently in his arms, unable to respond to their cries for help, while he calls God to account.

God's too good, he doesn't punish anyone now.

Vladimiro was on speaking terms with the Almighty. His chitchat with the divine surprised me. Vladimiro was once the Lord's most zealous of followers. But the old man can explain it: as we get older we begin to take liberties with the sacred. It's because we overcome our fear. Is it that the more we know the less we believe? He neither knows nor believes. Sometimes he even wonders:

Has God become an atheist?

Can it be that the old man is exempt from fear in his life? All alone like that, without a home of his own, a proper home. He challenges me on this point:

A proper home? Has anyone got more of a proper home than this?

Sometimes, in his illness, he senses that death is close by and on the prowl. But

Vladimiro knows a few tricks, and gives the one who has come to fetch him the slip. Even with teeth chattering and his eyes glinting with fever, he sings, his voice trembling as he pretends he's a woman. Women, he says, take longer to die.

Death likes to listen to a song. He stops thinking about me and dances.

And that's how life goes on, a game of hide-and-seek. Until one day, death steals a march and is the first to sing. But death is going to have to persist if he's to dislodge him. Vladimiro is well-ensconced on his bench. And he insists he's not of an age to go yet. The old are those who don't visit their own various ages.

In the meantime, Vladimiro sleeps little and light. His alarm clock is a toad. He sleeps with the amphibian tied to his leg. And he explains, in serious tone: the creature's only tied up to stop him taking off.

A toad doesn't fly because he's let water into his heart.

Now, everything is coming to an end. They're going to demolish the garden, the city is going to become more urban, less human. That's why I'm paying the old man a visit. I return to the reason for my going there:

Tell me about this business of the bank: are you really happy?

Vladimiro takes his time. He's seeking the best truth he can find. The smile vanishes from his face.

You're right. This cheerfulness of mine is a lie.

Then why are you putting on an act?

Did I never tell you about my late wife?

I shake my head. The old man tells me the story of his wife who died a lingering death full of suffering. A sluggish, putrefying disease. He would clown around in front of her all day, and crack jokes to scare away the crack of doom. The woman would laugh, who knows, maybe out of pity for the man in his kindness. It was at night, when she was asleep, that he would weep, crazy with despair.

It's like now: I only cry when the garden has gone to sleep.

My arm sneaks round his shoulder. It's time to say goodbye. I return to my senses with a far greater feeling of abandonment. Behind me, I leave Vladimiro, the avenue and a garden with its solitary bench. The last bench in the garden.

The Fat Indian Girl

I want to be like the flower that dies before getting old.

That's what Modari, the fat Indian girl, used to say. She didn't die, nor did she grow old. She just got fatter and fatter. By the time her adolescence was over, she'd grown huge, globese. She reclined on her bed cylindrically, unable to move, filling the feathery fabric with fluff. And because she cast so much shadow, moss even began to grow in the folds of her flesh.

Her life was one of distraction. They would turn the television on for her and leave her to bask in the suds of soap operas. Modari would cry, stare entranced and let out

377

378

A derelict building near Ponto de Ouro in southern Mozambique
Photo: J. Fox

Avenida 24 de Julho on Maputo is lined with 1970s apartment buildings
Photo: J. Fox

high-pitched peals of laughter, adding harmony to birdsong. Pressing the buttons on the remote control, she took possession of the world – everything was so easy, a touch was enough to change dreams. She could rewind life and cause time to pause in its tracks. Her destiny was, after all, at her fingertips. Modari lived her night in daytime, and her day by night. On the luminous screen, the girl peeled back time.

But so much substance sapped her strength. The fat girl couldn't sustain herself with so much sustenance. She had neither the strength to get up or sit down. Her flesh was unemployed, and her body as flaccid as an empty watermelon. A mere idea would cause her head to drop. By now, her family could tell the signs: if it was a good idea her head would droop to the left. A bad idea caused it to tilt onto the right shoulder.

For the good of the story, it must be said that she answered the call of nature right there, in the middle of her flesh. At a certain hour, a servant would come and clean her. He would undress the girl and ask her permission to wipe her crevices, folds and pleats with perfumed towels. He would lift her, turn her over and change her nappy with all the strength of a whale fisherman. Then, he would leave her, stark naked, like a mountain exposed to the cool air. Finally, he would help her to put on a light, transparent slip. The servant was by no means gentle with her. But she grew languid as his fingers brushed over her. And she would fall asleep with the remote control in her hand.

So that she wouldn't weaken further, they made a window in her room, far from prying eyes. They punched a hole through the wall, raising storms of dust. As it was impossible to move the fat girl, they covered her with a plastic sheet. Modari sneezed in soprano, more concerned with the television than the state of her lungs.

One day, a traveller turned up. The migrant brought her cloth, colours and perfumes from India. He was a sober, solitary man. He saw her and immediately fell in love with her great volume.

You've got so much woman inside you that if I was polygamous, I wouldn't need another one.

The man loved Modari but was finding it hard to get to the stage where his love might be consummated. He whispered passionately: If one day I manage to put it into practice with you ... But he was going to have to dig through more flesh than one of our miners deep down in the Rand.

From now on I don't want any servant to touch you.

He took charge of her ablutions himself. Modari took delight in being flushed and the man would dry her, apply soothing powders to her skin and rub her with lotions. It was during one of these sessions that the act of love took place. The visitor pushed back her legs as if he were casting aside the trunks of a pair of baobabs. They made love, and goodness knows how he managed to descend so far into her pulpsome network of caves. Straight afterwards, Modari felt light. With the remote control in her hand, she realised that at no time during their lovemaking had she let go of the little box of buttons. And so, bathed as she was in perspiration, she joked:

What do you like better, my love: to be panned or canned?

She felt so light that she tried lifting her arm. And she managed to. Delighted, she waggled her fingers on high like so many marionettes. On the following night, they made love again. And on the remaining nights too. Then, Modari realised that every time she made love, she got visibly thinner. After some days, Modari was getting out of bed and trying to take a few steps round the large room. Her consummate lover seemed more dissatisfied than a bee. He was so gnawed by love that he was losing his fingernails. His heart was suffering from an excess of access.

A month later, Modari was even dancing. She was slim, a picture of osseous elegance. Hundreds of kilos had evaporated, converted into heat and nothingness. Modari busied herself pulling in saris, tightening dresses, adding holes to belts. At first, her family was happy. But in time, they stopped rejoicing in the change. Modari was growing hollow-cheeked and scrawny. It was either one thing or the other: she was either ill or overly lovelorn.

Too much in love?

Modari rejected any advice. Love is like the sea: being infinite, it yearns to complete itself in other waters. I won't hold back, she shouted. And she went to speak to her man, who was compliant: they would love each other forever after, but she should leave the remote control on the bedside table. At least for the meantime. Amid laughter and lips, their bodies intertwined. For the first time that night, Modari felt the bite of tenderness. The taste of a kiss slithers between one's lips and teeth, between life and death. Blade and velvet, which of the two are touched in a kiss? Mouth to mouth asphyxiation: that's what a kiss is.

The following day, Modari, now shrunken to minuteness, was devoid of weight. Never before had a woman been seen with such poverty of flesh. To the extent that her lover was afraid:

No, Modari, I shouldn't touch you, your body can no longer provide love with its access.

Modari smiled: was her sweetheart scared she might die? She felt like answering that, because of love, she was all the while living infinite lives. In order to die now, infinite deaths would be required. Instead of this, she asked:

Don't you remember that, before, I wanted to be a flower? Well, answer me then: don't you find me scented?

He grabbed her hands as if summoning courage. And he announced that he had to go on a long journey when the sun next came up.

Tomorrow, my sweet love.

Modari moved away somberly. She remained like this, hushed, removed from the moment. The man thought she was weeping. But suddenly, she turned round, plying him with her laughter. Waving the remote control, she challenged him:

Mia Couto > Two Stories: Old Man with Garden at the Rear End of Time and The Fat Indian Girl

The modernist geometry of Maputo's skyline
Photo: J. Fox

Come and catch your rival here. Come on, you jealous thing!

He took her in his arms and cuddled her, vanquished and eager. Those who kiss are always princes. A kiss makes sleeping beauties of them all. The Indian girl surrendered as if asleep. Afterwards, the man looked at his own arms in surprise. There was no sign of anything or anybody. Modari had been extinguished. Her body had left her life, time had been exiled from her existence. Modari had departed for bygone times. The man even heard the remote control clatter to the floor somewhere in the room.

Isabel Hofmeyr
Seeing the Familiar: Notes on Mia Couto

Isabel Hofmeyr is Professor of African Literature
at the University of the Witwatersrand. She has
published widely in the field of South African
literary and cultural history. Her book *We Spend our
Years as a Tale that is Told: Oral Historical Narrative
in a South African Chiefdom* (1993) was shortlisted
for the Herskovits Prize. She has recently published
*The Portable Bunyan: A Transnational History of the
Pilgrim's Progress* (2004).

SEEING THE FAMILIAR: NOTES ON MIA COUTO

In "Two Thoughts on Drawing Beauty" (in this volume), William Kentridge contemplates the difficulties of seeing the familiar. How to bring the flat, semi-industrial, mine-dumped landscape of Germiston, east of Johannesburg, into view? How to slough off the established conventions of landscape painting into which the flat horizons and stark light of Germiston will not go? Kentridge ponders the process of being gradually re-educated by the terrain and finding the conventions for bringing newness into the world. Reframed in the terms of this collection, Kentridge asks how to render beauty through ugliness. How does one discover that quality of the unprecedented, the novel and the original with which beauty is associated in the drab mine-dumps of Germiston?

Mia Couto's stories provide one set of answers to this question. Set in unrelentingly ghastly post-colonial contexts, these stories offer ways of reconfiguring the world that challenge us to think about what beauty might be in the ugliness of political failure and poverty.

The first time I encountered Couto's stories it was precisely this quality which struck me. The setting was South Africa in the late 1980s, when two of his collections of short stories become available in translation as *Voices Made Night* and *Every Man is a Race.*[1] As I turned the pages, I had an electrifying sense of encountering a process of newness being brought into being. These were stories which shifted the axes of the world.

Couto's stories are set in Mozambique, a small and poor nation but one that shaped the narrative of the subcontinent in seminal ways. In 1975 Mozambique, conducting a guerrilla war in the name of socialism, gained independence from centuries of Portuguese colonial rule. In the darkness of apartheid, it was hard not to be touched by this incandescent revolutionary narrative in which the tiny and doughty Mozambique (along with the other Portuguese colonies in Africa, Angola and Guinea-Bissau) had thrown off Portuguese colonial rule. The struggle in Mozambique produced a quasi-religious historiography made up of stories of resistance and oppression, righteousness and evil. This template mapped neatly onto a similar narrative that was taking shape around the anti-apartheid struggle.

By the early 1980s, Mozambique had all but fallen apart. South African-sponsored terror, socialist autarky and protracted civil war had sundered what was in any event only superficially a country to begin with. This disintegration notwithstanding, the heroic anti-imperial narratives persisted. The tension between this triumphalist historiography and the reality of disintegration was considerable, yet one looked in vain for some alternative form of explanation which could capture the patent complexity of what was unfolding.

Against this background, discovering Couto's stories was like taking in huge draughts of invigorating air. Their opening paragraphs invited curiosity rather than that feeling of tired weariness when one can predict an entire story from its first

Washing day on the banks of the Lurio river in northern Mozambique
Photo: J. Fox

sentence. Couto's stories suggested a completely different landscape sedulously rooted in the complexity of post-colonial life. This was no longer a world of either/or, resistance or collaboration, virtue or vice.

Instead Couto's writing challenged these exhausted orthodoxies with a series of novel techniques. Instead of a Manichean world of good and evil, we were presented with a slithery continuum where, in a story like "The Private Apocalypse of Uncle Geguê", one could simultaneously belong to the state Revolutionary Guard, be a criminal and a part time member of Renamo (Mozambican National Resistance), the organisation that led the civil war against the Mozambican Frelimo-led socialist state. In the historiography of the time, such a continuum was unthinkable. Renamo, sponsored first by the Rhodesians and then by apartheid South Africa, was read as the incarnation of evil; Frelimo stood for anti-imperial righteousness. In Couto's story, by contrast, the world was full of "soldiers of no-one" who endlessly re-invented themselves in order to survive the cataclysmic circumstances of civil war.[2] As post-apartheid South Africa was to reveal, political activism and crime were not necessarily opposites, but rather a continuum where the resources of violence learned in one context could be adapted to another. The narrator of Couto's story, inducted into violence by his uncle Geguê, comments:

> With that weapon, I brought my wickedness to perfection. I broke into cattle pens, I emptied bottle stores. When I wasn't stealing things, a handkerchief over my mouth, I was a militia-man's auxiliary. I was at once a policeman and a burglar.[3]

The nameless narrator becomes a child soldier, a figure to appear prominently in the civil wars of Liberia and Uganda.

Couto's stories were also memorable for their unusual blend of violence, whimsy and humour. These were not acrid disavowals of the nation-state which have become so fashionable. Couto remains deeply committed to the idea of Mozambiqueness (*Moçambicanidade*) and captures the motivating force of this desire in complex ways. One favoured theme is that of public history, the site of the post-colony where performances of power are played out to create the illusion of a state. In this domain, Couto is less interested in the power of the state to compel or delude its citizens to internalise the idea of state. Rather, he is interested in the forms of desire that such a scenario awakens. His stories often investigate the quirkiness of public history: the outcast, homeless and crippled Rosa Caramela, who loves the statues in the parks she inhabits ("Rosa Caramela"); Uncle Geguê and his nephew, who keep encountering a soldier's boot which pops up throughout the story, like an idiosyncratic memorial ("The Private Apocalypse"); the character Zeca Tomé continually decorated with medals which bring disaster as the political regime changes ("The Swapped Medals").

388

Couto's use of humour is bravely inventive. One of his stories, "How Ascolino do Perpétuo Socorro Lost his Spouse", is an allegory of colonial rule, one of the few instances of an attempt to narrate colonialism in a comic rather than a tragic mode. Set in a house named Vivenda da Santíssima Palha (the House of Most Holy Straw), "more dreamt of than firmly fixed",[4] it tells the story of Ascolino do Fernandes Perpétuo Socorro, a Goan-born Mozambican and his strenuous attempts to love his distant, remote and barely-seen wife (who, as the story progresses, comes to represent Portugal). The story careens along comically with Ascolino routinely drinking too much and making suggestive overtures to his servant Vasco. His wife, Dona Epifânia, loses patience, packs up and goes home.

Many of his stories take up the theme of the deluded creativity induced by poverty. In a foreword to his collection *Voices Made Night*, Couto observes:

> The most harrowing thing about poverty is the ignorance it has of itself. Faced by an absence of everything, men abstain from dreams, depriving themselves of the desire to be others. There exists in nothingness that illusion of plenitude which causes life to stop and voices to become night.

His stories return again and again to this deluded creativity. In "The Whales of Quissico", Bento Joao Mussavele hears a rumour that there are whales that regurgitate commodities. He goes in search of the whales and drowns. In "The Girl with a Twisted Future", Joseldo Bastante hears a rumour from passing truck drivers that contortionists are much in demand in the circus world. He decides his daughter will become a contortionist and every night ties her to a barrel. She dies. In "So You Haven't Flown Yet, Carlota Gentina?" a man, influenced by his brother, decides that his wife is a witch. He pours hot water on her and she dies. In each of these plot lines, a protagonist hears a rumour and acts on that rumour with disastrous consequences for himself or someone else.

In exploring this set of motifs, Couto is able to provide a complex yet unsentimental view of those caught in the grip of poverty (his protagonists are generally the marginal of the marginal: orphans, widows, cowherds, children, blind fishermen). Through the theme of deluded creativity and obsession, he can also explore one of the great paradoxes of the post-colony, notably how the "citizenry contributes to its own capture".[5] Caught in the net of powerful obsessions, protagonists pour their creative energy into deluded projects and lose the ability to analyse their own situation with any critical distance.

His work has continued to forge a path of complexity. In his novel, *Under the Frangipani*,[6] he adopts the device of a deceased narrator. This is not a simple gesture towards the comforts of ancestral continuities. Instead, Couto uses the device as a way

389

to find a space from which to narrate the violent and venal excesses of the post-colonial state.

Through an exploration of the absurd complexities of post-colonial life, these stories offer us novel configurations of the beautiful and the ugly. The two stories of Couto in this volume continue that exploration. The first one, "Old Man with Garden at the Rear End of Time" tells us about a homeless man about to lose his last foothold in the world, namely a park where he lives. The story opens with a characteristic paragraph which offers us an imagist mini-archive of Mozambican history: the public garden created by Portuguese colonial rule; the remnants of this rule which still have a shaping influence in the present as the planks of the park bench press into the protagonist's flesh, creating an exo-skeleton; the protagonist's name (Vladimiro), inherited from a period of socialism, and its remaining markers (the street adjoining the park is Vladimir Lenin Avenue); and finally the spread of international finance capitalism in the form of a new bank, come to obliterate this little archive.

Like so many other Couto protagonists, this one is an outcast, a homeless vagrant sleeping rough. His only companionship comes from a frog and a community of prostitutes, or 'proxitutes', as he calls them, those, who like himself, must survive by creating proxy identities to present to the ever-changing world.

Yet, despite being so marginal, he still attempts to husband the remnants of the public park/nation, dying as his wife did, of a "sluggish, putrefying disease". During his long nursing of her he kept up a brave face, crying only privately and at night when she was asleep. Now, too, he keeps up a brave face, offering a series of cheerful public identities to the world, while at night he grieves for his dying park. However, the creativity that goes into this marginal life is also a deluded one. Like his companion frog who has lost the ability to fly because he has let water into his heart, Vladimiro has been saturated by his environment of poverty and want.

Like many of Couto's other stories, this one offers a vision of a fragile and briefly-glimpsed beauty in the midst of post-colonial administrative and bureaucratic dis-figurement. However, at the same time, the story highlights the deluded quality that often accompanies the creativity made in poverty.

"The Fat Indian Girl" is another mini-allegory on the state – this time, the bloated post-colonial state in an age of a globalised and all-consuming media regime. The Indian girl, existing entirely in and through soap operas, is vast yet empty, filled with nothing. She exemplifies the overfed few, living by remote control, sustained by soap opera and servants. She is the ugliness of the contemporary post-colonial state writ large.

The handsome prince falls for her excess and believes she can meet all of his desires. But in this reverse fairy tale, his kiss, instead of waking her up, puts her to sleep. For Couto, the excesses of the new world order are such that we can only think of them via reversed or anti-narratives. The ugliness of this world order challenges us to think things in reverse and upside down in order to try and make sense of what is happening. Through an economy of inversion and an aesthetic of juxtaposition, where the violent and the comic cohabit, Couto offers us a configuration of beauty and ugliness that provides novel insight into the complexities of post-colonial life.

Isabel Hofmeyr > Seeing the Familiar: Notes on Mia Couto

Notes

Notes Sarah Nuttall (pp. 6-29)

1. Kant, Immanuel, "On National Characteristics So Far as They Depend upon the Distinct Feeling of the Beautiful and Sublime" in *Race and the Enlightenment: A Reader*, Emmanuel Eze (ed.), Blackwell: Oxford, 1977, p. 57. Kant was drawing on Hume's work in which he challenged anyone to cite a single example in which a Negro had shown talents and suggests that the difference between blacks and whites is as great with regard to mental capacities as colour. In Kant's view "the religion of fetishes so widespread among them is perhaps a sort of idolatry that sinks as deeply into the trifling as appears to be possible to human nature ... The blacks are very vain but in the Negro's way, and so talkative that they must be driven apart from each other with thrashings" (*ibid.*, p. 57). In his "Lectures on the Philosophy of World History", Hegel argues that from a philosophical point of view, non-European peoples – American Indians, Africans, Asians – are less human than Europeans because, to varying degrees, they are not fully aware of themselves as conscious, historical beings (Eze, p. 109).

2. See Mbembe, Achille, *On the Postcolony*, University of California Press: Berkeley, 2001.

3. In 1906-7, Picasso wrote: "When I went to the Trocadero it was disgusting ... I wanted to get away. But I didn't leave. I stayed. I understood something very important: something was happening to me, wasn't it? The masks weren't like other kinds of sculpture. Not at all. They were magical things ... [Braque] loved the Negro pieces, but as I've said: because they were good sculptures. He wasn't ever afraid of them. Exorcism didn't interest him. Because he didn't feel what I called Everything, life, or, I don't know what, the Earth? Everything that surrounds us, everything that isn't us, he didn't them find at all hostile. Not even – imagine! – not even strange! He always felt at home. And still does. He doesn't understand these things at all: he isn't superstitious!" (Pablo Picasso, "Discovery of African Art 1906-7" in *Primitivism and Twentieth-Century Art: A Documentary History,* Jack Flam and Miriam Deutch [eds], University of California Press, Berkeley: Los Angeles and London, 2003, p. 34). Some of the more seminal critiques of the Museum of Modern Art's "Primitivism" exhibition in New York in 1984 in the end share Picasso's view of African objects (see Gikandi, this volume). Suggestive also of the relative currency of such views is Norman Mailer's *Portrait of Picasso as a Young Man: An Interpretative Biography*, Atlantic Monthly Press: New York, 1995; and his text on Zaïre, *The Fight*, Little, Brown & Company: New York, 1975, in which horror and fascination with the black body are commingled.

4. Fanon writes of the white child who sees him and exclaims: "Look at the nigger! ... Mama, a Negro!" He continues: "My body was given back to me sprawled out, distorted, recoloured ... The Negro is an animal, the Negro is bad, the Negro is mean, the Negro is ugly ... I sit down at the fire and I become aware of my uniform. I had not seen it. It is indeed ugly. I stop there, for who can tell me what beauty is?" (Franz Fanon, *Black Skin, White Masks*, Grove Press: New York, pp. 113-114).

5. Morrison, Toni, *The Bluest Eye*, Vintage: London, 1999, p. 95. Morrison writes further that beauty "originated in envy, thrived in insecurity, and ended in disillusion ... it was a wellspring from which she would draw the most destructive emotions ... curtailing freedom in every way".

6. *Ibid.*, p. 35.

7. Morrison, Toni, "Afterword", *The Bluest Eye*, p. 167.

8. *Ibid.*

9. It is important to note, however, that even earlier accounts were less culpable of the erasure of African agency than these 18th- and 19th-century versions. See for example Peter Mark, *Africans in European Eyes: The Portrayal of Black Africans in Fourteenth and Fifteenth Century Europe*, Syracuse Maxwell School of Citizenship and Public Affairs: Syracuse University, 1974; and Frank Snowden, *Blacks in Antiquity*, Belknap: Cambridge, MA, 1970.

10. Biaya, T.K., "The Arts of the Beautiful in Addis Ababa and Dakar", unpublished paper. Biaya continues by noting that "Within this hierarchy, the mulatto woman was placed at the top. Then there was the 'petite and beautiful Abyssinian', a nymphomaniac with skin of honey. The 'negress', black as the colour of night, was on the bottom rung of the ladder and, in the eyes of the white, represented both absolute taboo and maximum transgression."

11. Elizabeth Ezra argues this point and shows that behind the "love of the Negro" is a deep historical ambiguity, and a way for Europeans to project their own fears of difference onto otherness (Elizabeth Ezra, *The Colonial Unconscious: Race and Culture in Interwar France*, Cornell University Press: Ithaca and London, 2000). See also Patrice Archer-Shaw, *Negrophilia: Avant-Garde Paris and Black Culture in the 1920s*, Thames and Hudson: New York, 2000. Of further interest in this regard is Anne McClintock, *Imperial Leather: Race, Gender and Sexuality in the Colonial Contest*, Routledge: New York and London, 1995.

12. Clifford, James, "Negrophilia" in *A New History of French Literature*, Denis Hollier (ed.), Harvard University Press: Cambridge, MA, and London, 1989, p. 901.

13. *Ibid.*

14. *Ibid.*, p. 904. Like both of the systems of discourse discussed above, this ethnological system of thought displays a mix of aesthetic and political registers. Coinciding as it did with the rise of postwar anticolonial nationalism, it makes use of historical and ethnological data in order to develop an aesthetic discourse aiming to rehabilitate black cultures for the purpose of political liberation.

15. Miller, Christopher, *Theories of Africans: Francophone Literature and Anthropology in Africa*, University of Chicago Press: Chicago and London, 1990. Miller shows that the totality of African art is the cornerstone of Frobenius's anthropology – art is everything and everything is art; therefore art is functional and wastes no time or energy on false seductiveness: "There is nothing that tries to seduce through softness and sensitivity ... everything is functional, rough, austere, tectonic (Teutonic?)", writes Frobenius (quoted in Miller, p. 17).

16. Césaire, Aimé, *Une Saison au Congo*, Seuil: Paris, 1973, p. 94 (quoted in Miller, p. 16). Senghor subscribed to Frobenius's assertion of a fundamental unity and affinity between black African and German thought (Frobenius wrote: "The West created English realism and French

Beautiful Ugly: African and Diaspora Aesthetics

rationalism; the East, German mysticism ... The accord, with corresponding civilisations in black Africa, is complete") and immersed himself in German philosophy from Marx and Engels to Hegel, Husserl and Heidegger (quoted in Miller, p. 18).

17. Sartre, Jean-Paul, "Black Orpheus" (trans. of "Orphée Noir" by John MacCombie) in *Black and White in American Culture: An Anthology from the Massachusetts Review*, Jules Chametzky and Sidney Kaplan (eds), University of Massachusetts: Boston, 1969, p. 449.

18. See Thérèse Migraine-George, "Ama Ata Aidoo's Orphan Ghosts: African Literature and Aesthetic Postmodernity" in *Research in African Literatures* 34 (4), 2003, p. 89.

19. Sartre, p. 447.

20. Miller, p. 19.

21. Ouologuem, Yambo, *Bound to Violence* (quoted in Miller, p. 21). Despite his loftiness, Schrobenius is not above faking the "authenticity" of African objects to make a fast buck – a reference to Frobenius himself, who may well have absconded with one of the most important copper alloy casts in the treasury of the kings of Ife.

22. I am very grateful to Dominique Malaquais for her extensive discussions with me on Africanist art history, on which this section is based.

23. For decades – from the first major exhibits of African sculpture in non-ethnographic museums (in particular the MOMA show of 1935) until the 1970s, the very notion that Africans could think the concepts "art", "beauty" and "aesthetics" was considered largely untenable. This, of course, is intimately linked to the ideal of the "primitive", so essential to European self-constructions. What so attracts Euro-American artists to the objects created by Africans is the notion that they were "pure" – untainted by the kind of over-analysis and self-reflexivity from which artists like Picasso, Klee etc. want to move away. They are beautiful because their creators have no conception of beauty.

24. These notions had been in the air since the 1960s but it is with Robert Farris Thompson's *African Art in Motion,* California University Press: Los Angeles, 1974; and Warren d'Azevedo's *The Traditional Artist in African Societies*, Indiana University Press: Bloomington, 1973, that they enter the mainstream of scholarly discourse on Africa. It is noteworthy that Thompson is an art historian and d'Azevedo (like many of the authors whose work appears in his book) is an anthropologist: the lines are not as clearly drawn, even at this early point, as one might think.

25. This, of course, leads back to the history of collecting, in which attention was paid to general information about objects (how were they used?). Dealers, galleries and auction houses continue to treat objects in this fashion: collectors (whether they are institutions or individuals), too: what are looked for are representative pieces – representative of a group ("a good Lobi"; "a good Yoruba Epa mask") rather than representative of an artist.

26. See, for example, Christopher Steiner, *African Art in Transit*, Cambridge University Press: Cambridge, 1994; and Sydney Kasfir, "African Art and Authenticity: A Text without a Shadow", *African Arts*, 25(2), 1992.

27. Note the contradiction: it is only art if it has been created for use and used – i.e. if it is radically different from European art, which, it is held, is created for its own sake (all objects meant to be used being "artifacts" rather than "art"). The double standard is glaring. Again, we should not romanticise: there were real problems with the explosion of interest in African "tourist" art, as we will see via the work of Anthony Appiah and others, below.

28. Enwezor, Okwui (ed.), *The Short Century: Independence and Liberation Movements in Africa 1945-1994*, Prestel: Munich, with the Prince Claus Fund Library: The Netherlands, 2001.

29. Appiah, Kwame Anthony, *In My Father's House – Africa in the Philosophy of Culture*, Oxford University Press: Oxford and New York, 1992, p. 157.

30. Appadurai, Arjun, *The Social Life of Things: Commodities in Perspective*, Cambridge University Press: Cambridge, 1986, p. 54.

31. One important book which begins to address this problem is *The Art of African Fashion*, E. van der Plas and M. Willemsen (eds), Prince Claus Fund: The Netherlands and Africa World Press: Eritrea/USA, 1998. Although the book does not deal explicitly with African beauty, it does so implicitly with its focus on African fashion and the emergence of a new African aesthetic through the clothed body and the art of hairstyling.

32. Llosa, Mario Vargas, "Botero: A Sumptuous Abundance" in *Making Waves*, Farrar, Straus and Giroux: New York, 1996 (quoted in Christopher Steiner, p. xv).

33. Scarry, Elaine, *On Beauty,* Princeton University Press: Princeton, 1999.

34. *Ibid.*, p. 112. See Simone Weil, "Love of the Order of the World" in *Waiting for God* (trans. Emma Craufurd), Harper and Row: New York, 1951, p. 159.

35. Scarry argues for the ethical alchemy of beauty – as does Morrison, though they do so from completely different racial and philosophical vantage points. Morrison's complaint against normative understandings of beauty is their investment in a power of looking which is loaded with a history of racism, and she posits instead a notion of beauty invested, as we have seen, with a "more ethical" response to human bodies, by which she means that beauty may have as much to do with the body as a thing that feels rather than how it individually looks, and that in this capacity of bodies to feel lies the possibility of a universal recognition. For an extended discussion on this see Katherine Stern, "Toni Morrison's Beauty Formula" in *The Aesthetics of Toni Morrison: Speaking the Unspeakable*, Marc Connor (ed.), University of Mississippi Press: Jackson, 2000.

36. Donoghue, Denis, *Speaking of Beauty*, Yale University Press: New Haven and London, 2003, p. 172.

37. *Ibid.*, p. 44.

38. *Ibid.*, p. 29. Donoghue draws here from Josephine Miles, "Values in Language; or, Where Have *Goodness, Truth* and *Beauty* Gone?" in *Critical Inquiry*, 3(1), 1976.

39. Donoghue, p. 87.

40. Steiner, Wendy, *Venus in Exile: The Rejection of Beauty in Twentieth-Century Art*, University of Chicago Press: Chicago, 2001, p. xv.

41. *Ibid.*

42. *Ibid.*, p. 5.

43. *Ibid.*, p. 16.

Notes

44. *Ibid.*, p. 50.
45. *Ibid.*, p. xxiii.
46. Danto, Arthur, *The Abuse of Beauty – Aesthetics and the Concept of Art*, Carus Publishing: New York, 2002, p. xv.
47. Foster, Hal (quoted in Danto, p. 57).
48. Danto, p. 111.
49. *Ibid.*, p. 112. See also in this regard Susan Sontag, *Regarding the Pain of Others*, Farrar, Straus and Giroux: New York, 2003. Sontag argues that "To acknowledge the beauty of the photographs of the World Trade Centre ruins in the month following the attack seemed frivolous, sacrilegious. The most people dared say was that the photographs were 'surreal', a hectic euphemism behind which the disgraced notion of beauty cowered" (p. 76). She goes on: "Transforming is what art does, but photography that bears witness to the calamitous and the reprehensible is much criticized if it seems 'aesthetic'; that is, too much like art" (*ibid.*). Salgado, she also argues, has been the principal target of "the new campaign against the inauthenticity of the beautiful". She notes both the "sanctimonious Family of Man-style rhetoric that feathers Salgado's exhibitions and books which works to the detriment of the pictures" as well as the "focus on the powerless, reduced to their powerlessness" in the pictures, and finds it significant that the powerless are not named in the captions to his photographs (pp. 78-79).
50. Steiner, p. xvii.
51. Donoghue, p. 8.
52. Hickey, Dave, *The Invisible Dragon: Four Essays on Beauty*, Art Issues: Los Angeles, 1993.
53. Brand, Peg Zeglin, "Introduction" in *Beauty Matters*, Indiana University Press: Bloomington and Indianapolis, 2000, p. 6.
54. Schjeldahl, Peter, "Beauty is Back: A Trampled Esthetic Blooms Again" in *New York Times Magazine*, September 29, 1996, p. 161.
55. Beckley, Bill, and David Shapiro (eds), *Uncontrollable Beauty: Toward a New Aesthetics*, School of Visual Arts and Allworth Press: New York, 1998.
56. A point also made by Brand in *Beauty Matters*, p. 6.
57. One of the reasons for the difficulty of wresting a more capacious contemporary reading of beauty from a long and abstract philosophical tradition may be that while a theory of beauty may be concentrated on objects and appearances, aesthetics (of which a theory of beauty was long seen to be a part) is concerned with perceptions and perceivers. Donoghue writes: "The aesthetic claims to know nothing, but it also claims the wisdom of being beyond knowledge, or on the far side of it, in full possession of the self-evidence of human feeling and therefore having unique access to the universal patterns of human life" (p. 49). Epistemologically, aesthetics is far more interested in "the true" than in "the beautiful", since the beautiful requires a respect of things in themselves and for their own sake.
58. See, amongst others, Naomi Wolf, *The Beauty Myth: How Images of Beauty Are Used against Women*, William Morrow: New York, 1991; Sandra Lee Bartky, *Femininity and Domination: Studies in the Phenomenology of Oppression*, Routledge: New York, 1990; Nancy Friday, *The Power of Beauty*, Harper Collins: New York, 1996; Susan Bordo, *Twilight Zones: The Hidden Life of Cultural Images from Plato to O.J.*, University of California Press: Berkeley, 1997; Rose Weitz (ed.), *The Politics of Women's Bodies: Sexuality, Appearance and Behavior*, Oxford University Press: New York and Oxford, 1998; and Jacque Lynn Folton, *The Importance of Being Beautiful*, Harper Collins: New York, 1999.
59. See Donoghue, p. 29.
60. Bordo, Susan, "Beauty (Re)Discovers the Male Body" in *Beauty Matters*, Peg Zeglin Brand (ed.), p. 151. See also Germaine Greer, *Beautiful Boy*, Rizzoli International Publications: New York and London, 2003.
61. Taussig, Mick, "The Adult's Imagination of the Child's Imagination" and Martin Jay, "Drifting Into Dangerous Waters: The Separation of Aesthetic Experience from the Work of Art", both in *Aesthetic Subjects*, P. Matthews and D. McWhirter (eds), University of Minnesota Press: Minneapolis and London, 2003.
62. Araeen, Rasheed, "Conversation with Aubrey Williams" in *Third Text* 2, 1987-1988, p. 32 (quoted in Gikandi).
63. Why is it, he asks, that Picasso's intertextual relation to Gauguin or Cézanne was considered constitutive (hence conceptual) while his relationship to African objects was perceptual, a mere starting point to something more profound? A related question might be: why are African artists, whether of the pre- or early colonial period or of the contemporary period, perceived as having no knowledge of arts previous to their own? In this regard, see the egregious and widely read *History of Art* by H. and A. Janson (6th Edition), Pearson: New York and London, 2003, in which it is argued that abstraction in Africa resulted from the inability of sculptors to properly copy the work of their predecessors – their only model, since the conceptual evaded them completely
64. Enwezor, Okwui, "The Postcolonial Constellation: Contemporary Art in a State of Permanent Transition" in *Research in African Literatures*, 34(4), 2003, pp. 57-82.
65. *Ibid.*, p. 66. Enwezor continues: "Nearly a hundred years after the initial venture by Western modernists, it would have been clear enough to the curators at the Tate Modern that in terms of sheer variety of styles, forms, complexity, genres, plastic distinctiveness, stylistic inventiveness and complexity of sculptural language and conception, no region in the world approaches the depth and breadth of African sculptural traditions."
66. *Ibid.*, p. 67.
67. See Aidoo, Ama Ata, "Literature, Feminism and the African Woman Writer Today" in *Challenging Hierarchies*, Leonard A. Podis and Yakuba Saaka (eds), Peter Lang: New York, 1998, pp. 15-34.
68. Mbembe, Achille, "The Thing and Its Doubles" in *On the Postcolony*, University of California Press: Berkeley and London, 2001, p. 143.
69. *Ibid.*, p. 144.
70. *Ibid.*
71. *Ibid.*, p. 145.
72. Foster, Hal, "The 'Primitive' Unconscious of Modern Art" in *Primitivism and Twentieth-Century Art*, Flam and Deutch (eds), p. 384.
73. Ferme refers to but builds substantially on the earlier work of Sylvia Boone on forms of beauty amongst the Mende. See Sylvia Boone, *Radiance From the Waters: Ideals of Feminine*

Beautiful Ugly: African and Diaspora Aesthetics

Beauty in Mende Art, Yale University Press: New Haven, 1986.

74. Ferme, Mariane, *The Underneath of Things: Violence, History and the Everyday in Sierra Leone,* University of California Press: Los Angeles and London, 2001, p. 161.

75. Ibid., p. 162.

76. See, for example, H. Cole's work on Igbo masquerade and Wilfred van Damme, *A Comparative Analysis Concerning Beauty and Ugliness in Sub-Saharan Africa*, Faculteit van de Leteren En Wijsbegeerte, Rijksuniversiteit: Gent, 1987.

77. See also Biaya, "The Arts of the Beautiful in Addis Ababa and Dakar".

78. The "weakness of the spirit" which stemmed from immersion in the world of sensations produced, in this view, a world of fantasy and a propensity for phantasmagoria.

79. This was a great advance on Kant, who wished to dissociate beauty from the senses, and who more or less confined the relevant repertoire of affects to pleasure and pain (making an important exception for sublimity). Moreover, Hegel wrote, such an aesthetics concerns art "when works of art are treated with regard to the feelings they were supposed to produce, as, for instance, the feeling of pleasure, admiration, fear, pity and so on". Unfortunately, Hegel went on to argue that we did not need art at all, since philosophy could contain all these qualities of sensation, within the idea of "the Spirit". See Danto, p. 93.

80. Nietzsche, F., *La Philosophie a L'époque Tragique des Grecs*, p. 181.

81. Clifford, James, *Routes: Travel and Translation in the Late Twentieth Century*, Harvard University Press: Cambridge, MA, 1997.

82. Stein's descriptions recall aspects of Morrison's character Pecola, "plucking her way between the rims and the sunflowers, between Coke bottles and milkweed, among the waste and beauty of the world – which is what she herself was" (*The Bluest Eye*, p. 162).

83. Elaine Scarry reminds us how this notion of beauty as distributional has a long recorded history: "Wittgenstein speaks not only about beautiful visual events prompting motions in the hand but, elsewhere, about heard music that later prompts a ghostly sub-anatomical event in his teeth and gums. So, too, an act of touch may reproduce itself as an acoustical event or even an abstract idea, the way whenever Augustine touches something smooth, he begins to think of music and God" (*On Beauty*, p. 4).

84. Pinho in her essay quotes Paul Gilroy's notion of diaspora as "closely associated with the idea of sowing seed. This etymological inheritance is a disputed legacy and a mixed blessing. Diaspora posits important tensions ... between the seed in the bag, the packet, or the pocket and the seed in the ground, the fruit or the body"(Paul Gilroy, *Against Race – Imagining Political Culture Beyond the Color Line*, Harvard University Press: Cambridge, MA, 2000, p. 125).

85. The essays in the book are written by both local and metropolitan writers, but most of its contributors are based in Africa. The event that gave rise to this book was a symposium in Cape Town funded by the Prince Claus Fund for Culture and Development, The Hague, and convened by this editor and Cheryl-Ann Michael. As a consequence, a number of essays focus on South Africa. Nevertheless, the book stages a continental conversation, drawing essays and reflections from numerous African contexts.

86. I also argued that the dominant strands in Euro-American thought on beauty have been: (1) a concern with the *ethical* and moral force of beauty; (2) emphasis on the *power of that which/the one which is looked at* (the power of beauty); (3) *silence about the ugly* in some philosophical texts on beauty; (4) an ongoing engagement with *Euro-American modernism* as the primary site of enquiry; and (5) a focus on male bodies in particular within the vast "*beauty industry*" of the contemporary world. I suggested that African scholars, in their engagement with the question of beauty, have (1) undertaken the work of *decoding how the sign* of Africa is interpreted in the West, in particular in the ongoing reductive interpretations of a range of African texts, and on the failure of avant-garde theories of contemporary art in a globalising world; and (2) focused on a *spectral aesthetics* of "the other side" or "the underneath of things" imbued within the world of imagination and sensations.

87. See Nehamas, Alexander, "The Return of the Beautiful: Morality, Pleasure and the Value of Uncertainty" in the *Journal of Aesthetics and Art Criticism*, 58(4), 2000, p. 402. Nehamas recalls Nietzsche's idea that we remain fixed on what remains veiled, even after the unveiling (*The Birth of Tragedy*, Cambridge University Press: Cambridge, 1999, section 15).

88. I draw here on a point made by Denis Donoghue when he says that "beauty, whether we try to define it or not, should maintain its recalcitrance and go its own way". He suggests this as a way to maintain the difficulty of beauty as a concept rather than setting it down among "the standard values" as he fears the "return to beauty" is doing (p. 11).

Notes Simon Gikandi (pp. 30-59)

1. Araeen, Rasheed, "Conversation with Aubrey Williams" in *Third Text 2*, 1987-1988, p. 32.

2. Malraux, André, *Picasso's Mask*, Da Capo Press: New York, 1994, p. 10.

3. Writing to Kahnweiler August 11, 1912, about some masks he had bought, Picasso didn't hesitate to describe them as (stand-ins for) Africans: "We bought some blacks (*des nègres*) at Marseilles and I bought a very good mask and a woman with big tits and a young black" (quoted in Natasha Staller, *A Sum of Destructions: Picasso's Cultures and the Creation of Cubism,* Yale University Press: New Haven, CT, 2001, p. 318).

4. Araeen, Rasheed, *The Other Story: Afro-Asian Artists in Post-War Britain,* Hayward Gallery: London, 1989, pp. 16-50.

5. See Miller, D.A., *The Novel and the Police*, University of California Press: Berkeley, 1968, p. xii. Here Miller is discussing how "modern social organisation" has made even scandal "a systematic function of its routine self-maintenance". For my purposes one can substitute difference or primitivism in modernism for scandal. See for example the debates in *Pollock and After: the Critical Debate*, 2nd edition, Francis Frascina (ed.), Routledge: New York, 2000, especially the argument between T.J. Clark and Michael Fried, pp. 71-112.

395

6. My assumption here is that while the literature on black bodies and modernism has grown in recent years, as has that on race and modernism, most of it takes the African American, not the African, to be the representative black subject. See, for example, Michael North, *The Dialectic of Modernism: Race, Language, and Twentieth-century Literature*, Oxford University Press: New York, 1994; and the essays collected in *Race and the Modern Artist*, Heather Hathaway, Josef JaYab and Jeffrey Melnick (eds), Oxford University Press: New York, 2003.

7. Kahnweiler's comments were made in 1948 at the height of Picasso's canonisation; Daix was writing in the 1970s. Both are quoted in Yve-Alain Bois, *Painting as Model,* MIT Press: Cambridge, MA, 1990, p. 69.

8. Kahnweiler, Daniel-Henry, "Negro Art and Cubism", originally published in *Présence Africaine*, collected in *Primitivism and Twentieth-century Art*, Jack Flam and Miriam Deutch (eds), University of California Press: Berkeley, 2003, p. 284.

9. See Rubin, William, "Picasso in Primitivism" in *20th Century Art*, vol. 1., New York Museum of Modern Art: New York, 1984, p. 260.

10. See Kahnweiler, p. 285; Rubin, p. 17; and Bois, p. 73.

11. I pursue these questions in greater detail in *Unmodern Subjects: Race, Art, and African Difference* (forthcoming), from which this discussion is excerpted. Discussing the way the "ghostly" makes its way into the movement of European history, Jacques Derrida observes that "Haunting would mark the very existence of Europe. It would open the space and the relation to self of what is called by this name, at least since the Middle Ages" (Derrida, *Specters of Marx: The State of Debt, the Work of Mourning, and the New International*, trans. Peggy Kamuf, Routledge: New York, 1994, p. 4).

12. I develop this argument in "Race and the Idea of the Aesthetic" in *Michigan Quarterly Review*, XI (2), 2001, pp. 318-350. For the interplay of social ideals and ideas of pollution, see Mary Douglas, *Purity and Danger*, Routledge: New York, 1966, pp. 1-6.

13. Eliot, T.S., "War-Paint and Feathers", originally published in the *Athenaeum* on October 17, 1919, collected in *Primitivism and Twentieth-century Art*, p. 122.

14. *Ibid.*

15. See "Chronology" in *Picasso: The Early Years 1892-1906*, Marilyn McCully (ed.), National Gallery of Art: Washington DC, 1997, p. 48.

16. Staller, Natasha, *A Sum of Destructions: Picasso's Cultures and the Creation of Cubism,* Yale University Press: New Haven, CT, 2001, pp. 269-301.

17. *Ibid.*, p. 269.

18. *Ibid.*, p. 271.

19. For this argument I have relied on Staller and the essays collected in McCully.

20. Werth, Margaret, "Representing the Body in 1906" in McCully, pp. 277-288.

21. *Ibid.*, p. 277.

22. After 80 sittings, Picasso gave up "seeing" Gertrude Stein and turned to the mask as an alternative way of viewing. The significance of this turn from the human model to the mask is discussed by Michael Northy in *The Dialectic of Modernism: Race, Language, and Twentieth-century Literature*, Oxford University Press: New York, 1994, pp. 59-76. For a feminist reading of the *Portrait of Gertrude Stein*, see Tamar Darb, "To Kill the Nineteenth Century: Sex and Spectatorship with Gertrude and Pablo" in *Picasso's Les Demoiselles d'Avignon*, Christopher Green (ed.), Cambridge University Press: Cambridge, 2001, pp. 55-76.

23. These works are discussed in detail by Staller, pp. 296-301.

24. But in discussing notions of disorder, we need to keep Mary Douglas's dictum in mind: "Reflections on dirt involves reflection on the relation of order to disorder, being to nonbeing, form to formlessness, life to death" (p. 6).

25. Staller, p. 303.

26. Jameson, Frederic, *The Political Unconscious: Narrative as a Socially Symbolic Act*, Cornell University Press: Ithaca, NY, 1981, p. 280.

27. Malraux, p. 11.

28. This is not to deny Picasso's interested radical anticolonial politics; merely to raise the possibility that radical anticolonialism might have needed the valorisation of the primitive as part of its maintenance, a point that was to become more apparent with the rise of Surrealism. For Picasso and French colonialism in Africa, see "Colonialism, *l'art négre* and *Les Demoiselles d'Avignon*" in Green, pp. 77-103.

29. The quoted phrase comes from Robert Rosenblum, "Picasso in Gósol: The Calm before the Storm" in McCully, p. 268.

30. *Ibid.*, pp. 262-267.

31. As does Staller, p. 314.

32. Quoted in Staller, p. 316.

33. It would be interesting to compare Picasso's *Harem* with some of Matisse's Orientalist paintings. For the latter, see Roger Benjamin's *Orientalist Aesthetics: Art, Colonialism, and French North Africa 1880-1930*, University of California Press: Berkeley, 2003, especially ch. 7, pp. 59-90.

34. Malraux, p. 171.

35. *Ibid.,* pp. 11, 13.

36. Jameson, Frederic, "Beyond the Cave" in *Ideologies of Theory: Essays 1971-1986,* University of Minnesota Press: Minneapolis, 1988, p. 117.

37. Simpson, David, *Fetishism and Imagination*, Johns Hopkins University Press: Baltimore, MD, 1982, p. 11.

38. Rubin, p. 241.

39. *Ibid.*, p. 253.

40. *Ibid.*, p. 254.

41. *Ibid.*, p. 259.

42. *Ibid.*, pp. 260-262.

43. Culler, Jonathan, *The Pursuit of Signs,* Cornell University Press: Ithaca, NY, 1981, p. 102.

44. Rubin, p. 262.

45. Jenny, Laurent, "The Strategy of Form" in *French Literary Theory Today*, Tzvetan Todorov (ed.), trans. R. Carter, Cambridge University Press: Cambridge, 1981, p. 40.

46. Rubin, p. 265.

47. *Ibid.*

48. Bois, *Painting as Model*, p. 72.

49. Clifford, James, *The Predicament of Culture: Twentieth-century Ethnography, Literature, and Art*, Harvard University Press: Cambridge, MA, 1988, p. 190.

50. *Ibid.*, pp. 190, 193, 195.

51. Foster, Hal, *Recordings: Art, Spectacle, Cultural Politics,*

Beautiful Ugly: African and Diaspora Aesthetics

Bay Press: Port Townsend, WA, 1985, p. 184.

52. *Ibid.*, p. 182.

53. Thompson, Robert Farris, "Fang Mask" in *Perspectives: Angles on African Art*, James Baldwin *et al.* (eds), Centre for African Art: New York, 1987, p. 190.

54. *Ibid.*

55. The most notorious instance of this exclusion concerns the Baule artist, Lela Kouakou, who was invited to participate in a forum on African art but was allowed to comment only on works from his ethnic region because he was deemed incapable of providing "objective" aesthetic judgments, that is, those not bound by his "traditional criteria". See Susan Vogel, "Introduction" to *Perspectives: Angles on African Art*, Abrams: New York, 1987, p. 11. For a subtle discussion of this criterion of inclusion and exclusion see Kwame Anthony Appiah, *In My Father's House: Africa in the Philosophy of Culture*, Oxford University Press: New York, 1992, pp. 137-139.

56. The literature on African masks is too extensive to cite here, but see Z.S. Strother, *Inventing Masks: Agency and History in the Art of the Central Pende*, University of Chicago Press: Chicago, 1998, especially ch. 6, pp. 39-54.

57. Dramatic deployments of the mask in motion can be found in Chinua Achebe's *Arrow of God*, Heinemann: London, 1964; and Wole Soyinka's *The Road*, Oxford University Press: Oxford, 1965.

58. See Richards, David, *Masks of Difference,* Cambridge University Press, Cambridge, 1994, p. 204.

59. Roscoe, John, *The Baganda: An Account of their Native Customs and Beliefs,* MacMillan: London, 1911, p. ix. For Rattray, see *Religion and Art in Ashanti*, Oxford University Press: London, 1927.

60. What, for example, is the structural relationship between the destruction of the Kingdom of Benin by a British Expeditionary Force in 1897 and the availability of Benin sculpture to the British Museum? Should it surprise us that the rooted sculpture is now housed in a modern wing of the British Museum, paid for by a family that made its fortunes in the confectionaries of empire, and named after Henry Moore, a leading modernist and connoisseur of African art? For the Benin Expedition, see Annie E. Coombes, *Reinventing African Museums, Material Culture and Popular Imagination,* Yale University Press: New Haven, CT, 1994, pp. 7-28.

61. I had suggested a similar act of deritualisation, albeit too briefly, for T.S. Eliot in *Maps of Englishness: Writing Identity in the Culture of Colonialism,* Columbia University Press: New York, 1996, ch. 5, pp. 157-189.

Notes Achille Membe (pp. 60-93)

1. Adorno, T., *Introduction à la sociologie de la musique,* Editions Contrechamps: Paris, 1994, p. 38. See, too, *Aesthetic Theory*, trans. C. Lenhardt, Routledge & Kegan Paul: New York, 1982.

2. *Ibid.*, pp. 33-35.

3. Sève, Bernard, *L'altération musicale*, Seuil: Paris, 2002, p. 20.

4. On this kind of thinking, see G. Deleuze, *Francis Bacon. Logique de la sensation,* Seuil: Paris, 2003, pp. 57-61; and M. Merleau-Ponty, *Phénoménologie de la perception,*

Gallimard: Paris, 1945.

5. The following works are used in this study: Koffi Olomide, *Effrakata* (Next music/Sono, CDS 8919MD862, 2001); Papa Wemba, *Molokai* (Real World, LC3098, 1998); Werra Son, *Kibuisa Mpimpa. Operation Dragon* (CDJPS, 2001); J.B. Mpiana, *TH Toujours humble* (Sacem, s.d.); Extra-Musica, *Bon Pied Bon Look. Champion d'Afrique* (Declic Communication, 1997); Wenge Musica Maison Mère, *Solola Bien!* (CDJPS, 1999); Wenge BCBG, *J.B. Mpiana Souverain* (Simon Music-Sipe, s.d.); Koffi Olomide, *Attentat* (Sonodisc, 1999); Tshala Muana, *Malu* (CDJPS, 2002); Zaiko Langa Langa, *Eureka!* (CDJPS 217, 2003); Werra Son, *À la queue leu-leu* (CDJPS 234, 2003); Koffi Olomide, *Affaire d'Etat* (Next Music/Sono, CDS 8979, 2003); Papa Wemba, *Mzée Fulangenge* (Sono, CDS 8836-SD30, s.d.).

6. Agawu, Kofi, "African Music as Text" in *Research in African Literatures*, 32(2), 2001, p. 9.

7. See, for example, Kazadi wa Mukuna, "The Origin of Zairean Modern Music: A Socio-economic Aspect" in *African Urban Studies*, 5, 1979/1980, pp. 31-39; and "The Genesis of Urban Music in Zaïre" in *African Music*, 7(2), 1992, pp. 72-84.

8. Concerning non-customary centres, see V.Y. Mudimbe, *The Idea of Africa,* Indiana University Press: Bloomington, 1994, ch. 4.

9. Nkashama, Pius Ngandu (compiler), *L'Eglise des prophètes africains. Lettres de Bakatuasa Lubwe Wa Mvidi Mukulu*, L'Harmattan: Paris, 1991.

10. Hunt, Nancy, *Colonial Lexicon*, Duke University Press: Durham, 1998.

11. See Luise White, *Speaking with Vampires*, University of California Press: Berkeley, 2000.

12. Gondola, C.D., "Dream and Drama: The Search for Elegance among Congolese Youth" in *African Studies Review*, 42(1), 1999, pp. 23-48.

13. Martin, Phyllis, *Leisure and Society in Colonial Brazzaville,* Cambridge University Press, Cambridge, 1995.

14. Dorier-Apprill, Elisabeth (ed.), *Vivre à Brazzaville. Modernité et crise au quotidien*, Karthala: Paris, 1998.

15. Wa Mukuna, Kazadi,p. 80. Wa Mukuna cites such dances as the *mokonyonyon* (of the Tetela ethnic group) introduced in 1977 by the singer Papa Wemba, or Lita Bembo's *ekonda saccadé* (of the Mongo ethnic group), the Empire Bakuba's *kwasa-kwasa* (of the Kongo ethnic group) or the T.P.O.K. Jazz's *mayeno* (of the Bantandu ethnic group).

16. Read Sylvain Bemba, *Cinquante ans de musique du Congo-Zaire*, Présence africaine: Paris, 1984; and C.D. Gondola, "Musique moderne et identités citadines. Le cas du Congo-Zaire" in *Afrique contemporaine*, 168, 1983.

17. Read G. Ewens, *Congo Colossus: The Life and Legacy of Franco & OK Jazz*, Buku Press: Norwich, 1994, p. 94.

18. Read Kazadi wa Mukuna, "The Changing Role of the Guitar in the Urban Music of Zaïre" in *The World of Music*, 36(2), 1994, pp. 62-72.

19. *Ibid.*, p. 68.

20. Devisch, R., "Frenzy, Violence, and Ethical Renewal in Kinshasa" in *Public Culture,* 7(3), 1995, pp. 593-630; and "La violence à Kinshasa, ou l'institution en négatif" in *Cahiers d'études africaines*, 38(150-2), 1998, pp. 441-469.

21. Ngandu Nkashama, P., "Ivresse et vertige: les nouvelles danses des jeunes au Zaïre" in *L'Afrique littéraire et*

397

artistique, 51, s.d., pp. 94-102.

22. Jewsiewicki, B., "Vers une impossible représentation de soi" in *Les Temps modernes*, 620-1, 2002, pp. 101-105.

23. Jewsiewicki, B. and E. Mbokolo (eds), *Naitre et mourir au Zaïre. Un demi-siècle d'histoire au quotidien*, Karthala: Paris, 1993; Achille Mbembe, *On the Postcolony*, University of California Press: Berkeley, 2001; and Jean-Claude Willame, *L'automne d'un despotisme*, Karthala: Paris, 1992.

24. Cf. the special volume edited by J.L. Grotaers, "Mort et maladie au Zaïre" in *Cahiers africains*, 8(31-2), 1998.

25. Joris, L., *La danse du léopard*, Actes Sud: Paris, 2002.

26. Read F. De Boeck, "Le 'deuxième monde' et les 'enfants-sorciers' en République Démocratique du Congo" in *Politique africaine*, 80, 2000, pp. 32-57.

27. Read Soni Labou Tansi's novels: *La vie et demie*, Seuil: Paris, 1979; *L'Etat honteux*, Seuil: Paris, 1981; *La parenthèse de sang*, Hatier: Paris, 1981; and *Le commencement des douleurs*, Seuil: Paris, 1994.

28. Compare with the limited range of sounds within the convention of Western art music. It can be argued that until the development of electronic sound generators, this range remained confined within a relatively small compass. See Simon Schaw-Miller, *Visible Deeds of Music. Art and Music From Wagner to Cage*, Yale University Press: New Haven, CT, 2002, p. 8.

29. On the theme of the "scream" in contemporary African thought, see J.M. Ela, *Le cri de l'homme africain*, L'Harmattan: Paris, 1980.

30. For this discussion of ugliness I have used the study by Deleuze, *Francis Bacon*, pp. 28-61.

31. Read A. Artaud, *Le théâtre et son double*, Gallimard: Paris, 1964, especially the chapters on cruelty.

32. Berliner, Paul E., *Thinking in Jazz: The Infinite Art of Improvisation*, University of Chicago Press: Chicago, 1994.

33. In another context, see T. Rose, *Black Noise: Rap Music and Black Culture in Contemporary America*, Wesleyan University Press: London, 1994; and J. Attali, *Noise: The Political Economy of Music*, University of Minnesota Press: Minneapolis, 1985.

34. Mumbu, B., "Kinshasa, un scandale culturel" in *Africultures*, 53, 2002, p. 24.

35. There have always existed in the Congo hundreds of dance steps with evocative names: *boucher, caneton, choquez retarde, crapeau-crapeau, ekonda saccade, griffe dindon, kwasa-kwasa, masasi calculez, mobylette, mutwashi, nagez sous-marin, parachute, pompe bijection, volant, tsheke-tsheke, caneton a l'esema*, etc. See I. Ndaywel e Nziem, *Histoire générale du Congo. De l'héritage ancien à la République Démocratique*, Agence de la Francophonie: Paris, 1998, p. 481. The *soukous* and the *ndombolo* dominated the 1990s. Since 2000, a new dance, the *tshaku libondas*, has emerged in Ndjili. According to M. Tchebwa, "N'Dombolo: postulation identitaire de la mouvance post-Zaïko" in *Africultures*, 53, 2002, p. 39, it rests on the gestural fantasies of the *shegue* (streetchildren), and imitates the gestures of the parrot. It is a kind of dance theatre marked "by extremely mechanical gestures". The dancers spread their arms vigorously from the chest forwards, like the connecting rods of a steam train.

36. See *N'dombolo Fever. Laissez la fièvre vous envahir! Cours de danse africaine. Démonstrations et spectacles*, Maison Mère

Productions, 2002.

37. Rouget, G., *La musique et la transe. Essai d'une théorie générale des relations de la musique et de la possession*, Gallimard: Paris, 1990.

38. Nietzsche, F., *The Birth of Tragedy*.

39. Tchebwa, p. 39.

40. See E. Scarry, *The Body in Pain*, Oxford University Press: Oxford, 1985.

41. Nietzsche, F., *The Birth of Tragedy*, p. 48.

42. "Music," as C. Accaoui states in *Le temps musical*, Desclée de Brouwer: Paris, 2001, "shapes the time and time shapes music" (p. 8).

43. Nietzsche, *La philosophie à l'époque tragique des Grecs*, pp. 181-184.

44. Nietzsche, *The Birth of Tragedy*, p. 34.

Notes Rita Barnard (pp. 102-121)

1. Mda, Zakes, *The Heart of Redness*, Oxford University Press: Cape Town, 2000.

2. Appadurai, Arjun (ed.), *The Social Life of Things: Commodities in Perspective*, Cambridge University Press: Cambridge, 1986, p. 54.

3. Heathcote, Elizabeth, Interview with Dolly Parton, *Independent on Sunday*, 31 June 2002, L: p. 3.

4. Scarry, Elaine, *On Beauty and Being Just*, Duckworth: London, 2001.

5. *Ibid.*, p. 15.

6. *Ibid.*, pp. 6-7.

7. *Ibid.*, p. 57.

8. *Ibid.*, p. 17.

9. *Ibid.*, pp. 58-59.

10. *Ibid.*, p. 60.

11. *Ibid.*, p. 3.

12. *Ibid.*, p. 65.

13. *Ibid.*, p. 67.

14. Dollimore, Jonathan, *Sex, Literature, and Censorship*, Polity Press: Cambridge, 2001, p. 49.

15. Scarry, p. 49.

16. *Ibid.*, p. 18.

17. If I here seem to be unduly delimiting the potential flexibility and generosity of human perceptions, let me refine and rephrase the point somewhat. I am suggesting that people who have lived in a certain locale, operating under certain ideological constraints, may not only have difficulty, but a reluctance to claim certain objects around them as beautiful. Thus, even if they (we) might have an initial sensory experience of pleasure of the sort Scarry privileges, such experience may be censored or repressed so rapidly as to render it unavailable for discussion, verification and investigation.

18. *Ibid.*, p. 112.

19. *Ibid.*, p. 28.

20. *Ibid.*, p. 110.

21. *Ibid.*, p. 128.

22. Gordimer, Nadine, *The Conservationist*, Penguin: New York, 1978, p. 140.

23. Scarry, p. 124.

24. *Ibid.*, p. 123.

25. Mda, 2000, p. 1.

26. Clifford, James, *Routes: Travel and Translation in the Late*

Beautiful Ugly: African and Diaspora Aesthetics

Twentieth Century, Harvard University Press: Cambridge, MA, 1997, p. 39.

27. Robins, Steven, "Bodies out of Place: Crossroads and the Landscapes of Exclusion" in blank _____: *Architecture, Apartheid, and After*, Hilton Judin and Ivan Vladislavić (eds), David Philip: Cape Town and NAi: Rotterdam, 1998, pp. 458-459.

28. Mda, 2000, p. 29.

29. *Ibid.*, p. 36.

30. *Ibid.*, p. 28.

31. The idea of the multi-storey transit lounge is suggested by Amitav Ghosh's description of the restless cosmopolitanism of a traditional Egyptian village, where all the men seem to be inveterate travellers, rather than simple dwellers (cited in Clifford, pp. 1-2).

32. Mda, 2000, p. 30.

33. *Ibid.*

34. *Ibid.*, p. 307.

35. *Ibid.*, p. 308.

36. *Ibid.*, p. 34.

37. *Ibid.*, p. 33.

38. Clifford, pp. 20-21.

39. Mda, 2000, p. 39.

40. *Ibid.*, p. 70.

41. *Ibid.*, p. 10. For a fascinating report on the tendency of many black South Africans (and not only unsophisticated villagers) to find large women attractive, see Duval Smith's article on Johannesburg's Miss Fats 2001 beauty pageant: "Fat is where it's at, say new South African beauty queens" in the *Independent on Sunday,* 9 December 2001, W: p. 22. His interview with the winner Phidile Mbewe very effectively underscores the historicity and the class-determined malleability of standards of beauty: "AIDS had changed everything in South Africa and really improved the chances of large women," observed the two-hundred pound beauty queen. "Now the beautiful men in the fancy 4x4s want girls like us, because they can see that we are large and healthy, not thin and sick. Before the AIDS epidemic, those guys did not ever hoot at us" (p. 22). See also my essay "Contesting Beauty" for further details on South African beauty queens and standards of physical attractiveness.

42. Mda, 2000, pp. 78, 92.

43. *Ibid.*, p. 69.

44. Van der Berghe, Pierre L., *The Quest for the Other: Ethnic Tourism in San Cristóbal Mexico*, University of Washington Press: Seattle, 1994, p. 5.

45. Kincaid, Jamaica, *A Small Place*, Farrar, Straus, Giroux: New York, 1988, pp. 4-5, 13.

46. Mda, 2000, p. 5.

47. *Ibid.*, p. 61.

48. Becker, Rayda, "Homesteads and Headrests" in blank _____: *Architecture, Apartheid, and After*, Hilton Judin and Ivan Vladislavić (eds), David Philip: Cape Town and Nai: Rotterdam, 1998, pp. 79-81.

49. Mda, 2000, p. 54.

50. *Ibid.*, p. 47.

51. *Ibid.*

52. *Ibid.*, p. 300.

53. *Ibid.*, p. 114.

54. *Ibid.*, p. 71.

55. *Ibid.*

56. *Ibid.*, p. 48.

57. *Ibid.*, p. 185.

58. *Ibid.*, p. 61.

59. It is interesting to note in this regard that the cultural commodity that has the widest circulation in the novel seems to be a poster of a naked African mother and child, which, Mda tells us, is sold on the street in every village in South Africa. The popularity of this image is as understandable as it is politically suspicious in the contentious social world Mda evokes: by representing the mother and child as naked, the image simply dispenses with all the complicated negotiations about style, fashion and social identity that is one of the novel's chief preoccupations. It is no wonder that the poster appeals to the novel's most parochial character, and the one who is the least able to adapt to post-apartheid South Africa: the former Cherry Queen, Mrs Dalton.

60. Mda, 2000, p. 286.

61. *Ibid.*, p. 184.

62. *Ibid.*, pp. 285-286; and W*hen People Play: Development Communication Through Theatre*, Zed: London, 1993.

63. If anything, the novel as a whole seems to privilege a grassroots democracy and to validate local interests over international and especially national interests. The centralised governmental structure of the ruling party comes in for fairly direct criticism. Mda sympathetically records the concerns of various villagers about the lack of real local representation: the ANC, they complain, simply nominates candidates in rural elections without any consultation with the people of the area (p. 189). The geographies of power evident in the novel's aesthetic arguments also affect more directly political matters.

64. Mda, 2000, pp. 106, 168.

65. *Ibid.*, p. 169.

66. *Ibid.*, p. 229.

67. *Ibid.*, p. 234.

68. *Ibid.*, p. 1.

69. *Ibid.*, p. 175.

Additional references

Barnard, Rita, "Contesting Beauty" in *Senses of Culture*, Sarah Nuttall and Cheryl-Ann Michael (eds), Oxford University Press: Cape Town, 2000, pp. 244-362.

Dougary, Ginny, "Steel Magnolia" in *The Times Magazine*, 24 November 2002.

Gross, Terry, "Country Music Hall of Fame – Dolly Parton", interview with Dolly Parton, "Fresh Air", National Public Radio, 23 January 2001.

Huggan, Graham, *The Postcolonial Exotic: Marketing the Margins*, Routledge: London, 2001.

Marcuse, Herbert, "The Affirmative Character of Culture" in *Negations: Essays in Critical Theory*, Beacon Press: Boston, 1968.

Mayer, Philip and Iona, *Townsmen or Tribesmen: Conservatism and the Process of Urbanization in a South African City*, Oxford University Press: Cape Town, 1971 (1961).

Mda, Zakes, *Ways of Dying*, Oxford University Press: Cape Town, 1995.

Peires, J.B., *The Dead Will Arise: Nongqawuse and the Great Xhosa Cattle-Killing Movement of 1856-57*, Ravan Press: Johannesburg, 1989.

Steiner, Wendy, *The Trouble with Beauty*, Heineman: London,

Notes

2001.

Steiner, Wendy, *Venus in Exile: The Rejection of Beauty in Twentieth-Century Art*, Free Press: New York, 2001.

Notes Dominique Malaquais (pp.122-163)

1. Rampolokeng, Lesego, "Rap Attack" in *Blue V's*, Editions Solitude: Stuttgart, 1998, p. 10.
2. Dikeni, Sandile, *Telegraph to the Sky*, University of Natal Press: Durban, 2000.
3. Diabaté, Issa, "Les goûts" in *Revue noire*, 31, 1999, p. 28. My translation.
4. Dikeni, p. 38.
5. For discussions of *La nouvelle liberté* in the Douala press referenced in this paper, see: *Cameroun tribune* 2447 (8/8/96); *Challenge nouveau* (18/9/96); *Dikalo* 2 (9/8/96); *L'Effort camerounais* 52 (3-6/9/96); *Elimbi* 11 (19/8/96), 19 (27/11/96), 23 (9/1/97), 24 (16/1/97), 25 (23/1/97), 26 (30/1/97), 27 (6/2/97), 28 (13/2/97), 29 (20/2/97), 36 (23/4/97); *L'Expression* (22/4/97); *Mutations* 23 (10-16/12/96); *La nouvelle expression* 330 (1/8/96), 338 (30/8/96); *Planète jeunes* 23 (1996); *Ponda* 110 (7/8/96), 112 (20/8/96).
6. Over the past three years, I have had occasion to discuss Sumegne's statue with a range of political and economic leaders in Douala, from members of the mayor's entourage to bank directors. Few have anything good to say about the work – a point I will come back to later.
7. Statements by Sumegne cited herein, unless otherwise noted, stem from a series of interviews conducted with the artist in his studio in Yaoundé in 2000 and 2001.
8. *Planète jeunes*. My translation.
9. *Ibid.*
10. This and subsequent discussions of Doual'Art's philosophy are drawn from interviews conducted with its founders in Douala in 1998, 1999, 2000 and 2001.
11. The name *Elimbi* is drawn from that of a drum used for communication purposes by members of the Duala community prior to the colonial period.
12. Malaquais, Dominique, *Architecture, pouvoir et dissidence au Cameroun*, Karthala and Presses de l'UCAC: Paris and Yaoundé, 2002, p. 317.
13. *Ibid.*, pp. 272-273.
14. *Congelé* means "frozen". The allusion is to frozen foods that have exceeded their past-due date: once thawed, they stink.
15. Douala-Bell, Marilyn, personal communications, 2000 and 2001. I am grateful to Victor Kouankam for data with which he provided me from a series of interviews he undertook with *sauveteurs* concerning *La nouvelle liberté* in July and August 2000.
16. *Système D* is a French term that has been adopted in urban centres of Francophone Africa to designate women and men who toil in the so-called "informal economy". In Parisian French, the "D" of *Système D* stands for *démerde* (literally, "getting out of the shit"); in an African context, it becomes *débrouille* – literally "unravelling" and, in common usage, "making do".
17. See Allen Roberts "The Ironies of System D" in *Recycled, Re-Seen: Folk Art from the Global Scrap Heap*, Charlene Sheriff and Suzanne Cerny (eds), Harry N. Abrams: New York, 1996. The Rond-Point *sauveteurs* certainly think of the sculpture as theirs to sell in image form. On several occasions I was reprimanded for taking photographs of the statue, accused of taking business away from local image salesmen and photographers.
18. See Roberts, p. 86.
19. Malaquais, Dominique, "Blood/Money: A Douala Chronicle", *Chimurenga* 3, 2002.
20. Conversations with Komegne and fellow artists Louis Epée and Joel Mpa'a Dooh, Douala, September 2001.
21. Jameson, Frederic, "Postmodernism and Consumer Society" in *The Anti-Aesthetic: Essays on Postmodern Culture*, Hal Foster (ed.), The New Press: New York, 1998, pp. 129, 137.
22. Lest I be accused of hyperbole, an anecdote: a student of mine, writing about the near-total absence of works by 20th-century African artists in the modern and contemporary collections of major American museums, recently sought an interview with a curator of modern art at the Metropolitan Museum in New York. "No one," she was told, would "be willing to discuss this matter with [her]." In a similar vein, I was once asked by the chairman of an art history department at an Ivy League university whether the African continent provided enough material for me to fill a semester's worth of classes on architecture south of the Sahara.
23. Simone, AbdouMaliq, "Globalization and the Identity of African Urban Practices" in *blank _____: Architecture, Apartheid, and After*, Hilton Judin and Ivan Vladislavić (eds), David Philip: Cape Town and Nai: Rotterdam, 1998.
24. Simone, AbdouMaliq, "Spectral Selves: Practices in the Making of African Cities", paper presented at WISER (Wits Institute for Social and Economic Research), University of the Witwatersrand, July 2002, p. 2.
25. *Ibid.*, p. 1.
26. Interview with the artist, Douala, August 2001.
27. Yamguen, Hervé, *La machine à vapeur*, 2000. My translation.

Notes Pippa Stein (pp. 164-187)

1. Dell, E. (ed.), *Evocations of the Child: Fertility Figures of the Southern African Region,* Human and Rousseau: Cape Town and the Johannesburg Art Gallery: Johannesburg, 1998.
2. For an elaboration on the concept of slippability, see ch. 12 in D.R. Hofstadter, *Metamagical Themas: Questing for the Essence of Mind and Pattern,* Penguin Books: London, 1986.
3. "*Tula*" means "be quiet".
4. Morrison, T., *The Bluest Eye,* Vintage: London, 1999, pp. 13-14.
5. Laydevant, F., "La Poésie chez les Basuto" in *Africa*, 3, 1930, pp. 523-535.
6. Mbembe, A, "Translation and Tradition", paper presented at the Wits Institute for Social and Economic Research (WISER), University of the Witwatersrand, Johannesburg, 2002.
7. Hamilton, C., "Women and Material Markers of Identity" in *Evocations of the Child: Fertility Figures of the Southern African Region* in Dell, p. 26.
8. Kress, G., *Before Writing: Rethinking the Paths to Literacy,* Routledge: London and New York, 1997.
9. Appadurai, A., "The Capacity to Aspire: Culture and the

Beautiful Ugly: African and Diaspora Aesthetics

Terms of Recognition", paper presented at the Wits Institute for Social and Economic Research (WISER), University of the Witwatersrand, Johannesburg, 2002.

Notes Els van der Plas (pp. 188-201)
1. Riefenstahl, Leni, *Die Nuba*, Leni Riefenstahl Produktion: Pocking, Germany, 1973.
2. See Elaine Scarry, *On Beauty*, Princeton University Press: Princeton, 1999.
3. Sow stated this during an interview with the author at the conference on "African Aesthetics" in Cape Town in 2001.
4. Quoted in *Ousmane Sow, le soleil en face,* Le P'tit Jardin, 1999, which was published for Sow's exhibition on Pont des Arts, 20 March – 20 May 1999, Paris, France. This text is based on interviews between Ousmane Sow and Marie-Odile Briot, which took place on 17, 18 and 19 June 1998. The text is also available on the internet: www.ousmanesow.com.
5. Interview between Jan Hoet, Sofie Willems and Tom De Paepe, published on the internet in 2001: www.schamper.rug.ac.be.
6. From the introduction by Jan Hoet, *Documenta IX*, vols 1, 2, 3, Edition Cantz: Stuttgart, in association with Harry N. Abrahams: New York, 1992.
7. Sow, 2001.

Notes Mark Gevisser (pp. 202-221)
1. *King Kong* was an all-black musical about a black boxer written by Todd Matshikiza and produced in 1959. It broke the law by playing to mixed South African audiences, and most of its cast later went into exile in London.
2. *Drum* was a popular commercial magazine aimed at urban black audiences, which became the voice of contemporary black thought and culture in Johannesburg in the 1950s.

Notes Célestine Monga (pp. 222-235)
1. Magic System, *1er Gaou* (CD, 1999).
2. Veyne, P., "Plaisir et excès" in *Histoire de la vie privée*, vol. I, *De l'empire romain à l'an mil,* Philippe Ariès and Georges Duby (eds), Seuil: Paris, 1999, pp. 174-175.
3. Cioran, *Entretiens*, Gallimard: Paris, 1995, pp. 73-74.
4. *Ibid.*, p. 149.
5. Martin-Fuguier, A., "Les rites de la vie privée bourgeoise" in *Histoire de la vie privée*, vol. 4, *De la Révolution à la Grande Guerre*, Philippe Ariés and Georges Duby (eds), Seuil: Paris, 1999, p. 185.
6. *Ibid.*, pp. 185-186.
7. A columnist for the daily pro-government *Cameroon Tribune* wrote on 6 April 1988: "*un décret présidentiel relève-t-il un directeur ou un préfet de ses fonctions, le petit cercle d'amis et l'entourage familial expliqut l'événement aux villageois en disant: 'on lui a enlevé la bouffe'. Au contraire si c'est une nomination à un poste important, le commentaire triomphant devient: 'on lui a donné la bouffe'. Le plus embêtant, c'est que l'interessé lui-même, démis ou promu, est convaincu intimement qu'on lui a enlevé ou donné la bouffe*" (When a presidential decree removed a director or an official from office, his small circle of friends and family would explain this event to the villagers by saying: 'they have taken the food from his table'. If, on the contrary, a person was appointed to an important position, the triumphant comment would be: 'they have put food on his table'. The most disturbing aspect is that the person concerned, whether demoted or promoted, would be convinced that food had been taken or put on his table).
8. Bayart, J.-F., *L'État en Afrique: La politique de ventre*, Fayard: Paris, 1989, pp. 11-12.
9. Joiris, Daou V., "*Ce que 'bien manger' veut dire chez les Pugmyes Kola (gyeli) et Baka du Sud – Cameroun*" in A. Froment *et al.* (eds), *Bien manger et bien vivre – Anthropologie alimentaire et développement en Afrique intertropicale: du biologique au social,* Ortsom/l'Harmattan: Paris, 1996, p. 366.
10. See C. Monga, "Coffins, Orgies and Sublimation: Mismanaging the Economy of Death", paper presented at the African Studies Seminar, University of Chicago, February 1993.
11. Duby, Georges, "La vie privée dans les maisonnées aristocratiques de la France féodale" in *Histoire de la vie privée*, vol. 2, *De l'Europe féodale à la Renaissance*, Philippe Ariès and Georges Duby (eds), Seuil: Paris, 1999, pp. 53-160.
12. Borges, J.L., *Nouveaux dialogues avec Oswaldo Ferrari*, Éditions Zoé/Éditions de l'Aube: Paris, 1990, p. 150.
13. Dower, John W., *Embracing Defeat: Japan in the Wake of World War II*, W.W. Norton: New York, 1999, p. 91.
14. According to Carl Riskin, "Communal dining was wasteful both because the public food handlers and preparers did not have the same incentive to husband and economize on food that individual families did, and because the free supply system encouraged people to over-consume ("Seven Questions about the Chinese Famine of 1959-1961" in *China Economic Review*, 9(2), 1998, p. 116). He thus confirms the observations of G.H. Chan and J. Guanzhong Wen: "No one would take pains to economize his or her food consumption, knowing that every bit saved in a communal dining hall of this type would be consumed or wasted soon by others" ("Communal Dining and Causation of the Chinese Famine of 1959-1961", paper cited by Riskin).
15. A *feyman* is one of the new millionaires. See Malaquais, Dominique, "Sur la Feymania au Cameroon", paper presented at the conference of the African Studies Association, Houston, Texas, November, 2001.
16. The issue of number is important. A wedding is only considered to be "a success" if it has managed to assemble the greatest possible number of guests. A crowd being the primary criterion of success, guests will bring one or two additional guests who are not formally invited but who are received with open arms.
17. Labou Tansi, S., *L'autre monde: écrits inédits*, Revue noire: Paris, 1997, pp. 98-99.
18. Popular beers in West and Central Africa.
19. Following Lévi-Strauss, Bourdieu warns us that we should not allow ourselves to be misled by the banality of food, which has a special status in our sensorial repertoire: "It is probably in tastes in food that one would find the strongest and most indelible mark of infant learning, the lessons which longest withstand the distancing or collapse of the native world and most durably maintain nostalgia for it" (*Distinction: A Social Critique of the Judgement of Taste,*

401

Harvard Univeristy Press: Cambridge, MA, 1984, p. 70).

20. It is interesting to note the aggressive, sometimes violent rhetoric which accompanies reflections on consumption: one does not drink champagne, one "downs" it; one does not consume cheese, one "guzzles" or "kills" (*tue*) it.

Additional references

Barthes, Roland, "Toward a Psychosociology of Contemporary Food Consumption" in *Food and Culture: A Reader*, Carole Counihan and Penny van Esterik (eds), Routledge: New York, 1997.

Borges, J.L., *Histoire universelle de l'infamie*, Paris, 1935.

Brillat-Savarin, *Physiologie du goût*, Éditions du Raisin: Paris, 1930.

Brunel, Sylvie, *Ceux qui vont mourir de faim*, Seuil: Paris, 1997.

Ela, Jean-Marc, *L'Afrique des villages*, Karthala: Paris, 1982.

George, Susan, *Comment meurt l'autre moitié du monde*, Fayard: Paris, 1983.

Girrad, Luce, "Plat du jour" in *The Practice of Everyday Life*, vol. 2, *Living and Cooking*, Michel de Certeau *et al.* (eds), University of Minnesota Press: Minneapolis, 1998, pp. 171-198.

Girard, René, *La spirale mimétique: Dix-huit leçons sur René Girard*, Desclée de Brouwer: Paris, 2001.

Lévi-Strauss, Claude, *From Honey to Ashes*, Harper and Row: New York, 1973.

Lévi-Strauss, Claude, *The Origin of Table Manners*, Harper and Row: New York, 1978.

Lévi-Strauss, Claude, *Le totemisme aujourd'hui*, PUF: Paris, 1962.

Mintz, Sidney W., *Tasting Food, Tasting Freedom: Excursions into Eating, Culture, and the Past*, Beacon Press: Boston, 1996.

Moulin, Léo, *L'Europe à table: Introduction à une psychosociologie des pratiques alimentaires*, Elsevier Sequoia: Paris/Bruxelles, 1975.

Monga, Célestin, *L'argent des autres: banques et petites entreprises en Afrique – le cas du Cameroon*, LGDJ: Paris, 1997.

Slater, Don, *Consumer Culture and Modernity*, Polity Press: Cambridge, 1997.

Ye, Xiao, and J. Edward Taylor, "The Impact of Income Growth on Farm Households Nutrient Intake: A Case study of a Prosperous Rural Area in Northern China" in *Economic Development and Cultural Change*, 43, 1995, pp. 805-819.

Notes Françoise Vergès (pp. 236-251)

1. Alevins are newly-spawned salmon or trout, still carrying yolks.

Additional references

Appadurai, Arjun, "How to Make a National Cuisine: Cookbooks in contemporary India" in *Comparative Studies in Society and History*, 30(1), 1988, pp. 3-24.

Bistolfi, Robert and Farouk Mardam-Bey, *Traité du pois chiche*, Sindbad, Actes Sud: Paris, 1998.

Goody, Jack, *Cooking, Cuisine and Class*, Cambridge University Press: Cambridge, 1982.

Kehayan, Nina, *Voyages de l'aubergine*, L'aube: Paris, 2000.

Marie-France and Ivrin, *Le grand livre de la cuisine réunionnaise*, Graphica: Saint-Denis, 1984.

Millstone, Erik and Tim Lang, *Food Atlas*, Myriad Editions: Brighton, 2003.

Beautiful Ugly: African and Diaspora Aesthetics

Mintz, Sydney W., *Tasting Food, Tasting Freedom. Excursions into Eating, Culture and the Past*, Beacon Press: Boston, 1996.

Norbert, Elias, *The Civilizing Process*, Urizen Books: New York, 1978.

Notes Cheryl-Ann Michael (pp. 252-261)

1. Leipoldt, C.L., *Leipoldt's Cape Cookery*, W.J. Flesch and Partners: Cape Town, 1976, p. 14.

2. *Ibid.*, p. 29.

3. Duckitt, H., *Hilda's Diary of a Cape Housekeeper*, Macmillan: Cape Town, 1978, p. 29.

4. *Ibid.*, p. 66.

5. *Ibid.*, p. 3.

6. *Ibid.*, p. 71.

7. This usage offers an interesting dialogue with Pippa Stein's use of the "notion of slipping or slippability" (in this volume).

8. Mayat, Z. (ed.), *Indian Delights*, Booksite Africa: Johannesburg, 1993.

9. Gbadamosi, G., "The Road to Brixton Market" in *Travel Writing and Empire*, S. Clark (ed.), Zed Books: London, 1999, p. 188.

10. Soyinka, W., *Aké*, Arena Books: London, 1983, p. 115.

11. Rowling, J.K., *Harry Potter and the Goblet of Fire*, Bloomsbury: London, 2000, p. 221.

12. Bond, M., *A Bear Called Paddington*, HarperCollins: London, 1991, pp. 13-14.

Notes Patricia Pinho (pp. 262-285)

1. Gilroy, Paul, *Against Race – Imagining Political Culture Beyond the Color Line*, Harvard University Press: Boston, 2000, p. 125.

2. Raeders, Georges, *O Conde Gobineau no Brasil*, Paz e Terra: Rio de Janeiro, 1988, p. 96.

3. Brazil was the only Latin American country to participate in "The First International Congress on Races", held in 1911. On that occasion, anthropologist João Batista Lacerda presented his thesis "Sur les Métis", in which he contended that the process of miscegenation in Brazil would lead to a "whiter future". It would take three generations for the process of *whitening* to take place, lightening the Brazilian population both physically and morally (Lilia Schwartcz, *Racismo no Brasil*, Publifolha: São Paulo, 2001).

4. Usually Brazilian Indians are mentioned in schools only on the 19th of April, the "Day of the Indian", an occasion on which children are dressed as "Indians", that is to say as "Apache", "Comanche", or other North American ethnicities that never inhabited Brazil but became famous due to Western movies imported from the USA. Brazilian native peoples are also affected by racist representations, mostly through associating Indians with laziness and indolence, but usually the beauty of Indian women is mentioned as a positive trait together with the "heroic" characteristic of Indian men.

5. Appiah, Kwame Anthony, *Na Casa de Meu Pai – A África na filosofia da cultura*, Contraponto: Rio de Janeiro, 1997.

6. McClintock, Anne, "Soap and commodity spectacle" in *Representation, Cultural Representations and Signifying Practices*, Stuart Hall (ed.), Sage Publications: London, 1997,

p. 280.

7. *Catinga*: from the Tupi radical *cati*, strong smell; unpleasant smell of the sweat of blacks, and, in general, any bad smell of the body of people or animals, etc. (translated from *Grande Enciclopédia Portuguesa e Brasileira*. Editorial Enciclopédia Limitada: Lisboa and Rio de Janeiro, 1946).

8. Information collected during field research in Bahia, Brazil, in 1999-2000.

9. *Ibid.*

10. Hall, Stuart, "The Spectacle of the Other" in *Representation, Cultural Representations and Signifying Practices*, Stuart Hall (ed.), Sage Publications: London, 1997.

11. The soap opera was called *A Próxima Vítima* and was on air in 1995.

12. The *blocos* are the groups that parade on the streets of Salvador during Carnival. They are divided into two main categories: *blocos de trio* and *blocos afro*. The former's name come from their big trucks with sound systems called *trio eletrico*, and are known for being composed mainly of white high- and middle-class youth. The *blocos afro* are more thoroughly explained later in the text.

13. The "geographical discrimination" refers to the rejection of people who live in poor neighbourhoods, whose presence could "lower the level" of the carnival group and make them lose their targeted public composed of people of higher social strata, according to the directors.

14. Gilroy, Paul, *The Black Atlantic, Modernity and Double Consciousness*, Verso: London, 1993.

15. While Ilê Aiyê was the first *bloco afro* to be founded and is considered the most "traditional", Olodum is the most famous of Brazilian *blocos afro* and is regarded as the most "modern". Olodum was established in 1979 as part of the "re-Africanisation" of Bahia's carnival. The group created the stimulating rhythm of samba-reggae, an Afro-Atlantic fusion of regional Bahian samba with the beat and political message of Jamaican reggae. The rhythm became famous worldwide, attracting musicians like Paul Simon and Michael Jackson to record songs with Olodum.

16. Statistics show that in times of inflation Brazilian consumers tend to reduce the consumption of essential goods (food, clothes, etc.) but, surprisingly, the consumption of hair products, especially creams used for styling the hair, remains unaltered.

17. Ferme, Mariane, *The Underneath of Things: Violence, History, and the Everyday in Sierra Leone,* University of California Press: Berkeley, 2001, p. 58.

18. Erasmus, Zimitri, "Hair Politics" in *Senses of Culture*, Sarah Nuttall and Cheryl-Ann Michael (eds), Oxford University Press: Cape Town, 2000.

19. Bahia is commonly represented by the caricature of a dark person (tanned? black?) resting lazily in a hammock, drinking coconut water. The common image of São Paulo is a locomotive that leads Brazil forward and represents the hard-working quality of its (mainly white) people.

20. Souza, Neusa Santos, *Tornar-se Negro, ou As Vicissitudes da Identidade do Negro Brasileiro em Ascensão Social*, Graal: Rio de Janeiro, 1983; Amma-Psique e Negritude Quilombhoje (Various Authors), *Gostando Mais de Nós Mesmos. Perguntas e Respostas Sobre Auto-estima e Questão Racial,* Editora Gente: São Paulo, 1999; and Ronilda Ribeiro, *Alma Africana no Brasil: os Iorubás*, Editora Oduduwa: São Paulo, 1996.

21. Ribeiro, p. 171.

22. Every reasonable effort has been made to trace the holders of copyright material for this illustration. Any omission will be gladly rectified in future editions.

23. Ware, Vron, "What Makes You/Him/Her/Them/Us/ It White? The Making and Unmaking of Whiteness: A Global Project", paper prepared for the conference "The Burden of Race: 'Whiteness' And 'Blackness' in Modern South Africa", University Of Witwatersrand, Johannesburg, July 2001, p. 6.

24. Scarry, Elaine, *On Beauty and Being Just*, Princeton University Press: Princeton, 1999, p. 67.

25. "It may seem that in crediting the enduring phenomenon of beauty with this pressure toward distribution, we are relying on a modern notion of 'distribution'. But only the word is new. Plato's requirement that we move from 'eros', in which we are seized by the beauty of one person, to 'caritas', in which our care is extended to all people, has parallels in many early aesthetic treatises …" (*Ibid.*, p. 81).

26. Gilroy, 2000.

27. Hall, 1997, p. 229. Emphasis of the author.

28. Erasmus, p. 385.

29. Connerton, Paul, *How Societies Remember,* Cambridge University Press: Cambridge, 1989.

30. Gilroy, 2000, p. 104.

Notes Kamari Maxine Clarke (pp. 286-311)

1. Enwezor, Okwui, "Travel Notes: Living, Working, and Traveling in a Restless World" in *Trade Routes: History and Geography*, African Institute for Comparative Arts: Johannesburg, 1997, p. 7.

2. Òrìsàs are intermediary deities in the Yorùbá pantheon that are signified by humans to represent a range of characteristics and qualities.

3. Gilroy, Paul, *Against Race: Imagining Political Culture Beyond the Color Line*, The Belknap Press of Harvard University: Cambridge, MA, 2000.

4. On the grounds that Africans were barbarians void of Christianity and without the mental capacity to justify their liberty.

5. Hall, S. and P.D. Gay (eds), *Questions of Cultural Identity*, Sage: California and Thousand Oaks: London, 1996.

6. Note, the rural location, the signs of racial commonalities and African practices are not in and of themselves material differences that are adequate to link life in Òyótúnjí to that of life in West Africa. Likewise, evidence of musical preferences that blend "West African rhythmic" performers with "American rap songs" is not sufficient to distinguish difference of cultural production in the US from forms that may be simultaneously occurring in contemporary West African Yorùbá communities. Even as community life, imagined as part of the Òyó Empire, is not sufficient to render these differences as signs of disjuncture with a Yorùbá tradition. Instead, signs of the inauthentic and their ability to be classified in the eyes of the beholders as legitimate are dependent on the institutional forms of remembering and forgetting that typically shape the boundaries of social distinctions. I demonstrate how ritual practices are fashioned and refined to render a useable past

to those who travel to Òyótúnjí seeking assistance, and the interpretative constructions of particular kinds of ancestral connections with West Africa renders the meaning of the past – trans-Atlantic slavery – central to the formation of Òyótúnjí Yorùbá traditionalism. Thus, with linkages established, the power to establish the legitimacy of an African kingdom in South Carolina lies in the personal authority generated by religious ritual conducted by the revered subject.

7. The colours of the three flags are: red, green and gold; red and black; and white and black.

8. Many practitioners have lived in Òyótúnjí at some time and others have pursued ritual initiations there over a period of time. I conducted a population tabulation of residents every three months over a one-year period and found that over that period, the population shifted from 57 to 48 residents.

9. At one time many of the early residents were able to supplement their households with government assistance payments. However, in the late 1980s, the Òyótúnjí Ògbóni council outlawed Federal and South Carolina State Government assistance. This new law, as well as the increasing power of the Crown, made it increasingly difficult for many practitioners to make an adequate living on their religious trade alone. Unable to make ends meet, and in need of more political agency, hundreds of practitioners moved to US cities, forming Yorùbá satellite communities from which to continue their religious practices.

10. Althusser, L., "Ideology and Ideological State Apparatuses (Notes Towards an Investigation)" in *Lenin and Philosophy and Other Essays*, Monthly Review Press: New York, 1971, p. 93.

11. Durkheim, E., *The Elementary Forms of the Religious Life*, The Free Press: New York, 1915.

12. Hardt, M. and A. Negri, *Empire*, Harvard University Press: Cambridge and London, 2000.

13. Hernandez-Reguant, A., "Kwanzaa and the US Ethnic Mosaic" in *Representations of Blackness and the Performance of Identities*, J. Muteba Rahier (ed.), Bergin & Garvey: London and Wesport, CT, 1999.

14. Tsing, A., "The Global Situation" in *Cultural Anthropology*, 15(3), 2000, pp. 327-360.

15. Santería regulations required that ritual initiations had to be presided over by Babaláwos (the highest ranking priest – that of the Ifá Òrìsà) and as a young priest without a congregation of qualified African-centred priests, it was difficult for King to function in Santería religious circles within their support.

16. I use the word "ideology" not to revisit Marxian debates about political-based thinking. It is neither reflective of a class nor a coherent system of thought. Rather, I invoke it to describe a sphere of logics – a domain of seeing that allows people to classify, interpret and explain the world as they see it – sometimes producing contradictory results but shaped by particular fields of possibility through which meanings are channelled.

404

Additional references

Appadurai, A, *Modernity at Large: Cultural Dimensions of Globalization*, University of Minnesota Press: Minneapolis, 1996.

Ayorinde, C, *Identity in the Shadow of Slavery*. Continuum: London and New York, 2000.

Bakhtin, M.M., *The Dialogic Imagination: Four Essays*, University of Texas Press: Austin, 1981.

Castoriadis, C., *The Imaginary Institution of Society*, Polity Press: Cambridge, 1987.

Clarke, M. Kamari, *Mapping Yorùbá Transnationalism: Agency and Power in the Making of Òyótúnjí African village*, Duke University Press: Durham, NC, 2004.

Cooper, F., "What is the Concept of Globalization Good For? An African Historian's Perspective" in *African Affairs*, 100, 2001, pp. 189-213.

Darwin, C., *On the Origin of the Species by Means of Natural selection, or The Preservation of Favoured Races in the Struggle for Life*, John Murray: London, 1859.

Dominguez, V.R., *People as Subject, People as Object: Selfhood and Peoplehood in Contemporary Israel*, University of Wisconsin Press: Madison, 1989.

Ebron, P.A., *Performing Africa*, Princeton University Press: Princeton, NJ, 2002.

Featherstone, M., Lash, S. *et al* (eds), *Global Modernities*, Sage: California and Thousand Oaks: London, 1995.

Halbwachs, M., *The Collective Memory*, Harper and Row: New York, 1980.

Hall, S., "Culture, Community, Nation" in *Cultural Studies*, 7(3), 1993, pp. 349-363.

Jameson, F. and M. Miyoshi, *The Cultures of Globalization*, Duke University Press: Durham, NC, 1999.

Johnson, S., *The History of the Yorùbás: From the Earliest Times to the Beginning of the British Protectorate*, Routledge and Kegan Paul: London, 1921.

Jusdanis, G., *The Necessary Nation*, Princeton University Press: Princeton and Oxford, 2001.

Keane, W., "The Value of Words and the Meaning of Things" in *Eastern Indonesian Exchange*, 1995.

Koh, Harold Hongju, "How Is International Human Rights Law Enforced?" in *Indiana Law Journal*, 74, 1999, p. 1397.

Koh, Harold Hongju, "The 1998 Frankel Lecture: Bringing International Law Home" in *Houston Law Review*, 35, 1998, p. 623.

Lacan, J., *De la psychose paranoïaque dans ses rapports avec la personnalité suivi de premiers écrits sur la paranoïa*, Editions du Seuil: Paris, 1975.

Laitin, D.D., *Hegemony and Culture: Politics and Religious Change Among the Yorùbá*, The University of Chicago Press: Chicago and London, 1986.

Law, R., *The Slave Coast of West Africa, 1550-1750: The Impact of the Atlantic Slave Trade on an African Society*, Clarendon Press and Oxford University Press: Oxford and New York, 1991.

Martin Shaw, C., *Colonial Inscriptions: Race, Sex and Class in Kenya*, University of Minnesota Press: Minneapolis, 1995.

O'Donnell, Guillermo and Juan E. Mendez, *The (Un)Rule of Law and the Underprivileged in Latin America*, University of Notre Dame Press: Paris, 1999.

Sassen, S., *Losing Control? Sovereignty in an Age of Globalization*, Columbia University Press: New York, 1996.

Scott, David, "That Event, This Memory: Notes on the Anthropology of African Diasporas in the New World" in *Diaspora*. 1(3), 1991, pp. 261-284.

Shapiro, M., "Moral Geographies and the Ethics of Post-Sovereignty" in *Public Culture*, 6(3), 1994, p. 482.

Silverstein, M., "Shifters, Linguistic Categories, and Cultural

Description" in *Meaning in Anthropology*, K.H. Basso and H.A. Selby (eds), University of New Mexico Press: Albuquerque, 1976, pp. 11-55.

Young, R.J.C., *Colonial Desire: Hybridity in Theory, Culture and Race*, Routledge: London and New York, 1995.

Zizek, S., *Plague of Fantasies*, Verso: London and New York, 1996.

Zizek, S. (ed.), *Cogito and the Unconscious*, Duke University Press: Durham, NC, 1998.

Notes Rodney Place (pp. 312-336)

1. Quoted in *The Oxford Book of Short Stories*, V.S. Pritchett (ed.), Oxford University Press: New York, 1981.
2. *Couch Dancing,* Market Theatre, Johannesburg, August 1998 and The Castle, Cape Town, November 1998.
3. Maugham, W. Somerset, "Introduction" in *The Oxford Book of Short Stories,* V.S. Pritchett (ed.), Oxford University Press: New York, 1981.
4. Vladislavić, Ivan, *The Restless Supermarket*, David Philip, Cape Town, 2001.
5. *RETREKS* is a project that tracks the emergence of post-democratic metropolitan Johannesburg through four social viewpoints: yuppie/buppie suburbanites; cowboy and-girl Calvinists; Anglo-tribal aristocrats of KwaSandton; and new African immigrants into the city. The project proposes a cultural approach to urbanism in South Africa.
6. Koolhaas, Rem, *Conversations with Students*, Princeton Architectural Press: New York, 1996.
7. Koolhaas, Rem, *Delirious New York: A Retroactive Manifesto for Manhattan*, Monacelli Press: New York, 1995 (1978).

Notes Michelle Gilbert (pp. 336-367)

1. Mami Wata (pidgin for "Mother of Water"), half woman, half water spirit, is regarded as a deity who can bring luck or money to her devotees.
2. See Kwabena N. Bame, *Come to Laugh: A Study of African Traditional Theatre in Ghana*, Baafour Educational Enterprises: Accra, 1981; John Collins, "Comic Opera in Ghana" in *African Arts*, 9(2), 1976, pp. 50-57; John Collins, *Highlife Time*, Anansesem: Accra, 1994; Catherine M. Cole, "Reading Blackface in West Africa: Wonders Taken for Signs" in *Critical Inquiry*, 23, 1996, pp. 183-215; Catherine M. Cole, *Ghana's Concert Party Theatre*, Indiana University Press: Bloomington, 2001; Michelle Gilbert, "Concert Parties: Paintings and Performance" in *Journal of Religion in Africa*, 28(1), 1998, pp. 62-87; Michelle Gilbert, *Hollywood Icons, Local Demons: Ghanaian Popular Paintings by Mark Anthony*, Trinity College: Hartford, 2000; and Michelle Gilbert, "Shocking Images: Ghanaian Painted Posters / Images choc: peintures affiches du Ghana" in *Ghana: hier et aujourd'hui / Ghana: Yesterday and Today*, Musée Dapper: Paris, 2003, pp. 353-379.
3. On urban art, sometimes described as "sign-painter's art", see Susan Vogel, *Africa Explores: 20th Century African Art,* Center for African Art: New York, 1991, pp. 114-115; and see Georg Simmel, *Essays on Religion*, edited and translated by Horst Jurgen Helle in collaboration with Ludwig Nieder, Yale University Press: New Haven, CT, 1997, on how urban settings allow encounters to happen.

4. See Karin Barber, "Popular Arts in Africa" in *African Studies Review,* 30(3), 1987, pp. 1-78; and Bogumil Jewsiewicki, "Zairian Popular Painting as Commodity and as Communication" in *African Material Culture*, Mary Jo Arnoldi, Christraud Geary, and Kris L. Hardin (eds), Indiana University Press: Bloomington, 1996, pp. 334-355.
5. See Jean-François Bayart, "Africa in the World: A History of Extraversion" in *African Affairs,* 99(395), 2000, pp. 217-168.
6. Leach, Edmund R., "The Gatekeepers of Heaven: Anthropological Aspects of Grandiose Architecture" in *Journal of Anthropological Research*, 39(3), 1983, pp. 243-264.
7. In American minstrel shows, white actors enacted southern slaves: in the words of Kenneth Lynn, "a white imitation of a black imitation of a contented slave" (Jan Nederveen Pieterse, *White on Black: Images of Africa and Blacks in Western Popular Culture,* Yale University Press: New Haven, CT, 1992, p. 132). It was a way for whites to come to terms with the problems of slavery through the myth of the benevolent plantation.
8. "It was not *racist* but *about race* and racial affinity" and showed the burgeoning interest in the black Atlantic (C.M. Cole, 2001, p. 34; and 1996).
9. Men still play female roles in concert plays. Acting, as in early Hollywood and classical European theatre, is not considered a respectable occupation for women.
10. Van Dijk, Rijk, "From Camp to Encompassment: Discourses of Transsubjectivity in the Ghanaian Pentecostal Diaspora" in *Journal of Religion in Africa,* 27(2), 1997, p. 138.
11. The "crusades" of the Kristo Asafo church gradually developed into a play preceded by the comedian Nkomode (fig. 6 shows Nkomode as the joker, or "Bob"). Their concerts differed from those of other bands only in that they did not have deities (*ahosom*) in their plays. Yet Akrobeto, actor and playwright for Kristo Asafo, complained: "Now everyone is 'born again', so they don't want to dance to music that does not belong to Christianity. It is the same highlife, but unless they hear 'God, God, God' [they won't listen] ... If a song is about marriage and how Kwabena meets another girl, this is not the 'line of God', so if someone is a 'pure Christian', he won't listen to such a song. Pastors have become uncountable. Everyone has a church. If someone wants to come to concert, he feels shy because maybe someone will see him and report to his church and the pastor will cancel his membership."
12. See Michelle Gilbert 2000, pp. 30-32.
13. See Edmund R. Leach, "Anthropological Aspects of Language: Animal Categories and Verbal Abuse" in *New Directions in the Study of Language*, Eric H. Lenneberg (ed.), M.I.T. Press: Cambridge, MA, 1964, p. 39, on obscenity and animal abuse where he discusses these "... ambiguous categories that attract the maximum interest and the most intense feelings of taboo".
14. Among the Akan, as among the English, the most common insult is to call someone an animal, *aboa*, or to say they are meat, *nam* (with the implication of cannibalism?); someone who feels slighted will remark "I am a person" (and so worthy of respect).
15. European witches were believed to be able to metamorphose into werewolves due to their pact with the devil.

405

16. See Michelle Gilbert, "The Person of the King: Ritual and Power in a Ghanaian State" in *Rituals of Royalty: Power and Ceremonial in Traditional Societies*, David Cannadine and Simon Price (eds), Cambridge University Press, Cambridge, 1987, p. 312; and "The Leopard Who Sleeps in a Basket: Akuapem Secrecy in Everyday Life and in Royal Metaphor" in *Secrecy: African Art that Conceals and Reveals*, Mary H. Nooter (ed.), The Museum for African Art: New York, 1993, p. 134, on *esen*. Among the Asante they could neither be flogged nor killed (R.S. Rattray, *Religion and Art in Asante*, Oxford University Press: London, 1927, p. 279).

17. On Mark Anthony, see Michelle Gilbert, 2000, pp. 8-11. NB: all the concert paintings referred to in this essay are by Mark Anthony.

18. See Birgit Meyer, "'If You Are a Devil, You Are a Witch and, if You Are a Witch, You Are a Devil.' The Integration of 'Pagan' Ideas into the Conceptual Universe of Ewe Christians in Southeastern Ghana" in *Journal of Religion in Africa*, 22(2), 1992, p. 104, on *obonsam*, its translation of Christian devil, African evil spirits and witchcraft; and its relation to gods (*abosom*) and giants (*sasabonsam*).

19. Viewers of the paintings, educated and semi-literate alike, recognise what is portrayed. "I don't believe in such crap! I am a Christian; I went to school!" (*Menye saa neama ndi; mi ye Kristoni, maako suku*) exclaimed a schoolteacher examining a painting of deities, witches and sacrificial rites. As for those who do believe the ideas portrayed in the paintings, she said witheringly: "These people, their eyes are not open" (*nkrofuo wei dee omo ani mmue*). However much the Christian or non-Christian audience is lured, attracted or repulsed by the sensationalism of the painted images, the moral message of the play is a readily recognisable one of good versus evil.

20. Biebuyck, Daniel, *Lega Culture: Art, Initiation and Moral Philosophy among a Central African People*, University of California Press: Berkeley, 1973, pp. 177-178.

21. Horton, Robin, *Kalabari Sculpture*, Nigeria Department of Antiquities: Lagos, 1965, p. 23.

22. See Mariane C. Ferme, *The Underneath of Things: Violence, History and the Everyday in Sierra Leone*, University of California Press: Berkeley, 2001, pp. 162-163; and Ruth Phillips, *Representing Woman: Sande Masquerades of the Mende of Sierra Leone*, UCLA Fowler Museum of Cultural History: Los Angeles, CA, 1995, p. 90. See also the anti-aesthetic of the Mende *gongoli* mask (Phillips, 1995), and the review by Wilfred Van Damme, *A Comparative Analysis concerning Beauty and Ugliness in sub-Saharan Africa*, Rijksuniversiteit: Gent, 1987, p. 57f, of deliberately ugly masks by Igbo, Bangwa and Bamana.

23. See Michelle Gilbert, "Sources of Power in Akuropon-Akuapem: Ambiguity in Classification" in *Creativity of Power: Cosmology and Action in African Societies*, William Arens and Ivan Karp (eds), Smithsonian Institution Press, Washington DC, 1989, pp. 59-90.

24. See Ferme, 2001, p. 161.

25. See Inih A. Ebong, "The Aesthetics of Ugliness in Ibibio Dramatic Arts" in *African Studies Review*, 38(3), 1995, p. 51.

26. "Acceptable" expressions of obscene and vulgar language and gesture, including mock copulation, are seen in joking repartee and mimed dances at funerals and in women's funeral and puberty songs (*bra goru*). While cathartic, these do not elicit laughter from the viewers, who here are also the participants.

27. See Paul Gifford, *African Christianity: Its Public Role*, Indiana University Press: Bloomington, 1998, chap. III, on Christianity in Ghana; see also Birgit Meyer, "'Delivered from the Powers of Darkness' – Confessions of Satanic Riches in Christian Ghana" in *Africa*, 65(2), 1995, pp. 236-255.

28. Meyer, 1995, p. 237.

29. *Ibid.*, p. 238.

30. *Ibid.*, p. 244; and Birgit Meyer, "The Power of Money: Politics, Occult Forces, and Pentecostalism in Ghana" in *African Studies Review*, 41(3), 1998, p. 24.

31. Meyer, 1995, p. 249.

32. Akurang-Parry, Kwabena O., "Passionate Voices of Those Left Behind: Conversations with Ghanaian Professionals on the Brain Drain and its Net Gains" in *African Issues,* African Studies Association, XXX/1, 2002, p. 58, records that remittances to Ghana form the fourth biggest source of foreign exchange transfer after cocoa, gold and tourism.

33. Akyeampong, Emmanuel, "Africans in the diaspora: the diaspora and Africa" in *African Affairs*, 99(395), 2000, p. 186. He notes that even menial jobs in the West yield foreign currency that translates generously into devalued home currencies.

34. *Ibid.,* p. 207.

35. As in Cameroon, the Democratic Republic of Congo and Sierra Leone: see Peter Geschiere, *The Modernity of Witchcraft: Politics and the Occult in Postcolonial Africa,* University Press of Virginia: Charlottesville and London, 1997; Filip De Boeck, "Domesticating Diamonds and Dollars: Identity, Expenditure and Sharing in Southwestern Zaire (1984-1997)" in *Globalization and Identity: Dialectics of Flow and Closure*, B. Meyer and P. Geschiere (eds), Blackwell: Oxford, 1999; and Rosalind Shaw, "The Production of Witchcraft/Witchcraft as Production: Memory, Modernity, and the Slave Trade in Sierra Leone" in *American Ethnologist*, 24(4), 1997, pp. 856-876.

36. For example *People and Places* and *The Spectator*.

37. See Birgit Meyer, "Popular Ghanaian Cinema and 'African Heritage'" in *Africa Today*, 2000, pp. 92-114; and "Money, Power and Morality: Popular Ghanaian Cinema in the Fourth Republic" in *Ghana Studies*, 4, 2001, pp. 65-84, on Ghanaian videos as vehicles of morality.

38. One, called *Witches*, concerned a group of witches who feared that their kingdom was declining as their numbers dwindled; so instead of just killing people in lorry accidents and sucking their blood, they decided to convert some of them to witches. However, many of those they wanted to convert were Christians and their witches' power was not as strong as the Christian power, so in the end they did not succeed.

39. *Sasabonsam* are dangerous and said to be taller than giants, with thorns and hair all over their bodies. They live especially in the *onyaa* (silk cotton; *Bombax: ceiba pentandra*) and *odum* (*Erythleum guiniese*) trees that overlook the towns, and when they catch an animal, they do not eat its flesh but take its blood instead (cf. witches that suck the blood of humans) (GTV, August 2000).

40. See M. Gilbert, 1987, pp. 308-309; and 1989.

41. Covens of witches – generally women and mostly post-

Beautiful Ugly: African and Diaspora Aesthetics

menopausal – are active at night. Always envious of others, they mostly destroy those within their own lineage. In the past, witches were killed; since their blood must not be shed, they were strangled. Christians formerly denied the existence of witches and because those accused sometimes took refuge within the church, some said that witches filled the mission churches. Pentecostals take the threat of witchcraft seriously and claim that the power of God can reveal and purify witches.

42. See P. Geschiere, 1997, on the Cameroon.

43. See Misty L. Bastian, "'Bloodhounds Who Have No Friends': Witchcraft and Locality in the Nigerian Popular Press" in *Modernity and its Malcontents: Ritual and Power in Postcolonial Africa*, Jean Comaroff and John Comaroff (eds), University of Chicago Press: Chicago, 1993, pp. 129-166, on Nigeria.

44. See P. Geschiere, 1997, p. 143; and R. Shaw, 1997, p. 860.

45. See Alma Gottlieb, "Witches, Kings, and the Sacrifice of Identity or The Power of Paradox and the Paradox of Power among the Beng of Ivory Coast" in *Creativity of Power: Cosmology and Action in African Societies,* W. Arens and I. Karp (eds), Smithsonian Institution Press: Washington DC, 1989, pp. 245-272, on the Beng of Côte d'Ivoire.

46. The opposition of white/good, black/evil, and angel/devil is a familiar missionary trope that was used on political banners for the 1996 election campaign, and was the subject of light-hearted, ironic joking on talk radio/popular music stations in the late 1990s.

47. Here a myth from Eastern Europe (about Count Dracula, a real person in 15th-century Transylvania, who was a sadist and rumoured to be a vampire) and a novel (by Bram Stoker in 1897) have been taken on by Hollywood and the West and in turn by the West African imagination. Vampire stories intrigue the public: there have been over 200 films and scores of books on the subject. See Hans Askenasy, *Cannibalism: From Sacrifice to Survival*, Prometheus Books: Amherst, NY, 1994, p. 160.

48. See Ernie Wolfe III, *Extreme Canvas: Hand-painted Movie Posters from Ghana*, Dilettante Press/Kesho Press: New York, 2000, p. 196, for an unsigned, undated poster for the Ghanaian video *False Witch.*

49. See Bogumil Jewsiewicki, *Cheri Samba: The Hybridity of Art*, Contemporary African Artists Series #1, Galerie Amrad African Art Publications: Westmount, Quebec, 1995; Henry J. Drewel, "Mami Wata Shrines: Exotica and the Constitution of Self" in *African Material Culture*, Mary Jo Arnoldi, Christraud Geary and Kris L. Hardin (eds), Indiana University Press: Bloomington, 1996, pp. 308-333; and Rush, Dana, "Eternal Potential, Chromolithographs in Vodunland" in *African Arts*, 32(4), 1999, pp. 60-75, on Mami Wata.

50. See Ernie Wolfe III, 2000, p. 44, for a poster of *Splash* painted by the artist Leonardo in 1991; and pp. 222, 223 for others, including two entitled *Laal Paree: Indian Splash.*

51. See Brian Larkin, "Indian Films and Nigerian Lovers: Media and the Creation of Parallel Modernities" in *Africa*, 67(3), 1997, pp. 406-440, on the appeal of Indian videos in Nigeria.

52. I am grateful to Rukhsana Siddiqui, who clarified this point for me.

53. For the 1997 A.B. Crentsil play *In This World, if You Do Not Allow Your Brother to Climb, You Will Not Climb (Ama won yonko antwa nkron. . .),* see M. Gilbert 2000, p. 20, plate 14.

54. Painted in 1995, this was bought by Kwame Nti for his Katakyie Professionals concert band in 1997.

55. Blue skin is symbolic of the Hindu god Krishna.

56. Painted in 2001 for Kaakyire Kwame Appiah's concert called *Agya Nyame* (God the Father).

57. See Michelle Gilbert, "The Christian Executioner: Chieftaincy and Christianity as Rivals" in *Journal of Religion in Africa*, 25(4), 1995, pp. 352-356.

58. By the end of the 1990s, TV sets were widespread and films of all types were broadcast on GTV, so most people now watch at home. The use of hand-painted video posters declined after the introduction of free off-set printed paper posters. See Ernie Wolfe III, 2000.

59. See Ernie Wolfe III, 2000 for examples of these posters.

60. "The brutality of embrace, penetration of the vampire's teeth, sucking of hot blood, the passionate moment of transformation – this is sexy stuff indeed . . ." (Anne Rice in a *Playboy* interview about her vampire books, in H. Askenasy 1994, p. 161).

61. *Fufuu* is boiled and mashed cassava with yam or plantain that is pounded in a wooden mortar until it becomes an elastic doughy mass. It is eaten with soup.

62. The 19th-century slave trader Theodore Canot, alias Theophile Conneau, describes in his autobiography a case in which, following the advice of a "soothsayer", Amara Lalu of Madine grabbed his two-year-old son and threw the infant into a rice mortar and "smote [him] into a mummy" with a pestle. See Adam Jones, "Theophile Conneau at Galinhas and New Sestos, 1836-1841: A Comparison of the Sources" in *History in Africa*, 8, 1981, pp. 93-94 and note 41, p. 102.

63. See Ezio Bassani, "Un Cappuccino nell'Africa nera del seicento: I disegni dei *Manoscuitti Araldi* del Padre Giovanni Antonio Cavazzi da Montecuccolo" in *Quaderni Poro*, 4, 1987, colour plate 24, for an illustration from Father Cavazzi's Araldi manuscripts. I thank Adam Jones for this information.

64. Reidorf, C.C., *History of the Gold Coast and Asante*, 2nd edition, Ghana University Press: Accra, 1966, p. 153.

65. As an allegory for civilised/savage worlds, Ghanaians view neighbouring Nigerians in much the same way as 19th- and early 20th-century Christian Europeans viewed Africans. See W. Arens, *The Man Eating Myth: Anthropology and Anthropophagy*, Oxford University Press: New York, 1979, on the fact that believing that "others" are cannibals (and thus wicked, depraved, dangerous and akin to animals) is universal. Arens argues that, excluding survival conditions, old accounts of cannibalism are not credible and few believable modern accounts exist (but see Ross Bowden, "Maori Cannibalism: An Interpretation" in *Oceania*, 55(2), 1984, pp. 81-99). Anecdotes about cannibalism have fascinated Europeans at least since Herodotus reported on the Scythians' practices. True or not, people believe cannibalism to exist, as may be seen in the recent rash of rumours in Malawi that the government is colluding with vampires to collect human blood for international aid agencies in exchange for food. Ritual sacrifice certainly existed throughout much of West Africa and there are numerous accounts of recent war atrocities – for example, the UN report that the Movement for the Liberation of

Congo (MLC) "... cut out the hearts and other organs of their victims and forced families to eat them" (*L.A. Times*, January 16, 2003, A: p. 60). Human sacrifice was legally abolished in 1844 in the Gold Coast, but continued secretly for some time (see M. Gilbert, 1995, pp. 352-356 and notes pp. 378-9; and Clifford Williams, "Asante: Human sacrifice or capital punishment? An assessment of the period 1807-1874" in *The International Journal of African Historical Studies*, 1988, pp. 433-441, on the Asante).

66. *Kelewele* is ripe plantain, mashed or cut into little pieces, mixed with ginger and pepper, formed into little morsels and deep fried.

67. I am grateful to Mary Esther Dakubu for telling me of this belief from the Upper West Region of Ghana; it was related to her by Joseph Kabom.

68. English children's picture books, including learners' books on dinosaurs, are readily available in Ghana.

69. See M. Gilbert, 2000, pp. 26-29 and 35-69, for the text of this play: *When a Royal Dies, We Take Him Home (Odehyee wu a yede no ko fie)*.

70. The idea of anthills being sacred ground is widespread in West Africa (see I.A. Ebong, 1995, on Ibibio).

71. Clothing is a "social skin" that marks social beings everywhere (T.S. Turner, "The Social Skin" in *Not Work Alone*, J. Cherfas and R. Lewin (eds), Sage: Beverly Hills, CA, 1980). The purposefully created "sculpted body" of the *macho* youth that can be displayed as part of his "self" and that becomes an inseparable part of his identity is just as much a case of postmodern culture being inscribed directly on the body as is the latest fashion (*la sape*) worn by the *sapeurs*, the Congolese youth, in Brazzaville and Paris (see Ch. Didier Gondola, "Dream and Drama: The Search for Elegance among Congolese Youth" in *African Studies Review*, 42(1), 1999, pp. 23-48).

72. Most focus on polygyny, co-wife rivalry, orphans, jealousy and envy, wealth and poverty, morally good and bad character, chieftaincy and Christianity.

73. By the age of 20, they either find a job or are pressured to be more serious because they have made a girl pregnant. See B. Meyer, 2000, on the videos that Ghanaian women bring home to view on television.

74. See Brian Larkin, "Piracy, Infrastructure and the Materiality of Media Flows in Nigeria" (ms.), African Studies Association 45 Annual Meeting, Washington DC, 2002, on how distortion from piracy and the fact that viewers are watching a dub of a dub produces aesthetic standards for new videos.

75. Quoted by Deirdre Evans-Pritchard, "Other Considerations" in *Extreme Canvas: Hand-painted Movie Posters from Ghana,* Ernie Wolfe III (ed.), Dilettante Press/Kesho Press: New York, 2000, p. 47.

Additional references

Appiah, Peggy and Kwame Anthony Appiah with Ivor Agyeman-Duah, *Bu Me Be: Akan Proverbs*, The Centre for Intellectual Renewal: Accra, 2003.
Barber, Karin, John Collins and Alain Ricard, *West African Popular Theatre,* Indiana University Press: Bloomington, 1997.
Fabian, Johannes, "Popular Culture in Africa: Findings and Conjectures" in *Africa*, 48(4), 1978, pp. 315-334.
Fabian, Johannes, *Remembering the Present: Painting and Popular History in Zaire,* University of California Press:

Berkeley, 1996.
Gilbert, Michelle, "From Highlife to Hellfire: the Art of Mark Anthony", paper presented at the 12th Triennial Symposium on African Art, Virgin Islands, 2001.

Notes Isabel Hofmeyr (pp. 380-387)

1. Couto, Mia, *Voices Made Night*, translated by David Brookshaw, Heinemann: Oxford, 1990; and *Every Man is a Race*, translated by David Brookshaw, Heinemann: Oxford, 1994.
2. Couto, Mia, "The Private Apocalypse of Uncle Gegué" in *Every Man is a Race*, p. 21.
3. *Ibid.*, p. 19.
4. Couto, Mia, "How Ascolino do Perpétuo Socorro Lost his Spouse" in *Voices Made Night*, p. 29.
5. Atieno-Odhiambo, E.S., "Democracy and the Ideology of Order in Kenya" in *The Political Economy of Kenya*, Michael G. Scharzberg (ed.), Praeger: New York, 1987.
6. Couto, Mia, *Under the Frangipani*, David Philip: Johannesburg, 2001.

Beautiful Ugly: African and Diaspora Aesthetics

Index

409

Beautiful Ugly: African and Diaspora Aesthetics

413